The People and the Book

Essays on the *Old Testament*, contributed by
H. R. HALL, S. A. COOK, G. R. DRIVER,
A. C. WELCH, T. H. ROBINSON, J. E.
MCFADYEN, W. F. LOFTHOUSE, A. S. PEAKE,
W. E. BARNES, W. O. E. OESTERLEY, H. W.
ROBINSON, R. H. KENNETT, I. ABRAHAMS,
G. H. BOX, G. BUCHANAN GRAY

Edited by

ARTHUR S. PEAKE

(Hon. D.D. Oxford and Aberdeen)

*Rylands Professor of Biblical Exegesis in the University of Manchester;
President of the Society for Old Testament Study, 1924*

OXFORD
AT THE CLARENDON PRESS
M DCCCC XXV

Oxford University Press

London   Edinburgh   Glasgow   Copenhagen

New York   Toronto   Melbourne   Cape Town

Bombay   Calcutta   Madras   Shanghai

Humphrey Milford Publisher to the UNIVERSITY

ESSAYS

by Members of the Society for

Old Testament Study

Printed in England
At the OXFORD UNIVERSITY PRESS
By John Johnson
Printer to the University

CONTENTS

Contents

a 3

INTRODUCTION

THE present work owes its origin to a request from the Society for Old Testament Study that I should edit a volume of essays. I accepted the task with not a little hesitation because my time was already deeply pledged ; but I recognized how great a service such a volume might render in the present situation and felt that I ought not to decline it. Its completion has been delayed by various causes on which I need not dwell, but the delay has not been altogether a disadvantage since it has enabled us to take fuller account of recent work. The Society left me quite free to plan the volume, select the contributors, and make arrangements for the publication. But it gave approval to the scheme I put before it and helped me with suggestions. I desire to express my gratitude to it for its confidence and interest and to the contributors for their kind and loyal co-operation. I am also grateful to the Delegates of the Oxford University Press for undertaking the publication and especially to Mr. J. de M. Johnson, the Assistant Secretary, for his counsel and help. The contributors have been left free to deal with the subjects allotted to them in their own way, along the general lines indicated to them. No uniformity of view has been sought for or indeed desired. In a field where so much difference of opinion exists it is well that the student should have it forced upon his attention. Even in such a matter as the transliteration of proper names the writers have been left free to follow their own preference.

The Society was formed in the first instance to bring together Old Testament scholars for the discussion of problems and for communications on researches undertaken or conclusions reached by its members. But it has also been our intention to promote the study of the Old Testament, to deepen interest in it, and justify its right to a prominent place in religious education and the theological curriculum. Wherever our help or guidance is sought, there we accept the duty of meeting the demand to the best of our ability.

Two reasons in particular made the publication of such a volume timely. We were conscious in the first place of a tendency to relegate the Old Testament to a position of relative insignificance. Partly this has been due to the franker recognition of its very mixed character and the persistence of lower elements in it alongside of the more elevated, partly to the results of Higher and Historical criticism and of Biblical Theology. But whatever our individual views on these matters, we are united in the conviction that the classical literature of Israel possesses for ourselves an inestimable value. It ranks beyond dispute with the other great literatures of the world ; it is the monument of a religious development unique in history ; it is indispensable for all who desire to understand the Christian religion. Indeed the Christian, while claiming that in Jesus revelation attained its summit, is also committed to the belief that this is but the final stage of a long and gradual process Divinely planned from the outset and guided to that goal. Of that process the Old Testament is our only record. We trust accordingly that the present volume will do something to check the suspicion that the Old Testament has been discredited and that modern culture can with impunity neglect it.

In the second place we desire to explain the present situation in Old Testament study. The modern reader who has no independent knowledge of the subject is not unnaturally bewildered when he finds eminent scholars offering him certain critical conclusions as assured results, and on the other hand is told that the critical movement has received a decisive check and that traditional beliefs are on the high road to rehabilitation. On this Professor McFadyen has spoken so fully in his article and has given so balanced and trustworthy a sketch of the real position that it is unnecessary to speak at length. It is now nearly forty years since I began to take an interest in Old Testament problems, and during the greater part of that period prophecies of a reaction have been a fairly constant feature. To bring the matter to an issue, it may be simplest to quote a paragraph from my Inaugural Lecture at the University of Manchester written just over twenty years ago :

'We need then have no fear of a reaction such as is constantly foretold, though it is quite probable that deeper study and widening knowledge may correct many critical conclusions, sometimes in the direction of tradition, but sometimes in the other direction. We need not hesitate to claim that many assured results have been reached, which the future is not likely to reverse. Among these I may enumerate the analysis of the Pentateuch into four main documents, the identification of the Law on which Josiah's Reformation was based, with some form of the Deuteronomic Code, the compilation of that Code in the reign of Manasseh at the earliest, the fixing of the Priestly Code to a date later than Ezekiel ; the highly composite character of some parts of the prophetic literature, especially the book of Isaiah ; the post-exilic origin of most of the Psalms and large parts of the book of Proverbs, the composition of Job not earlier than the Exile and probably later, the Maccabean date of Daniel and the slightly earlier date of Ecclesiastes. On all these points it would be possible to name dissentient voices, but speaking generally these results would probably secure the adhesion of most Old Testament critics.'

This summary of accepted results still, I believe, holds good on the whole, and it would even now, I think, command the assent of most Old Testament scholars. It is therefore still premature to suggest that the foundations on which the accepted critical structure has been built are showing signs of collapse. Even if there is a strong tendency at certain points towards a more conservative view, it is in some cases counter-balanced by a movement towards a more radical position. Even where the absolute dating has been altered the relative dating may remain. Hölscher, it may be said, abandons the pre-exilic date of Deuteronomy, the authenticity of the greater part of Ezekiel, and the identification of Ezra's Law Book either with the Pentateuch or the Priestly Document. It is highly improbable that his view of Ezekiel will be accepted ; and if so it is not likely that his date for Deuteronomy can be maintained. But the significant thing is that he retains the relative chronology identified with the Grafian theory— Deuteronomy, Ezekiel, the Priestly Document. Hölscher himself speaks of Wellhausen's convincing proof of the post-exilic origin of P.

I have just used the term ' Grafian theory '. It should be definitely limited to the view that the Priestly Code is the latest of the main documents, that it is the outcome of a development initiated by Deuteronomy in which the closing section of

Ezekiel constitutes the middle term. But an unfortunate usage has grown up of extending it so as to cover a particular theory of Israel's religious development. This extension leads only to confusion. It is true that leading Grafian scholars—I name especially Kuenen, Wellhausen, Stade, and Duhm—put forward a view of the early history of religion which many scholars, probably with justice, regard as too depreciatory. But these scholars themselves accept the Grafian theory in the strict sense of the term. Their loose terminology provides quotations which opponents of criticism are all too ready to use in proof of their contention that the Grafian *criticism* is fast going the way which the theory it displaced has already gone. I have drawn attention to this point in the introduction to the English translation of Sellin's *Introduction to the Old Testament*, a book which was made accessible to English readers, not only for its great intrinsic merits, but in order that students might see for themselves how far the author is in agreement with the generally accepted critical position and how far he is in disagreement or strikes out fresh lines of advance. On the latter question the reader will find excellent guidance in Dr. McFadyen's essay, but I hope that he will also study Sellin for himself.

The most notable advance in Old Testament scholarship has been due by common consent to the enlargement of our horizon by discoveries in the lands with which Palestine was in contact and in Palestine itself. Israel and the Old Testament have been taken out of their former isolation. It was therefore essential to the scheme of this volume that the relations of Israel with the surrounding peoples should receive due attention. Accordingly Dr. Hall has dealt with the history of these peoples and Dr. Stanley Cook with their religion. Thus the history, literature, and religion of Israel are placed in their context. It will be a gratification to all lovers of Biblical scholarship that the name of one of our foremost Hebraists and Old Testament scholars is worthily represented by his son, who has written on the languages of the Old Testament with a similar attention to their affinities with other languages of the Semitic family. For the sketch of the history we are indebted to Professor Welch, whose striking volume *The Code of Deuteronomy* has attracted much attention and is discussed in Dr. McFadyen's essay. To the criticism of the Old Testament two essays have been devoted. Of the article on critical results and theories I have already spoken. It seemed expedient to include an account of critical method, so that the novice might see how the critic sets about his work and why he claims that his task is forced upon him by the phenomena which his documents present and how they supply the material which renders their analysis possible.

But the history of Israel and the criticism of its literature are not in themselves of such importance that we should devote so much time and labour to their investigation. The goal of our study is to understand the religion. Since the national history was the source from which this came and the medium through which it was developed, we must know the history that we may understand the religion. Inasmuch as the history is accessible to us only in literary records we must examine these by critical methods. In this way we can break up our documents into their elements, arrange these in their chronological order, test them for their historical trustworthiness, and finally submit the story they relate to critical examination. Even if at the end of the process not a few questions admit of different answers or have received no answer at all, yet other problems have been certainly or probably solved and we have provided the only basis on which a scientific history of the religion can be erected. To that history four essays have been devoted. It was desirable to reserve the treatment of the cultus for a separate essay, and Dr. Oesterley has accordingly sketched the development as a connected whole. This has had the additional advantage of relieving the other three essays from some discussions for which otherwise they would have had to make room. While the middle period, though it has its own perplexities, could for the most part be covered by simple narrative and exposition, the uncertainties which gather about the earliest and the latest stages necessitated the devotion of much space to the discussion of problems. In his *Einleitung in die drei ersten Evangelien* (2nd edition) Wellhausen said: 'Under the quiet influence of Strauss "The Life of Jesus" which used to find a place on the programme of theological literature and theological lectures has recently shrunk so much that it appears as "Problems in the Life of Jesus".' Something similar might be said with reference to the early history of Hebrew religion. If at some points it may seem that agreement is growing, on others the divergence of opinion is still acute; moreover, new questions continue to arise. We may hope that in the Life of Jesus, as in the History of the Religion of Israel, problems will more and more give way to generally accepted solutions, but assuredly in neither field is such a consummation at present in sight. The best service that can be rendered to the student is to put the position before him as it really is, rather than to delude him into an unjustified optimism. New evidence may settle some issues which are at present in debate, but it may also unsettle some conclusions which have been generally accepted and it is almost certain to raise new problems.

In view of the growing interest in psychology the presence of Principal Wheeler Robinson's essay will occasion no surprise. But it will open quite a new field to many Old Testament students, and it is to be hoped will enable them to enter into the consciousness of the Hebrews which was so alien from our own that a strong effort of sympathetic imagination is needed before we can appropriate it. Special importance also attaches to the psychological investigation of the prophetic state given in his essay.

There is much in the volume which reminds us of the kinship between the Hebrews and their religion and the surrounding peoples and their religion. It seemed desirable accordingly to include an essay which should exhibit the differentia of Hebrew religion and the contribution which it made to religious development. This is naturally treated by a Christian scholar from the standpoint of one who believes that this development was Divinely designed to culminate in Jesus as the supreme revelation of God. But those who would refuse to accept this position will probably be prepared to recognize that the Old Testament did make a contribution to religion of unique elevation and value. In this connexion a warm welcome will be extended to the admirable article by Dr. Abrahams.

In recent years the value of the Jewish interpretation of the Old Testament has been much more generously recognized. Jewish scholars might no doubt have done more in the past to guide their Christian colleagues into a fuller knowledge and fairer judgement of this and other fields of Jewish theology. Happily the signs are multiplying of their willingness to share the treasures of their learning with their Gentile colleagues. The sympathetic but discriminating account and estimate given by Dr. Abrahams will make a truer valuation of Jewish exegesis possible to many readers.

Lastly, the value of a study of the Old Testament for the fuller and truer interpretation of the New Testament is brought out by Canon Box. That the Old Testament deserves loving study for its own sake and amply repays it is a conviction in which the writers of this volume are united. But they recognize with equal conviction that it is the indispensable approach to the right interpretation of the New Testament. This will probably be admitted for the Synoptic Gospels, for the Acts of the Apostles, and for some other writings in the New Testament. Speaking as one whose work has been fairly evenly divided between the Old Testament and the New, I cannot refrain from adding that not a little recent work on the Pauline theology would have been at once strengthened and corrected if the scholars responsible for it had been more thoroughly grounded in the Old Testament.

The closing paper falls outside the scheme of the volume. It represents, probably imperfectly, the Presidential Address given to the Society by Dr. Gray. Had he been spared to us he would have made his own contribution to the volume. If he had published the Presidential Address it would no doubt have been more complete in substance and more finished in form. But as it is it seemed to us, though brief, to be so valuable that we desired to include it in the volume, and are grateful to Mrs. Gray for her cordial permission to print it and to Dr. T. H. Robinson who prepared it for publication.

It was on the same evening as that on which the Address had been delivered that Dr. Gray and the other members of the Committee invited me to undertake the editorship of this volume. He was spared to preside over our summer meeting to which I submitted my scheme for the volume. When we met for our next winter session our first duty was to express our sense of the irreparable loss to scholarship and of our own loss as a Society which we had sustained by his sudden death. His colleagues desire to mark at once their personal affection for him and their sorrow at his untimely death by dedicating this collection of essays to his memory. For a short time he was my colleague and for many years one of my dearest and most intimate friends. I watched his development with the keenest interest and his achievements with increasing pride, and looked forward with quiet confidence to a still more brilliant sequel. Nor can I covet higher praise for the volume it has been my privilege to edit than that it should not be unworthy of the scholar and the friend to whose unfading memory it is our joy to dedicate it.

ARTHUR S. PEAKE.

September 15, 1925.

ISRAEL AND THE SURROUNDING
NATIONS

It is inevitable that we should be accustomed to regard the relations of Israel with the surrounding nations from the point of view of Israel rather than that of her neighbours. It is difficult to put ourselves in the position of the other nations, of the Goyyim rather than that of the Chosen People, and to see with their eyes rather than with hers. Yet if we are to envisage the situation of Israel in ancient history we must attempt to do so. This essay has therefore been written with the aim of familiarizing students with the notions as to the relations of Israel with the surrounding nations that present themselves to the minds of non-Hebrew or even non-Semitic scholars. It is written from the standpoint of Mizraim and the Goyyim, of the Philistines, of Kaphtor and Yavan, of Babel and Assur. Let us see what they have to tell us of Israel.

We shall find that they have very little to tell us directly. Only once does the name of Israel occur clearly and unmistakably in an Egyptian inscription; rarely do tribal names occur in Egyptian inscriptions and Palestinian cuneiform letters that have doubtfully been identified with that of the Hebrews. Yet the one incontrovertible mention, in the inscription of Meneptaḥ of the thirteenth century B. C.,[1] places Israel in Palestine, and near where we should expect to find her from the Bible narrative. Israel was there, and was growing to nationhood amid the fastnesses of Mount Ephraim and Judah, but she was not yet important enough to attract much attention from Egypt. Yet she must have been sufficiently important to be

[1] See p. 16, below.

B

mentioned more than once; and it must be remembered that
there are probably thousands of Egyptian inscriptions yet to
be discovered, in more than one of which we may yet find
mention of Israel. It is in Palestine itself probably that we
may with most confidence look forward to the discovery of such
inscriptions; and the recent finds of important Egyptian
monumental stelae of the kings Seti I and Rē'masesu or
Rameses II (14th and 13th century B. C.) at Beth-shan [1] are
an earnest of others that may yet be found which will tell us
more of Israel from the Egyptian point of view. On one of
these stelae indeed has been deciphered a mention of the
'Apuri, 'Aperiu or 'Eperiu (the final -*u* is the Egyptian plural
form, corresponding to the Hebrew -*im*), who are spoken of
in papyri of the same period as slaves in Egypt, and later, under
the XXth Dynasty (about 1170 B. C.) as slaves in the mines of
Sinai.[2] Whether they were 'Ibhrim or Hebrews we shall
know later. It has been supposed that the Khabiru of the
el-Amarna letters (14th century), who are shown as invading
and conquering Palestine at the time of the weakness of the
Egyptian heretic-king Akhenaton in face of the rebellion of the
Amorite princes of central Syria led by Aziru and his sons, were
none other than the Hebrews in the act of entering and occupying
the Promised Land. These Khabiru are mentioned by the
Hittites, probably at an earlier date, and still earlier in Babylonia.[3]

Going further back again we come to the vexed question
of the date of the Exodus, which, it seems to me, we

---

[1] C. S. Fisher, *Philadelphia Museum Journal*, Dec. 1923; Ovenden,
P. E. F. Q. S., 1923, p. 147 ff.; and Hall, *Anc. Hist. Near East*, 6th ed.
(1924), p. 599.

[2] See Peet, *Egypt and The Old Testament*, pp. 123–5; Jirku, *Die Wanderungen der Hebräer*, p. 23 ff.; Burney, *Israel's Settlement in Canaan*, p. 62;
and Heyes, *Bibel in Ägypten*, p. 154 ff. The 'Aperiu are mentioned also in
a romance dealing with the time of Thutmosis III (*c.* 1470 B. C.), but this
may be later than his time.

[3] See later, pp. 7 ff., 14 ff.

must put back to the beginning of the sixteenth century, and identify simply with the expulsion of the Hyksos from Egypt, as Josephus supposed. Although rejected by many first-rate authorities on the Hebrew and Biblical side (e. g. by Dr. Burney),[1] I am not without support in this view from those who deal at first hand with Egyptian as well as Semitic lore : I may quote Sir Ernest Budge [2] and Dr. Alan Gardiner [3] in my support, for instance. But here we are dealing wholly with our individual views of the probabilities. We lack all precise monumental statements like those of the stelae of Meneptah ; we have not even the precarious foundation of identification of names in the Amarna letters. It is merely a matter of what we think most likely.

Going further back, again, we have nothing, so far as Israel is concerned, nor should we expect to find anything, since Israel as a separate nation did not then exist.

Returning to the period succeeding the mention by Meneptah, while the nation was slowly growing up it was natural that it should not bulk largely in the minds of its neighbours. Not till the founding of the kingdom and above all the reign of Solomon was Israel great enough to attract much attention. We know (as yet) nothing of Solomon from non-Hebrew sources. But this defect may be remedied any day by some lucky Egyptian excavation. The Hebrew account is definite enough for us to see that he was a very real monarch of energy, wealth, and power, that he controlled a wide realm, traded afar, and took the daughter of a Pharaoh to wife. Unluckily the Egypt of the day was weak and not given to chronicling the names of successful rivals and compeers. Still, we have a hope of hearing something about David and Solomon from contemporary Egyptian sources. Babylonia was no longer, Assyria

---

[1] *Israel's Settlement in Canaan*, p. 91 ff.
[2] *Egypt (Home University Library*, 1925), p. 110.
[3] ' The Geography of the Exodus,' *Journ. Eg. Arch.*, x (1924), p. 88.

was not yet, in such close relations to Palestine as to give us any information. But two centuries later, after the campaign of 853 B. C. had brought Assyrian armies into Palestine, and the defeat of Ahab and his allies at the battle of Ḳarḳar is chronicled by the Assyrian annalists, we have the two histories, the annals of Israel and Judah and those of Assyria and Babylon recovered by Layard and his successors, set out for us plainly side by side and confirming or correcting each other at every point. A side-hint from the foreign point of view is given us by the Moabite Stone, with its chronicle of the revolt of Mesha', king of Moab, which comes into direct connexion with the Old Testament narrative. Still, we have only the cuneiform records to read parallel with those of the Bible until the Captivities, the destruction of Nineveh, the fall of Babylon, and the favour of the Persian to the remnant of Judah. And with the Diaspora our story ends.

It is naturally from the side of Egypt that we have the earliest definite mention of Israel. Could we read more of the Hittite records, or anything of the Minoan, we might possibly hear more of the folk of Palestine from the former than the single mention of Khabiru already noted, but from the latter we need not expect any information. Even as kingdoms Israel and Judah were too insignificant to be mentioned by any other nation than those brought into direct contact with them, like the Egyptians or Assyrians.

We begin our study then with Egypt. Assuming for the moment that the sojourn of the Israelites in Egypt and the story of Joseph is to be assigned to the period of the Hyksos, have we any Egyptian hint of an earlier sojourn that may be brought into connexion with the story of the visit of Abraham ? Semites were always making their way into Egypt, in single spies when the native power was strong, in battalions when it was weak ; the fleshpots of Egypt were always an attraction, whether to the desert Arab or to the fellah of Palestine. It has

been supposed that an actual Semitic invasion took place
during the interval between the VIth and XIIth Dynasties,
though not, it seems to the present writer, on very strong
grounds.[1] Is the Abrahamic tale, however, a faraway reflection
of this? It is, of course, not impossible that the Abrahamic
tribe may have passed from Hebron into Egypt for a space and
then returned. Of the truth to life of the description of Egypt
in the Biblical story of Abraham's visit the Egyptologists are
well aware; but the description as it stands may have been
written at any time: it is not necessarily the Egypt of the
XIIth Dynasty that is described: there is no historical indication in the tale, and it may after all be nothing but a doublet
of the story of Jacob's going down into Egypt, and have no
historical value whatever, just as the tale of Abraham and
Abimelech (Gen. xx) is obviously merely a doublet of the
exactly similar tale of Isaac and Abimelech in Gen. xxvi:
even the name of the king of Gerar is the same in both stories.[2]
Also plagues are mentioned in both tales concerning Egypt,
as sent by the God of the Hebrews to torment Pharaoh and
his people. In fact, if Jacob went down into Egypt so did
Abraham. The procession of Abishai and his Semitic immigrants pictured on the walls of the tomb of Khnumhotep
at Beni Hasan [3] has been regarded as a possible representation
of the coming of precursors of the Israelites, and so in a sense
it is, since it is an interesting picture of one of the many
groups of Semitic immigrants that were filtering into Egypt,
and even reached Upper Egypt, at this time, to culminate in
the armed invasion of the Hyksos.

[1] This has been deduced from certain indications in early papyri, but as
yet no monumental confirmation of the idea has been obtained.

[2] The description of Abimelech in Gen. xx as a Philistine is naturally
a later interpolation. It does not occur in the Isaac version of the story.
The Philistines were of course not in Palestine until at least eight centuries
after the Abrahamic epoch (see p. 24 ff.).

[3] Newberry, *Beni Hasan*, i, Pl. xxviii.

We have, of course, no contemporary mention of the Hebrews or Israelites as such in the scanty Egyptian record of the expulsion of the Hyksos, as preserved for us by Manetho and on the monuments. Josephus, however, who transcribed the otherwise lost fragments of Manetho that relate to the Expulsion, did so because he believed that the Expulsion and the Exodus were the same event.

The Hyksos invasion was a Semitic invasion; the Hyksos were Semites. Their name in Egyptian means ' princes of the Arabs '; the proper names of their kings, when not Egyptian imitations of Egyptian regal appellations, were Semitic, such as Khayan, 'Ant-hal, Yepeq-hal, and others.[1] The Egyptian tradition preserved in Manetho brings them from Palestine : the Egyptians we know called them Asiatics, shepherds, ' who are an abomination unto the Egyptians '. Their kings assumed the insignia of the pharaohs and ruled as Egyptian monarchs ; just as Joseph and his pharaoh did, they ruled the land and performed the usual duties of the pharaoh and his court in ministering to the well-being of their subjects in times of stress and dearth. Then, the day came when a pharaoh arose who ' knew not Joseph ', and the Israelites according to their tradition were commanded by their God, speaking through the mouths of Moses and Aaron, to leave Egypt. While historically the Hyksos were expelled by the arms of the native Upper Egyptian kings, the Israelites passed out of Egypt by the same route as the Hyksos. The most modern exegesis (that of Dr. Gardiner),[2] holds that they went out of the Gate of Pelusium along the shore of lake Serbonis (where probably enough, I would suggest, some of the pursuing Egyptian chariots were engulfed, perhaps in a sea-storm that drove the waters of the Mediterranean landwards, in the bog of the ' Sea of Reeds '),

[1] Hall, *Anc. Hist. Near East*, p. 217.

[2] *Études Champollion*, p. 205 ff., *Journ. Eg. Arch.*, x (1924), p. 87 ff. ; cf. Naville, *ibid.*, p. 18 ff. for the other view.

and then inland into the wilderness and to Sinai, whether the historical Sinai of tradition or a Horeb out beyond in the land of Edom. The Hyksos went by the same route, pursued by the Egyptian pharaoh Yaḥmase or Amōsis and his host from Avaris, which probably is Pelusium,[1] to the Negeb where the town of Sherohan was the scene of their last defence before they disappeared, a broken and disorganized band, into the east.

Dispassionate objective consideration of the two stories, one historical, based on contemporary monuments, the other traditional, and coloured by national partiality, leads, if one entirely disregards all prepossessions and realizes how legend can transmute the history on which it is based, to the conclusion that Josephus may have been right, indeed that he very probably was right. Stated periods of years, especially when given in round numbers, can be disregarded in legend. The attribution of the Exodus to the reign of Meneptaḥ (*c.* 1220 B. C.), hitherto generally accepted as a probable guess, has always suffered from the reproach of being almost impossibly late. If the expulsion of the Hyksos (*c.* 1580 B. C.) is too early for the Exodus, where in the history of the great and powerful XVIIIth Dynasty can we find a probable place for an event which, like the Exodus of tradition, presupposes internal trouble and weakness in Egypt, until the reign of Akhenaten? Of all theories, to place the Exodus, say, in the reign of Amenhotep II, in order to agree with traditional dates, seems to the historian of Egypt the least probable. If it took place then, however, and the Khabiru are still to be regarded as the Hebrews, the sojourn in the wilderness, too, is reduced to nothingness, is a mere fiction.[2] That we cannot believe: the legend is too

[1] Gardiner, ' The Delta Residence of the Ramessides,' *Journ. Eg. Arch.*, v (1918) ; ' The Ancient Military Road between Egypt and Palestine,' *ibid.* vi (1920).

[2] Dr. S. A. Cook seems to me to treat this view with far too much deference in his note in *Cambr. Anc. Hist.*, ii, p. 356, in which he treats it as one

circumstantial for that. The ancestors of at least a part of the Hebrew nation abode for a long period in the deserts, in Sinai and Edom, between their departure from Egypt and their entry into Palestine. And if this entry was part of the invasion of the Khabiru in the days of Akhenaten, what more likely period for their Exodus from Egypt can be found than that, two hundred years earlier, when the Semitic Hyksos were expelled from the Nile-land?

It is difficult to suppose that their incoming took place later. If we accept Meneptaḥ as the pharaoh of the Exodus we must place it at least a generation later than his time (about 1190–1180 B. C. ?) as Dr. Burney does.[1] But on this theory we have only a century for the events of the period of the Judges up to the high-priesthood of Eli and the Philistine subjugation of Israel (*c.* 1080). And it cannot have taken place *after* the coming of the Philistines into Palestine, which we know took place about 1200 B. C., or the Philistines would have been mentioned in the accounts of Joshua's invasion. Israel, too, is mentioned as a settled country in Palestine by Meneptaḥ, about 1220. Israel was already there then. Are we to suppose two Israels, one a settlement of a sept that had already left Egypt before the main Exodus or had never gone there, as we have to do if the Exodus took place at the end of Meneptaḥ's reign? It

of the two views of which most can be said in favour ; viz., the XVIIIth Dynasty possibility and the XIXth Dynasty possibility. These are his alternatives (2) and (3) ; (1) Expulsion of the Hyksos and (4) XXth Dynasty he rejects. From the Egyptian point of view I entirely disagree, and regard alternatives (1) Expulsion of the Hyksos and (3) XIXth Dynasty as having much in their favour, though (3) must, for me, be finally abandoned in favour of (1) ; while Dr. Burney (*loc. cit.*) accepts (3) but rejects (1), while agreeing with me as to the impossibility of (2). The other two alternatives (2) XVIIIth Dynasty and (4) XXth Dynasty both appear to me equally impossible, for different reasons : (4) is quite impossibly late, of course, and would make nonsense of all the Jewish legends and annals. I agree with Dr. Cook on this point.

[1] *Israel's Settlement in Canaan*, p. 95 ('soon after 1200').

has been thought that there are traces of such tribes that had remained behind in the mention by Thutmosis III of towns in Palestine perhaps called Yaḳeb-il (Jacob-el) and Yeshap-il (Joseph-el), and for other reasons.[1] It is true that Hebrews and Israelites are themselves to be differentiated at first, and there was always a duality in the nation. This may point to fusion of an Aramaean (Abrahamic) and an Edomite stock in South Palestine before the going down into Egypt, or were the Hebrews who went down into Egypt properly speaking Israelites and had the Khabiru of the Amarna letters, who invaded Palestine from the north-east, never been there? Is the duality due to this?

One of the great objections to placing the Exodus before the reign of Rameses II is the mention of Pithom and ' Raamses '. But such names of well-known Egyptian cities could enter the legend later when stories of the tasks of Israelite prisoners, captured in the wars of Rameses II, in Egypt had taken its place in it, and the mention of Raamses may well show that the legend began to take its final form during the period of Ramessid domination in Palestine in the thirteenth and twelfth centuries when the young nation was making in Mount Ephraim and the wilds of Judah. At this time 'Aperiu prisoners are actually spoken of as working at the building of the name-city of Rameses in the Delta (Pelusium?).[2]

[1] On these disputed points see Cook, in *Cambr. Anc. Hist.*, ii, p. 296 ff. The present writer takes a somewhat more hopeful view than Dr. Cook of the possibility of reconstituting the early history of Israel from the admittedly often self-contradictory Jewish legends aided by contemporary monumental evidence. At any rate, it is the duty of the historian to try to make as probable a reconstruction as he can on the basis of our knowledge, which means fitting the native legends preserved in the Old Testament as plausibly as he can into the framework provided by the contemporary data, at first Egyptian chiefly, later Assyrian. And as time goes on we shall be able to do this with greater certainty. Personally I am not disposed to admit that we have not reached quite reliable results already, especially on the archaeological side.

[2] Fisher, *Philadelphia Museum Journal*, 1923, p. 234; and cf. Jirku,

Other names in the story are even later and belong to recensions of the eleventh and even far later centuries. Such are Zaphnathpaaneakh, a name of a form unknown in Egypt until the eleventh century and not current after the ninth,[1] and Potiphar and Potipherah, which belong to the ninth at earliest and may be as late as the sixth or later. Evidently we must be critical of the names, and 'Raamses' has no historical value as proof of the late date of the Exodus. Yet it is interesting to find in the same story in its final form as we have it such late names as Potiphar and Potipherah (evidently given later and to purely legendary Egyptians, as typical Egyptian names of the time when the story, perhaps, was first written down), and such early ones as Moses, Hur, Phinehas, Hophni (?), and Levi, which may well be the historical names of tribal leaders of the Exodus and of the period of the Judges, preserved as those of national leaders well might be.

One hypothesis is as good as another, and personally I think the view of Josephus more probable than the guess of the moderns: the Exodus is the Expulsion of the Hyksos looked at from the peculiar angle of Jewish tradition. The story of the Hebrews in Egypt is what we should expect a memory of the rule of the Hyksos to become in later legend. Joseph represents the Semitic Hyksos régime in Egypt. The king who favoured him was a Hyksos: the king who knew him not was

loc. cit., p. 24. This will not affect our date for the Exodus. In legend events are constantly misplaced in time, and the works of the Hebrew prisoners in Rameses' time could quite well be antedated to the period of the Hebrew stay in Egypt under the Hyksos. Rameses II was the pharaoh of the Oppression, but not the pharaoh who knew not Joseph.

[1] That is if we identify it with Steindorff as the Egyptian Žed-pneter-ef-'ankh : if we adopt Mr. Engelbach's ingenious suggestion that it is a misunderstood surname (Žed-nef-Pi'ankh, (Joseph) ' called Pi'ankh '), the name will be even later (see *Journ. Eg. Arch.*, 1925, p. 204). On the whole subject of these Egyptian names in the Biblical record see my *Anc. Hist. Near East*, pp. 405, 406.

Amosis. Moses, the Hebrew with an Egyptian name and a Nubian wife, and Aaron his brother may have been historical leaders of the Hebrew tribe of Hyksos. The Egyptian names of the priestly clan, preserved to the last at Shiloh until David's supersession of the ancient Exodic priesthood by the Jebusite high-priesthood of Jerusalem after his capture of the city, are significant. There is little doubt that the Hebrews had imbibed something of the Egyptian culture, especially in the matter of religious rites. Such things as the Ark are clearly Egyptian, and the Golden Calf was as much Egyptian as it was Canaanite. Was it nothing but an image of Hathor, the Egyptian tutelary goddess of the desert, and specially of Sinai? The Hebrews probably ' spoiled ' the Egyptians quite as much in the matter of ideas as in that of riches. It is conceivable, by the way, that the Hyksos may have got away a good deal of treasure with them. And then Egypt was the land of gold, which the mines of Nubia gave her.

It is a hypothesis that has much probability in its favour, and it allows for the sojourn in the Wilderness the period of two hundred years, succeeding the expulsion of the Hyksos, that saw the vengeful dominance of Egypt in Palestine and Syria. During those two centuries we find no trace of the Hebrews in Palestine but the doubtful mention of the Jacob-el and Joseph-el towns, noted above. These may, if their names are really to be interpreted thus, have belonged to an Israelite sept left behind when the rest went forward into Egypt with the Hyksos, or one that had pressed forward after the Expulsion and had reached Palestine while the rest were wandering in Edom, waiting for the opportunity to enter the Promised Land from which their ancestors had come down into Egypt in the days of the Hyksos. It is true that, as Dr. Burney objects, this view entirely dissociates Joshua from Moses, if the sojourn in the Wilderness is supposed to have lasted more than a generation, but, after all, one is dealing with legend, and associations of legendary personages are not always to be taken literally. It is likely enough that the events of the sojourn in the Wilderness have been compressed, and the two outstanding leaders, one at the beginning of the period and the Exodus, the other at the end of it and the Conquest, have been approximated in time, and considered to belong to immediate generations.

During this period Phoenicia was held close to Egypt by her ancient bond,[1] and served as the regular base of Egyptian campaigns in Syria, at any rate in the time of Thutmosis III. Holding Phoenicia and Syria, Egypt naturally dominated Palestine also, and the way from Pelusium to Gaza and so into the Vale of Esdraelon often saw the march of the Amenhoteps and Thutmosis northwards through Canaan. Thutmosis III took this route in his first campaign when he made his phenomenally swift march from Gaza by the Wady Arah to Megiddo, and there defeated the ban and arrière-ban of the Canaanite chiefs, who had taken advantage of the pacific reign of his sister Hatshepsut to throw off the Egyptian yoke. The list of the booty taken at Megiddo shows that the Canaanites had developed a luxurious civilization, of which few relics have been revealed yet by archaeological exploration. The excavations of Taanach and Megiddo have, however, yielded results of much interest; and especially at Taanach certain cuneiform tablets have been found that give us an insight into conditions in the time between the reigns of Thutmosis III and Amenhotep III (1450–1400 B.C.).[2] They are letters from and to Ishtar-washur, the local chief, which show that Egyptian

---

[1] Phoenicia had been closely connected with Egypt from the earliest times. Gebal (or Kapun, as the Egyptians called it), Byblos, the modern Jebeil, was practically an Egyptian overseas colony with regular Egyptian temples as early as the time of the Pyramid-builders, when King Snefru sent his ships there to fetch the cedar and pine-logs for Egyptian buildings from Mt. Lebanon. Gebal was also specially connected with Egyptian religion, as the Osiris myth shows.

[2] For references see *Anc. Hist. Near East*, p. 247.

travelling inspectors and even residents watched the conduct of the local chiefs, who had to send their sons to be educated at the Egyptian court and were expected to send their regular tribute to the coffers of the Egyptian god Amen of Thebes, to whom all foreign conquests were, so to speak, dedicated. It is to this period of a *pax aegyptia*, the days of Egypt's greatest and least disputed power, extending from the Sudan to the Euphrates, that some would ascribe the Exodus and the disturbances it must have caused in the Delta and on the border ! [1]

The cuneiform tablets show that the culture of the country was largely Babylonian, as was that of all Western Asia south of the Taurus, and even, as we shall see, to some extent north of it. The Canaanites were never egyptianized, though the Phoenicians were so, partially. But even they were preserved from becoming entirely egyptianized by their Semitic language and religion, which indeed, soon began to exercise a reflex influence upon Egypt herself.

Whether the religious heresy of Akhenaten is to be ascribed to Semitic influence it is difficult to say. It was certainly of Heliopolitan origin, and the sun-worship of On, the probably somewhat esoteric doctrine of the Heliopolitan priests, the ' wisdom of the Egyptians ' in which Moses was proficient, was perhaps ultimately of Semitic origin, and must from its environment have always been subject to Semitic religious influences. Whether other influences from Turco-Aryan [2] Mitanni or from the Hittites of Anatolia also helped to move thinking Egyptians in the direction of the new heresy it is as yet difficult to decide ; but such influences would hardly be monotheistic in tendency. The political effect of the forcible introduction of the mono-theistic Sun-worship into the Egyptian dominions by Akhenaten we know. In conjunction with the restless intrigues of

[1] See *antea*, p. 7, and note.
[2] For the mixed Mitannian nationality see Hall, ' The Hittites and Egypt.' in *Ramsay Anatolian Studies*, p. 175.

certain Lebanese and South Palestinian princes (some of the latter of foreign non-Semitic origin, Hittite or Mitannian or both), probably encouraged by the ambitious Hittite king, Supilul or Shubbiluliuma,[1] it brought about the turmoil into which the Khabiru came, entering Palestine very much as the Hebrews did into the Promised Land, if they were not, as seems highly probable, the Hebrews themselves.[2]

We hear from the letters discovered at Tell el-Amarna and Boghz-Kyöi of what happened; of how Egypt lost Phoenicia in spite of the fanatical loyalty of such princes as Ribadda, and how even the whole south of Palestine was lost to her. We hear of the cities of Canaan; of Jerusalem now for the first time, the little city on the slope of Ophel, whence ' Abd-Khiba the king wrote to warn the pacificist pharaoh that he was losing the whole land, and to complain that black Sudanese troops stationed there were oppressing the population. Jerusalem is an important place. We can see how it was that it bid defiance to the inroad of the Hebrews, and continued to be a burgh of its Canaanite inhabitants, the Jebusites, when the less fenced cities of the land had fallen before the arms of Joshua. It has been supposed that Jerusalem was the site of a temple of the monotheistic worship of the Sun-disk set up by Akhenaten in Palestine and called Khinatuna by the Canaanites; but it is more probable that this was at Bethshemesh ('Ain Shems), an ancient city of old devoted to the worship of the Sun and possibly connected with On, or at Hannathon, north of Carmel.[3]

In spite, then, of some difficulties, the probability that the Khabiru of Akhenaten's day were the Hebrews of Joshua's seems to me to be great, in view of the name (an absolute philological equivalent of 'Ebher or 'Ibhrim), and the difficulty of finding

[1] For the name see Hall, ' Egyptian Transliteration of Hittite names,' *Journ. Eg. Arch.*, viii (1922), p. 219 ff.

[2] See p. 2.

[3] Cook, *Cambr. Anc. Hist.*, ii. 399.

any other period earlier or later when the Hebrews could have entered Palestine from the desert, as the Khabiru did.[1]

The Khabiru (*Sa-Gaz*)[2] are first met with before 2000 B.C. in the days of Rim-Sin and Hammurabi,[3] and somewhat later under the early Kassites, as tribal levies in Southern Babylonia. They were dwellers, probably, on the outskirts of the desert who took service with the princes of the plain. Later we find them up north, as warriors of the Hittites. Like Abraham, they move from Ur to Harran, so to speak. And the resemblance may mean a real identity.[4] A branch of the race moves very early (the Abrahamic migration) into Southern Palestine, eventually with the Hyksos into Egypt and out with them again, and returns to the desert. This is Israel.[5] Then after two centuries the Hebrew-Israelite invasion takes place at the same time, the main body of the Khabiru moving from the north-east into Syria, while Joshua's force attacks from the east. That is the theory. It is difficult to square the events of the Joshua-Saga with those in the Amarna letters, but how far can tradition be trusted in details? The names of Joshua and his paladins do not occur in the Amarna letters. But we never hear in them the names of the actual leaders of the Khabiru, unless a certain Tagi is to be regarded as one of their

[1] The identity of Khabiru and Hebrews is accepted by most scholars, e. g. by Burney and Jirku, among others, without question. Cf. Dhorme, *Rév. Bibl.*, 1924, p. 33. The objections of Landsberger (*Z. Assyr.*, 1924, p. 213 ff.) which are purely philological, do not convince the historian. Cf. Lewy, *Z. Assyr.*, 1925, p. 26, n. 4.

[2] The absolute identity of Khabiru and *Sa-Gaz* is proved (Jirku, *loc. cit.*, p. 13; Weidner, *Boghazköi-Studien*, 8 (*Politische Dokumente aus Kleinasien*), p. 31, n. 9).

[3] There is even a possible mention as early as the time of Sargon of Agade (*c.* 2750 B.C.); see Jirku, *loc. cit.*, p. 14.

[4] Jirku, *loc. cit.*, p. 28.

[5] Here I do not follow Jirku, who makes the Israelites and Hebrews originally two entirely distinct peoples (p. 32).

chiefs, and names, even those of the principal actors in legend, are often untrustworthy. Are those in the *Chanson de Roland*, other than that of Charlemagne himself, historical? How far can we trust the names and the details in our traditional accounts of the conquest of Britain by the Saxons and Angles? It is unlikely that Hengest and Horsa were the real names of the Kentish invaders, since both names mean the same thing, and the white horse was and is the old Saxon emblem.

The curtain falls for half a century, and rises again when the young king of a new dynasty (itself probably of half Semitic origin in the Delta), Seti I., reasserts Egyptian domination in Palestine, and sets up his stelae of conquest and ownership at Bethshan, at Tell esh-Shihab near Mzerib beyond Jordan, at Kadesh on the Orontes (Tell Nebi Manduh), and even so far north as Ḥoms.[1] In the wars that ensued between Egypt and the Hittites over prostrate Palestine, Egyptian occupation of the 'Heerstrasse' from Gaza to Bethshan and the ford of the Jordan was more closely riveted than under the XVIIIth Dynasty, as we see at Bethshan, which must have been an important fortress, commanding as it did the way from the vale of Esdraelon across the Jordan into Syria. Rameses II also set up his stelae there, and on one of them the people of the 'Aperiu are mentioned, as we have seen. These again may be the Hebrews, who must, *ex hypothesi*, now have concentrated in the fastnesses of Mount Ephraim, but were unable to face Egypt in opposition.

The conclusion of peace between the Hittite king, Khattusil, and Rameses II about 1279 B. C. left Southern Palestine to Egypt, though she lost Syria, and certainly Northern Phoenicia. Fifty years later under Meneptaḥ, the successor of Rameses, we have the first undoubted historical mention of Israel, in the famous passage of his inscriptions, in which he says : ' Isirail is wasted : he hath no seed.' Israel is mentioned now as one of the

[1] *Cambr. Anc. Hist.*, ii. 319 ; and see *antea*, p. 2 ; and *P. E. F. Q. S.*, 1923, pp. 130 ff. For Kadesh see Pézard, *Syria* (1922), p. 89 ff.

chief nations of Palestine : ' Plundered is Canaan with every evil : Ashkelon is carried away ; taken is Gezer ; Yenoam is made as a thing that is not ; Israel is wasted, he hath no seed ; Palestine has become as a widow before Egypt.' [1] And the special mention of Israel looks as if the tribesmen of Mount Ephraim had, with the Canaanites of Ashkelon, Gezer, and Yenoam, been among the prime movers of revolt.

At this time indeed the Israelites seem to have developed in their new home with considerable energy, which had carried them not only across the Jordan but also northwards into the Vale of Esdraelon and down to the sea, where we find in the neighbourhood of Mount Carmel the settlement of Asher and Dan on the sea-coast, which soon afterwards disappeared in the turmoil of the Philistine invasion. It is to this period of expansion,[2] which the Philistine domination soon brought to an end, that the victory of Deborah and Barak must be assigned, and the struggle with Meneptaḥ also, which may have been directly caused by the defeat of the Canaanitish chariotry under Sisera at Taanach, the event that placed Israel not only in the position of dominator of Canaan, but also athwart the Egyptian line of advance into Syria. If the empire re-established by Seti I and maintained against the Hittites by Rameses II was to be preserved, Meneptaḥ had to strike, and it would seem that he did, with effect. The southern coast-cities must have opposed him as more or less subject-allies of Israel, with the result we know from his stele. Egypt no doubt regained the *Heerstrasse* to Galilee, Bethshan, and the Jordan, cutting off Dan and Asher and even probably Gilead from the south. Twenty years later the Philistine invasion took place and reduced Israel, first to a century of nullity, and then to the century of actual servitude from which David rescued her.

The Philistine invasion brings totally new forces upon the

---

[1] See *antea*, p. 1.
[2] For this see E. Meyer, *Israel u. ihre Nachbarstämme*, pp. 472 ff.

C

scene, to consider which we must digress from the story of
Egypt's relations with Israel, to take it up again later when we
come to deal with the Philistine domination in Palestine. This
is also a convenient point at which to break off from Egypt for
a space in order to discover possible early relations with Israel
of the other surrounding nations.

The mention of Babylonia, in the first place, brings the story
of Abraham into our view. Whatever the standpoint from
which we regard it, there can be little doubt that it represents
a historical tradition of connexion with Palestine of a tribe
originally settled in Mesopotamia, the Khabiru or Hebrews in
fact, which was the direct ancestor of the Israelite Hebrews who
went to Egypt. Abraham's visit to Egypt may be a mere
doublet of the legend of Joseph. But the connexion with
Harran and Ur of the Chaldees is more definitely historical,
as the probable fragment of historical legend preserved in
Genesis xiv shows. Here we have Abraham brought into
hostile contact with 'Amraphel king of Shinar, Arioch king of
Ellasar, Chedorla'omer king of Elam, and Tid'al king of the
Goyyim, who are probably the historical king Hammurabi, of
the Amorite dynasty of Babylon, an unidentified king of Larsa,
a king of Elam not known from inscriptions but whose name
must have been Kudur-Lagamar, and a king of the Hittites
(Goyyim, or ' Gentiles ') with the common Hittite appellation
Dudkhalia, which was known already well before 2000 B. C.
in Anatolia,[1] and is no doubt much older than this. So
much our modern knowledge tells us. Such a collocation of
names belongs to about 2000 B.C., and it is evident that tribal
tradition preserved the tale of an ancient collision of the
primitive Hebrew semi-nomads with the powers of Mesopotamia about that time.[2] And it was precisely at this date that
Khabiru warriors took service as warriors with the princes

---

[1] Sidney Smith, *Cappadocian Texts*, i, p. 21.
[2] *Anc. Hist. Near East*, p. 194.

of the plain (see above, p. 15). We see these Abrahamites (Khabiru?) as a tribe of Amurru unsteadily wavering between Syria and Mesopotamia like the tribes of Aramaeans along the Euphrates in later times. Gradually the Israelite branch came to a temporary rest in Southern Palestine, from which the Israelites may have more than once gone down into Egypt as Abraham was supposed to have gone, until, carried along probably by the momentum of the host that moved down from Syria, they finally entered Egypt as part of the Hyksos invasion.

With Southern Palestine we hear of few direct Babylonian connexions at this time, though with Syria, the North-Phoenician coast, and the Amanus region the Babylonians had been in direct communication a thousand years and more before, when we see the rulers of Sumer and Akkad passing through the Cedar Forest (Amanus) and the Silver Mountain (Taurus) in their expeditions to the ' Upper Sea ' (the Mediterranean). And just as we see that Semitic folk were settled beyond Taurus in the region of Argaeus (Caesarea Mazaca) [1] possibly in the time of Sargon of Akkad (*c.* 2800 B. C.) where (until they were expelled or died out some centuries later) they lived spreading the knowledge of Babylonian culture and especially the cuneiform script among the Anatolians, with whom it was to abide for centuries, so no doubt in the early part of the third millennium the same knowledge passed southwards from Syria into Palestine and Phoenicia, and the knowledge of cuneiform writing and Euphratean religion was grounded which later on we find a part of Canaanite civilization. The Canaanites naturally used a Semitic script for their own Semitic language, and they must have begun to do so many centuries before the Amarna period, indeed before the Hyksos invasion, since after it one would expect (judging by the considerable amount of Egyptian culture adopted by the Hyksos) that the Egyptian script would have had considerable chance of being brought back by them

[1] S. Smith, *op. cit.*, and see Hall, in *Ramsay Anatolian Studies*, pp. 171, 172.

modified in some way to serve Semitic needs. It is highly probable, as a matter of fact, that some such script as this, modelled upon the Egyptian, was actually in use in the border-lands of Egypt as early as the time of the XIIth Dynasty (2000 B. C.) when it was used in the Sinaitic peninsula, at Sarābīt al-Khādim;[1] and many centuries later, under the XIXth Dynasty (*c.* 1250 B. C.), at Byblos in Phoenicia,[2] we find it already developed into the Phoenician-Aramaic alphabet, the origin of the Greek and our own. But this curious script never came to its own until it had become simplified to the alphabetic form : until then the cuneiform syllabary, more adapted to writing Semitic than any script partaking of the cumbrous complications of the Egyptian possibly could be, remained in general use. Indeed, we do not know that David's scribe Shavsha, who has a Babylonian name, was not a Babyl-onian who wrote in cuneiform, though it seems more probable that he used Aramaic, since we find it used not only two hundred years before at Byblos but a century later by Ahab's scribes at Samaria and by those of the Judaean capital on Ophel.[3]

The Babylonian influence on Palestinian culture was un-doubtedly great. Space fails us here in which to follow various lines of argument that might establish here a con-nexion and there a parallel; the great instance of the adoption of cuneiform and the well-known connexions of Mesopotam-ian and Canaanitish-Syrian religion, typified in Ishtar-Ashtoreth-Astarte and Dumuzi-Tammuz-Adonis, are sufficient for our purpose. The early Canaanitish culture, of which we obtain hints from the Bible, and from such Egyptian records as those of Thutmosis III, must have been, as was to be ex-

---

[1] Gardiner, 'The Egyptian Origin of the Semitic Alphabet,' *Journ. Eg. Arch.*, iii (1916), p. 1 ff. ; Cowley, 'The Origin of the Semitic Alphabet'; *ibid.*, p. 17 ff.

[2] Dussaud, 'Les inscriptions phéniciennes du tombeau d'Ahiram', *Syria*, v. 135–57.   [3] *P. E. F. Q. S.*, 1924, p. 183 ff.

pected, a mixture of Babylonian and Egyptian influences grafted on to a native substratum that does not seem to have been of much account, judging from the results of excavations. The result of the mixture was, however, not un-luxurious (see p. 12). Later on Palestine was more affected by Syrian culture, and Syrian influence is specially to be observed in the Northern Kingdom, where also, as was natural, Phoenician influence was much stronger than in the South. Indeed, foreign influences in culture, in religion, and in art, to us seem soon to have different-iated Israel from Judah, and the Solomonic culture seems to have departed from Jerusalem to the more congenial soil of Samaria.

In Syria there was a strong native culture-element, less Egyptian influence than in Phoenicia, and more of Hittite ; while at the same time the Syrian strongly affected the Hittite, so that a Syro-Hittite *Mischkultur* arose among the Aramaeans, which must have exercised the greatest possible influence on the civilization of the Israelite Kingdom, but would not be apparent there earlier than the Disruption.

We have mentioned the Hittites : Tid'al, king of Goyyim, otherwise Dudkhalia, king of Khatti, the Anatolian Hittites, is a figure whose true significance has only been apparent of late years.[1] We now see that there existed in Anatolia, beyond

---

[1] The same may be said of Chedorla'omer of Elam ; but the Elamites, whose culture was akin to that of the Sumerians of Babylonia, rarely can have appeared in the West, and one cannot speak of any specifically Elamite influence there, though it has recently been suspected. On the Hittites see Hogarth, in *Cambr. Anc. Hist.*, ii, pp. 252 ff. and 540 ff., and in *Ramsay Anatolian Studies*, p. 225 ff. ; Hall, *ib.*, p. 165 ff., and Cowley, Schweich Lectures, *The Hittites*. Although the characteristic hieroglyphic script of the Hittites is found most developed in the late sculptures of Carchemish and rarely in Anatolia at all, I cannot agree with Cowley that the Hittites only adopted it at a late period, and originally wrote in cunei-form, which we find in use at Boghâz-Kyöi in the Amarna period. This seems against all probability. The cumbrous hieroglyphic system must

the confines of the Semitic world, from comparatively early times a civilization which although it owed much to Sumerian culture exercised through the Syrians (whose native culture was equally influenced by the Sumerians), and through the medium of Assyria and the Semitic colony in the Argaeus region, was at the same time so strongly marked by individual characteristics that it bears the stamp of a nationalism almost as definite as that of Egypt. It was a culture ruder than the Egyptian or the Babylonian or than the Minoan that adjoined it on the west, to which also it probably was related racially as well as culturally. The Hittite tablets of Boghâz-Kyöi show us a loose confederation of Anatolian nations, some speaking Asianic tongues, others a mixed language, half Aryan, called Luvian, which was perhaps related to the speech of the presumably pre-Aryan Minoan Greeks, and another, purely Aryan in structure but with a large non-Aryan vocabulary, which was the tongue of the ruling race, to which the kings belonged. And the certainly Aryan words in the Hittite vocabulary were west-Aryan, and related more to Latin than to Greek. But the religion of this Hittite ' empire' seems to us more Asianic than Aryan ; and Anatolian religion bore this Asianic character to the last, with its worship of the mother Kybele and her husband-son Atys, related certainly on the one hand to Minoan religion and on the other to Syrian, rather than to anything which we can regard as Aryan Greek. We know something of the history of the Hittite kings from about 1600 B. C. And one of them employed Khabiru soldiers. This, if the Khabiru are the Hebrews, is the first connexion between them and the Hittites that we know. From the Hebrew side we hear of ' children of Heth' in Palestine. And there is

---

surely be the older, retained for nationalist reasons till quite late times for monumental inscriptions, while ordinary correspondence was conducted in cuneiform or possibly in linear hieroglyphs, such as those on the leaden tablets from Assur (Andrae, *Hettitische Inschriften auf Bleistreifen*, 1924).

(called by the Assyrians Ashgūza, the Greek Σκύθαι), Japheth and Togarmah, all represent the Anatolians and peoples of Armenia and the North generally ; while Madai are the Medes, from the eighth to the sixth centuries—the time from which the genealogy evidently dates—closely connected in the popular mind as enemies of Assyria with the Scyths and Kimmerians, the Umman-Mandā, as the Assyrians called the Northern tribes. Tiras is no doubt Tyrsenoi, Tursce (= Italy), and Javan (Ἰάων) is the Ionians (= Greeks generally) with his sons Elishah (the ancient Alashiya : ? the west Cilician coast), Tharshish (Tarsus, or Tartessos = Spain), Kittim (Kition = Cyprus), and Dodanim or possibly Rodanim (Rhodes). On this explanation the genealogy of Javan is circumscribed, with the exception of Tharshish, to the coast from Cilicia and Cyprus to Rhodes, where the Ionians and semi-Greeks related to the Ionians dwelt, who would have been already known to the Hebrews in the eighth century. Tharshish may originally have meant Tarsus, and been transferred to Tartessos later when the Phoenician voyages to Spain became well known. Since Tiras is pretty certainly Etruria, Italy, Tharshish may well later have meant Spain, as the mention of its ships may indicate. The distinction of Tiras as a son of Japheth, and brother not son of Javan, shows that the racial distinction between Greeks and Etruscans was well understood, so that why Tharshish is a son of Javan is difficult to explain if it was originally Tartessos, whereas we know that there were Ionian settlers in the neighbourhood of Tarsus at least as early as the beginning of the seventh century, when Sennacherib's generals warred with them, and probably much earlier, as is indicated in the story of Mopsos and his colonists.[1] Rodanim, which should be Rhodes, evidently stands for the Aegean Greeks generally. But is it not possible, I would ask, that the

---

[1] Hogarth, in *Cambr. Anc. Hist.*, ii. pp. 545, 547. Mr. Hogarth brings the expedition of Mopsos into direct connexion with the Philistine invasion, which seems a likely suggestion.

original reading was Donanim (= Danuna, Δαναοί), which would be a much better equivalent for the continental Greeks? I commend this suggestion of mine to the experts in textual emendation. It is perhaps surprising that Rhodes should be omitted if Cyprus is mentioned; but Cyprus naturally was well known to the Hebrews, and all other Semites, as pre-eminently the home of the Javanites and would in no case have been left out of the list. In later days Javan was always used as the Hebrew name of the Hellenes, as the Romans, taking another of their sectional names to represent the whole, called them Graeci. But the days when Japheth was to dwell in the tents of Shem, when Alexander was to hellenize the eastern world, and the Maccabees were to bid defiance to Hellenism, are outside my scope.

We return along the dusty road of history a thousand years, to the days when Krēthi and Pelēthi, sons of Japheth indeed, if not of Javan, but unknown to the later compilers of genealogies, also dwelt in the tents of Shem as predecessors of the Macedonian and his epigoni, and were finally conquered by that earlier Judas Maccabaeus, Elhanan or Ba'al-hanan (?) called David, the son of Jesse.[1]

We hear nothing from the Egyptians of the doings of the Philistines in the Shephelah, nor for a century do we hear much of them in Jewish story, except the tale of Shamgar, which points to successful local resistance against the invaders. The Philistines established themselves in the cities of the seaboard and inland as far as Ziklag (a non-Semitic name) and Gath, and modern excavation has found the traces of their settlement here and there in the shape of the pottery of debased Aegean type but mostly made locally. These finds show that later on the Philistines penetrated so far inland as Bethshemesh in the south, as we shall see they also did in the north as far as Bethshan. In the

[1] See S. A. Cook, in *Cambr. Anc. Hist.*, p. 393 ff. (after Sayce, *Hibbert Lectures*, 1887, p. 53 ff.).

story of Samson also we seem to hear echoes of Aegean culture. Whether Samson is partly a solar hero, a sort of Gilgamesh perhaps, may be debated ; but when placing his exploits in Philistia the Jewish chronicler gives us an insight into Philistine manners and customs that certainly echo our other knowledge of ancient ways.[1] Bethshan was reached during the second period of the Philistine expansion, when Israel was conquered and enslaved by the Philistines, an event of which we have in the Bible an account that obviously bears the stamp of genuine history. The date of this conquest may be placed about 1080 B. C., at the end of the high-priesthood of Eli,[2] and it was the result of the single victory of Eben-ha-ezer and the capture of the sacred ark of Yahweh. The Philistines held down the Israelites in the hills by a system of garrisons (*neṣībim*), the forging of iron weapons was forbidden to the Israelites, and the possession of Bethshan ensured for the conquerors the passage over Jordan.[3] The religious revolt of Saul and Samuel in Gilead, followed by the capture of Geba' and the victory at Michmash, resulted in the expulsion of the foreign overlords. But the struggle was not decided till the slaying of Saul and Jonathan (largely owing to the defection of David) on Mount Gilboa once more placed the Israelites and their king Ishba'al under the control of the Philistines and the chief of their confederacy, Achish. Elhanan (?) or David's unification of the kingdoms of Hebron and Mahanaim and capture of Jerusalem moved Achish to advance against him, and the battle of Ba'al-perazim reversed the verdict of Eben-ha-ezer. The subjection of the greater part of Philistia to David followed, and the Pelethites and Cherethites entered his service as the mercenaries of the successful condottiere who had established the Hebrew kingdom in ancient Jerusalem and now perhaps

---

[1] See my *Anc. Hist. Near East* (6th ed., 1924), p. 418.
[2] Meyer, *Israeliten u. ihre Nachbarstämme*, p. 381, *n*. 1.
[3] *Anc. Hist. Near East.*, p. 423.

took the name David as being that of a local Jebusite god, Daudoh.[1]

Egypt, however, had not lost sight of her ancient rights in Palestine, and it is probable that the Philistines were driven to invoke her aid. She was, however, now weak, and her kingdom divided between the Priest-kings and the Tanites of the XXIst Dynasty. One or two of the Tanites, as Siamon, were monarchs of some energy, and it is probable that Solomon deemed it politic to conciliate him and take his daughter to wife, probably with the Philistine city of Gezer, which the pharaoh (? Siamon) [2] had captured, as dowry. The advent to power of the more energetic Libyan-Bubastite XXIInd Dynasty meant more direct interference in Palestine on the part of Egypt, and the revolt of Jeroboam, who had Egyptian connexions, is to be connected with the expedition of the pharaoh Sheshenk or Shishak I, who, about 930 B. c., in the fifth year of Rehoboam, besieged and took Jerusalem. Whatever outward show of allegiance the kings of Judah and Israel may at first have observed towards Egypt, Shishak and his successors took no steps to revive the empire of the Thutmosids and Ramessids in Palestine, and very soon all pretence at real political control was abandoned by the Egyptian court. Too weak to rule, it continued, however, to influence the course of events in Palestine by constant intrigues. Egypt probably had largely

---

[1] See Cook, *loc. cit.* Daudoh is mentioned by Mesha' of Moab in the Moabite Stone as a deity of his enemies, as also is Yahweh. It is conjectured by Frazer, *Adonis, Attis, Osiris*, 3rd ed., i. p. 19 *n.*, that David assumed the name of the city-god on his capture of Jerusalem.

[2] Chronology will hardly allow the taker of Gezer to have been Shishak, as Peet, *Egypt and the Old Testament*, p. 163, suggests. We have no knowledge that Shishak attacked Palestine at all till the time of his great expedition against Jerusalem, which took place in the twenty-second year of his reign. If Solomon was an old man by 935, he is more likely to have married, middle-aged, a daughter of Siamon (reigned *c.* 970–950) than, when old, a daughter of Shishak (reigned 927–940).

brought about the always threatening division of the kingdom,
for the power of Solomon, so close to the borders, must have
been to her an alarming portent. Her present object was
to keep the two kingdoms as much as possible embroiled with
each other and with their neighbours. Military intervention
had no prospect of success after the significant defeat of
Zerah ' the Ethiopian ' (probably Osorkon I of Egypt) by
Asa about 895.[1]

Between the two branches of the Israelitish-Hebrew race
and their immediate neighbours relations had never been good.
They were always regarded as intruders : they had displaced
Amalek and the Edomites in the south, the Canaanites everywhere, when they had not exterminated them ; and Moab,
Ammon, and Midian to the East loved them not. During the
period of the Judges war was constant with all these, when the
Philistine power was not felt. And at one time ' Israel was
brought very low because of Midian '. Saul and Samuel finally
defeated Amalek, and David disposed of Ammon and, for the
time, of Moab and Edom, so that probably his name, as Ba'al-
hanan, appears in the lists of the kings of Edom. And then
the Aramaeans of Syria entered the lists against the powerful
Israelite king, with the result that Damascus was annexed to the
kingdom of David and Solomon. The North-Syrian princes
who since the destruction of the Hittite power had been independent of foreign control, and at this time probably formed
a loose confederation under the king of Hamath, were too far
away and too powerful to be attacked by David, who was always
a prudent warrior. His friendship with To'i of Hamath
is chronicled, as are also his relations with Hiram of Tyre. The
Phoenician cities, now entirely divorced from Egypt, flourished
with their commerce on the main, and peaceful commercial
relations with them as with North Syria were characteristic
of the policy of David and Solomon, who controlled the trade

[1] The name ' Zerah ' is probably corrupted from an original (O)zerakh(on).

routes from Gaza to Tadmor and from Ezion-geber to Damascus and Tyre.

Events took a new turn when the battle of Ḳarḳar in 853 B. C.[1] brought the Assyrians into Palestinian affairs for the first time. Assyria had now succeeded to the ancient power of Babylon. In the days of the Amarna letters, five centuries before, she led rather a precarious existence among the contentions of the surrounding great powers, Babylon, Mitanni, Egypt, and Khatti. Ancient days, when she already dominated western Anatolia, were even then long past. She had no power in the West, from which she was barred by Mitanni and by the conflicting Hittite and Egyptian spheres of interest in Syria. Babylon still was actively interested in Palestine on account of her caravans, but claimed no hegemony there as she did over Assyria : her kings fully recognized the legal rights of their brothers of Egypt as kings of Canaan, from whom the Semitic kinglets received the holy oil of their unction. The contemporary conquest of Mitanni by Supilul the Hittite and the later elimination of the Hittites themselves by the Philistines gave Assyria room to breathe. The nation developed, and in the ninth century the cruel conqueror Ashur-naṣir-pal gave the peoples a foretaste of the wrath that was to come to them from Assyria. Ashur-naṣir-pal took from Babylon her control over the Aramaean states of the Middle Euphrates ; Carchemish of the Hittites followed Bit-Adini of the Aramaeans in paying tribute : Syria and Phoenicia submitted. His successor, Shalmaneser III, consolidated these conquests. Bit-Adini and Irkhuleni of Hamath summoned to their help Ben-Hadad II of Damascus, who now maintained there the royalty that had been set up when Rezin revolted from Solomon towards the end of the wise king's reign and southern Syria was lost to Israel. And with Benhadad marched Ahab of Israel,

---

[1] For the date see Forrer, *Chronologie der neuassyrischen Zeit*, M. V. A. G., 1915.

whom the Damascene king had compelled to acknowledge his overlordship. With Ahab came Egyptians, the 'thousand men of Muṣri' mentioned as with the allies.[1] The confederacy was defeated at Ḳarḳar, in the Orontes valley, but Shalmaneser's force was too shattered to pursue the enemy; while at the same time Ahab took the opportunity of the losses of the Syrians to attack Benhadad in alliance with Jehoshaphat of Judah, only to be defeated at Ramoth-Gilead.[2] The Syrians were, however, exhausted and took no further revenge on Ahab, who himself lost Moab to the native rebel Mesha‘, which Ahab and Jehoram were unable to recover. We hear of the other side of this war from the Moabite Stone, on which Mesha‘ records his slaughter of the Israelites and how he dragged the sacred vessels of their god Yahweh before his god Chemosh. Edom then revolted from Judah. Syrian overlordship in Israel was still claimed, and when in 841 Shalmaneser defeated Hazael on the slopes of Hebron, Jehu sent the famous embassy to the Assyrian which is recorded on the 'Black Obelisk' in the British Museum. Israel now for the first time paid tribute to Assyria, which was renewed fifty years later by Jehoahaz to Adadnirari III, who was the first Assyrian to enter Palestine, for he records that not only the House of 'Omri (Israel) but also Edom and Philistia submitted to him and paid him tribute. Judah is not mentioned and was no doubt considered a mere vassal of Israel. Edom also submitted as a separate kingdom. The victories of Jehoash and Jeroboam II over Syria, which resulted in the capture of even Hamath by the Israelites, followed.

The appearance of the Assyrians on the borders of Egypt and the threatening power of Israel under the aegis of Assyria must have caused a considerable stirring among the dry bones on the banks of the Nile, and one of the chief pre-occupations

[1] There is no doubt that these were Egyptians, and not a contingent from the northern Muṣri (see Olmstead, *History of Assyria*, p. 134).
[2] Some would place Ramoth-Gilead *before* Ḳarḳar.

of the rulers of Egypt was to stave off the danger that threatened their country from Assyria. Too weak to do this by force of arms they bent themselves to effect it by political intrigue, in which, as the depositaries of an ancient and worldly-wise culture, they were adept. The Philistine cities were naturally inclined to look to Egypt for help against the Assyrian domination in Palestine, which again materialized, after a temporary obscuration of Assyria, in the reign of Tiglath-pileser III. The appeal of Ahaz of Judah to Tiglath-pileser for aid against the Philistines and their allies of the kingdom of Israel, perhaps eager for revenge on Judah for the temporary domination by Azariah,[1] brought Assyria into the field once more and the Philistines were the chief object of attack. The Philistines apparently still retained at least a semblance of their foreign nationality, as their names such as Rukipti and Ikaushu (Achish) at this period show. They were still not wholly assimilated to the Semites, as perhaps they were later in the time of Nehemiah,[2] though the tradition of western origin was never lost among them, and was naturally revived in Hellenistic and Roman times, when Zeus Kretagenes ('Marnas') was worshipped at Gaza, and the name of Minoa was borne by the same Philistine town.[3] Their foreign origin perhaps moved the Philistines of the eighth century to resistance against a Semitic domination more threatening than that of Israel or Judah or even Damascus, and they naturally turned to Egypt for help. None came, however, in material guise: Egypt was now in the last throes of the dynastic quarrels of the XXIInd and XXIIIrd Dynasties; the Memphite-Saite

[1] It seems to me more probable that 'Azriyau of Yaudi' was Azariah of Judah than that he was a North-Syrian prince (*Anc. Hist. Near East*, p. 463).

[2] *Cambr. Anc. Hist.*, ii, p. 289.

[3] Hall, *Oldest Civilization of Greece*, p. 340. *Cf.* G. F. Hill, *Life of Porphyry Bishop of Gaza by Mark the Deacon*, p. xxxii ff. Mr. Hill notes the constant enmity of Gaza to the Jews, in Maccabaean times as earlier.

princes were coming forward as supplanters of the Bubastites
of the Delta, and the Ethiopians were preparing to seize the
derelict inheritance of Thebes.   When Tiglath-pileser took
Gaza in 734, Hanun its king (a Semitic name here) fled for
refuge to Egypt; Rukipti of Askalon submitted, and Philistia
was annexed to Assyria as far as the border of Egypt. But the
revolt of Hoshea of Israel, again probably relying on at least the
hope of Egyptian assistance—though how it could be expected
under the circumstances of Egypt at the moment it is difficult
to understand—followed, with its result, the capture of Samaria
and captivity of Israel, following that of Damascus.

The fate of Palestine seemed assured when, probably about
721, hope of assistance from the Nile-land was renewed by the
Ethiopian conquest of Egypt under the king Pi'ankhi.   In 720
Sib'e, ' the *turtan* ' (commander-in-chief) of Egypt ', probably
the Ethiopian prince Shabaka, then perhaps commanding in
Egypt for pharaoh Pi'ankhi,[1] actually invaded Palestine in arms
against Assyria, bringing with him the exiled Hanun, and was
routed at Raphia.   Shabaka probably fled to Nubia, abandoning
the Delta to the Saite princes Tefnakhte (Tnephachthos) and
Bocchoris.   The latter was probably mixed up with a new
Philistine revolt in 715, when Ashdod revolted under a Greek
adventurer, a ' Yavāni ' from Cyprus or Ionia, and was of
course defeated.   In 712 Shabaka returned to Egypt and destroyed Bocchoris, but it was not till 700 that he, again now in
alliance with Hezekiah of Judah and the national party in
Philistia, tried conclusions with Assyria, and was again defeated
at Eltekeh.   The siege of Jerusalem by Sennacherib's generals
followed, and the valiant resistance of Hezekiah atoned for his
political stupidity; for Egypt was, indeed, as the Rab-shakeh
said, ' a broken reed, upon which if a man lean, it shall pierce

---

[1] On the probable identity of Sib'e with Shabaka, in spite of many
objections, see my *Anc. Hist. Near East*, p. 472.   In 2 Kings xvii the mention
of Seve (So) or Sib'e (= Shabaka ?) seems to be displaced from 720 to 726 B.C.

his hand'. Shabaka now died, and the struggle of his second successor, Tirhakah, against Assyria, with its alternations of success and defeat, followed. In 671 Esarhaddon conquered Egypt. Since the battle of Ḳarḳar, nearly two centuries before, fear of Assyria had dominated Egyptian policy in Palestine. She had with the feeble means at her disposal, of intrigue rather than of war, opposed the enemy with at any rate the result of staving off actual invasion from herself, though with uniformly disastrous results to her friends. But now the blow fell, and for the first time for a thousand years Egypt was conquered and occupied by a Semitic enemy. Tirhakah, however, was not defeated : the retirement of Esarhaddon was followed by his return to Egypt, and it was not till 663 that Ashurbanipal finally overthrew his successor Tanutamon, took Thebes, and enslaved Egypt.[1] Psamatik, son of Niku, of the Saite house, who had been the faithful servant of Assyria, ruled as an Assyrian satrap, with the Assyrian name Nabu-shezib-anni, till the growing weakness of his overlord, wearied by the succession of Elamite wars, enabled him gradually to throw off the yoke and ascend the throne as pharaoh. Still, however, even at the end of his long reign, when Assyria, in the throes of dissolution, was encircled by the forces of Nabopolassar of Babylon and Uvakhshatra (Kyaxares) of Media, he regarded himself as the ally of Assyria, and came to the help of her last kings on the Euphrates (616). The destruction of Nineveh in 612[2] left Egypt face to face with Nabopolassar, and the advance of Psamatik's successor, Niku II (Necho), to Carchemish (609–605), in the course of which he defeated Josiah, the ally of Babylonia, at Megiddo, ended in the victory of the Babylonian and the

[1] For the date, which now seems certain, see *Anc. Hist. Near East*, 6th ed. (1924), p. 502 ff. The recalculation is based on Forrer's conclusions, *M. V. A. G.*, 1916, see above p. 34.

[2] See C. J. Gadd, *The Fall of Nineveh* (1923) and *The Expositor*, Feb., 1925.

retreat of the Egyptian again to his own soil. Palestine now fell to Babylonia, whose rule was accepted everywhere except in Judah, where Necho's nominee, Jehoiakim, was left undisturbed for the time, till his fanaticism, in spite of the warnings of the prophet Jeremiah, led him into the mad adventure of defiance that ended in the Captivity of Judah (586) by Nebuchadrezzar.

Israel and Judah were now both destroyed and carried away captive. But whereas Israel disappeared into the East, never to return, Judah abode in mourning ' by the waters of Babylon ', remembering Zion, until the tolerant policy of the Persian conqueror of Babylonia and the eastern world enabled a remnant to return and rebuild the Temple. It was only a remnant. The Nabataeans had occupied the vacant territory of Judah to the south, and the Samaritans held the old kingdom of Israel. There was no room for more than a remnant. And the Diaspora had already begun. Jewish mercenaries had taken service in Egypt, where also numbers of Hebrew merchants had already congregated, forming communities of settlers such as that of which we have recovered a priceless record in the papyri of Elephantine, which prove the existence in a city of the far south of Egypt, on the borders of Nubia, of a regular Ghetto, quite of the sort which existed later at Rome and still later all over Europe, the last specimen of which (apart from Russian Poland), survived at Frankfurt-on-the-Main till the beginning of the nineteenth century. At Yēb (Elephantine) these transplanted Jews were polytheists, and had not a mere synagogue, but a temple, their own temple with sacrifices to Ya'u or Yahweh and his contemplar goddess 'Anath and the deities Bethel, 'Ishum, and Herem, an institution which was regarded with great disfavour by the native priests of the Egyptian god Khnum. The papyri tell us much of the struggle of the Jews of Elephantine with these priests, and of their appeal towards the end of the fifth century (408 B. C.) against Egyptian exactions to Bagoas, the Persian governor of Judah : [1] the Persian had now ruled in Egypt, with short intervals of native revolt, for more than a century. The tale of the Jews at Yēb and Jerusalem under new Persian patrons is a presage of what was to come in the later centuries ; of the Diaspora and the ceaseless striving to rebuild Zion. For the time the surrounding nations had conquered, and Zion existed again only on sufferance, to be exposed soon to a denationalizing influence more powerful than any other, that of the descendants of Javan, who came, more and more powerful Philistines, in the train of Alexander. Idumaeans and Nabataeans, her old foes of Edom and Midian, had fallen to the wiles of pagan Hellas : should Judah escape ? The Maccabaean reaction warded off the serious danger of absolute drowning in the sea of Hellenism ; but when Rome came as the heir of the Macedonian and a more powerful leveller than he, the ' end of the auld sang ' was at hand. Judah, even after she was permitted to dwell again in Zion and Aelia Capitolina was no more, never existed again as an independent state in the Promised Land. The strength of the surrounding nations and the dispersal of her people to the ends of the earth rendered a restoration of the kingdom impossible.

H. R. HALL.

[1] See *Anc. Hist. Near East*, p. 546, for references ; and the latest work on the subject, Cowley, *Aramaic Papyri of the Fifth Century* B. C., Oxford, 1923.

[ADDITIONAL NOTE.—On p. 11 it might be added that if the Golden Calf was the Goddess Hathor, the Brazen Serpent may very well have been the Delta-Goddess Buto, whose symbol was a serpent borne aloft upon a standard. An inscription from Deir al-baḥri in Egypt mentions Hathor as ' the Cow of Gold ' (Hall, *Hierogl. Texts*, v, pl. 40, p. 11 : see Spiegelberg, *Äg. Zts.* 1923, p. 56). Pp. 8, 16. I am glad to see that J. W. Jack in *Expository Times*, 1924, pp. 40–4, agrees that the Israel stela proves conclusively that the Exodus took place before the time of Meneptaḥ.]

THE RELIGIOUS ENVIRONMENT
OF ISRAEL

In recent years the study of the religion of Israel has been powerfully stimulated by our increased knowledge of its environment. It has thereby become possible to consider the way in which Yahwism was influenced by the religious conditions that prevailed over the great area of which Israel formed only a very small part. Just as the ' external history ' of Israel involves that larger background of events in which she was inextricably interwoven, so the comparative, historical, and other departments of the science of religion place Yahwism upon a larger canvas, and study it in its place among the religions of the ancient world. Indeed, so much has been written on this subject that only a very general notion of the field thus opened up can here be given.

The comparative study of religion is symptomatic of the progress of research as a whole, and the endeavour to interpret ancient cults moves *pari passu* with the modern developments of thought. The study is relatively modern, and many preliminary steps were necessary. It began virtually with John Spencer, whose work on the ritual laws of the Hebrews (1685) ' may justly be said to have laid the foundations ', though he was more concerned to defend the rationality of the Mosaic legislation than to pursue the method of comparison.[1] The next real landmark consists in the researches of William Robertson Smith (1846–94), himself responsible for the estimate of Spencer just quoted. He collected considerable stores of illustrative material, opened up many new lines of

[1] H. P. Smith, *Essays in Biblical Interpretation* (Boston, 1921), pp. 106 ff.

inquiry and established fundamental principles,[1] thus placing the study of ancient religion upon a new basis. The course of subsequent research cannot here be described, it must suffice merely to emphasize the profound difference between the modern and the early works on our subject.

Now, the collection of material is but a very preliminary undertaking. So many questions arise, such sweeping conclusions are apt to be drawn, that it is more important that the reader should know something of the principles of the scientific study of religion and be able to realize its possibilities and limitations, than that he should be presented with a quantity of miscellaneous evidence, or with a finished sketch *ex cathedra* which would be a reconstruction needing justification.

To start at the beginning, then. The religious beliefs and practices of Israel find numerous analogies or parallels in the neighbouring lands. Thus, there are similar religious ideas in Moab (viz. in the inscription of Mesha, *c.* 850 B. C.), similar sacrificial ritual in Phoenicia, South Arabia, and Babylonia. This similarity is of course striking when the languages are akin ; but even in Egyptian, a language quite distinct from Semitic, there are interesting resemblances to Old Testament or to Semitic thought, as regards imagery, ideas, &c. Excavation in Palestine has revealed many traces of Mesopotamian, Egyptian, Hittite, and Aegean contact, and when we turn from material objects to beliefs or rites comparison at once takes us far afield. In all cases we have to ask, have we the results of borrowing, of direct or indirect influence; or are the resemblances due to common origin and to causes which lie outside our inquiry ? Very difficult questions arise, but at the outset we have merely

[1] Notably in *Animal Worship and Animal Tribes among the Arabs and in the Old Testament* (1880) ; art. ‘ Sacrifice ’, *Ency. Britannica* (1886) ; *Kinship and Marriage in early Arabia* (1885, 2nd edition, 1903), and *Religion of the Semites* (1889, 2nd edition [by the author] 1894, 3rd edition in preparation [by the present writer]).

to register the similarities. Further, we should notice that whatever geographical position, or trade-routes, or the vicissitudes of history might lead us to anticipate, we are not confined, as regards beliefs and practices, by geography or history. As every one knows, much valuable work has been done in tracing resemblances (1) between ancient Babylonia, Egypt or Palestine and the modern East, and (2) between the ancient and modern East and Africa, Australia, &c. For merely comparative purposes distance in space and time is not necessarily relevant—*at the outset*.

But everywhere, by the side of resemblances, there are differences. They begin at once—within Israel itself, or in the differences between the Israelite and Phoenician sacrificial systems, and so forth. *At the outset*, however, the resemblances are the more significant, and time has only enhanced the measured words of Driver in 1899 :

' The general result of the archaeological and anthropological researches of the past half-century has been to take the Hebrews out of the isolated position which, as a nation, they seemed previously to hold, and to demonstrate their affinities with, and often their dependence upon, the civilizations by which they were surrounded. . . . Their beliefs . . . their social usages . . . their religious institutions can no longer be viewed, as was once possible, as differing in kind from those of other nations, and determined in every feature by a direct revelation from Heaven; all, it is now known, have substantial analogies among other peoples.' [1]

The relationship which we find between Israel, the old Oriental peoples and even rudimentary peoples, is precisely as significant as that among organisms. The similarities between the lower and the higher orders, and between prehistoric and existing types, are just as fundamental from one point of view as are the essential differences from another. That real

[1] *Authority and Archaeology Sacred and Profane*, ed. Hogarth (2nd edition, 1899).

continuity which can be traced among peoples widely severed in space and time is precisely as significant as the dissimilarity, and so much confusion is engendered by writers who stress the one group of facts to the exclusion of the other, that an ability to recognize both groups is indispensable for any serious study. Our starting-point must be the frank recognition that there are as essential resemblances between religions as between man, the rest of the primates, and the lower orders. We shall, then, not be perplexed at the striking resemblances, and we can endeavour to understand more clearly the striking differences.

The discovery of resemblances leads to questions of their real value—for they vary greatly—and of the inferences that can be based upon them. And at once we encounter the inevitable limitations of mere comparison. For example, the Ark of the Covenant has been supposed to be a seat, an empty throne, a chest containing some sacred object or fetish, and one perhaps carried about on a boat, a cart, &c. The Ephod, in turn, has been taken to be a loin-cloth, a plated image, the clothing worn by the image, and—on occasion—by the priest or diviner, &c. In every case it is possible to adduce interesting parallels ; but we cannot necessarily prove that our particular explanation excludes others and is alone correct. The comparative method affords parallels, suggests explanations ; it is highly stimulating, but, in itself, it is inconclusive. The golden bells on the high-priest's garment might be explained by the common belief that the noise would frighten away evil sprits : but a noise might also be made to arouse a deity, and it has even been suggested that the ceremonial trumpet-blowing in Israel served this purpose. Yet, in either case the question is whether such motives prevailed in Israel, and we have to be sure that the particular explanation we prefer is in harmony with the ideas of the age.

Thus, if we take the contents and symbolism of Solomon's

Temple, for the brazen serpent, pillar, cherubim, molten sea, and the rest, parallels can be found in the ancient world. But it does not follow that each object meant for Israel what its parallel did for Mesopotamia, Egypt, &c. From the Old Testament itself we can see how the trans-Jordanic altar could be explained as a mere memorial (Joshua xxii), and how Jacob's pillar at Bethel could be primarily the abode of a spirit (Gen. xxviii. 16 ff.). We might, suppose, therefore, that the Temple-objects were gradually bereft of the meaning they have elsewhere, or even that they had been borrowed unintelligently, and were meaningless from the first. The comparative method views things in isolation, but our inter-pretation depends upon their context, and, consequently, it is significant that (1) as regards, e. g., the Nehushtan (2 Kings xviii. 4) there is much miscellaneous evidence for the venera-tion of serpents in Palestine, and that (2) the view that the molten 'sea' had a cosmical meaning and referred to the world-ocean and Marduk's conflict with the dragon finds some support in the Biblical references to Yahweh's power over the ocean and his defeat of the dragon. In this way we can recover much of the ancient thought of Israel, and we pass from the external comparison of beliefs and rites to the ideas that lie beneath them and give them life.

Starting with the belief that Samson's strength lay in his hair, we extend our inquiries and reach two important ideas : (1) that a man's strength, life, or soul was something tangible, material, concrete ; and (2), that it could be taken by an enemy, or protected by a god, or otherwise preserved. In two remarkable passages in the Old Testament we read that a man's soul could be bound in a bundle with Yahweh, and that it could be snared.[1] We are entitled to conclude that such

[1] 1 Sam. xxv. 29 and Ezek. xiii. 17–21 : see J. G. Frazer, *Folk-lore in the Old Testament*, ii. 503 ff. The significance of the former passage was also pointed out by the present writer in an essay on ' Israel and Totemism '

ideas were neither exceptional nor isolated in Israel; there
must have been others implicated in them, though of course
we cannot determine precisely how far we may supplement
or reconstruct them from what we know of other lands. Another
important fact emerges. The belief that one's soul is in safety,
and other 'spiritual' ideas of trust and confidence, or of
anxiety and fear, are obviously psychological, resting upon
appropriate emotions, convictions, &c. So also the world-
wide tabus with their fear of the contagion of holiness or of
uncleanness—familiar in the Old Testament—have a psychological foundation; and he who breaks one may even die,
overwhelmed by his fears of the consequences. On the other
hand, 'spiritual' beliefs and ideas are primarily clothed in
highly concrete form; they express themselves perceptually,
so that ideas of the safety or danger of the soul can be vividly
realized when 'the blood is the life', or the soul is supposed—
outside Palestine at least—to inhabit some such object as
a tree or a stone. In the incisive words of Robertson Smith:

'Redemption, substitution, purification, atoning blood, the garment
of righteousness, are all terms which in some sense go back to antique
ritual. But in ancient religion all these terms are very vaguely defined;
they indicate impressions produced on the mind of the worshipper by
features of the ritual, rather than formulated ethico-dogmatical ideas;
and the attempt to find in them anything as precise and definite as the
notions attached to the same words by Christian theologians is altogether illegitimate . . . in primitive life all spiritual and ethical ideas
are still wrapped up in the husk of a material embodiment.' (*Religion
of the Semites*, p. 439.)

The importance of this principle has hardly yet been fully
realized. David's belief in a bundle of life conceivably took
some material form, as elsewhere, where the soul has an actual
material embodiment; for, if the life of the nation could be

(*Jew. Quart. Rev.*, 1902, p. 446 f.): for the latter passage see also *Ency.
Biblica*, art. 'Dress', col. 1141.

embodied in the visible king (2 Sam. xxi. 17), a man's life
might have a no less visible vehicle. Certainly the 'cup' in
Jer. xxv. goes back to ceremonial scenes such as are represented
on Hittite reliefs; and when the god takes the 'hand' of a
man, Babylonian ritual shows that this could be a realistic
ceremony. If sins are blotted out or washed away, there are
—outside Palestine at least—magico-religious practices which
serve this purpose. Again, elsewhere at least, the 'spiritual'
resemblance to a god is preceded by a 'ceremonial' one
(toilet, dress, &c.); and 'spiritual' ideas of rebirth find their
prototype in highly realistic practices. In fact, the transition
from the perceptual or ritual to the spiritual or conceptual,
is so well attested that we have to expect it and determine
to which stage our data belong. Thus the 'Rock of Israel'
(2 Sam. xxiii. 3) may be pure metaphor, or some apparent
'magic' or 'fetishism' may reflect no lowly recognition of
a spiritual power. Our horizon is immensely widened as we
see into the modes of life and thought of ancient peoples,
although our limitations become painfully obvious.

Again, from the story of Saul's visit to the witch of Endor
we pass to divination, resort to oracles, ordeals, and the means
of learning the will of the gods, and utilizing their might.
There are fundamental convictions of man's power, either
directly or indirectly through the gods, and of his ability to
cope with life's problems. For example, we have much evidence
for resort to sacred places in the hope of procuring offspring;
and the widespread cult of Oriental mother-goddesses, and
the numerous Astarte-figurines in and around Palestine
supplement Israel's ideas concerning Yahweh's power over
life and death. Now, human societies have everywhere their
systems—often very complex—of belief and ritual, and early
religion is very practical. In necromancy, divination, Astarte-
worship, and all else that prevailed in and around Palestine,
there were well-understood forms of cult. The more developed

we find these to be, the more important is the problem of the early growth of Yahwism as the religion of a newly introduced god—a problem quite distinct from that of the history of prophetic reform. Yahwism, like Christianity in its day, had to take an attitude to the current religions : some elements it naturally accepted, to others it was antagonistic. And we have to bear in mind that, in the very nature of the case, Yahwism, as a practical religion, must have incorporated all the usual essential elements of a social-religious cult. Consequently, the student has to look for their traces, explain their absence, or observe the forms they take.

It is to be observed also, that the rudimentary ideas of the powers of gods and spirits, and of causes and effects in general, paved the way for the theology and philosophy of the more advanced stages of culture. There is a certain continuity between the lowest and the highest religions ; there is a transition ' from religion to philosophy '.[1] Much has yet to be worked out, but we are already entitled to look for the bridge between early Egyptian mythology and the strange syncretisms of the Greek period, and to search for links between old Oriental thought and the ' Wisdom ' literature. The idea of Wisdom in Prov. viii is hardly mythological, but it has a mythological parentage, even as germs of the Logos-idea have been claimed in early Babylonian conceptions of the Word. Caution is needed throughout in tracing such connexions, but it is instructive to notice the persistence of semi-mythological conceptions in the late apocryphal writings, and the antiquity of ideas of gods and of causes which represent early tendencies to reflect upon the nature of deity and the origins of things.

Once more the limitations obtrude themselves. Thus, the account of the Nephilim in Gen. vi. 4 obviously implies a much

---

[1] See Cornford's brilliant book, *From Religion to Philosophy : a Study in the Origins of Western Speculation* (London, 1912).

fuller record of these prehistoric giants and their exploits; and, in fact, in *late* sources we find *late* references to the fall of angels. The old myth has been lost—it would clearly be out of place in Genesis—and it would be rash to reconstruct the details from the late references. We might, perhaps, distinguish among these the earlier elements from the later, but the isolated verse is a 'bone' of some 'skeleton', though by no means of the sort of 'skeleton' which we find later. We are tempted to reconstruct the missing 'skeleton'; but reconstruction, always legitimate within limits, is always dangerous. Every case must be taken on its merits. A study of the world-wide stories of a Tree of Life has suggested a reconstruction of the original account of which that in Genesis is only one version; and the stories of the birth of Moses and other heroic figures have induced the conjecture that originally the Pharaoh proposed to kill all the male children because he had been warned that a child would be born who would rob him of his throne and life.[1] The method is ingenious; but it has led to wayward and extravagant fancies, as when sweeping resemblances have been claimed between Babylonian, biblical, and Homeric literature on the basis of a certain similarity among a few 'bones'. Every significant datum implies other data, but there are always differences. Although no two animals and no two plants are exactly alike, we have the sciences of zoology and botany; but the data of the world of beliefs and practices have not yet been wrought into a science. The differences are often most fundamental. Ps. civ has points of contact with a hymn of the Egyptian reforming-king Ikhnaton; but the psalm is theistic in a way that the hymn is not, and its background is Palestinian. The biblical accounts of the Creation and Deluge differ in spirit from the Babylonian originals or parallels. The Hebrews (or

[1] See, respectively, Frazer, *Folk-lore*, i. 51 f.: Gressmann, *Mose und seine Zeit* (1913), p. 5.

Israelites) differed psychologically from the Babylonians (or Assyrians); human sacrifice and ceremonial licentiousness appear to be more inveterate in Syria and Palestine than in Babylonia, Arabia, or Egypt. There are differences of temper and thought between Semites and Greeks, even as there are between the Indian and the Persian religions; and every estimate of Israel's debt to her neighbours must take into account such facts as these.

Relatively lofty ideas prevailed outside Israel; and, conversely, the cult of Yahweh came to involve much that called forth the prophets' condemnation. The licentious cults of Palestine might have originated, as Indian religion suggests, in rites of mystical union with the deity, and have been sustained by rudimentary ideas of the cause of natural growth; but although we have none of the ancient invocations to Astarte, a prayer in 105 lines to her counterpart Ishtar is ' one of the finest Babylonian compositions that has yet been recovered ' (L. W. King). Here we read :

I pray unto thee, lady of ladies, goddess of goddesses !
O Ishtar, queen of all peoples, directress of mankind ! . . .
All mankind, the whole human race, boweth down before thy power.
Thou judgest the cause of men with justice and righteousness . . .
Where thou lookest in pity, the dead man lives again, the sick is
     healed ;
The afflicted is saved from his affliction, when he beholdeth thy face !
I, thy servant, sorrowful, sighing, and in distress cry unto thee.
Look upon me, O my lady, and accept my supplication, . . .
May thine eyes rest with favour upon me ;
With thy glorious regard truly in mercy look upon me ! . . .
My heart hath taken wing, and hath flown away like a bird of the
     heavens ;
I moan like a dove, night and day . . .
Forgive my transgression, accept my supplication ! . . .
How long, O my lady, wilt thou be angry and thy face be turned away ?

How long, O my lady, wilt thou rage and thy spirit be full of
  wrath ? . . .
Let my prayer and my supplication come unto thee,
. And let thy great mercy be upon me,
That those who behold me in the street may magnify thy name,
And that I may glorify thy godhead and thy might before man-
  kind ! . . .[1]

It is of interest, too, in view of the Jewish traditions of
Nebuchadrezzar to note his own prayer to Marduk upon his
accession to the throne :

'Without thee, O lord, what would happen unto the king whom
thou lovest and whose name thou dost call? As it appeareth good
unto thee, hast thou directed his name aright ! A straight path dost
thou grant unto him ! I am the prince who obeyeth thee, the creation
of thy hand. Thou art my creator, and the sovereignty over the
hosts of men hast thou entrusted unto me. According to thy mercy,
O lord, which thou hast extended over all of them, incline unto compassion thine exalted power and the fear of thy god-head set within
my heart. Grant (unto me) that which may seem good unto thee.'

We are gradually learning much of the religious background
of the Ancient East, and much has been collected which proves
extremely suggestive for the general study of Israelite religion.
Thus the history of Islam, its sects, and the recent rise of
Babism is highly suggestive : in the work of founders of
religions and sects, in the vicissitudes of new religions and
in their relation to the old we have material which helps us
to estimate more truly the work of Moses and the reformers of
Yahwism. Of special interest is the speedy growth of false
tradition in Babism, conflicts in regard to fundamental doctrines,
the diversity of opinion relating to the authorship of various
Bābī writings, and the appearance of different 'official'

[1] L. W. King, *The Seven Tablets of Creation*, i (1902), pp. 222 ff.   The
prayer of Nebuchadrezzar is from his *Assyrian Language* (1901), pp. 191 ff.

histories and recensions.[1]   Special problems similar to those
in Israel appear elsewhere in the relation between orthodox
Islam and the popular religion, where the *Welis* and saints
correspond *mutatis mutandis* to the Baals and local gods of
old. We learn the ' sort of thing ' that could have happened,
and approach the question of the centralization of religion
in Israel with a wider knowledge. If we cannot always tell
how Israel was influenced by her environment, we at least
know more of the usual relations between greater and lesser
gods, the co-ordination of different cults, the effects of war
and of alliance, and so forth.

Of supreme interest is the ebb and flow of religion. It is
noteworthy how such ethical gods as Varuna and Ahura-
Mazda (virtually his later counterpart) stand at the head of
the long development of Indian and of Zoroastrian religion,
the more interesting because, while the latter god was doubtless familiar to the Jews and other peoples of the Achaemenid
age, the former was known in the fourteenth century B. C.—
at all events to the Hittites and to the· Mitannians of North
Syria, and the latter, or a kindred Iranian people, left traces
of their influence in Palestine. Again, as we observe the
deterioration of ethical religion as Varuna came to occupy
a secondary place, we can the better appreciate the work of
the prophets in purifying and reviving Yahwism. Ancient
India also illustrates the growth of a priesthood and of a magico-
religious theory of priestly sacrifice—to which Judaism affords
some parallels ; while, nearer home, Egypt shows us the
powerful priesthood of the XIXth Dynasty gradually usurping
monarchical power, and Mesopotamia furnishes other examples
of typical relations between the ecclesiastical and the secular
arm. In this way the kingship and priesthood of Israel, even
if not positively influenced by the environment, can be more

[1] E. G. Browne, *Materials for the Study of the Babi-Religion* (1918),
pp. xxi, xxiii f.

vividly apprehended ; and light is thrown upon ideas of a priestly king or royal priest, and their significance for the conception of a Messiah (cf. pp. 64, 69 f.). Moreover it can safely be said that the elaborate priestly ritual, as preserved in the Pentateuch, is an unintelligible phenomenon in the history of religion if we retain it at the beginning of Israel's career as a nation.

The decline of an ethical religion is partly the inevitable price of the adjustment of the teaching of individualist reformers to the social-religious cult of the community. It is helpful, therefore, to understand (1) the Egyptian monistic reform of Ikhnaton and its failure (cf. p. 68 f.), and (2) the successful reorganization of Israel after the Exile amid the death of all creative power in Egypt and Babylonia. And when a religion dies, the varied results can be studied in the sporadic traces of old Oriental ideas among the Mandaeans and the people of Harran, or in the debt of Egyptian Christianity to the survivals of the old Egyptian religion, or in the almost complete extinction of the South Arabian civilization. Thus does the environment of Israel afford invaluable suggestive material for the story of the birth, career, and death of religions, and we can study the religion of Israel as that, not of a book, but of a people, whose history extends over only a small portion of the entire period during which Oriental religion is now known to us.

Since the religion of Israel is conceived as one of other religions—the differences which give it its permanent value not being ignored—the same or similar fundamental principles are assumed to prevail throughout. This is important in view of certain far-reaching principles and theories which may be briefly noticed. (1) The antiquity of sundry beliefs and practices *outside* Israel does not prove, as is sometimes thought, that they must be no less ancient *within*. There are catalogues of ethical and other offences in early Babylonia and Egypt—in the former, in the shape of questions (e. g. 'Has he separated brother from brother?'), in the latter, as denials (e. g. 'I have not dealt falsely against men'). There are also ancient psalms, prayers, and gnomic utterances, so that it might be urged that Palestine must have possessed ethical codes before Moses, psalms before David, and proverbs before Solomon. Indeed, such is the general culture of the Amarna age that—on *a priori* grounds—Palestine might fairly be credited with a very rich literature long before the entrance of Israel.

On the other hand, the low level of Arab culture at the rise of Mohammed shows how a people can be indifferent to a higher civilization; Palestine excavation does not reveal any considerable influence of Babylonia; and the many traces of Egyptian influence do not prove that Egyptian ethical and other ideas entered and took root. The Amarna tablets themselves do not, on various internal grounds, suggest that writing was in universal use. Moreover, Oriental literature was often copied and recopied, and ancient Babylonian legal usages are found in the fifth century B. C. at Elephantine in Egypt, and, much later, in the Talmud. There were several periods when Babylonia or Egypt could exercise influence upon Palestine, and the question of the earliest date when, say, the Egyptian story of the Two Brothers could have entered Palestine is not so important for us as the date of the passages where presumed traces are found (viz. in the story of Joseph and Potiphar's wife.) It is probable that some Israelite circles were more in touch with the neighbouring lands than others; but the evidence for a certain independence in archaeology, thought, and religion must be weighed against the arguments for the imposition of any culture from without. It should also be observed, in passing, that since Babylonia, in its turn, was susceptible to external influence (West Semitic, or 'Amorite', as it has been called), the apparent 'Babylonian' elements in the Old Testament may have come from another and nearer source common to both.

(2) Another very important assumption is that primitive traits are necessarily early. If this were so, and if Palestine enjoyed an advanced state of culture at an early period, then these traits must be very ancient indeed, or they must be treated as survivals. As a matter of fact, the Code of Hammurabi (*c.* 21st cent. B. C.) represents a relatively more advanced society than either the Israelite or the Assyrian laws. The Assyrian laws are in certain respects the crudest, perhaps typical of a fiercer temperament ; but the Babylonian retain the *lex talio* and collective responsibility (contrast the individualism of Jeremiah and Ezekiel), and some of the penalties are ferocious. We have to understand, therefore, that social institutions (marriage, property, &c.), economic conditions, material civilization, and humanitarian and ethical ideals do not move at the same pace. Human sacrifice persisted among the Carthaginians, and Phoenician myth virtually justified what the much earlier story of Abraham and Isaac relegates to the past. So, while Yahweh accepts the animal substitute (Gen. xxii), the Carthaginians, at a much later date (310 B. C.), ascribed their disasters to their religious negligence, in offering up for sacrifice bought children in the place of their own. Again, difference of *milieu* is to be considered. There was always a difference between the wild tribes of the desert and the settled population, whether under a Solomon or a Herod ; and at various times, owing to historical causes, the desert influence would be especially strong—not only when the Israelites entered, but when Sargon introduced desert tribes into Samaria (715 B. C.), and also later. At periods of disintegration primitive features are invariably more prominent, and the assumption under consideration has the merit of making us ask ourselves what we really mean by ' primitive ', ' crude ', or ' rudimentary ' traits. The period of the sixth

century B. C. was certainly one when such traits would predominate, and, consequently, each piece of evidence taken by itself conveys no indication of its precise date.

Hence, we must be prepared for the antiquity of culture in and around Palestine, and must also do justice (*a*) to the rudimentary or primitive elements which attract attention because of the simple conditions they imply, and (*b*) to the absence of the influence which we might otherwise have expected. This leads us to two widely opposed theories—that of Semitic totemism and that of the various Pan-Babylonian schools.

(3) The theory of a primitive Semitic totemism was brilliantly initiated by Robertson Smith. Since his day an immense amount of work has been done, and naturally the study of totemism no longer stands where it did. Although so far-reaching a theory cannot be discussed here, it has much in its favour. In totemism a social group stands to the totem (a species of animal or plant, generally edible, or to an object or class of objects) in an intimate relation of friendliness or of close kinship ; the totem is not in any sense an equal, but it is treated as a cognate, respected, not eaten or utilized save under certain restrictions ; the members of the group, too, are usually prohibited from marrying others of the same group. There are various modifications, even individuals can have their totems ; but what is essential is the all-round rudimentary character of the group. *Totemism* is found in Africa outside the Semitic area, but there it is hardly so ' primitive ' as that of Central Australia. *Totemic* features are found in early Egypt—natural enough in view of the proximity of negro tribes. But the *totemistic* or *theriomorphic* features of later Egypt—the worship of living animals which so amazed the Greeks—belong to an age when the national religion was decaying and the civilization had long passed far beyond the rudimentary stages.

We should not call these relatively late cults in Egypt, where each district had its own sacred animal, real totemism ; but they illustrate some of its elements. Animal traits—theriomorphism—in themselves do not spell totemism, but they invariably deserve attention. Animal names (e. g. Caleb ' dog ') may become entirely meaningless (like our ' Mr. Lamb ') ; but they are frequently significant, even when they are not totemic, betokening *originally* some recognition of the animal's power, some contact between man and the animal, some latent conviction that the two are not disparate. Animal names predominate in South Palestine (Judah–Edom) as against the North; and, as Buchanan Gray pointed out, if such names were harmless, it is difficult to see why they should have tended to disappear. ' They do not prove a totem stage in the development of Israel ; but it so far favours a totem theory that they receive from it a reasonable explanation.'[1] Moreover, when we consider the many names containing the divine element (Josiah, Hilkiah, &c.), it is astonishing to find in the age of Josiah such proper names as ' coney ' (Shaphan son of Azaliah), ' mole or weasel ' (Huldah), and ' mouse ' (Achbor son of Micaiah [i. e. ' Who is like Yah ? ']) ; for not only are their owners connected with the temple, but Ezekiel's vision (viii. 10), somewhat later, especially mentions the temple cults headed by Shaphan's son, the pourtrayal upon the walls of creeping things and abominable beasts, and the women weeping for Tammuz, the god especially associated with the swine. Of course, at times of disturbance and decadence obscure and old-time cults will come to the fore, but while this would mean that the animal-cults were quite exceptional at this age (*c.* 600 B. C.), it also implies that they were a reassertion of what had once been more familiar. In any case the ' bones ' indubitably point to a very remarkable ' skeleton '.

[1] G. B. Gray, *Hebrew Proper Names* (1896), p. 114 : cf. also id. *Ency. Biblica* ' Names (Place-) ' col. 3316 ,§ 104.

From the evidence for ' sacred ' animals among the Semites
and their association with certain deities, there is no doubt
that they played a large part in ancient life. The ' sanctity '
of both animal and human blood implies that animal and
human life were not thought of as necessarily different in
kind. Animal imagery and animal symbolism, too, indicate
that in certain respects the animal was more powerful than
man. And of such stuff is totemism made. But totemism
is on a consistently low level, and whereas at the stage of
anthropomorphism the animal imagery may still be freely
utilized, the lower stage is below the anthropomorphic. Until
conceptions of human personality were well established, the
idea of superhuman power, skill, &c., did not naturally clothe
itself in anthropomorphic form. Dr. Farnell,[1] in a happy
phrase, speaks of the ' unstable anthropomorphism ' of
Babylonia ; and it is natural to infer that, as we get back to
ruder stages, the anthropomorphism will become weaker, the
animal elements stronger. On theoretical grounds, at all
events, a theriomorphic or totemic stage preceded the anthropomorphic, the resemblances point to a continuity between
the stages, and a primary totemism of some sort alone appears
to account for certain later and higher developments. Our
evidence for the Semites is admittedly incomplete, and we
do not know what ' real ' totemism would be twenty-five,
thirty, or more centuries ago—even that of Central Australia
has a history behind it—but Robertson Smith's theory is
still, in the present writer's opinion, the best guide to all
the facts.

In marked contrast to this general evolutionary attitude,
(4) various ' Pan-Babylonian ' theories prevail. They are
influenced less by the ' primitiveness ' of the nomadic Semites,
and more by the advanced culture of Babylonia, Egypt, &c.

---

[1] L. R. Farnell, *Greece and Babylon : a comparative sketch of Mesopotamian, Anatolian, and Hellenic Religions* (1911).

One type in particular postulates an elaborate cult or teaching, which stood at the head of the history of positive thought.[1] It begins with a laborious and invaluable collection of *motifs* which recur in legend and myth—the marriage of the king's daughter, mysterious births, dragon conflicts, &c. These *motifs* have found their way into history, so that the old Sargon of Babylonia and Alexander the Great are embellished with mythical *motifs*. But since, conversely, perfectly circumstantial things are said of purely fictitious creations, each case must be taken on its merits, and the stories of Samson may present an inextricable fusion of mythical *motifs* and the traditions of some actual hero. Next, the *motifs* are essentially astral. The forty days of the disappearance of the Pleiades are days of storm and misfortune, the number is typical of want and privation. The five intercalary days (the $5\frac{1}{4}$ epagomena) explain the five kings conquered by Joshua. Goliath's height was really 5 ells and a span (the 6 ells is a misunderstanding). To be brief, there was a *façon de penser*—innumerable *clichés* floating about ready to be utilized. Comparison shows that they are world-wide, they link on to one another and admit of being systematized. Ultimately, from the scattered ' bones ' the ' Pan-Babylonists ' build up ' skeletons ', grandiose systems —a teaching, an astral *Weltanschauung*. The antiquity of Babylonian culture gives that land the first place, and a vast doctrine, a prehistoric ' pre-theology ', is supposed to have spread over the ancient world, into Egypt, Greece, and India, Mexico, &c. In its light the Old Testament and ancient literature are freely interpreted. The writings of this school must be read to be believed ; they contain much that is of permanent

[1] See A. Jeremias, *Handbuch der altorientalischen Geisteskultur* (Leipzig, 1913) : cf. his *Old Testament in the Light of the Ancient East* (1911). These contain fuller references to the pioneering work of Hugo Winckler and others. For some criticisms of ' Pan-Babylonism ' see W. L. Wardle, *Israel and Babylon*, ch. xii.

value enwrapped in theories to which, it must be confessed, it is difficult for the sceptic to do justice. In fact, we have a theory of a prehistoric theory.

When we talk of the ' patience of Job ', or of ' Philistinism ' there lies behind us the Bible. Mohammedan literature, in turn, presupposes the Koran. In like manner, a vast positive system is here postulated ; it has been built up, regardless of the limitations of the comparative method. Of course, strange systems once prevailed : the Chinese Yang and Yin illustrates how upon a few fundamental ideas an organized and remarkable body of thought can be constructed, and once established can hold its own. But this system is a purely theoretical construction. It is as though, from the fragments of innumerable skeletons, none complete, it was possible to formulate the sort of animal from which they all could be derived. The method is unnatural ; beliefs and customs cannot be treated in this manner.

It is argued that this system, or teaching, once inaugurated, set the standard. Women were veiled because Ishtar was veiled. People spoke of gods, heroes, heavenly bodies, and celestial phenomena in a certain fashion, and thus arose *clichés* or ' properties ' for more mundane affairs. There was (so the theory urges) a pre-established harmony between the celestial and the terrestrial : ' naturally in practice it is things terrestrial which are imagined in the heavens, but in theory [i. e. this ancient teaching] it is the other way, the type is in the heavens.' That is to say, men spoke of combats of deities, the movements of heavenly bodies, and so forth, in terms of mundane life, but the teaching starts with this positive doctrine—cosmical, celestial, call it what we will. Now there is a very profound truth in this. Men seek to imitate the gods, but the conceptions of the gods have first been influenced by a knowledge of men. In Egypt homely lessons were inculcated by the Osiris myth. The New Jerusalem owes itself to the Old, but the New alone inspires and stimulates. Religion takes up and gives new life to the 'non-religious' elements which it assimilates, and so, this strange theory of a primitive widespread teaching illustrates a very important fact when it recognizes the influence upon men of a super-sensuous, religious, romantic, or artistic treatment of things.

We perceive how, not the empirical facts themselves, but an idealization of them, influences mankind, and how we can follow a development from some positive initial, religious, or other stage—e. g. the introduction of such ethical gods as Yahweh, Varuṇa, and Ahura-Mazda (cf. p. 52)—although in reality, the new stage had behind it a history which in very many cases has been lost, or, as in the question of the Babylonian origin of Yahweh, is relatively unimportant. Hence the 'Pan-Babylonist' theory, in its various forms, is exceedingly stimulating and suggestive, and the extravagant forms it has taken should not blind us to its many valuable aspects. Among various 'technical' objections to it is the assumption of the migration of entire systems of thought. It applies equally to a recent theory of the Egyptian origin of all civilization.[1] This too, is based upon the 'comparative method', and it is fortified by the evidence for ethnical movements and trading-journeys and by the superior antiquity of a land so centrally situated as Egypt. Once more a grandiose system is built up, and a Frankinstein is constructed; in Procrustean manner new data are found to fit the theory admirably. Theories of sweeping Egyptian influence in Old Testament literature are not new; but the Asiatic or Semitic influence upon Egypt is well marked in historic times, and, although Egyptian influence in Palestine is indubitable, Egypt was also prepared to recognize Palestinian gods and permit a considerable measure of independence. Influence is not so simple and one-sided

[1] See the works of W. J. Perry, and the bibliography in M. A. Canney, *Givers of Life* (1923), pp. 104 ff.

a process as the theory assumes, and what is known of the ancient Oriental world places it beyond serious consideration.

Confronted with sweeping theories of the influence of A over B one must ask, what stage do we suppose B had reached previously? what are the conditions of a successful or permanent influence? what of the counter-influence of B upon A? and what of the ability of a migrating body to maintain its cultural unity intact? All such theories, audacious in their sweep and in their disregard for the minutiae of criticism, involve just those intricate problems which always engage the biblical student, viz. the relations between Israelites, Canaanites, and others, or between reforming figures (e. g. the prophets) and the people, the clash of religions, and the development and decay of religious and other ideas. They entail problems of methodology—and the questions which are apt to spring first to our lips are commonly the hardest to answer.

Gradually all such theories as these force a more careful analysis of both modern and ancient thought. For example, there are certain parallels between Israelite and other prophecy, certain *motifs* can be found elsewhere; but these only force us to recognize the *differentiae*, just as the sources of Shakespeare's plots or of Coleridge's *Ancient Mariner*, though necessary subjects of research, enable us to understand more clearly the essential nature of originality, genius, and personal influence. Again, much has been written in recent years of monotheistic tendencies in the Ancient East—the net result has been to compel us to analyse more closely our ideas of monotheism. We perceive the influence of a centralizing rule and a centralizing religion; the co-ordination of ideas of causes of things, and the play of opposing causes—the conflict of good and evil. In the readiness to use the same general term (*El, Elōhīm,* and the like) there is a consciousness of some fundamental similarity underlying different deities. In the Code of Hammurabi we find ' God ' behind or, in some way, other than, the recognized gods, and the whole history of religion implies that there is a Power greater than inherited or established conceptions of the gods. We are led to the psychological aspects—the psychological ability to assimilate and develop the idea of God. Much can be said about different forms and developments of the idea—and here external influences play their part ; but our inquiries take us, on the one hand, into the technicalities of the Science of Religion, and, on the other, to the fundamental question whether, by definition, mono-theistic, henotheistic, or other conceptions of ' God ' can originate from purely human or mundane experience.

Enough to observe that all these modern studies of Israel's environment have given us an immensely fuller and more powerful stock of knowledge, and not of Israel alone. As has been said, one tendency is to emphasize the progressive development of religion in its evolutionary aspects ; the other stresses the effect of new initial steps or of positive systems imposed from without or brought by immigrants or conquerors. A complete synthesis must appreciate the truth in both tendencies. Both processes have been at work in the history of religion, even as, in the history of individuals, the individual partly develops his own private world of life and thought, and partly is constantly indebted to some new and external stimulus. The history of the several religions is that of a certain unfolding, development, and deterioration, by the side of new stages of inspiration and rejuvenation. The old philosophy of history in Judges ii is in this respect profoundly true. The grandiose and bizarre theories of sweeping influences, to which we have referred, are incredible, unnatural ; we need theories and explanations which we can test by what we find within ourselves. The intricate facts of the influence and counter-influence of peoples and religions are not more com-plex as between man and man. And here the facts lie at hand. The great problems of ancient culture turn upon the possibility

and the nature of the influence of one man upon another—
questions which in this age of keen reforming activity are
extremely topical. Thus does the study of the religion of
Israel and its environment move *pari passu* with a better
knowledge of human personality.

What has just been said concerning influences leads us to
notice very briefly (1) the part played by the kingship in
developing ideas of personal religion, and (2) their extension
or ' democratization ' at certain historical periods. The kings
were typically the representatives of the deity, his lieutenant,
or even his embodiment. At the same time, they represented
the people, whose political and general prosperity was bound
up in them. So intimate was the relationship that the king's
character affected land and people, and if he offended the gods,
his realm would suffer, whereas the divine favour ensured
victory, good harvests, health, and happiness. ' The kings
had to exercise special precautions in all their acts—official
and otherwise. A mis-step, a failure to observe certain rites,
a neglect of any prescribed ceremonial, or a distinctly ethical
misdemeanour, or act of injustice or cruelty, might be fraught
with the most dire results.' [1] In Egypt the divine nature of
the kings was very realistically expressed. The Pharaoh was
of divine ancestry, chosen and begotten by the god, and when
Sinuhe, a fugitive in Syria in the Middle Kingdom, told forth
the praises of his king, ' the god who has none like him, before
whom no other existed ', we may suppose that the sentiment,
part of ancient ideas of the divine kingship, would not be
meaningless to the Semite, although such ideas cannot be
explicitly traced in Palestine before the Amarna age.

Properly speaking, the king was inferior to the deities. He
must appeal to them, carry out their behests, and, primarily,
there is not that attitude, characteristic of Magic, wherein,
instead of appeal or prayer, there is command or spell. Thus,

[1] M. Jastrow, *Religious Belief in Babylonia and Assyria* (1911), p. 241.

in the poetical account of the victory of Ramses II over the Hittites, the king, hard pressed and deserted, invokes his god :

> What is in thy heart, my father Amon,
> Does the father ignore the face of a son ?
> I have made petitions, and hast thou forgotten me ?
> Even in my going stood I not on thy word ?
> I never broke the decrees thou ordainedst. . . .
> Made I never for thee great multitudes of monuments ?
> I filled thy holy house with my prisoners,
> I built for thee a temple of millions of years,
> I have given all my goods to thee by decree,
> I give thee the whole of every land for offerings to thy holy altar,
> I have slain for thee myriads of oxen
> With all perfumes sweet to smell. . . .
> Amon, behold this has been done to thee out of love,
> I call upon thee, my father Amon. . . .
> I find that Amon is worth more than millions of troops
> More than hundreds of thousands of chariots. . . .

And the result :

> Amon came because I cried to him,
> He gave me his hand and I rejoiced,
> He cried out to me, ' My protection is with thee,
> My face is with thee, Ramses, loved of Amon,
> I am with thee, I am thy father,
> My hand is with thee,
> I am more excellent for thee than hundreds of thousands united
>   in one.' [1]

In Egypt the future life is at first reserved for royalty, but the reward must be earned. When the king dies, ' the sky weeps for thee, the earth trembles for thee, clouds darken the sky, the stars rain down '. His death was an almost cosmic event and naturally, since all prosperity was bound up

---

[1] Sir Flinders Petrie, *History of Egypt*, iii (1905), pp. 55–61.

F

in his person.[1]   But he does not reach his heaven by virtue of his rank ; there are certain ethical requirements. And these requirements, demanded of *the* man, the king, and then of the great men, the nobles, are ultimately for every man. The hymns, prayers, and records of all these distinctive individuals are, therefore, exceedingly instructive, because they show us an early form of personal religion. In Babylonia there was a ritual atonement in which the king took the prominent part. He implores the gods to return to their city, to look upon the thirsty and the suffering, and he prays that his sins may be released and his iniquity taken away. Consequently we can mark how the king's character could affect ordinary religious conceptions. When Ashurbanipal tore out the tongue of those who had spoken impiously against his god Ashur, when righteousness and loyalty were as closely associated as wickedness and rebellion, we can see how the behaviour of the distinctive individual—the king—was a tremendous power for good or for evil, for elevated or for low ideas of the Divine.

The city and local gods bestowed life, health, strength, victory, and prosperity ; they stood to the members of the locality in much the same way as the ruler to his people. But they were more immediate, even as the local chieftain was at hand to listen to complaints ; whereas the great king was somewhat inaccessible. In Egypt the ruler of a nome will assert, ' I did that which the god of the city loved,' or it is said of the nomarch : ' thy city-god, thy father loves thee.' The local chief or nomarch stood to the local cult as the Pharaoh did to the national religion. No doubt he would be influenced by the religious ideas of the Pharaoh, and the cult of the city-god would involve a certain amount of personal religion. In Egypt we often find him invoked to protect his faithful worshipper from the perils that beset the dead soul.

[1] Cf. Frazer, *The Golden Bough : The Dying God*, p. 14 f.

Now the ideas and usages established through the individual *par excellence* did not necessarily disappear when the kingship decayed or individualism grew stronger. At periods of social and political confusion individualistic tendencies are more powerful, and all transitional periods play a very important part in extending the beliefs, ideas, and practices which had once been confined to special circles. Dr. Warde Fowler (*Roman Ideas of Deity*, p. 102, f.) has remarked that when the medieval forms of religion were gradually changing in the fifteenth and sixteenth centuries A. D., we find a greater prominence of individuals and of individual thought. He observes very similar features in the Greek and Roman world at the rise of Christianity. It was a period of individual as opposed to national religion, and ideas of personality and personal worth were uniquely developed. A few centuries earlier we encounter another period of dislocation, at the downfall of the Assyrian Empire (seventh century) : a period of transition between the Old Oriental and the Indo-European (Persian, Greek, &c.) epochs of civilization, and one especially familiar to us for the individualistic teachings of the Hebrew prophets Jeremiah and Ezekiel.

But still earlier there are other significant periods. In Babylonia the age of Hammurabi (21st cent. B. C.) was one of political triumph ; civilization reached a relatively lofty height ; society was complex. Hammurabi's code represents a considerable amount of individualism, though the unit is the family ; the wife, children, and slave are parts of one unit, and share the responsibility. However, there was a downfall and many centuries elapsed before the land recovered itself sufficiently, and, after the rise and fall of Assyria, enjoyed a brief revival (sixth cent. B. C.). In Egypt the fall of the Old Kingdom (about 2700 B. C.) marks a period of disorganization, which increased the strength of the nomarchs and the local powers. The Middle Kingdom reveals the effects, and in the Twelfth Dynasty, approximately the age of Hammurabi, there is once more a high state of culture and diversity of thought. Especially noteworthy is the fact that the king sometimes seems to be more truly a god than the deities themselves—a significant aberration. The age was introspective, contemplative, and critical. The literature reflects magic and superstition, pessimism and scepticism, the consciousness of prevalent corruption, fickleness and untrustworthiness. In many senses the age was a ' live ' one.

The Middle Kingdom passed away, the Hyksos invaded the land. In time Egypt expelled the foe, religion and society were reorganized, and we enter upon the New Kingdom about 1580 B. C. There is closer intercourse with Asia, and Egypt became a world-empire. All conditions of life rapidly changed. There is a gradual democratization, and, characteristically enough, the costume and toilet of the ' upper classes ' are adopted by the ' lower '. The most remarkable of individualistic acts was the reform of the young Amenhotep IV, or Ikhnaton (about 1375 B. C.). The particularistic and exclusive myths were dropped.

' There are no references to the ancient solar myths, such as the combat of the sun with the dragon monster, to his voyage in his morning and evening barques, to the ancient and magical names. Not the fabulous adventures of an anthropomorphic sun-god, but the beneficent works of the divine sun, move the poet's admiration and gratitude.' [1]

The god Aton is at once a father and a mother to Egyptian and barbarian ; the Syrians and the Ethiopians are subjects of his providential care. The religion was universal, without the associations of the national and local cults. The zealous

[1] G. F. Moore, *History of Religions* (1914), i, p. 184. See, in general, J. H. Breasted, *Development of Religion and Thought in Ancient Egypt* (1912) pp. 312 ff. : *Cambridge Ancient History*, ii. 109 ff. (Breasted), 203 ff. (Peet).

king desecrated the holy places, banished the name of Amon, and destroyed the effective beliefs of the people. The reform ended, as it began, in violence; but although the old *régime* returned under Tutenkhamon, later religion was not uninfluenced by Ikhnaton's ideas. 'The human and beneficent aspects of Aton, in his care for all men, had taken hold upon the imagination of the thinking classes and we find the same qualities now attributed to Amon' (Breasted). The belief in an intimate and personal relationship between the worshipper and his god becomes more widespread, and—quite in harmony with this 'immediacy'—the characteristics of magic and fetishism come to the front. A stimulus is given to personal piety and religion, the individual has to find an outlet in ways that seem good to him—and both good and bad results follow. Similarly, when the life beyond death was extended outside the great men and the ordinary individual became an Osiris, the destiny of Osiris was open to all. But all must prove themselves morally acceptable, and thus the Osiris faith could become a great power for righteousness among the people. On the other hand, religious feeling decayed, the sense of individual responsibility weakened, and 'magical' means were taken to preserve a man from his fate. The ethical aspects were lost, and the Book of the Dead with its 'Negative Confession' became little more than an automatic charm.

The kingship, at its best, developed ideas of the relations between the individual and his god. The king was intermediate between the gods and the people, and to the people he could be a more real and tangible deity than the god or gods whom he served. It is of the greatest interest, therefore, that the petty kings of Syria and Palestine in the Amarna age (*c.* 1400 B.C.) freely recognized the divine or semi-divine character of their Egyptian overlord. No doubt it was partly conventional; but we are entitled to conclude that ideas of human representatives of the gods were familiar. There was a ' monarchical ' as opposed to a ' priestly ' type of religion ; and the local kinglets themselves, like the nomarchs of Egypt, doubtless stood in a very special relationship to the local deities. The phraseology of the Amarna Letters shows how they *did* address their sacred king, and how they *could* address their own deities ; and there is a variety of expression and metaphor which finds parallels in even the later writings of the Old Testament, and also implies a considerable wealth of thought and language. It is safe to infer, therefore, that a well-developed religious usage was established in Palestine before the fourteenth century B. C. awaiting invading Israelites and other settlers.

Details must be sought elsewhere.[1] It must suffice to refer to the Palestinian cities dedicated to Amon-Re of Egypt and to the Egyptian temples in Palestine with all their symbolism. There were deities which naturally had some meaning for the people, e. g. Shamash, the sun-god, god of justice, Addu or Adad (Ramman), god of the fierce storm and the beneficent and fertilizing rain. The name of Baal was known : he was a great god to whom the Pharaohs of the XIXth and XXth Dynasties loved to compare themselves. In a cuneiform tablet found at Taanach Akhi-yawi invokes the ' lord of the gods ', and tendencies to unite Shamash and Addu indicate that a co-ordinating or monotheistic (strictly ' henotheistic ') spirit was in the air. The name Akhi-yawi itself probably corresponds to that of Ahijah (Akhiyyahu); but although the god Yahweh may have been known, there is nothing to suggest that he was prominent. Powerful deities were, however, known, and the question, based on external data, as to what Palestine could offer the invading Israelites is not less important than that, based on the internal criticism of the Old Testament, as to the earliest forms of Yahwism.

[1] See, on the religion of the Amarna Age, the present writer, *Cambridge Ancient History*, ii. 336–51, and the literature, ib., p. 665 f.

The Amarna Age was one of a veritable internationalism. Perhaps its most arresting feature is the discovery that a certain similarity of idea can be traced over a large part of the ancient Oriental World. From the naturalism and love of truth which distinguish the religion and art of Ikhnaton, we can turn to the traces in Mitanni in North Syria (which had dynastic connexions with Egypt) of the prominence of the idea of Truth and Order (*arta*), familiar in the old Indian religion (*rita*), where it is associated with the ethical god Varuna, already referred to. Besides the solar god of justice, the Hebrew word for Righteousness in the compounds Melchizedek, Adoni-zedek, &c., contains related ideas of Right and Justice, but viewed from a distinctively social and religious aspect. That is to say, just as an age may be marked by ruling conceptions of a general character, widely distributed, though varying in form (cf. pragmatism, anti-intellectualism and direct action; nationalism and self-determination), so in the fourteenth century B. C. we find a series of fundamental inter-related ideas, but varying everywhere according to the land or circle where they appear.[1] Accordingly, at this age, when political and social barriers were being broken down, we have to recognize both the advanced character of the old religions and a certain similarity of ideas. But not only are there striking differences of form, only in Palestine do we find any real continuity and development.

A few centuries later, and the age in and about the sixth century B. C. is one of upheaval and of widespread religious unrest. Once more continuity and development distinguish Palestine in contrast to the Egyptian and Semitic empires. Confucius and Lao-tse, Gautama and the founder of Jainism, Zoroaster, Orphic cults, and the height of Israelite spiritual idealism in the Deutero-Isaiah—these present us with facts of outstanding significance, and it is precisely the old idea

[1] See further ib., pp. 397–403, and the literature, p. 670.

of Righteousness which gains a new prominence. No similar movement intervenes between the fourteenth and the sixth centuries, and it is true that the smaller area at the earlier period is historically more closely interconnected than are the vaster reforming movements at the later. But, like the third supreme period of religious unrest and development, that at the rise of Christianity in Palestine, these far-reaching events make us realize that the history of religion is something profounder than the internal developments of a land, a people, or a single religion. As we place the religious development of Israel upon that wonderful background which we are slowly recovering, the more impressive is the picture we gain of the Divine Process working among men. New and absorbing inquiries are opened up, as this sketch has endeavoured to explain, and the great values of religion, so far from suffering any loss, admit of being restated in a newer and a truer history of the past.

S. A. COOK.

THE MODERN STUDY OF THE HEBREW LANGUAGE

ἡ γὰρ τῶν λόγων κρίσις πολλῆς ἐστὶ πείρας τελευταῖον
ἐπιγέννημα—Longinus, περὶ ὕψους, 6.

THE writer was once asked how there could be any progress
in the study of Hebrew, and whether there was any work left
for scholars but to look up what the Jews had said and base
modern and possibly improved translations of the Old Testament on their versions and commentaries. The present essay
is an endeavour to answer this question along one of the many
lines of investigation now followed by the critic. It is the
writer's purpose to show how the student works and what
means there are, outside the sacred books themselves, for
increasing our knowledge of Hebrew and for solving many of
its still unsolved riddles; for it must never be forgotten that
classical Hebrew is not a language well known, like Greek, from
a vast body of very diverse types of literature but one confined
to a small set of books handling almost exclusively a single
theme, and that consequently, even within the narrow limits
of that theme, there must necessarily be, owing to the lack of
any other documents from which to draw comparisons, much
that is obscure.

By far the greater part of the Old Testament is written in
Hebrew; but Aramaic is the language of a few chapters in
Daniel (ii. 4–viii. 28), and of certain documents quoted in Ezra
(iv. 8–vi. 18 and vii. 12–26), as well as of an ancient gloss in
Jeremiah (x. 11), while in Genesis (xxxi. 47) the heap called
Gal'ēd by Jacob received from Laban the Aramaic name of
Yĕghar-sāhădhûthâ 'the heap of witness'. Here Laban and
Jacob represent respectively the 'Syrians', as the English

versions usually call the 'Aramaeans', and the Israelites, whose territories met on the north-eastern border of Gilead and who spoke distinct languages. The first of these two languages is called in the Old Testament 'Aramaic' (2 Kings xviii. 26 = Isa. xxxvi. 11, Ezra iv. 7 and Dan. ii. 4) or, in the Greek version, 'Syriac', and sometimes by Syriac writers 'Chaldee'. The second is described as 'the lip (*i.e.* tongue or speech) of Canaan' (Isa. xix. 18) or 'Jewish' (2 Kings xviii. 26, 28 and Neh. xiii. 24) in the Bible ; but the later Jews came to call Hebrew *lĕshôn haqqōdesh* 'the sacred tongue', while the term *'ibhrîth* 'Hebrew' is first found in native sources in use among the Palestinian Rabbis. The stories of Laban and Jacob at Gal'ēd as well as of the Rabshakeh prove that speakers of 'Jewish' and 'Aramaic' were unintelligible to each other. The only other language mentioned by name is that of Ashdod (Neh. xiii. 24), by which Philistian is probably meant ; of this, however, and of Ammonite (Deut. ii. 20) nothing, while of Amorite (Deut. iii. 9) very little, is known. Moabite (Deut. ii. 11) has been shown by the 'Moabite Stone' to be almost identical with Hebrew, and Sidonian (Deut. iii. 9) is hardly more than a name for the Phoenician language, in which a number of extant inscriptions is written and which is closely related to Canaanite. Apart from a number of Assyro-Babylonian loan-words which have been assimilated by Hebrew, Daniel's second name Belteshazzar (Dan. ii. 26), and the name of the Feast of Pûrîm 'lots' may be mentioned as purely Babylonian ; the latter is particularly interesting, for a comparison of the phrase 'they cast *pûr*' (Esther iii. 7), and a passage in a recently discovered Assyrian code of laws, in which occur the words 'for his second share he shall cast a pebble (*pûru*, used like the Greek ψῆφος 'pebble' and 'lot') with his brothers' proves that it is a Babylonian word brought back by the Jews from the exile.[1]

[1] G. R. Driver in the *Journal of Theological Studies*, xxiii, 92, p. 408. (Johns, *Assyrian Deeds and Documents*, vol. iv, p. 66.)

A few Egyptian words have also crept into the Old Testament, especially in the narrative of Joseph, such as *yĕ'ōr* ' the Nile ' (Egyptian *'io'r* ' watercourse ').

Hebrew, Aramaic and the cognate languages are all branches of the Semitic family. These languages stand far more closely together than, for instance, French, Spanish and Italian ; but Ethiopic, like Rumanian, is in many respects furthest removed from the common type. Many words in daily use run through the whole group : for example Ass. *bîtu*, Hebr. *bayith*, Aram. and Syr. *baythâ*, Arab. *baitu* and Eth. *bēt* ' house '. Yet great caution must be observed in explaining an unknown word in one language from the cognate word in another, since each acquires a special connotation which can only be determined by its usage in any given language, while a comparative study of the root will only give its basic, underlying significance ; thus from the root underlying Ass. *ezib*, Hebr. *'āzabh* and Aram. *'ăzabh* ' left ' are formed derivatives with such different connotations as ' except ' and ' divorce ' in Assyrian, ' desert ' a wife (Isa. liv. 6) and ' wares ' (as ' left ' in the purchaser's hand) in Hebrew, ' celibate' in Arabic and ' widowed ' in Ethiopic. This will suffice to show that comparative philology is a two-edged weapon which must be used prudently but may be productive of the most valuable results, especially in the case of a dead language like Hebrew which, in that it offers a very limited field, is naturally remarkable for a large number of rare or unknown words.

The name ' Semitic ' or, as it is sometimes called, ' Shemitic ', applied to this group of languages, is based on the fact that most of the nations which speak or spoke them are derived, according to the genealogy accepted by the Jews (Gen. x–xi), from Shem, the son of Noah ; Shem's sons are there said to be Aram (whence ' Aramaic ') and Arphaxad, whose grandson is Ebher (whence ' Hebrew ') the ancestor of Abraham, the father of Ishmael, from whom sprang the nomadic Arabs (whence ' Arabic '). But further, this table resting rather on geographical and political than on ethnographical principles, Asshur (whence ' Assyrian '), Elam and Lud appear among the sons of Shem, because the Elamites and Lydians were united under Assyrian rule at the time when the table was drawn up, although it is known that the two last-mentioned races were not Semitic either in race or in speech.[1] The outstanding feature which distinguishes the Semitic languages from all others is the fact that almost all words go back to triconsonantal roots, although it must be admitted that there is considerable plausibility in the hypothesis which would refer them ultimately to roots of only two consonants. But, as the languages are exhibited to us in extant documents, roots consisting of only three consonants constitute the vast majority of words. The few quadriliteral roots, which are rare except in Ethiopic, can hardly be primitive ; on the contrary, the isolated biliteral roots which have survived denote relations, such as *'ābh* ' father', parts of the body, like *yādh* ' hand ', or natural objects, like *'ēṣ* ' wood ', and belong to the primitive stock whence all the Semitic languages are sprung. Of the artificial biliteral roots postulated as original by some scholars, one example will suffice : the common root of two consonants underlying the Hebrew *ṣār* ' enclosed ', ' besieged ', *ṣārar* ' bound ', ' was restricted ', Arabic *'aṣara* ' confined ' and Hebrew *'āṣar* ' stored up ' (*viz.* shut up in a treasure-house), Hebrew *'āzar* ' restrained ', Arabic *ḥaṣara* ' surrounded ', with which the Hebrew *ḥāṣēr* ' enclosure ' is cognate, Assyrian *qaṣāru* ' to join together ' and Hebrew *qāṣar* ' harvested ' (*viz.* bound up the sheaves) is supposed to be *SAR* ' surround '[2]; but, though the theory may be true, it can never be proved, since the original Semitic speech, if indeed there was such a common speech, is lost beyond all hope of recovery and is therefore outside the bounds of practical philology.

[1] Schlözer in Eichhorn, *Repertorium* (1781), viii. 161.
[2] Burney, *Judges*, p. 96.

Equally characteristic is the importance assigned to the consonants, by which in almost every instance the meaning is expressed, while the vowels only serve to indicate modifications of the radical sense ; for example, *qāṭal* ' he killed ', *qěṭōl* ' kill ', *qôṭēl* ' killing ', *qāṭûl* ' killed ', and so on, all go back to the root *qṭl* ' kill '. Similarly, too, by doubling the consonants or by a change in the vowels, a number of themes can be formed, modifying the original denotation of the stem ; thus the simple intransitive verb *qādhash* ' was sacred ' yields, by doubling the middle consonant, a transitive form *qiddēsh* ' consecrated ', of which the passive *quddash* ' was consecrated ' is coined by changing the vowels. Other modifications are effected by the addition of prefixes, as *niqdash* ' showed oneself sacred ', *hiqdîsh* ' regarded as sacred ' and *hithqaddēsh* ' kept oneself sacred '. Of the various shades of meaning which the Hebrews could express by this means the ordinary reader of the English Bible can have no idea ; yet Hebrew was the least richly endowed in this way of all the Semitic languages, in that it used ordinarily only five themes, two of which had passive forms, whereas Assyrian possessed ten, Arabic nine together with their corresponding passives, and Ethiopic at least twelve ; and each language could create at will a number of rarer forms, so that in Ethiopic, for instance, the grammars record a possible total of more than twenty derived themes. But it is only fair to add that few verbs in practice employ more than half a dozen themes. These formations have the additional advantage that they do away with the need of a number of auxiliary verbs and of periphrastic constructions, and to a certain extent obviate the difficulty caused by the complete absence of compound words.

So thoroughgoing, in fact, is the aversion from compound words that the well-known Hebrew word *ṣalmāweth* ' valley of death ', which the Massoretes vocalized as one word, composed of *ṣēl* ' shadow ' and *māweth* ' death ', is now universally read *ṣalmûth* ' darkness ', through a comparison of the Ethiopic *ṣelmat* ' darkness ', which shows that the *th* or *t* are the feminine terminations indicating an abstract noun. Apart from proper names, the only undoubted compound in the Old Testament is the Hebrew *bĕlîyaʿal* ' Belial ', which is supposed to be formed from *bĕlî* ' without ' and *yaʿal* ' profit ', an assumed derivative from the same root as *hôʿîl* ' profited ' ; in Syriac the well-known *bĕʿeldĕbhābhâ* ' enemy ' is a loan-word from the Assyrian *bêl dabâbi* ' possessor of a plea ', *viz.* an adversary at law.

A great weakness in the Semitic languages is the possession of only two tenses. In this respect Hebrew, which failed in the classical period to invent any compound tenses, comes off worst ; for the Biblical language had only two tenses, the one expressing completed action and the other incomplete action, whether past, present or future. Yet Babylonian from the earliest time possessed also a present tense, and Aramaic as early as the fifth century B. C. had devised a present, an imperfect of habitual action, and a pluperfect, by prefixing the substantive verb to the perfect, imperfect or participle, as the case might require, just as English can distinguish between ' did ', ' is doing ' and ' was doing '. Phoenician apparently did the same, while Arabic, especially in the modern dialects, has created in this way a set of tenses as complete as that of most European languages ; modern Syriac has gone almost too far, having three presents and two preterites, as well as a perfect and an imperfect.

A striking peculiarity of this group is that all the Semitic languages express the genitive by the so-called ' construct case ' ; that is to say, not only is the dependent noun put in the genitive case, but the governing noun, whatever its case should be in relation to the syntax of the sentence, is also inflected, being put in the construct case. In Hebrew, owing to the almost total loss of the case-endings, this is often obscured but can be seen in the feminine singular and the masculine plural : for example, *baʿălāh* ' mistress ' but *baʿălath habbayith* ' mistress of the house ', and *bĕʿālîm* ' masters ', ' inhabitants ' but *baʿălēy hāʿîr* ' inhabitants of the city '.   There is, however, one mark of Semitic speech, namely, the preference for the co-ordination over the subordination of clauses, owing to the paucity of conjunctions, which can be recognized by the reader who is ignorant of Hebrew ;   for the translators of the Bible have not infrequently preserved the flavour of the Hebrew original in such passages as ' This do and live ' (Gen. xlii. 18) where we should say ' Do this that ye may live ' or ' If ye do this, ye shall live '.

Some account must now be given of the principal Semitic languages.   As they appear in history, Assyrian is the earliest, and Hebrew the second language, followed closely by Aramaic, in the pre-Christian era ;   Syriac coincides roughly with the Christian epoch and later Aramaic with the development of Judaism, while Arabic does not appear, at least as a literary language, till the seventh century A. D., when the Muhammadan conquests caused it rapidly to supplant the older languages. But philologically, Arabic is in some respects the oldest, while Hebrew is almost the latest, member of the family ;   that is to say, classical Arabic preserves many grammatical features which represent a primitive stage, almost before any decay had set in, while Hebrew, even in the earliest form in which we know it, already exhibits phenomena which have only taken place quite recently in modern Arabic.

The Semitic languages fall roughly into four geographical groups ;   the eastern, comprising the Assyro-Babylonian language, the northern, which is practically coterminous with the Aramaic dialects, the western, of which the principal representative is Hebrew, and the southern, embracing Arabic and Ethiopic.   Only Arabic and Abyssinian, the modern representative of Ethiopic, are still spoken by any considerable number of persons ;   the use of a dialect of Syriac or Aramaic by

Nestorian Christians in a few districts in the mountains to the north-east of Mosul, and of Aramaic in the village of Maʿlûlâ in Syria is hardly more worth recording than is ʾĔliʿēzer ben Yĕhûdhāh's attempt to revive a classical Hebrew among Jews. Perhaps that which distinguishes most clearly the southern from the three other groups is the grammatical peculiarity known as ' broken plurals ', of which there are some twenty-nine varieties in Arabic and about eleven in Ethiopic. To take an illustration from Arabic, *durrah* ' a pearl ' has not only the regular plural *durrât*, formed by substituting *-ât* for the termination *-ah*, but also *durar*, formed by internal inflexion within the word. Some words have several plurals, not infrequently with different meanings : for example, the Arabic *ʾamr* ' order ', ' thing ', has the two plurals *ʾawâmir* ' orders ' and *ʾumûr* ' things '. The attempt to discover ' broken plurals ' also in Hebrew has not proved successful ; such a word as *zākhûr* (*zĕkhûr*) ' male ' which, it has been suggested, is a ' broken plural ' of *zākhār* ' male ', meaning ' males ' can in every case be taken equally well as a singular by regarding it as a collective and by substituting ' every male of thine ' for ' all thy males ' (Exod. xxiii. 17 and xxxiv. 23 ; Deut. xvi. 16 ; cp. xx. 13, R. V.).[1] Yet, although the southern group is thus clearly marked off from all the other languages in this respect, in others the distinction breaks down ; so Hebrew and Arabic, of the northern and southern branches respectively, agree against the rest in the possession of a definite article which is prefixed to the noun, while Sabaean, the dialect closest akin to Arabic, adds an *-n* and Aramaic an *-â* at the end of the word for the same purpose ; against this, Assyrian and Ethiopic agree in the complete absence of any definite article. Again, in Hebrew the old passive is already dying out and in Ethiopic is quite extinct, while it is in full use in Arabic. Another division of the languages into a Western and an Eastern group is less clearly

[1] Margoliouth in Hastings, *Dictionary of the Bible*, vol. iii, p. 28 a.

HISTORICAL TABLE OF THE SEMITIC LANGUAGES

[Assumed parent-language, subdivided into four principal groups.]

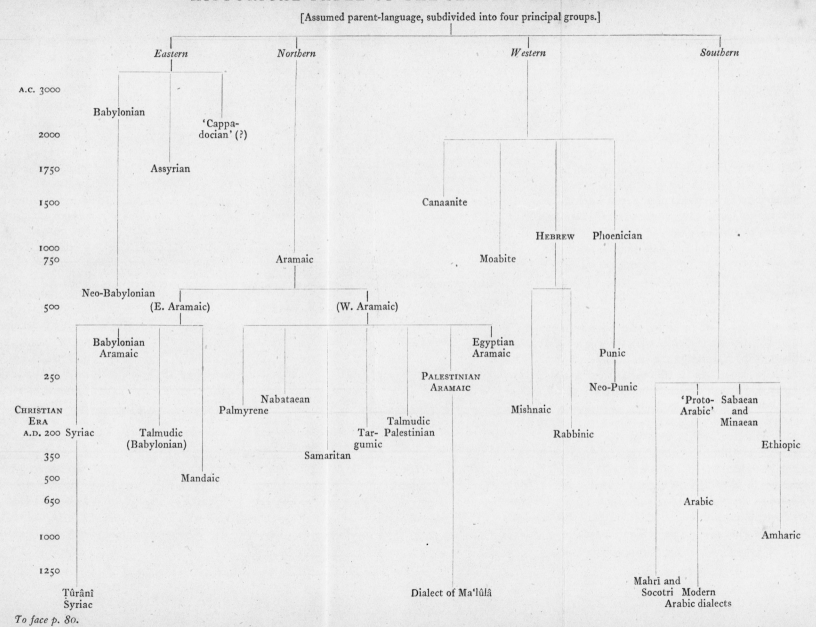

Eastern	*Northern*	*Western*	*Southern*

A.C. 3000 — Babylonian — 'Cappadocian' (?)

2000

1750 — Assyrian

1500 — Canaanite

1000
750 — Aramaic — HEBREW   Phoenician — Moabite

Neo-Babylonian

500 — (E. Aramaic) — (W. Aramaic)

Babylonian Aramaic — Egyptian Aramaic — Punic

250 — PALESTINIAN ARAMAIC — Neo-Punic — 'Proto-Arabic'   Sabaean and Minaean

Palmyrene   Nabataean — Mishnaic

CHRISTIAN ERA
A.D. 200 — Syriac   Talmudic (Babylonian) — Tar-gumic   Talmudic Palestinian — Rabbinic   Ethiopic

350 — Samaritan

500 — Mandaic

650

1000 — Arabic   Amharic

1250

Tûrânî Syriac   Dialect of Ma'lûlâ   Mahrī and Socotri   Modern Arabic dialects

To face p. 80.

defined in point of accidence but has a clear distinction in the syntax, both in the peculiar use of the tenses and in the fact that in the latter the verb is thrown to the end of the sentence whereas in the former it generally stands at the beginning. The Eastern, further, is marked off from all the other branches by its employment of a non-Semitic script. But such groupings are all more or less arbitrary and hardly serve any useful purpose ; the simplest and therefore, it may be, the best is to set on one side the Assyro-Babylonian language and on the other a branch subdivided into Hebraeo-Phoenician and Aramaic on the one and the southern languages on the other hand.[1]

Before the decipherment of the Accadian [2]—or Assyro-Babylonian—language, scholars were primarily dependent on Aramaic and Arabic for the interpretation and understanding of the Hebrew language. As soon as Arabic began to be studied by European scholars, it became immediately apparent that its vast vocabulary would explain many Hebrew words, whose meaning had long been forgotten, and laws analogous to ' Grimm's law ' in the Aryan languages were formulated to govern the interchange of consonants between the various Semitic languages. An interesting instance is to be found in the Hebrew word *qā'āth* conventionally rendered ' pelican ', although this meaning does not suit the context of at least three of the passages where it occurs ; twice it is mentioned among unclean birds (Lev. xi. 18 and Deut. xiv. 17), twice as inhabiting ruins (Isa. xxxiv. 11 and Zeph. ii. 14) and once as an example of loneliness (Ps. cii. 7). Yet the pelican can hardly be considered unclean, since it feeds solely on live fish, nor does it inhabit ruins but marshes, and it builds its nest in high trees. Now the root *qā'*, whence *qā'āth* is formed by the addition of the feminine termination -*āth*, does not occur in Hebrew ; but

[1] Nöldeke in the *Encyclopaedia Britannica*, vol. 24, p. 621.
[2] The early decipherers wrongly used ' Accadian ', the language of Agade, for Sumerian, the pre-Babylonian, non-Semitic language of Mesopotamia.

in Arabic it is found in the reduplicated form *qa'qa'* ' cawed ', ' croaked '; the *qā'āth* is therefore the bird that caws or croaks, *viz.* the jackdaw which, unlike the pelican, is abundant in Syria, Palestine and Mesopotamia, and satisfies the requirements of all the passages quoted above. Finally the Syriac and Arabic versions translate it by a word meaning ' rook ', ' crow ' or ' jackdaw ', instead of ' pelican ', which goes back to the rendering of the Septuagint in these passages [1].

Syntactically, Arabic appears on the whole to have preserved the greatest resemblance to the parent Semitic tongue, and in it very many features are preserved more faithfully than in the cognate languages—for instance, nearly all the original abundance of consonants and many grammatical distinctions which elsewhere are more or less obscured ; especially with regard to grammatical forms, Hebrew has lost much that is still preserved in Arabic ; but it must always be borne in mind that this greater richness of Arabic is in part the result of later development. Thus the Hebrew letter *'ain,* it is well-known, stands for two earlier letters which still survive in Arabic, *'ain* and *ghain,* the latter being distinguished in writing by a supra-linear point. The Septuagint knew the distinction, for it represents *gh* by *g,* as in Γάζα ' Gaza ', which is *'azzāh* in Hebrew but *ghazzah* in Arabic. It is therefore possible to separate *'ebhrāh* ' wrath ' from *'ābhar* ' passed beyond ', ' over-stepped ', with which it is usually connected on the supposition that it means ' overflowing ' and thence ' arrogance ' or ' wrath', and compare it with the Arabic verb *ghabira* ' bore rancour ' and the noun *ghibr* ' rancour '.[2] A signal instance of the lateness, on the contrary, of some of the phenomena exhibited by Arabic is to be found in the case of the relative pronoun *allādhī* ' who ', ' which '; its true nature as primarily a demonstrative pronoun is proved by the cognate *hallāzeh* ' this ' in

[1] G. R. Driver in the *Journal of Theological Studies*, xxii, 88, pp. 382–3.
[2] G. R. Driver, *ibid.*, xxiii, 89, p. 69.

Hebrew, since the relatives were in the Semitic languages as in Greek adaptations of originally demonstrative pronouns.

Of grammatical distinctions the most noticeable is the survival, in Arabic as in Babylonian, of case-endings both in the singular and in the plural; in the loss of these terminations, Assyrian, Hebrew even in its earliest known form, spoken Arabic, at any rate, from the second century of the Muslim era onwards and its modern dialects are almost in the same stage of development. The simple forms are -*u* (nom.), -*a* (acc.) and -*i* (gen.) in the singular, and -*û* (nom.) and -*î* (acc. and gen.) in the plural. In Hebrew there survive a few traces of a nominative singular in -*û* or -*ô*, the former being confined to proper names like *Mĕthûshā'ēl* Methushael, meaning ' man of God ' (in Babylonian, *mutu sâ ili*), and the latter to a few phrases, found chiefly in elevated style, such as *ḥayĕthô 'ereṣ* ' beasts of the earth ' (Gen. i. 24) for the more usual *ḥayath 'ereṣ* (Gen. i. 25). The *i*- termination, indicating the genitive, does not occur ; where -*î* is found in Hebrew, it represents a binding-vowel sometimes found attached to the construct case in old Babylonian, like -*i* in *mukinni Ishtar* ' the stablisher of Ishtar ' (Code of Hammurabi, iv a, 48). From this and similar passages it is clear that -*i* could be used in the construct case in place of the regular case-ending, here for the nominatival -*u* (*mukinnu*, as in iv a, 40), as well as instead of the regular shortened form without a termination (*mukîn*, as in ii a, 24).[1] The ending -*a*, which originally indicated the accusative, lingers on in two usages in Hebrew as unaccented *āh* : (i) when attached to a noun to express motion towards a place, as in *habbáyĕthāh* ' to the house ' from *habbayith* ' the house ' ; (ii) as a meaningless termination added to nouns, as to *láyĕlāh*, ' night ' properly the accusative of *layil* ' night ', and so on. In this degradation of the accusative Hebrew is in the same stage as modern Greek, in which ἡ νύχτα ' the night ' has replaced the classical ἡ νύξ ;

[1] G. R. Driver, *ibid.*, xxvi, 101, pp. 76-7.

so in the Arabic spoken now in the Syrian desert, where the old ending of the accusative in its indefinite form *-an* is affixed in all cases to indefinite nouns, the modern Arab says *jâ'ani rijjâlan* ' a man came to me ', but *jâ'ani-'rrijjâl* (without a termination) ' the man came to me '.[1]

In yet another case Biblical Hebrew and modern Arabic exhibit the same stage of degradation. In classical Arabic the feminine singular of the noun takes the termination *-at* or, with the case-ending, *-atu*, which in modern Arabic has been weakened to *-ah*, so that *sanat(u)* ' year ' has become in modern Arabic *sanah*; similarly, for the usual form *shēnāh* ' sleep', there once occurs *shĕnāth* as an archaism in Hebrew (Ps. cxxxii. 4). That language shows indeed further symptoms of decay than Arabic ; for, whereas the third person singular of the perfect ends in *-at*, as for instance in *qatalat* ' she killed ', both in classical and modern Arabic, it has become *-āh* in classical Hebrew ; thus, although the normal form would be *'āzĕlāh* ' she went ', *'āzĕlath* survives only in an ancient poem (Deut. xxxii. 36). This *th*, however, reappears regularly before pronominal suffixes ; and its antiquity is further attested by the agreement of all the other Semitic languages in preserving it. Again, Hebrew in *tishmĕ'û* ' you will hear ' agrees with the modern Arabic *tismi'û* against the classical *tasma'ûna* ; yet over 300 forms with *-ûn*, such as *tishmĕ'ûn* (Deut. viii. 20), occur in the older books of the Bible. In fact, as Gesenius long ago remarked, the modern popular Arabic often agrees with Hebrew against the classical or literary Arabic, many grammatical forms existing in the written language having in the popular language dropped out of use, precisely as happened in Hebrew.[2]

Since the case-endings have, to all practical purposes, dis-

---

[1] Wetzstein in the *Zeitschrift der Deutschen Morgenländischen Gesellschaft*, vol. xxii, p. 113.

[2] S. R. Driver, *Hebrew Tenses*, p. 243 n. 1. See also G. R. Driver in the *Journal of the Royal Asiatic Society*, 1920, pp. 305–18.

appeared from Hebrew, the explanation of a construction may have to be sought in those languages which have similar terminations still in use. From Arabic it is learnt that the predicate stands in the accusative in virtue of its limitative sense ; thus the Arabic *jâ'a râkiban* ' he came riding ', in which the participle is in the accusative, shows that in the Hebrew *hālōkh 'ārôm* ' to walk naked ' (Isa. xx. 2) the adjective is probably to be regarded as standing in the same case. Again, in Hebrew the verbal idea may be strengthened by placing the infinitive of the same verb before it, as in *môth tāmûth* ' a dying thou shalt die' or ' thou shalt surely die ' ; in Assyrian the infinitive, which always (as usually in Hebrew) precedes the finite verb, stands usually in the nominative case, as in *tabâlum tatbal* ' taking away, hast thou taken away ? ' or ' hast thou surely taken away ? ' Hence it is evident that the infinitive is properly exclamatory, so that *tabâlum tatbal* should be translated literally : ' a taking away ! hast thou taken away ? ' This is probably the true explanation also of the Hebrew idiom.

Of Ethiopic less need be said, for it hardly appears before the third century of the Christian era and throws but little direct light on the earlier languages. Its principal value to the student of Hebrew lies in the fact that in all but a few of the earliest inscriptions it is written in a fully vocalized script— a peculiarity which it shares with the languages written in cuneiform alone. Thus it confirms the tradition of the Massoretes that the Hebrew vowels were subject to modification in the neighbourhood of gutturals ; for in it they are demonstrably even more susceptible to their influence than in Hebrew. Thus in the imperfect, whereas the prefix in Hebrew takes *i* or in Ethiopic *e* in the regular verbs (as in the Hebrew *yiqṭōl* or the Ethiopic *yeqatel* ' he kills '), both languages agree in preferring *a* when the initial consonant is a guttural, as, for example, in Hebrew *yaḥbōl* and in Ethiopic *yaḥabel* ' he binds '. As this variation is otherwise confined to Hebrew, it might at first sight be supposed to have been due to a liturgical tradition in the public reading of the Hebrew scriptures. There is again a curious parallel between the forms of the first and second persons of the perfect in Hebrew, as well as in Aramaic and Arabic, on the one side, and Ethiopic on the other. In all the Semitic group the perfect is inflected by adding to the simple verbal form certain pronominal elements ; thus, in Assyrian, are formed *qirbâkû* ' I was near ' and *qirbâta* ' thou wast near ', the pronominal elements being -(*â*)*kû* from the independent pronoun *anâkû* ' I ' and -(*â*)*tâ* from *attâ* ' thou '. In Hebrew, however, and those languages which in this resemble it the suffix is -*t* in both persons, resulting in the forms *qārabhtî* ' I approached ' and *qārabhtâ* ' thou didst approach ' ; in the Ethiopic *qarabkū* ' I approached ' and *qarabka* ' thou didst approach ', on the contrary, this element is -*k* in both persons. Till the discovery of Assyrian it was much debated which was the original form, but now there can be no doubt that in the original Semitic speech -*k* indicated the first and -*t* the second person ; both Hebrew and Ethiopic have gone through the remarkable process of assimilating the two persons to one another for the sake of a fictitious uniformity, the only difference being that whereas Hebrew, Aramaic, and Arabic have assimilated the first to the second person, Ethiopic has done the reverse. But for this the consensus of all the other languages against Assyrian (and Samaritan, curiously enough, in verbs alone whose final consonant is weak) would have led scholars to a false conclusion.

The vocabulary of Ethiopic, though full of peculiar and even of non-Semitic words, to a large extent resembles that of Arabic, yet its coincidence with Hebrew and Assyrian against that language in a number of common words has caused it wrongly to be classified as more closely akin to the northern or eastern than to the southern group. For instance, the Ethiopic *'esāt* ' fire ' agrees with the Assyrian *'ishatu* and the Hebrew '*ēsh* against the Arabic *nâru*, the Ethiopic '*eben* ' stone ' with the Assyrian *abnu* and the Hebrew '*ebhen* against the Arabic *ḥajar*. Yet its preservation of two distinct sounds for the Hebrew letters *ḥêth* and *ṣādē*', the structure of its words and its inflexions, the frequent termination in a short vowel, the presence of broken plurals and of the verbal themes, and the possession of a host of roots common to the two languages, place it indubitably in the same class as Arabic ; but the regular definition of the accusative, although it follows Hebrew in dropping the other cases, and the distinction of the subjunctive from the indicative show an affinity with Assyrian equally with Arabic. At the same time it shares with Assyrian alone one defect in the absence of a definite article and one dubious advantage in the ability to attach two pronominal suffixes, one expressing the direct and the other the indirect object, to the verb. The Ethiopic negative '*ī*, which corresponds to the Assyrian *ai* or *ê* , is the negative element in the Hebrew name ' Ichabod ' or rather '*ī-khābhôdh* ' no glory ' (I Sam. iv. 21) ; this same particle, which occurs often in late Hebrew, is found once more also in the Old Testament, in '*ī-nāqî* ' not innocent ' (Job xxii. 30). There are few passages in the Old Testament which Ethiopic by itself serves to elucidate, so that one may perhaps be quoted. In the verse ' I will turn thee about, and will lead thee on (*shishshē'thîkhā*), and ' will cause thee to come up from the uttermost parts of the north ' (Ezek. xxxix. 2) the verb *shishshē'* is completely unknown, and various attempts have been made to emend it— needlessly, for it has been shown that, since Ethiopic has a simple *s* where Hebrew prefers *sh*, it is the causative conjugation of a verb cognate with the Ethiopic *sōsawa* ' entered in ' and that it therefore means ' caused to enter in ' or ' brought in '. The passage, then, should be translated : ' I will turn thee about and will bring thee in,' and so on.[1] One last point

---

[1] Gesenius-Buhl, *Hebräisches und Aramäisches Handwörterbuch*, p. 866 a.

in which Ethiopic may help the student of Hebrew may perhaps be mentioned, before passing on to a language of far greater, if not of supreme, importance for that purpose. A common word for ' God ' in Ethiopic is *'amlāk* ' gods ', properly a plural of which the polytheistic origin was forgotten after the Ethiopians had been converted to Christianity; is then the Hebrew *'ělōhîm* ' God ', which is also plural in form, as is also the determinative *ilâni* (plur.,) used instead of *ilu* (sing.) ' god ' in speaking of the eponymous god of the *Khâbiru* in the Hittite texts,[1] equally a relic of heathenism and not a ' plural of majesty '? There are, certainly, many passages where it is used both of heathen gods and of superhuman beings, including God and angels, still to be found in the Old Testament, and the use of a ' plural of majesty ' as used of a god is unknown, apart from this example in the Hittite texts, in cuneiform literature.[2]

The decipherment of the Assyrian language seventy-five years ago proved a turning-point in the study of the Hebrew language; for it became immediately evident that Babylonian and Assyrian were the closest relatives of Biblical Hebrew. The language was originally called Assyrian because the earliest documents to be interpreted were in the northern, that is the Assyrian, dialect; but historically Babylonian, being found on documents dated far back into the third millennium B. C., preceded Assyrian, which hardly appears till a thousand years later. Yet the differences are slight and chiefly phonetic; for instance, Babylonian substitutes *g* for the Assyrian *q* and often changes *m* into *w*.

Of primary importance in the decipherment of Assyrian are the syllabaries drawn up by native scribes, which give lists of Sumerian ideograms—that is, words in the old Sumerian language from which the Babylonians borrowed the cuneiform script together with their phonetic spellings and their Assyrian equivalents as well as a number of synonyms; many also

---

[1] Jirku, *Die Wanderungen der Hebräer*, pp. 16–20.
[2] Dillmann, *Lexicon Linguae Aethiopicae*, p. 151.

give alternative ways of spelling the Assyrian word. For instance, a recently published syllabary gives the Sumerian sign *BI* (which it also spells out *bi-i*, indicating its pronunciation *bi*, since the sign bears also other syllabic values), and then explains it by a number of Assyrian synonyms for ' to speak', amongst them *nabû* ' to proclaim', *qabû* ' to say', *dabâbu* ' to speak', *shasû* ' to call' and *khapû* ' to utter'. Two of these words will interest the Hebraist ; *nabû* is well-known as the root from which the Hebrew *nābhî'* ' prophet' is sprung and *dabâbu*, which is chiefly used as a legal term, meaning ' to sue', shows the root of the Hebrew *dibbāh* ' whispering', ' defamation'. But *khapû*, which has not occurred hitherto, is an even more interesting word, for it explains the passage translated in the Revised Version : ' And the children of Israel did secretly (*yᵉḥappᵉ'û* from *ḥāphâ*) things that were not right against the Lord their God and they built them high places in all their cities ' (2 Kings xvii. 9). Now the Hebrew verb *ḥāphâ*, which is otherwise unknown, has been assumed to be a variant form of *ḥāphāh* ' covered' and to connote here ' hid their actions', ' did secretly '; but *ḥāphāh* means ' covered' the head in mourning or ' overlaid' one material on another and contains no implication of secrecy, nor, indeed, does such a meaning in the least suit the context, since the building of high places could hardly be kept secret. The Septuagint translated the verb ' were clothed ', making nonsense of the passage ; but the Targûmîm and the Syriac version have ' spoke against the Lord ' rightly, as the discovery of the Assyrian verb *khapû* ' to utter ', cognate with this unknown Hebrew *ḥāphâ*, proves. The passage should therefore be rendered : ' And the children of Israel uttered words that were not right against the Lord their God,' just as of old they had often murmured against Moses and Aaron.[1]

A secondary source of information exists in interlinear texts ; for on many liturgical tablets the text was written in Sumerian, which survived as a dead language for ecclesiastical purposes like Latin in the Roman church, but was furnished line for line with a Babylonian translation.

Before turning to the actual languages in which the Old Testament is written, it will perhaps be well to give a few concrete examples of the light shed on them by Assyrian. The origin of many words can be traced back to Assyrian and even to Sumerian ; in fact, the common word *hêkhāl* ' temple ' or ' palace ' goes back to the Sumerian *Ê* ' house ', and *GAL* ' great ', which were combined into *Ê.GAL* ' palace ' and passed over into Babylonian as *êkallu* ' palace ' ; only in Hebrew did it acquire the special connotation of ' temple ' as well as of ' palace '. Another example is the Hebrew *mallāḥ* ' sailor ', a loan-word from the Assyrian *malakhu* ' sailor ', which goes back to the Sumerian *MA* ' ship ' and *LAKH* ' to go ', the sailor being one who ' goes in a ship ' ; the Hebrew *mallāḥ* was probably, in its turn, the word from which *melaḥ* ' salt ' for obvious reasons was derived. The true explanation also of the tower of Babel is now known ; the word has nothing to do with the verb *bālal* ' confounded ', as popular Jewish etymology fancifully supposed (Gen. xi. 9), but is the Babylonian *Bâb-ili* ' gate of God ', the reference being to the stage-towers reaching up to heaven for which Babylon was famous. The Rabshakeh is the *rab shākê* ' chief of the magnates ' and the Tartan is the *tartânu* ' commander-in-chief ', a noun derived from *têrtu* ' command ', which is identical with the Hebrew *tôrāh* ' law '. These three nouns are formed by prefixing *t* to the stem *arû* or *warû*, as seen in the Ethiopic *warê* ' information ', which only occurs in Assyrian in the second theme *ûrû* ' to give an oracle ' ; the latter verb in turn explains clearly the *'ûrîm* ' oracles ' of the Hebrews. It is also not impossible that the Massoretes—the Jewish scholars who inserted the vowels in the text of the scriptures—mistook the origin also of *tummîm*, when they punctuated it as the plural of *tōm* ' completeness ' used intensively in the sense of ' perfection ' ; it is far more probably connected with the Babylonian verb *tamû* ' to speak ', ' to swear ', ' to charm ', in the second theme *tummû* ' to cast a spell upon ', ' to bewitch ' a person. Consequently the Urîm and Tummim will mean ' Oracles and Spells ' rather than ' Lights and Perfections ', as suggested in the margin of the Revised Version (Exod. xxviii. 30) and will be a relic of heathenism which received a new and more spiritual interpretation at the hands of Moses.[1] Another important term is *'ēl shaddai*, the archaic title for the Lord which the Revised Version renders conventionally ' God Almighty ', but which is to be explained from the fact that the Babylonians at times called their god *shadû rabû* ' the great mountain ' or *ilu shadû'a* ' god my mountain '; so the Hebrew *'ēl shaddai* (which should probably be vocalized *shādhai*) means ' God the mountain ' and is to be compared with the title of ' the Rock ' so often applied to Him by the Israelites.

Elsewhere the study of Assyrian has confirmed the Massoretic text against too ready emendation. Thus in the passage ' as soon as the commandment came abroad ' (2 Chron. xxxi. 5) the verb *pĕrōṣ* is mistranslated ' came abroad ', on the supposition that it was connected with *pāraṣ* ' broke through ' used metaphorically of a command being spread abroad over the land; there is, however, a second verb *pāraṣ* ' issued an edict ', ' ordained ', occurring only here and once again (1 Chron. xiii. 2) in Hebrew, cognate with the Assyrian *parâṣu* ' to decree ' and the Arabic *faraḍa* ' ordained '.[2] Of these external sources, indeed, available for the interpretation of the Old Testament Assyrian, partly because it existed contemporaneously with Hebrew, partly on account of the vast and as yet largely unexplored riches of its vocabulary, is now by far the most important.

Peculiarly interesting is the light shed by Accadian on the

[1] Kennedy in Hastings, *Dictionary of the Bible*, vol. iv, p. 838 b.

[2] G. R. Driver in the *Journal of Theological Studies*, xxiii, 89, pp. 72–3. Cp. Delitzsch, *Prolegomena*, pp. 69–71, on *māḥaṣ* ' dipped ' in Ps. lxviii. 24.

Semitic tense-system and thereby on that of the Hebrew language. The assumed parent language, from which both Accadian and Hebrew were derived, started with a single form —for example, *zakir* ' mentioned ' ; this form was in all likelihood nominal or rather adjectival in origin and therefore connoted merely a state, in this case the state of being mentioned. But the being in a state implies that that state has been brought about by a preceding action, while the distinction between passive and active is often unimportant : thus *kasap nadin* could be rendered either ' the silver has been given ' or ' he has given the silver ', and *kasap makhir* ' the silver has been received ' or ' he has received the silver ', without any essential difference to the sense intended by the speaker. The early Semites resolved this ambiguity by means of case-endings, which the Babylonians naturally retained, whereas the Hebrews were able at an early period to dispense with them. For, when Accadian and Hebrew broke away from the parent language, one emphasized the first and the other the second aspect of the original form : Accadian, adopting the stative sense and retaining the *i* under the second vowel, developed out of its primary, intransitive usage the ' permansive ' *zákir* ' was mentioned ', although traces of the active sense lingered on in the much rarer use of the permansive as an active tense, meaning ' has mentioned ' ; Hebrew, on the contrary, developed the transitive sense, which it marked by substituting *a* for *i*, in its ' perfect ' *zākhar* ' has mentioned ', and confined the intransitive sense to a few verbs, with which it retained the old *i* lengthened to *ē*, such as *kābhēdh* (Babylonian *kabit*) ' was honourable '. A third class, which had from the beginning been only stative, differed in having *u* in place of *a* or *i*, like the Babylonian *maruṣ* ' was ill ' and the Hebrew *qāṭōn* ' was small '. That both the Eastern and Western group have a class of *u*-verbs marks this distinction also as very early, if not actually primitive.

The Western group preserved very few instances of the double—intransitive and transitive—use of this form. Occasionally, as always in Accadian, it was both intransitive (passive) and transitive (active) at the same time, like the Hebrew *mālē'*, which corresponds to the Accadian *mali* 'was filled' or 'has filled'. Sometimes, especially in Arabic, the distinction came to be marked by a change of vowel, as in the Arabic *mali'a* 'was full' and *mala'a* 'has filled'. More often, however, the languages of this group employed a derived theme to give both an intransitive sense to a transitive root, as Syriac in *'ethmlī* 'was filled' from *mlâ* 'has filled', and a transitive sense to an intransitive root, as Hebrew *nilqaḥ* or *luqqaḥ* 'was taken' from *lāqaḥ* 'has taken', where Accadian had only *liqi* to signify both 'was taken' and 'has taken'. Another and a rarer method of obviating the uncertainty of the primitive form was to make use of verbs from different roots, as Hebrew used *ḥākham* 'was wise' beside *shāphaṭ* 'judged', where Arabic by a modification of the second vowel made two words derived from a common root, *ḥakuma* 'was wise' and *ḥakama* 'judged', serve the same purpose.

Now this tense connoted what was past and complete; the next stage was to invent one expressing incomplete—*i. e.* in the first instance, present and future—action. In the permansive or perfect, as the case might be, the person was denoted by affixing the required pronoun in an elementary form. Thus from using the adjective followed by the pronoun as a predicate, as in *kabtu attâ* 'honourable (art) thou', it had been a natural step to inflect the permansive *kabit* 'was honourable' by affixing a fragment of the pronoun to form (out of *kabit* + *attâ*) the composite *kabtâta* 'thou art honourable'. The new tense was therefore formed by prefixing the pronominal element, and the combination of *attâ* + *zákar* gave rise to *tazákar* 'thou dost mention' or 'wilt mention', describing an incomplete—*i. e.* present or future—act. This tense was taken over by Accadian in its original sense ; but Hebrew failed to adopt it, the reason being that *izákar* would have become in that language *y^ezakkar* or *y^ezakkēr*, and so been almost or wholly identical with the imperfect of the Pi'ēl. Exactly analogous, it should be noticed, was the disappearance of the passive of the Qal, which became *zukkar* (from *zukir*) and so was lost through its identity in form with the Pu'al or passive of the Pi'ēl. Hebrew made up for the absence of a purely present and future tense partly by a wide use of the participle, partly by freely developing one side of the third primitive tense.

The third tense, and the last to be required, was one connoting incomplete action in past time ; for (a) *zákar* expressed simply what was past and complete without any inherent reference to the active or passive nature of the act or state described, and (b) *izákar* was originally confined to what was present and future and only incidentally incomplete. As tenses formed by the affixing and prefixing of the pronominal element already existed, the only possible course in forming a new tense was to modify the vowels of one of these two tenses : this was done by modifying the more recent formation so as to produce *izkur* ' he was mentioning '. That this was derived from the form *izákar* and not from *zakir* is clear from three facts : (i) it expresses a more complex idea than either of the other tenses ; (ii) it is explicable only as being a shortened form of *izákar* and not as derived from *zákar* by the addition of a pronominal prefix ; (iii) in Ethiopic the corresponding form *yezker* is the subjunctive, *viz.* a shortened form derived from the indicative *yezáker*. In point of usage, however, the distinction between complete and incomplete action in past time is often immaterial, so that *izkur* soon came to be used also as meaning ' he mentioned ', of complete or historic action in the past ; this process was further aided by the ambiguity attached to the meaning of the form *zakir* in primitive usage. Now, once again, Accadian and Hebrew, in taking over this tense, emphasized different aspects of it : Accadian developed its historic sense in the 'preterite', Hebrew its incomplete sense in the 'imperfect'. Yet in both languages there are vestiges of the other sense. In Hebrew, on the one hand, such idioms as that of the imperfect after 'āz ' then ', as in 'āz yāshîr (impf.) yisrā'ēl ' then sang Israel' (Num. xxi. 7), and perhaps also of the imperfect after ' wāw consecutive ' go back to the historic sense of the primitive tense. To the same origin must be referred the interesting use of the imperfect instead of the perfect in Arabic after lam ' not ', as in lam yaqtul, compared with lâ qátala ' he did not kill '. In Accadian, on the other hand, traces may be found of its occasional use of emergent action—*i. e.* of action regarded as incomplete from the point of view of the preceding act. An example may perhaps be seen in the opening lines of the Babylonian *Epic of Creation* (i. 1–5) : ' When on high the heavens were not named (nabû—permansive), beneath the earth was not called by name (zakrat—permansive), Apsû and Mummu went on to mingle (ikhuqû—preterite) their waters ', and so on ; here the permansives, which express a state resulting from an action, are contrasted with the preterite, implying an act emerging from what preceded. Compare the words in Genesis (i. 2–3) : ' and the earth was (hāyᵉthāh—perfect, corresponding to the permansive) waste and void . . . and God went on to say (way-yōʼmer—imperfect corresponding in form to the Babylonian preterite) ', and so on. Here the perfect takes the place of the permansive and the imperfect of the preterite, each bearing the force of the corresponding tense.[1] Once again, therefore, the two languages adopted and developed different aspects of the same original tense, while hints of the other meaning borne by the primitive tense could still be detected in both languages.

---

[1] Burney in the *Journal of Theological Studies*, vol. xx, pp. 208–9.

Thus a comparison of the two languages or rather of the two groups, makes it possible not only to reconstruct the original tense-system of the primitive Semites but also by that means to explain the perplexing differences between the Eastern and the Western systems, especially how the tense *izkur-yizkōr* seems to bear opposite connotations in the two groups ; at the same time it lights up the apparent contradictions in the use of the Hebrew imperfect. Both the Accadian and Hebrew languages are now seen to have passed through the same stages : each took over the primitive system, dropping what it could not use and emphasizing those aspects of the original tenses which it required to develop, yet retaining relics here and there of the other usages exhibited by them.

It remains to account for one more difficulty—that generally after the precative particle *lû* and always after the prohibitory particle *lâ* Assyrian apparently uses the preterite tense. How this could have arisen is the question, unless the Assyrian *izkur*, like the Hebrew *yizkōr*, meant originally ' he will mention ' or ' remember '. For then in Assyrian *lâ tizkur* would have come to mean ' do not mention ' in the same way as *lō* ' (*'āl*) *tizkōr* ' thou shalt not remember' passed into ' do not remember' in Hebrew; but, since *tizkur* can bear only a past significance in Assyrian, this explanation is not possible. Now, the imperative was expressed as abruptly as possible and therefore bore a superficial resemblance to the shortened form, whichever that was, the Assyrian *zukur* ' mention ' to the preterite, the Hebrew *zĕkhōr* ' remember ' to the imperfect (future) and the Ethiopic *zeker* ' remember ' to the subjunctive. Since, however, there was, properly speaking, no first or third person in the imperative, the requisite forms were invented by prefixing the same pronominal elements as those used in these persons of the preterite or imperfect, giving the forms *izkur* ' let him mention ' and *nizkur* ' let us remember ', to which the particle *lû* was always prefixed, giving *lizkur* (*lû izkur*) ' let him mention' and *lû nizkur* 'let us mention'; the same forms were naturally employed in these persons after *lâ*, yielding *lâ nizkur* 'let us not remember'. Since *lû* and *lâ* implied a precative and a prohibitory sense respectively, there was no risk of confusion between these forms, though identical in appearance, when used as preterites and when they served as subjunctives or imperatives. By false analogy an improper second person of this pseudo-subjunctive tense, similar to that of the preterite or imperfect or subjunctive, as the case might be, came to be used in all the Semitic languages in prohibitions instead of the proper imperative, just as in prohibitions the • Romans, from having to say *ne meminerit* and *ne meminerimus*, came to use also *ne memineris*, to the exclusion of the imperative in such sentences.

A few words must now be said about Aramaic, a language of more than philological interest to the Hebraist, since certain short portions of the Old Testament are written in it. The Aramaeans were a wandering race, whose earliest emigrations from the Arabian peninsula may be dated as far back as the twenty-eighth century B. C.; on the one hand their roving nature connects them with the nomad Arab, while the appearance of certain characteristically Arabic words and idioms in the Aramaic inscriptions of the Nabataean kingdom (overthrown by Trajan in A. D. 105) proves an early linguistic connexion; on the other hand that same feature, as well as their position as a trading people, connect them with the Hebrews, the vocabulary of whose language is largely identical with that of Aramaic. The sources for the pre-Christian are as scanty as those for the subsequent period are abundant. There is a small number of inscriptions of the early Syrian kingdom belonging to the seventh and eighth centuries B. C., a very few from Babylonia, Asia Minor and Arabia between that period and the fourth century, some inscriptions on stone, potsherds and *papyri* of the fifth and sixth centuries from Egypt, besides the famous series of *papyri*, found at Elephantine in Egypt, which belong to the fifth century, certain Aramaic passages in the books of Ezra and Daniel, and lastly the inscriptions of the Nabataean kingdom, some of which are found in the Sinaitic peninsula, and those relating to the kingdom of Palmyra, which run from about 10 B.C. to the overthrow of Zenobia in A.D. 273. There are also not a few cuneiform tablets of the Assyrian and Neo-Babylonian kingdoms to which Aramaic endorsements have been added. Not only, therefore, do these documents themselves speak for the wide diffusion of Aramaic, but the references in the Old Testament to a variety of scattered Aramaean states vouch for the same fact.

Before coming to the problem of the dialects, which is of considerable importance as affecting the date of the book of Daniel, it will be well to point out the outstanding characteristics of the Aramaic language. In the first place, unlike Hebrew and Arabic it has, properly speaking, no definite article prefixed to the noun but attaches a long -*â* to the end, as in *bayĕthâ* 'the house' as distinct from *bayith* 'a house', for which Hebrew says *habbayith* and Arabic *albaitu*. In the course of time this -*â*, the so-called 'emphatic' ending, lost its force, so that there was no essential difference between *bayĕthâ* and *bayith*, both meaning either 'the' or 'a house'; the force or weakness of this ending, however, varies somewhat from dialect to dialect. The second important difference lies in the tenses; for the Aramaeans seem very early to have been sensible of the imperfections of the Semitic system. They therefore made great use of the active participle; in the first place, standing alone with the personal pronouns it serves as a future and as a present with the sense of a *futurum instans* and often as a pure present; secondly, in past time, though sometimes used alone, especially in place of a perfect in historical narrative, it is more often employed in dependence on the various parts of the verb 'to be', forming with it a compound tense. Thus, while

the participle *'ābhêdh 'ănâ* means ' I am doing ' in the sense of
' I am now doing ' or ' I am on the point of doing ' and the
imperfect *'e'ĕbhêdh* ' I might, should do ' is chiefly confined to
modal, conditional and subordinate clauses, the compound
tenses *hăwêth* (perf.) *'ābhêdh* ' I was doing ' or ' I used to do ',
'ehĕwĕ' (impf.) *'ābhêdh* ' I shall be doing ' and *hāwênâ* (ptcp.)
'ābhêdh ' I repeatedly do ' form a series of tenses totally unknown to Hebrew, which is almost limited to the imperfect
to express all these shades of meaning. Again, while in Hebrew
the perfect has to serve both as a perfect and as a pluperfect,
Aramaic has devised a pluperfect by prefixing the perfect of
the verb ' to be ' to the perfect, so that *'ăbhadh* ' he did ' can
be distinguished from *hăwāh 'ăbhadh* ' he had done '. In
addition to this, it early developed a number of subordinate
conjunctions, of which Hebrew shows a singular lack. It was
the flexibility thus given to the language, combined with the
greater wealth of its vocabulary, which gave it so great an
advantage over Hebrew and led to its supplanting of that
language ; at the same time the simplicity of its alphabet
in comparison with the cuneiform script and syllabary made it
inevitable that it should displace sooner or later the Accadian
language. Throughout the duration of the Assyro-Babylonian
empire there are indications that a large proportion of the
population were Aramaean ; but it is probable that it was the
short dominion of the Chaldaeans which gave to Aramaic its
preponderance in Mesopotamia.

The Aramaic sections in Ezra are the letter to Artaxerxes and
his reply (Ezra iv. 8–23), and the following passage (Ezra v. 1–
vi. 18, the last verse of the preceding chapter being a connecting
link, also in Aramaic), which is probably an extract from the
same source as the two letters. The nature of this source is
uncertain, but it appears to have been a thoroughly trustworthy
document, although the edicts contained in it, as far as their
form is concerned, are open to the suspicion of having been

coloured by their transmission through Jewish hands. The
dialect is that generally known as the Western or Palestinian
Aramaic.[1] Of this it is an older form than that employed in the
Aramaic section of Daniel (Dan. ii. 4–vii. 28) ; for example, in
Ezra the pronominal suffixes of the third and second persons
plural are -*kom* or -*kôn* ' you ', ' your ' and -*hom* or -*hôn* ' them ',
' their ', but -*kôn* and -*hôn* in Daniel, as in Palmyrene and
usually in the later period ; again in Ezra the pronoun of the
third person plural is *himmô* ' they ', as always in the Egyptian
papyri, while in Daniel there occurs not only *himmôn* but
'*innôn*, the latter being a characteristically later form. In the
verbs, it should be noticed, the causative theme is always
marked, as in the earlier inscriptions and the Egyptian *papyri*,
by the prefix *ha-*, except that '*a-*, the usual prefix in late
Aramaic, occurs once in Daniel. These and a number of
other peculiarities prove, by comparison with extra-Biblical
Aramaic documents, that the dialect of Daniel is later than
that of Ezra, the former tending to agree with the later and
the latter with the older texts which have been preserved.
Now it has been laid down that, in regard to the date of the
book of Daniel : ' the Persian words presuppose a period
after the Persian empire had been established : the Greek
words demand, the Hebrew supports, and the Aramaic permits,
a date after the conquest of Palestine by Alexander the Great
(332 B. C.).' [2] In view of recent attacks made upon this
statement, based chiefly on the ground that the language of the
Aramaic *papyri* from Elephantine, of the fifth century B. C.,
so closely resembles that of the book of Daniel that that book
may safely be held to be rather the work of Daniel himself, who
was living in the third year of Cyrus (535 B. C.), than a compilation of the middle of the second century B. C., it may be
well, while refraining from a recapitulation of the old arguments,

[1] S. R. Driver, *The Literature of the Old Testament*, p. 549.
[2] S. R. Driver, *The Book of Daniel*, p. lxiii.

to adduce some fresh points in favour of the critical view. A calculation of the relative frequency of *z* beside *d*, of *q* beside *'ayin* and of *sh* beside *th* shows a steadily increasing preference for the weaker letter even within the series of dated *papyri*; outside these, the order thus reached makes Ezra roughly contemporaneous with the *papyri* and Daniel considerably later. Further, of the Aramaic dialect current in the East when Daniel was supposed to be living there, a few words are known; yet in every case Daniel exhibits the later, non-Ninevite, form. Lastly, the curious mistranslation of the name Belteshazzar (Dan. iv. 8) shows the author of the book as ignorant of Babylonian as of Eastern Aramaic!

The language of the Egyptian hieroglyphics is only half-Semitic and throws very little direct light on Hebrew. Some of the personal pronouns resemble closely those of the Semitic languages: thus the Egyptian *'nky* and the Hebrew *'ānôkî* ' I ', are evidently identical, and *sw* ' he ' and *sy* ' she ' are clearly cognate with the Babylonian *shû* ' he ' and *shî* ' she '. The Egyptian has also a pseudo-participle which is not only used very much as the permansive in Babylonian, but is also inflected with pronominal affixes almost identical with those in the latter language: so in the singular the Egyptian *-kwy* corresponds to *-kû* ' I ', *-ty* to *-tâ* (masc.) and *-tî* (fem.) ' thou ' and *-ty* to *-at* ' she ', although Babylonian has no termination for the first person to compare with the Egyptian *-y* or *-w* ' he '; in the plural the Egyptian *-win* corresponds to *-(â)aî* ' we ', *-tiuni* to *-(â)tunû* (masc.) and *-(â)tinâ* (fem.) ' you ' and *-w* to *-û* ' they '. The vocabularies are less similar, but there are not a few roots common to both languages; for instance, the Egyptian *myw* and the Babylonian *mû* ' water ', the Egyptian *ḥshb* and the Hebrew *ḥāshabh* ' reckoned ', *ptḥ* and *pāthaḥ* ' opened ', *mwt* and *mûth* ' to die ' are clearly identical. Again the Egyptian numerals *sn* ' two ' and *sfḥ* ' seven ' clearly show the same origin as the Hebrew *shĕnayim* ' two ' and *shebha'* ' seven '. There is also

a causative theme of the verb, marked by a *s-* prefix, as in
Babylonian. So rarely, however, does Egyptian solve a difficulty in the Hebrew text that it may not be amiss to cite one
instance. In the verse: 'Have I not written unto thee
excellent things of counsels and knowledge?' (Prov. xxii. 20)
the word *shālīshôm* or *shālīshîm*, conventionally rendered
'excellent things', has long been a puzzle; in appearance it
is a corruption of the numeral *shĕlōshîm* 'thirty', which the
old interpreters regarded as meaningless in this connexion.
Now in the conclusion to a collection of Egyptian proverbs the
author writes: 'Thou hast seen these thirty chapters, how
joyful and instructive they are'; and, since several other
sayings in this section of the Hebrew book (Prov. xxii. 17-
xxiv. 22) seem also to go back to the same original, it is not
unlikely that *shĕlōshîm* 'thirty' is a literal but here senseless
reproduction of the words of the Egyptian sage.[1]

The Semites seem to have overrun Assyria and Babylonia,
Syria and Palestine in a succession of waves, welling up from the
Arabian peninsula through the pressure of an expanding
population. The first wave flowed along the valley of the
Euphrates and Tigris into Assyria, where by intermarriage with
the savage highlanders of the mountainous country beyond it
they gave birth to the cruel and warlike Assyrian. The next,
generally known as the Amorite, poured out of Arabia early in
the third millennium B.C., and divided into two groups: the first
settled in Babylonia and by fusion with the civilized Sumerians
produced the cultured Babylonian race; the second overran
Syria and Palestine, and from it there sprang, by the union of
these Amorite invaders with the pre-Semitic element—a short,
dark-skinned race found elsewhere along the shores of the
Mediterranean Sea—the Canaanites of early Hebrew history.
Thirdly, in the fourteenth century B.C. there began that

[1] Erman, *Eine ägyptische Quelle der 'Sprüche Salomos'* in the *Sitzungs-
berichte der preussischen Akademie der Wissenschaften*, 1924, xv, pp. 89–90.

Aramaean invasion which led to the founding of an Aramaean kingdom at Damascus in Syria. The Amorites and Aramaeans, indeed, were peoples closely akin both in habits and apparently also in speech; in fact, the Aramaeans are little more than the descendants, if not of those Amorites who were left behind on the occasion of the previous migration, at least of their closest kin.

Of this Amorite language there is only one word preserved in the Assyrian inscriptions, where there is several times mention of a certain chamber built ' like a Hittite temple ' into the gate of palace or city, known as the *bît khillâni* ' in the tongue of the land of Amurrûm ' but called in Assyrian *bît appâti* ' house of outbuildings ' (Winckler, *Sargon*, pp. 128–31, l. 161, *al.*) ; this ' Amorite ' word *khillāni* is cognate with the Hebrew *ḥallôn* ' window ', so that it means literally ' window-house ', used somewhat loosely like the Hebrew word in the description of Ezekiel's temple (Ezek. xl. 16 ff. ; xli. 16). Now the word *khillâni*, although *bît khillâni* may denote a structure borrowed from the palaces of Palestinian princes, is not Canaanite, since that language, like Phoenician and in this instance Hebrew, prefers an *û* or *ô* to *â*, but has rather the colour of Aramaic, which like Arabic adopts *â* for *ô* ; that this is a characteristic of ' Amorite ' is confirmed by the fact that in certain proper names of the first or Amorite dynasty of Babylon and in the name of a certain prince in southern Palestine the god whom the Hebrews called Dāgôn appears as Dagan. Further, the mention of the Hittites in connexion with the *bît khillâni* makes it probable that it is not so much of Aramaic as of Amorite origin ; for the Amorites are known from other sources to have had close relations throughout their history with that people. In fact, there can be little doubt that ' Amorite ', which probably lay closer to Aramaic than any other Semitic language, was the prevailing speech of the desert for many centuries and only yielded very gradually to the advance of Aramaic.

Of the early history of the Hebrew language very little till recently was known; almost, like Greek, it seemed to be already at its first appearance fully developed, both in accidence and syntax; even the inscription on the Pool of Siloam, dated about 700 B. C., proved to be written in a pure and idiomatic style, and showed perhaps only a single archaism, which is found also in Biblical Hebrew—namely, the use of the suffix -*ōh* for -*ô*, ' him ', ' his '. Even more remarkable is the fact that the Moabite Stone, which is placed about 850 B. C., exhibits a language almost identical with Hebrew, apart from a few unimportant dialectical variations. But the discovery in 1888 at Tell-el-'Amarnâ in Egypt of several hundred clay-tablets containing letters from the petty kings and princes of Syria and Palestine to their Egyptian overlords, Amenhotep III (about 1395 B. C.) and Amenhotep IV (about 1370 B. C.), revealed elements of the pre-Hebraic speech of those countries.

It is usually said that, when Sargon conquered the West and made it all ' to speak one language ', the use of Babylonian became universal from the hill-country of Elam to the Mediterranean Sea; but, if this were so, it is striking that in these letters it is common Babylonian words for ' hand ', ' arm ' and so on that require ' Canaanite glosses ' to explain them. The diffusion of pure Babylonian in the extreme west must, on the contrary, have given rise to a very brief domination of that speech over the vernacular of the people, if the divergence was so great. Now there lived between Babylon and Jerusalem from the earliest times a Semitic people, the Amurrû or Amorites, of whose language something has already been said; this race spread over the whole Syrian desert from the river Orontes in the north, over Phoenicia and over Palestine, right down to Babylonia, where they constituted an important element in the population. In the west there sprang up princes here and there like Aziru in the extreme north and Sihon and Og beside the Jordan; yet this people never formed a united nation but lived more like the Arab tribes of the Syrian desert at the present time, now independent, now subject to their powerful neighbours, the Hittites on the north or the Egyptians on the south. Of an Amorite empire there is no trace; their greatest power came when an Amorite family founded the first dynasty of Babylon (*c.* 2225–1926 B.C.). There their authority lasted some two centuries and fell before the Cassites; so in Syria, perhaps 500 years later, they gave way before the well-organized Phoenicians, and so some time earlier in Palestine they seem to have been driven out of the fertile plains and confined to the hill-country by the invading Canaanites. Ulti- mately even in the desert they were supplanted by the more versatile Aramaeans, who seem to have begun to pour up from Arabia five or six centuries before the Amorites established a dynasty of their own on the throne of Babylon. But it was this people, rather than temporary Babylonian invaders, who carried the use of clay-tablets to Canaan and Phoenicia, and it was a form of their speech, fused with that of the invading Canaanites, which in all probability constituted the basis of the language in which the correspondence of the local rulers found at Tell-el-'Amarnâ was written. In the verbal forms the principal peculiarity, the substitution of *a* for the Baby- lonian and Hebrew *i* in the prefix of the imperfect is known to be ' Amorite '; so also may well be the use of the tense corre- sponding in form to the Babylonian preterite as a present. A number of proper names, for instance, of the first or Amorite dynasty of Babylon, such as *Yashmakh-êl* for the pure Babylonian *Ishme-el*, which corresponds to the Hebrew ' Ishmael ' ' God hears ', prove that this *a* is characteristic of the Amorite dialect.[1] Amorite must, however, have become to a large extent assimi- lated to Babylonian, especially during the Amorite supremacy in Babylonia, and had adopted a number of common Babylonian words. It was these words which the Canaanite scribes glossed

[1] Ranke, *Early Babylonian Personal Names*, pp. 24–38.

with the corresponding terms in their own native tongue ; the latter shows in them, as far as an opinion can now be formed, a closer affinity with Phoenician than with Amorite. That these languages were quite distinct is implied in the preservation of two different names for Mt. Hermon, the Amorite *Sĕnîr* and the Sidonian (or Phoenician) *Siryôn* (Deut. iii. 9) ; another trace of Amorite influence on a dialect of Hebrew will be noticed later.

Before proceeding to the glosses it will be as well to give some general account of the peculiarities which distinguish the language of these letters from pure Babylonian. In the permansive or perfect the first person singular has *t* instead of *k* in the pronominal affix, the form *naṣrâku* ' I have preserved ' having been replaced by *naṣrâti*, which is almost identical with the Hebrew *nâṣartî* ; in the imperfect the prefix of the third person masculine is *ya-* or *yi-* instead of the Babylonian *i-*, so that *imlik* ' he takes counsel ' has given way to *yamlik* or *yimluk*, which closely approximates to the Hebrew *yimlōkh* ' he will rule '. In certain groups of letters, however, *i*-forms are exclusively used. Equally fluctuating is the prefix of the first person ; for, although *i-* is regularly preferred to the Babylonian *a-*, there are even a few instances of *e-*, as in Biblical Hebrew ; so *ishmi* and *eshmi* ' I hear ' are closer to the Hebrew *'eshma'* than to the Babylonian *ashme*. In the syntax too they exhibit one important divergence from Babylonian : the tense which bears the form of the Babylonian preterite begins to be used, as in Hebrew, in a present sense, so that *yipushu* means ' they do ' rather than ' they have done ', as it must do in classical Babylonian, and the permansive regularly serves as a perfect with a transitive sense. Yet, although it is no more correct to claim that the Canaanite glosses represent primitive Hebrew than this Babylonian dialect, the part played by both in moulding the mixed language of the Hebrew invaders must not be overlooked.

The language of the glosses is generally known as ' Canaanite ' *par excellence* (although many scholars are inclined to regard that of the letters in general as Canaanite, interspersed with pure Babylonian words, often translated into the native speech), from the fact that Syria and Palestine collectively are called the land of *Kinakhkhni*, that is of *Kěna'an* ' Canaan ', in these letters. From these glosses, which number nearly a hundred, it is clear that of the known Semitic languages Canaanite is, if not the immediate parent of, at least the speech most closely related to Hebrew, as a few examples will show. The Babylonian *arkishu* ' behind him ' is glossed by the Canaanite *akhrunu*, the equivalent of the Hebrew *'akhǎrônô*, *ina qâtishu* ' in his hand ' by *badiu*, the Hebrew *běyādhô*, and so on. Certain regular peculiarities are due to the fact that they belong to another dialect than Hebrew and in fact show it to be in some respects closer to Phoenician than to Hebrew ; for example, *o* is replaced by *u*, just as the Hebrew *shôphēṭ* ' judge ' appears in Phoenician as *sufet* (Livy's *sufetes*). More interesting still, several well-known archaisms of Biblical Hebrew occur among them ; so the archaic *pānêmô* (instead of *pěnêhem*) ' before them ' is to be recognized in *panima*, *taḥtāmô* (instead of *takhtām*) ' beneath them ' in *takhtamu*, and *'ābhědhat*, (instead of *'ābhědhāh*) ' has been lost ' in *abadat*, which reveals the old termination already discussed. There are also indications that the case-endings were in full use, for the nominative seems to end regularly in *-u* and the genitive in *-i*. These glosses also indicate that the Massoretic vocalization of the Hebrew text *may* reflect a late tradition, as already suggested ; for instance, *laqakhu* represents the Hebrew *lāqěḥû* ' they have taken ', *yazkur* the Hebrew *yizkōr* ' he will think ', *yukabid* the Hebrew *yekhabbēdh* ' he honours ' ; in each case the Canaanite form is closer to the Arabic (as seen in *yazkuru* and *yukabbidu*) than to the Hebrew vocalization. Other words, on the contrary, like *meshalime* ' one who has made peace ', which approximates more closely to the

Hebrew *mĕshallim* than the Arabic *mushallimu*, make it evident that the Massoretic vocalization may often represent a very old tradition.

The primitive form of the Hebrew language cannot, however, be reached by the simple expedient of referring it to the Canaanite glosses and comparing the variations in the vocalization of the few words found there with that reflected spasmodically in the transliteration of Hebrew words into Greek characters in the Septuagint or in the other versions. Such agreement may, indeed, be seen in the treatment of the so-called ' segholate ' nouns, in which an *e* has been inserted under the second radical of certain originally monosyllabic nouns to help the pronunciation ; for example, the Hebrew *béṭen* ' belly ' was originally *baṭn(u)* as the Canaanite *baṭnu* shows and as is confirmed by the transcription of such nouns in Greek letters by Origen, who writes αρς for *'éreṣ* ' land ' ; when the termination *-u* was lost, *baṭn* was found difficult to pronounce by the Hebrews (as by many modern Arabs in Syria and Palestine) [1] and became *béṭen* through the insertion of a helping *e* in the final syllable and the assimilation of the *a* of the first syllable to that vowel; another example is *shakhri*, corresponding to the Hebrew *shá'ar* ' door ', whose original form *sha'r* is confirmed by the cognate word in Arabic, *tha'ru* ' gap '. There is evidence, further, that before the weak letter *y* the short vowel of the preposition was merged by crasis with the following vowel, as is attested both by the gloss, already cited, *badiu* for *bĕyādhô* and by the recorded fact that Ben Naphtali is said to have read *lîsrā'ēl* where Ben Asher preferred *lĕyisrā'ēl* ' to Israel ' ; but no proper trace of such a crasis appears in the Hebrew language as handed down. Yet again, the imperative of the first theme appears in the Biblical text as *zĕkhōr* ' remember ' ; but that it was once pronounced *zukur* with an

[1] G. R. Driver, *A Grammar of the Colloquial Arabic of Syria and Palestine*, p. 19.

equal stress on both vowels can hardly be doubted when the Canaanite *nupul* ' fall down ' is compared with Origen's transliteration of *lĕḥam* as λοομ ; both the Babylonian *zukur* ' mention ' and the Ethiopic *zéker* ' remember ' confirm this accentuation. The facts of the case are perhaps that the Massoretic tradition represents rather the liturgical pronunciation of Hebrew, and that this, while giving roughly the position of the tone, at least as recited in the synagogue at the time when the Massoretes were engaged in vocalizing the sacred text, none the less exaggerates the actual practice ; but it does not normally represent the primitive pronunciation, which can now only be somewhat hazardously conjectured from such sources as those indicated in this and the preceding paragraph.

There is another factor to be considered in looking for the sources whence Hebrew sprang. The Hebrews were immigrants into Canaan and, although they found a Semitic race already settled there, they naturally did not speak a language identical with that of the Canaanites, however closely it resembled it. A proof of this can be seen in the fact that Hebrew is a mixed language ; for its vocabulary is demonstrably drawn from two sources, from an eastern Semitic and a southern Semitic stock. There are in Hebrew not a few synonyms, one of which finds a parallel in Accadian and the other in Arabic and often in Aramaic. The most noteworthy are the two words for ' God ', *'ēl* and *'ĕlōhîm*, the first cognate with the Babylonian *ilu*, the second with the Arabic *'ilâh*, and the two pronouns of the first person singular, *'ānōkî* and *'ănî*, which reflect the Babylonian *anâkû* and the Arabic *'anâ* respectively. Similarly *nāthan* ' gave ' represents the Babylonian *nadin* but *yāhabh* the Arabic *wahaba*, *ḥārûṣ* ' gold ' the Babylonian *khurâṣu* but *zāhābh* the Arabic *dhahab*, *'ărî* ' lion ' the Babylonian *arû* but *lābhî'* an Arabic root which is current, as it happens, only in the feminine *labû'atu* ' lioness '. Another series of doublets, exemplified by the verbs *rā'āh* and *ḥāzāh* ' saw ', corresponding to the Arabic *ra'ā* and the Aramaic *ḥăzāh* respectively, confirms an Aramaic contribution to the Hebrew vocabulary. A careful search will reveal many more alternative words of the same kind, but the few cited here should suffice to establish the Babylonian and the Aramaeo-Arabic source of certain elements in the Hebrew language.

Both Canaanite and Phoenician, it has been remarked above, show a marked predilection for *û* and *ô* respectively where Hebrew has sometimes *ô* and sometimes *â* in place of the Arabic and Aramaic *â*; thus the Hebrew nominal termination -*ôn* occasionally gives place to -*ān*, as in *shulḥān* 'table' and *qurbān* 'gift'. Sometimes alternative forms occur side by side, as *kĕthōbheth* and *kĕthābh* 'writing' and possibly in *shiryôn* and *shiryān* 'armour'; similarly, the Phoenician name *Ḥîrôm* is Hebraized, if the Massoretic punctuation is correct, as *Ḥîrām*, though the true form also is preserved. Apart from its concurrence with the Canaanite vocalization, there is little trace of a direct Phoenician element in Hebrew; for *ḥārûṣ* 'gold' may come as well from an Accadian as from a Phoenician source. The Canaanite strain is clearly visible in *ṣō'n* 'sheep' and *rō'sh* 'head', which go back rather to the Canaanite *ṣûn(u)* and *rûsh(u)* than to the Aramaic *ṣân* and *rôsh* or the Arabic *ṣa'n* and *ra's*, although the retention of the *'āleph* in Hebrew shows that *â* was the original vowel; similarly, Hebrew prefers *zĕrôă'* 'arm', after the Canaanite *zurukh*, to a form with *ā* as seen in the Aramaic *dĕrâ'* and the Arabic *dhirâ'*. This fluctuation, then, in the use of *â* and *ô* reflects the part played by Canaanite and to a less degree by Phoenician in moulding the Hebrew language.[1]

It is possible to go further than this, for the Hebrews themselves acknowledged an Aramaean origin (Deut. xxvi. 5), which is hardly at variance with other genealogical indications (Gen.

---

[1] Bauer u. Leander, *Historische Grammatik der Hebräischen Sprache*, i, pp. 15–19, 21 and 23–4.

x. 22). The Aramaeans were a wandering commercial people—perhaps not a nation but clans or families animated by a common purpose—of Semitic origin; they first overflowed from the Arabian peninsular about the twenty-eighth century B. c. and continued for many centuries in increasing numbers to overrun, in more or less peaceful penetration, the Semitic world, of which in the course of time their language became the *lingua franca*. The roots also of Arabic seem to be embedded in Aramaic, if the right conclusion is drawn from inscriptions as well as from grammar. Not only, indeed, as already pointed out, is one element in Hebrew of southern Semitic origin, but those words also which are common to Hebrew and Arabic are almost always to be found also in Aramaic. It is therefore in the highest degree probable, at least on linguistic grounds, that the Hebrews were one wave—the second of which there is any record—of the *Khâbiru*, marauders who invaded Canaan ' from beyond ' the river ; [1] but, unlike the *Khâbiru* who harassed it during the Egyptian suzerainty, they succeeded in obtaining a permanent foothold in the land and eventually became masters of it. There a fusion was effected between their own dialect of the original Aramaeo-Arabic and the native Canaanite languages; that also in its turn had already been largely influenced by both, by the neighbouring Phoenician language and the Amorite dialect which had preceded the Aramaeo-Arabic speech and which, having been introduced by the Amorite dynasty of Babylon during their supremacy, had lingered on long after their passing away as a literary or written language throughout the west ; of this fusion was born the Hebrew language. The commercial ability of the Jews is but another proof of their kinship with these early wandering Aramaean traders.

Semites are found in Canaan, according to the Egyptian

[1] The Babylonian *khâbiru* is philologically identical with the Hebrew '*ēbher*.

sources, as early as the fourth millennium, that is, about the same time as they appeared in Babylonia; they are said to bear, as far as pictures go, a specifically Jewish type of feature, from which it has been inferred that Hebrew also was brought into Canaan at that time. This is held to be confirmed by the close resemblances existing between Accadian and Hebrew, which would prove that the forefathers of the historical Hebrews and the primitive Babylonians were once in close relation to one another in Arabia, the cradle of the Semites; whence they spread north-eastwards and north-westwards as did the Arabs long afterwards, there to give birth to two distinct races. The Babylonian language then came under strong foreign influences, to which it to a certain extent succumbed, while Hebrew remained relatively pure, being affected only by later Semitic influence, Phoenician on the north and Aramaean on the east. The objections to this view are clear: (i) to identify, from a few early sculptures, the primitive Semites in Canaan with the historical Jews is precarious; for it is notorious that the same physical characteristics have always distinguished all Semites; (ii) it has been shown that there are other languages bearing a stronger resemblance to Hebrew than Assyrian, notably the language of the letters found at Tell-el-'Amarnâ and that of the Canaanite glosses; (iii) that this assumed Hebrew existed for three thousand years uncontaminated in a country overrrun by Hyksos, Mitanni, Hittites and Aryans, whereas Babylonian submitted so readily to external influences, is an extremely rash assumption; and (iv) Hebrew is demonstrably a mixed language. Is it not far more probable that the early Semites of the Egyptian monuments were the forerunners of the people who spoke the language of the Canaanite ' glosses ' and that the *Khâbiru* and other Hebrew immigrants entered the land well within historical times, bringing with them a dialect of the language spoken by the Semitic nomads and traders of the desert, which by fusion with the 'Canaanite' and the neighbouring languages gave birth to Hebrew? This accounts for the proto-Aramaic as well as for the Canaanite or Phoenician elements in Hebrew, while the undercurrent of the Babylonian is due to the strong hold which that language had obtained in Canaan during the Babylonian supremacy and which was continued indirectly by the Amorite or western variety of the latter language down to the establishment, it may be, of the kingdom.

Amorite influence, then, lingered on for some time, and is indeed to be recognized in one dialectical form. It is known that the Amorites, like the Arabs, substituted *s* for *sh*, saying *samsu* for *shamshu* 'sun', and this is precisely what happened when the Ephraimites said *sibbŏleth* for *shibbŏleth* 'stream' (Jud. xii. 6). There are several other indications of dialectical variations in the Old Testament. Instead of *'ēdh* 'witness' the Gileadites used *shōmēā'* (Jud. xi. 10), a word cognate with the Assyrian *shâme'ânu* and the Ethiopic *samā'ī*. The particle *shā-* or *she-* for *'ǎsher* 'who', 'which', in some of the early narratives, may well be a mark of the northern Palestinian dialects; the same is probably true of certain infinitives found in the narrative of the Elohist, *dē'āh* for *da'ath* 'to know', *něthōn* for *tēth* 'to give', *hǎlōkh* for *lekheth* 'to go', and so on. Again, such alternatives as *zā'aq* and *ṣā'aq* 'cried out' and *'ālaz* and *'ālaṣ* 'exulted', as well as forms like *mělōkhāh* for *molkhāh* 'be king' (Jud. ix. 8), and the substitution of *'el* 'unto' for *'al* 'upon' in certain writers, may perhaps be traced to different dialects; but it is difficult to speak with any certainty on this point. The occurrence, indeed, both of *zě'aq* and *ṣě'aq* 'cried out' in the Aramaic of the Egyptian *papyri* points to the possibility of alternative forms within the same dialect.

In the later books of the Old Testament Hebrew came under strong neo-Aramaic and even under foreign influence. The

Aramaic which thus colours later Hebrew is not that of the early inscriptions but a modified variety, in which the original Semitic spirants have become explosives, as exhibited in the change of the old Aramaic *nĕṣar* ' kept ' into *nĕṭar*. Examples of these Aramaisms are *bar* for *bēn* ' son ', *zĕmān* for *'ēth* ' time ', *shāhēdh* for *'ēdh* ' witness ', *rā'a'* for *rāṣaṣ* ' broke ', and *nāṭar* for *nāṣar* ' kept ; orthographically, a sign of Aramaic influence is the writing of the termination *-āh* as *-â* and in syntax the use of the preposition *lĕ* ' to ' in place of the accusative to mark the direct object and the formation of compound conjunctions like *shallāmāh* for *pen* ' lest '. The poverty of the Hebrew vocabulary, further, required the introduction of many foreign loan-words, among which may be cited the Assyrian *'iggereth* ' letter ', the Persian *pardēs* ' park ' (whence the English ' paradise '), *'appedhen* ' palace ', and *dāth* ' law ', even though there was a good Hebrew word already in use. More remarkable still, in some cases Hebrew words exchanged their proper meaning for that borne by the cognate word in Aramaic ; thus the Hebrew *ṭa'am* ' taste ', ' judgement ', came to mean ' decision ', ' decree ', in imitation of the Aramaic *ṭĕ'êm* ' command '.

It has already been pointed out that Hebrew accidence has broken down and that in this respect it is comparable with modern colloquial Arabic. Not only does the accusative serve in place of all the cases of the singular, but the same process has also taken place in the plural ; both Assyrian and Arabic show that *-îm* was the ending of the oblique case and that the nominative must have terminated in *-ûm*, while the Canaanite glosses appear to confirm this ; for beside the regular *shamema*, corresponding to the Hebrew *shāmayim*, explaining the Babylonian *shamû* ' heaven ', there occurs also the form *shamuma*, which may be the old nominative, although actually the word glossed by it stands in the oblique case. Another form due to the same cause is the indeclinable relative *'ăsher* ' who ',

' which'; this is nothing else than the construct case of a lost word meaning ' place (where) ', as the Babylonian *ashar* ' the place of', 'where' from *ashru* ' place' shows. This will readily be compared with the use in modern Greek of ποῦ ' where' and in Bernese German of *wo* ' where ' as indeclinable relative particles, denoting ' who ', ' which,' in the vernacular speech.

Against these symptoms of decay must be set the fact that a certain number of old phrases have persisted, though frequently obscured by the theological prejudices of the Massoretes. For example, in view of the words : ' No man shall see me and live ' (Exod. xxxiii. 20) it became an established doctrine among the Jews that the result of seeing God was death ; consequently in the phrase ' to see the face of God ' the verb ' to see ' is vocalized as a passive and the noun ' face ' is taken as an adverbial accusative meaning ' in the face ' or ' presence of', so that the whole phrase may be translated ' to be seen ' or ' to appear before God '. But there is at least one archaic phrase which has escaped notice, in spite of an extreme anthropomorphism which has caused modern scholars to doubt the genuineness of the text. Undoubtedly the words : ' Thy throne is God for ever and ever ' (Ps. xlv. 7) are unexpectedly anthropomorphic, and various attempts have been made to emend the passage ; thus, the Revisers treated the divine name as a vocative, translating the line : ' Thy throne, O God, is for ever and ever,' even though a direct invocation of God in the midst of words addressed to an earthly king is out of place ; others read *kisě'ăkhā khě'lōhîm* ' thy throne is like God', that is, like God's throne, for *kisě'ăkhā 'ělōhîm* ' thy throne is God ', assuming that the preposition *khě* ' like ' has fallen out after the final *kh(ā)* in the preceding word, by haplography. But no such emendation is necessary, for ' thy throne is God' is an archaic form of *comparatio compendiaria* which has survived unaltered in an early poem ; its genuineness is attested by a passage in the Babylonian *Epic of*

Creation, which itself comes down from a very early period; there it is said of Marduk: *segarka (il)Anum* ' thy word is the heaven-god ' (iv. 4 and 6), *viz.* like that of the heaven-god. In fact, the phrases ' thy throne is God ' and ' thy word is the heaven-god ' are precisely parallel expressions, each in its own language a rare relic of a primitive syntax.

It will, perhaps, be well to remark a few other peculiarities which can but be regarded by western readers as more or less grave defects. The most noticeable is the paucity of adjectives, whereby Hebrew is driven to clumsy periphrases with nouns; for example, ' a perfect and a just weight ' is in Hebrew ' a whole stone and righteousness ' (Deut. xxv. 15), ' divers weights ' is ' a stone and a stone ' (Deut. xxv. 13) and ' with a double heart ' is ' with a heart and a heart ' (Ps. xii. 13). Neither is there any comparative or superlative of adjectives nor any word for ' than ' in Hebrew; the preposition *min* ' from ', out of its partitive use as seen in such sentences as ' Israel loved Joseph out of (*i. e.* more than) all his sons ' (Gen. xxxvii. 3), came to be used in both superlative and comparative expressions; so ' the great one from his brethren ' (Num. xiv. 12) means ' the greatest of ' or ' among his brethren ', ' great out of all gods ' (Exod. xviii. 11) means ' greater than all gods ', and so on. In regard to the verbs, apart from the inadequate system of tenses, it should be noticed that the connotation of the derived themes may be almost ambiguous; ' thus *siggēl*, the second theme of *sāgal* ' stoned ', means both ' pelted (a person) with stones ' (2 Sam. xvi. 6) and ' cleared (a place) of stones ' (Isa. v. 2). Lastly, there is no verb ' to have ' nor, strictly speaking, ' to be ' in Hebrew, although Assyrian possesses both, and the speaker is compelled to have recourse to various circumlocutions in place of the latter and to omit the former entirely. Thus, to express ' it is not in me ' the Hebrew says ' not in me it ', and for ' it is not with me ' he says ' nothingness with me ' (Job xxviii. 14); for ' they have ears but hear not' he says 'two ears to them and they hear not' (Ps. cxv. 5).

In conclusion, a few interesting Hebrew idioms may be brought to the reader's notice. In three the peculiarity lies in the striking use of ellipse or aposiopesis. The most note-worthy is the method of making an emphatic statement as a negative and a denial as an affirmative condition of which the apodosis is suppressed. Thus the words 'as thy soul liveth, I will not do this thing' (2 Sam. xi. 11) are in the original : 'as thy soul liveth, if I do this thing!', the suppressed apodosis being 'God curse me' or the like; the full phrase appears occasionally in such passages as 'God do so to thee and more also if thou hide anything from me, &c.' (1 Sam. iii. 17) which means ' thou shalt surely not hide from me, &c.' This remark-able phrase has even turned up in a newly found Assyrian code of laws, where the statement ' He surely said it' appears in the conditional form : 'if he said it not!'[1] Another expressive ellipse occurs in the common phrase 'to see one's desire upon one's enemy'; thus 'I shall see my desire upon mine enemies' (Ps. cxviii. 7) is tersely expressed in Hebrew by the two words *'er'eh bĕsōnĕ'āy,* 'I shall look upon mine enemies'. This forcible idiom was transplanted by the Jews resident in Egypt into Aramaic, where it occurs twice in one of the *papyri* found at Elephantine.[2] Similarly, the well-known sentence 'let my right hand forget her cunning' (Ps. cxxxvii. 5) is in Hebrew briefly expressed by *tishkaḥ yĕmînî* 'let my right hand forget'. Another construction, used by Semites in elevated style but strange to Western ears, is the insertion of a secondary subject, also in the nomina-tive case, when the primary subject is personal, to indicate the instrument. So 'I did call upon the Lord with my voice' (Ps. iii. 5) is in Hebrew 'my voice—I cried unto the

[1] Scheil, *Lois assyriennes*, § 48, l. 17.
[2] Cowley, *Aramaic Papyri*, 30, 16 and 17.

Lord' and 'I called unto him with my mouth' (Ps. lxvi. 17)
is 'my mouth—I called unto him'. This idiom, which occurs
chiefly with the parts of the body such as the voice and the
mouth, as above, or the hand and the soul and also with such
external instruments as the sword (Ps. xvii. 13) and even horses
(Hab. iii. 15), is purely poetical. It has also recently been found
in a Babylonian chronicle written, it is interesting to note, in
verse, with the hand as the secondary subject; the words there
are : *ishallal qâtâsha* 'he—his two hands—tears (it) down'.[1]

In general, the Old Testament comprises too narrow a field
and therefore supplies insufficient material for the study of
classical Hebrew, while the Semitic script allows but a very
inadequate representation of phonetic and even of grammatical
details, and especially of dialectical variations. Nevertheless,
certain characteristics of the Hebrew language are well defined.
The first point to be remarked is that almost all words can be
traced back to roots denoting originally something that can be
grasped by the senses; intellectual ideas, therefore, are
expressed largely by roots of concrete significance and the
passions by words indicating primarily the organs of the body.
Thus the radical idea underlying the root *bîn* 'to understand'
is seen from the Arabic *bâna* 'was separated' to be 'to separate'
and so 'to distinguish', and that of *bāṭaḥ* 'trusted' appears as
'to cast oneself at a person's feet for protection', as the Arabic
baṭaḥa 'threw a person on his face' and *inbaṭaḥa* 'prostrated
oneself' show; again *ḥēmah* 'anger' is derived from the
root *yāḥam* 'was hot'. So abstract an idea as 'patient' demands some such paraphrase as *'erekh rûăḥ* 'long of breath', of
which the reverse is *qĕṣar rûăḥ* 'short of breath', namely
'quick to anger'. In the same way *kĕlāyôth* 'kidneys' is used
figuratively of the affections or of character; consequently
there can be little doubt that, when *kābhôdh* 'glory' is found
in the Massoretic text in parallelism with *nephesh* 'soul' (Gen.
xlix. 6 and Ps. vii. 6) or with *lēbh* 'heart' (Ps. xvi. 9 and cviii. 2)

[1] Smith, *Babylonian Historical Texts*, p. 86, l. 18.

in the sense of ' feelings ' or ' disposition ', the original text had *kābhēdh* ' liver ', since the Assyrian *kabittu* ' liver ' is normally so used and in Aramaic there occurs the derivative verb *'ethkabbad* ' was liverish ', namely ' was angry ', the liver being regarded as a seat of the emotions. The same root has a wider usage; the *kābhēdh* ' liver ' is so called as being the ' heavy ' organ, from the root *kābhēdh* ' heavy '; but the Hebrew, being unable to conceive an abstract root denoting ' honour ', used the same verb *kābhēdh* ' was heavy ' to mean also ' was honoured '. This same inability is at the bottom of many Semitic grammatical conceptions; for instance, there is no neuter form either in Hebrew or in any other Semitic language. Consequently, Hebrew very frequently uses either the feminine singular of the adjective in place of an abstract noun, as *nĕkhônāh* ' steadfastness ', which is properly the feminine singular of the adjective *nākhôn* ' steadfast ', or the feminine plural, as *nĕkhōhôth* ' upright things ' for ' uprightness ' from *nākhōăh* ' upright '. Abstract formations are a characteristic sign indeed of late Hebrew.

Another result of this defect is the extreme paucity of particles and the almost complete absence of subordinate conjunctions; hence the Semitic sentence is a succession of short sentences linked together by simple co-ordinate conjunctions. The principal mark, therefore, of Hebrew and especially of classical Hebrew style is that it is what the Greeks called λέξις εἰρομένη ' speech strung together ' like a row of beads. It was not till a late period that this deficiency began to be made good by the borrowing of a number of particles, both simple and compound, from Aramaic. It will, therefore, be readily understood that philosophical reasoning and sustained argument were beyond the grasp of the Hebrew intellect or, at any rate, beyond its power of expression. Further, the fact that the fundamental conception of the Hebrew mind was nominal, whereby the Hebrew thought in nominal rather than in verbal sentences, resulted in the development of a system of tenses without, primarily, any sense of the order of time. This made possible

' the ease and rapidity with which a writer changes his standpoint, at one moment speaking of a scene as though still in the remote future, at another moment describing it as though present to his gaze. Another characteristic is a love for variety and vividness in expression so soon as the pure prose style is deserted ; the writer, no longer contenting himself with a series, for instance of perfects, diversifies his language in a manner which mocks any effort to reproduce it in a western tongue ; seeing each individual detail he invests it with a character of its own—you see it perhaps emerging into the light, perhaps standing there with clearly cut outline before you—and presents his readers with a picture of surpassing brilliancy and life '.[1]

It was precisely this which made the language so perfectly adapted not only to the needs of the ordinary Jewish writer but above all to the prophet. The historian and the lawyer strung his facts loosely together, careless of the underlying connexion of thought and regardless of the philosophy either of history or of law ; the scene or the fact alone it was that mattered to him. The prophet, too, saw in his visions a scene, and saw it as a series of facts with surpassing vividness and in burning words described it detail by detail as it stood out before his eyes. The order of time or the date at which an action took place was of no consequence ; to him it was at the moment, and there was need only to define the action as complete or incomplete, emergent or continuing. The lesson, too, to be drawn from the vision was both momentary and eternal, outside the series of time ; and both were written down as a series of facts ' strung together ' by simple co-ordination, with but sufficient variation in the tenses to make clear the proper sequence of events.

G. R. DRIVER.

[1] S. R. Driver, *Hebrew Tenses*, pp. 5–6.

THE HISTORY OF ISRAEL

Our only source of information as to the primitive history of Israel is derived from the traditions which were current among the people. These agree in representing the nation as aliens and conquerors in Palestine, and as having become a homogeneous people with a common stock of traditions and ideals, only after the settlement in Canaan. With this the character of the early tales is in entire agreement. For these were originally grouped round certain heroic figures, and the religious character which attaches to many of them shows that their place of collection, if not of origin, was a religious centre. Since, however, early Israel was a loose confederation of clans, each figure round which a number of stories gathered was originally, not a national, but a tribal, leader. Since also the original sanctuaries were tribal, rather than national, centres, it is natural to suppose that each shrine originally collected the tales which referred to its own origin and to the history of the tribe which frequented it. It is necessary to recognize that the combination of the local traditions which referred them all to a united Israel is a later process. There remains an original divergence which has only been partially obscured.

Thus one series of traditions, grouped round the name of Abraham, is chiefly localized at sanctuaries in Southern Palestine. These, while they more immediately connect the race with Harran in Mesopotamia, derive it ultimately from Ur, which the later Jews regarded as the ancient city of Babylonia. Another series of tales, however, is gathered round the name of Jacob, and is more closely associated with the shrines of Central Palestine. These bring the people from North-East

Syria, and, saying nothing about Babylonia, describe the fore-father of their race as having been a wandering Aramaean. The distinction between the North and South, which thus appears at the beginning, persists through all the later history and profoundly influences the fortunes of the nation. It may be doubted whether the identification of Ur with the famous city of South Babylonia was ever more than a guess : but several other considerations serve to confirm the impression that Israel was part of the Aramaic stock and found its way into Palestine from the North-East.

Before reaching their new home, however, the clans are said to have gone down into Egypt and to have received there some of the strongest influences which made them into a nation. Here again the traditions are not uniform. There are indica-tions of a tradition which regarded certain clans as having been settled without ever passing into the Nile-valley. Efforts have been made to identify the particular sections, but, in the uncertainty of our sources of information, these cannot be said to offer very sure conclusions. The tribes, which went down to Egypt, received through their stay there so profound an impression that they became the dominating section of the national life, and they naturally impressed their view of the history on the entire community. It is possible that some of the newcomers remained in Palestine, while others were drawn further in the wake of the Hyksos, after these had come to dominate Egypt.

Hebrew tradition, then, brings one section of the people into direct contact with Egypt. And Palestine, at the time of Israel's conquest, was more or less under Egyptian control. It becomes natural to look for further light to the records of that country. Unfortunately the information these afford is meagre and very inconclusive : but two items of somewhat cardinal importance seem clear.

The first is supplied by the Tell-el-Amarna letters. A

number of these consist of appeals for help from the chiefs of the Egyptian garrisons in Palestine during the reign of Amenhotp IV, *circa* 1350. The men complain that the country is being overrun by two bodies of invaders, called Sagaz and Habiru. Since the letters are the statements of army-captains, who regard the newcomers merely as troublesome neighbours, they cannot be treated as scientific documents on the questions as to the original home of the strangers, the route by which they arrived, or the relation which may have obtained between the two bodies. Yet it is clear that the Sagaz chiefly vexed the Northern borders, while the Habiru disturbed the Centre and the South. And from the fact that the expression ' gods of the Sagaz ' sometimes takes the place of ' gods of the Habiru ' it is natural to conclude that the invaders had a certain community of race and religion. The larger question, however, is whether one or both of these were Israel, and whether their invasion represents the conquest of Palestine. Now the equation of Habiru with 'Ibhrim or Hebrews is philologically perfect : and it is very difficult to believe that at this particular date a people invaded Palestine, whose name is practically identical with that of a section of Israel, and yet which had no connexion with the Hebrews. If, however, the equation should be accepted and the Habiru of the letters identified with the invaders from Egypt, the natural, though not necessary, conclusion will be to set the beginning of Israel's conquest of Palestine about the middle of the fourteenth century.

This conclusion is supported by the second clear item of evidence from the Egyptian records. Mineptha, *circa* 1220, claims to have defeated the people of Israel in the course of a campaign into Syria. In this period Egypt, having recovered from the internal weakness which had befallen it under Amenhotp, was seeking to reassert its dominant position in West Asia. It is unnecessary to take too literally the statement of the Egyptian that he had practically extinguished the nation :

royal bulletins have never been perfect historical documents. But it is also impossible to ignore that he wrote of Israel as a people, and as already settled in the country. This of course implies that the invaders in the first quarter of the thirteenth century had not only broken into Palestine, but were sufficiently possessed of their new settlements to be recognized as having a national life and even as being the dominant race in certain parts of the land.

The two items of evidence from the Egyptian records support each other in making it difficult to maintain the customary date of the Exodus in the period of Mineptha, i. e., in the thirteenth century. That cardinal event in the life of the people more probably took place under Amenhotp II, *circa* 1445, or somewhat later.

On this view of history the Israelites derive from North-East Syria, out of which they may have been thrust by that advance of the Hittites, which later gave so much trouble to the Egyptian kings. Certain clans drifted into Palestine, where some settled among the native population, as allies or as subjects. These remained, and their lower status in purity of blood and religion may be the reason why the Biblical records call them the descendants of concubines. But a larger contingent found a temporary lodgment in the Negeb, where they were able to maintain their original character and a closer cohesion. From there they transferred themselves to Egypt, following in the wake of their fellow-Semites, the Hykso invaders. On the Hykso collapse they made their escape and were fortunate enough to escape with some cohesion. These clans formed the most important part of the future nation, not merely because they were brought into contact with the civilization of the Nile valley, but because they came under the influence of Moses. From him they received a profound religious impulse, which gave them so strong a sense of their distinct and common character that, after the escape from Egypt, their loose federation of clans was able to resist the disintegrating influence of the desert life. Instead of dissolving into wandering Bedawin, they found their way under their leader to Kadesh, which became for a period their religious and social centre. The rudiments of law were framed into a simple code, an organization for worship and justice was instituted. The chief bond, however, was devotion to a common God, Yahweh. He, and He alone, was acknowledged as the deity of the federation. Since the principal task for which the tribes united was defence or conquest, He was naturally regarded as pre-eminently the God of war. But everything common to their national life was also placed under His authority. By His direction they sought to determine their internal social regulations as well as their external warlike activities. Since He was peculiarly the God of the federation, Israel learned to realize its unity as a people through its devotion to Yahweh, and such cohesion as the clans possessed came from their common faith.

How long the tribes remained near Kadesh it is impossible to say. The forty years assigned by tradition to the desert wanderings is too recurrent a period in their history to be trustworthy. But what gave them opportunity for a forward movement was the weakening of Egypt's hold on Palestine in the period of Amenhotp IV. They attacked the new country in the earlier half of the fourteenth century. The Egyptians had withdrawn their garrisons or abandoned them, and the only enemy the invaders had to meet was the native Canaanites, already weakened by the long period of Egyptian domination.

For the story of the conquest the sole source is Hebrew tradition. The character of this is changed, for the stories are no longer grouped round religious centres, and there begin to appear literary records, such as the song of Deborah and a few extracts from a book of the wars of Yahweh. But all the tales of the conquest have been submitted to a drastic revision which had for its aim to bring them into an artificial unity.

The leading characteristics of this revision are easily recognized. Later Israel, conscious of its unity and proud of its distinctive character, was incapable of conceiving that it had once existed as a loose federation. Accordingly, when it recast the traditions of the conquest, it represented this as carried out by a homogeneous people in one campaign under a single leader. Inevitably also it gave the place of honour to that section of the nation which, having come under the influence of Moses, preserved the strongest national type and became the representative of the dominant civilization. To it the leader at the conquest was Joshua, who crossed the Jordan at Jericho, captured the central position of Benjamin, and lodged Israel in the heart of its new land. From there he carried his victory forward into Judah, and even succeeded in striking down a Canaanite coalition on the highlands of Galilee. Having thus reduced the country to a *tabula rasa*, he divided it among the tribes.

How artificial the process of unifying the tradition was, is most clearly seen in connexion with the conquest of the South. One account represents Caleb as conquering Hebron on his own initiative ; another regards him as acting at the instance of his tribe, Judah ; a third makes Joshua, the representative of Israel, commission him to his task. The process is clear. First the tribe has drawn to itself the exploits of local clans, then the national leader has absorbed the tribe and its traditions.

The matter is not so easily resolved in connexion with Central Palestine. But here too there is evidence of a tradition which represented Jordan as having been crossed opposite Shechem and which made that town the site of the first Israelite sanctuary in Palestine. It is significant that one of the Tell-el-Amarna letters states that the Habiru have already by that time possessed themselves of this district. And it is equally significant that the Hebrew story of conquest does not relate the capture of Central Palestine. It only ascribes the foundation of the sanctuary there to Joshua. Apparently the tradition of the independent character of this settlement was too strong for it to be put under the Southern leader. The later revisers could ignore the local record of the conquest of Ephraim, but they could not venture to set it down as one of the triumphs of Joshua.

Probably then Palestine was entered at three places, by way of the Negeb, by the Jordan ford at Jericho, and opposite Shechem. It is more difficult to determine the relation in which the threefold advance stood. One Hebrew tradition makes Judah cross at Jordan, and then, after the fall of Jericho, branch off to seek its independent settlements in the South. So long as Jerusalem was Jebusite, however, their road was hopelessly barred. The story may preserve the memory of the fact that the conquest of the South was later than the break-through at Jericho. And, since we hear of the failure of an initial effort in the Negeb, it may also mark that the task was made easier by Joshua's victory. The weakened Canaanites offered less resistance. The fresh advance will then have been made from Kadesh, and Caleb, by his capture of Hebron, will have made Judah the dominant power in the South. Until, however, it had assimilated the alien elements in itself, and had captured Jerusalem, it remained separate from its brethren.

It is a harder task to define the relation between the invasion at Jericho and that opposite Shechem. It might be possible to suppose that the invaders of Central Palestine moved out from Kadesh and that the assaults in the North and South took place about the same time, even as part of a common plan. This would explain why the Hebrew tradition does not connect Joshua with the conquest of Mt. Ephraim. When the Southern invaders reached Bethel, they found Central Palestine already occupied. The later historians, who aimed at unifying the traditions, could not ignore the story of the independent conquest of the North nor bring it under Joshua. All they could do was to represent him as having acknowledged their place in the confederation of Israel. And this was done by representing Joshua as having built the altar at Ebal. Since the binding tie of the confederacy was their faith, the recognition of any tribe naturally took the form of common worship. And since the invaders at Jericho were the purer in faith and in blood, the admission into the federation of Israel came from their leader.

But such an act of deliberate recognition hardly suits the idea that the Northern invaders had already formed part of the confederation at Kadesh. It rather points to their occupation having been independent and earlier than that of Benjamin. And other facts point in the same direction. Thus some possession of Shechem is constantly ascribed to Jacob. If Knudtzon's reading of one of the Amarna tablets is correct, Shechem appears to have been in the hands of the Habiru even before the Egyptian garrisons were withdrawn. If some of the settlers on Mt. Ephraim were lodged there by an earlier and independent advance, it becomes easier to understand certain phenomena of their later religious history. Not having come under the influences which made the unity of Israel at Kadesh, they were less deeply convinced of the unique character of Yahweh. The Abimelech story shows them mixed with Canaanite elements and inclined to a religious syncretism. The code of Deuteronomy shows what vigorous efforts were needed to preserve the purity of their faith. And to the end they were inclined in their historical records to use the more general and colourless name of *El* as well as the distinctive Yahweh for the name of their deity. The invasion of Central Palestine may have been effected by a tribe which was never in Egypt. But they received from the South an accession of strength, physical and moral, which made them dominant; yet they remained Jacob and Joseph, Ephraim and Manasseh. The double name points to a double strain.

These are questions which are unsettled, which perhaps can never be settled. At least the initial conquest was sporadic, carried out by individual tribes under their own leaders. It was gradual and slow instead of being effected in one rush. And in several districts it was incomplete. But it made the confederacy dominant in Palestine and gave it a quickened sense of its distinctive life. Much, however, remained to be done. The native Canaanites were cowed, but were far from being vanquished. The success of the invaders tempted the hungry marauders of the desert to follow their example, and the new land must be protected against their raids. Some internal order was needed in the federation itself. For all these purposes an organization of the scattered clans was necessary. How these tasks were faced and with what success is told in the traditions which have been collected in the book of Judges.

These also have been submitted to a revision which, though not so thorough as that of the book of Joshua, betrays some of the same characteristics. The tales have been allowed to retain more of their original form, but they have been fitted into a framework which represents their heroes as rulers over a united Israel, and as following one another in a chronological sequence. In reality there was as yet no united Israel. Gideon leads his own clan of Abiezer to repel a local razzia of the Midianites. Ehud hurls back the king of Moab who is seeking to follow Joshua's example and become master of Benjamin. Jephthah frees Gilead from the Ammonites. All these are mere clan or tribal leaders. As for Samson, he is not able to free Dan from the pressure of the Philistines, far less to govern Israel. The stories are local, and the men they celebrate are not necessarily consecutive in date. The attack of Moab on Benjamin may well have coincided with, rather than preceded, Ammon's invasion of Gilead : the two little kingdoms may have been seeking to follow in the steps of the successful invaders.

Apparently the Canaanites, rallying in the North, made

a desperate effort to break the yoke of the conquerors. The
challenge to their supremacy and to their faith revealed the
latent unity of the tribes and showed them to be capable of
combining against a common danger. The song of Deborah
breathes the pride of a people which is finding itself in a mutual
task, but it also reveals the need of some central authority to
make the unity complete and permanent. At least the victory
was so signal that the original inhabitants ceased to be a danger.
The situation, as between Canaanite and Israelite, varied in
different parts of the country. In certain districts the new-
comers were definitely superior, notably round Hebron, in the
Ephraim highland and in Benjamin. In others they were as
definitely inferior, especially in parts of Galilee. Here and
there the relation was one of alliance. Thus Gibeon was
admitted on terms to the federation, and Abimelech, himself
a half-caste, attempted to combine the races. But Palestine
definitely ceased to be Canaanite.

The other task of the tribes was to maintain the land they
had won against attacks from the outside. Its traditions
uniformly reveal Israel as successful in beating back new invaders, except on the West, where Dan was unable to resist the
advance of the Philistines. When, however, the tribe sought
a new home in the North it could traverse the country with
ease. Evidently Central Palestine was in secure possession.
The new-comers had even succeeded in establishing some civil
order, for Micah's protest against the theft of his property by
the band reveals the temper of a man who is annoyed by an
unaccustomed outrage. The basis of a national life had been
laid. What was needed was some authority to represent the
fundamental community of race and faith, and make it effective
against outward attack and inward division. The community of
spirit was there, for Deborah had appealed to it with success.
But it was weak, for certain districts failed to respond, and,
when the immediate danger had passed, the tribes lapsed into

their easy isolation, and were capable of the jealousy which made Ephraim resent the success of one of its own clans under Gideon.

The task was not easy, for the conditions of the conquest had helped to isolate the clans. Jerusalem was still in the possession of the Jebusites, and, when Dan was driven out, a barrier was run across the country which shut off Judah into an enclave. The strong belt of towns along the vale of Esdraelon remained Canaanite, and so separated Ephraim from Galilee. The deep trough of the Jordan valley has always divided Eastern from Western Palestine. There was grave danger that Israel might divide into four sections, each of which followed its own independent course. What at first threatened to make permanent the cleavage between Judah and Israel was the influence which led to a closer union. The rise of the Philistine power on the Western coasts made it essential that, if the people were to preserve their national existence, they must combine. The danger of the Canaanite rising had produced a temporary union, but, when that rising was crushed, the union it had summoned into life died down. The Philistines could not be finally crushed. The enduring threat they constituted to Israel's independent life made it necessary to discover a permanent unity which alone could resist them.

If the Philistines did not arrive in Palestine precisely during the period of the Israelite conquest, they must then have received an accession of strength. Arriving from the Mediterranean, probably from Crete, they built or conquered their famous five towns in the lowland along the coast. Their situation gave them economic strength, since they were posted on the trade-route and could take toll from the caravans. Defeat in open battle did not break men who rallied behind their fortified walls and thence defied the efforts of the unskilled Highland clans. They were also strong in the Western power of combination and their close-knit organization lent them marked superiority. The result was that, after driving Dan from its first settlements, the Philistines penetrated into Benjamin, destroyed Shiloh with its sanctuary and, if they did not overrun Ephraim, held the passes into the North country. Israel was cut in two. And this was no Midianite razzia ; it was a conquest.

Naturally resistance began where the danger was greatest and where the pulses of independent life beat most strongly— in Benjamin. Naturally also their religion, which gave the people their sense of a distinctive life and of a common bond, supported with all its power the Benjamite who began the resistance. As the faith was the flag to which the clans rallied when the Canaanites rose in the days of Deborah, so Saul's more desperate adventure found a strong ally in the prophetic party which itself makes its appearance in the period of the national danger. Samuel is represented as having stirred up and sent out the new leader. Saul was able to free his own tribe and thus to open communication with and win support from Ephraim. But, though he succeeded in driving back the Philistines into the low country, he could never break them. They remained a danger during his lifetime, and the constant threat of their return made it natural that Israel retained the new authority which alone prevented the country from being again overrun. How necessary the king and the kingdom had become to the national life is most clearly proved by the fact that, though Saul early in his reign quarrelled with the prophetic order which had done so much to make his kingdom possible, the people supported him to the end. How far he succeeded in extending his power is uncertain. He must, however, have had firm footing beyond Jordan, for one of his famous victories was gained in delivering Jabesh Gilead from Nahash of Ammon, and after his death his son established a short-lived kingdom in Eastern Palestine. The scene of his final defeat and death, Mount Gilboa, near the plain of Esdraelon, points to the kingdom having held real power in Ephraim. Either Saul actually controlled Central Palestine and was threatening to cross into Galilee. In that case the Philistines marched North to protect the trade route along Esdraelon. Or his increasing power in Ephraim had made his enemies uneasy. Then they may have attacked by way of the great plain, because Saul securely held the direct route into Benjamin by Beth-horon.

The first kingdom ended in disaster, but not until it had done its work. It had succeeded in uniting several of the tribes, not in a spasmodic effort, but in a permanent union. This feature sets Saul's deed beyond what was accomplished by the preceding judges, and makes it a new beginning in the nation. Israel began to feel itself as Israel through him. And even after he fell at Gilboa, Israel could not forget what it had won. Saul prepared the way for an abler and more fortunate successor.

At first the situation seemed hopeless enough. David was head of a petty kingdom at Hebron, subject to the Philistines, while Ishbaal held precarious rule at Mahanaim. The two could not fail to conflict, since Ishbaal was driven on to assert his authority over his father's native tribe, and no ruler of any ambition could be content to remain permanently pent in the Negeb. The debated territory became the scene of border scuffles at which the Philistines looked on placidly while the rivals weakened each other. So soon, however, as David mastered his opponent, their jealousy was roused. For a time Judah was overrun and its king was a fugitive.

David restored the situation by a master stroke. The narrative of this period of his life is scanty and hopelessly confused so that the causes which led to a dramatic change of fortune cannot be discovered. But he succeeded in capturing Jerusalem and made it his capital. The natural strength of the city gave Israel what it needed in its struggle with the Philistines—a rallying place in the event of defeat. Yet it meant much more. So long as David's capital was Hebron he remained merely the leader of Judah. Jerusalem, lying on the confines of two tribes, had no tribal associations. The city also had defied both Judah and Benjamin, and had only been mastered by a united effort. It was peculiarly adapted to become the centre of united Israel, and, to emphasize the fact, David brought into it the ark, the emblem of Ephraim's religion. From this time Judah emerged from its isolation, and all his life the new king was diligent to mark that he regarded himself as more than the head of a tribe.

David was fortunate in the date of his accession. He came to the throne when the great powers of the Nile and the Euphrates valleys were incapable of interfering in Syria. Egypt was busy with internal difficulties; Assyria was paralysed by frontier troubles. There was an opportunity for an able man to build up a strong kingdom in Palestine, and the new king had the capacity which could seize the opportunity. When the minor states beyond Jordan took alarm at finding a strong ruler instead of the weak Ishbaal as their neighbour, David was prompt to accept their challenge. Ammon, Moab, and Edom were effectually humbled or made subject, and the more distant Syrian principalities along the North-east frontier were made tributary. The kingdom extended from the roots of Lebanon to the Negeb, and from the Mediterranean to the desert.

Its strength, however, depended on two factors, one external, the other internal. The situation could not fail to be gravely changed, when one or other of the greater powers recovered from its temporary weakness. As serious was the difficulty of maintaining the cohesion between Northern and Southern Israel. The ease with which that bond could be loosened by an appeal to the old spirit of independence was shown in the later years of the king. The rebellion of Absalom in Judah and of Sheba in Ephraim revealed the weakness of the union which David had been careful to maintain.

How long a period should be given to the conquest and settlement it is hard to determine. Hebrew tradition assigned 480 years as intervening between the Exodus and Solomon's building of the temple. The statement is late and is generally regarded as an artificial calculation based on the 12 high priests, whom I Chron. vi. 3–10 mentions between Eleazar, Aaron's son and Azariah, priest under Solomon, to each of whom the conventional forty years of a generation have been allotted. But the explanation is one of those which fail to explain, since it is natural to ask why exactly twelve priests were given to the period. It is more probable that tradition handed down a round number of 500 years, and that the later men turned it into 480, in order to find room for twelve priests corresponding to the twelve tribes. If then Solomon's date is *c.* 970, Hebrew tradition roughly carries back the Exodus to the middle of the fourteenth century.

Solomon's task was to consolidate the kingdom his father had won. The frontiers were secure, especially after an alliance was entered into with Phoenicia. From its control over the trade routes which ran across its territory the state could draw considerable revenues. The king gave large attention to the development of this trade. For administrative purposes he divided the country into districts which he placed under the charge of royal officials. He enlarged the new capital, building in it a palace, an armoury and a temple. But all this offended some of the strongest elements in the national life. The subdivision of the country ran counter to the tribal feeling, since the new districts ignored the original clans and the royal officials supplanted the local leaders. For the building of the temple Solomon must employ Phoenician workmen, and, since Israel never developed an independent religious art, this meant that the royal chapel was full of heathen symbolism. Semitic dislike to centralization, human resentment of taxation, and offended religious feeling combined to lay on the people's loyalty to the central authority a greater strain than it could bear. The institution of the kingdom had changed the whole basis of the national life. The 'elders' and local leaders administered after a law which all men recognized and remained responsible to the community with which they were in close contact. The hereditary king governed by his own will and was responsible to no one. His officials and the new men who carried on the increasing trade were equally remote from contact with and responsibility to the community. The new relations with the outside world into which the nation was carried implied a certain change in religious attitude. The older system had an ethical basis, and the new kingdom as yet had none. Hence the prophetic party began to drift into opposition; and some of them were found supporting Jeroboam when the rupture came after Solomon's death.

That disruption made Ephraim the centre of Israel's life for several generations, since the Northern kingdom was the larger, the wealthier, and religiously the more vital section of the people. Judah dropped into a backwater, where all its tasks were simplified. Its internal politics were easily determined, for the tiny kingdom practically represented the old tribe and the king claimed and received the old loyalty of the clan. Sitting apart on its eagle's nest of the Judaean highland, its relations to the outside world were chiefly dependent on its relation to its stronger neighbour in the North. When its kings refused to accept the division, they could become an irritation or even a weakness to Ephraim, but no more. When they had the political sagacity to acquiesce in the situation, they might become its allies. Israel's life now centred not in Jerusalem, but in Samaria.

The task which lay before the Northern kingdom was a serious one for two reasons. Since it included several tribes, it was internally less homogeneous than Judah. No sooner then had its kings rebelled against centralization than they found themselves compelled to erect a strong authority among a people which derived its existence from a successful resistance to this inevitable task. Ephraim could the less evade the difficult duty, because externally the kingdom was in contact with the world. Damascus was rising to influence on its Eastern flank, and Phoenicia bordered it on the north-west. The great route between Asia and Africa ran through its territory, and the powers, which it might have linked by trade, had recovered from their weakness and were preparing to use it for war. Jeroboam's kingdom must enter into relations to all these.

What at first impelled these powers, Egypt on the one side, Damascus first, Assyria afterwards on the other, to press into Syria was more than ambition. A minor factor was the need on the part of the treeless lands for the control of the timber-forests on Lebanon. A larger factor in the situation was that the Mediterranean and its coasts were beginning to influence the Eastern world in a new way. Phoenicia had grown rich and powerful through holding the monopoly of that trade. Through its ports of Tyre and Sidon all the traffic from Syria and the Euphrates valley found its way westward. It was impossible that Damascus or Assyria should permanently acquiesce in a condition of things which shut them off from the command of their own trade. Now, since the territory of Israel lay in the way, the Northern kingdom was inevitably swept into world politics, as Judah was not.

Damascus began the pressure; it was aiming at a route which would have brought it to the open sea at Akko. As its success would have amputated Israel and threatened the Phoenician monopoly, it was the evident interest of the two kingdoms to combine against the aggressor. About this period the dynasty of Jeroboam had fallen and given place to a usurper, the army-captain, Omri. He was shrewd enough to grasp the situation and strong enough to take the necessary measures for meeting its danger. He entered into league with the king of Tyre and made peace with Judah. The alliance was cemented on both sides by intermarriage of the royal houses. Ahab, the crown prince of Israel, was married to Jezebel a princess of Tyre, and later Athaliah, a daughter of Ahab, was given in marriage to the king of Judah. The league with Phoenicia enabled the dynasty to make head against Damascus, though Ahab during part of his reign was evidently hard-pressed. In another direction, however, it had mischievous consequences. The king remained personally loyal to the national religion, for he gave his children names compounded with Yahweh, but he found it necessary to tolerate the worship of the Tyrian deities in a way which appeared like apostasy to the more zealous prophetic party. Jezebel, also, accustomed to Tyrian methods of dealing with troublesome subjects, resented the limits set to the king's authority in Israel. The Hebrew kingdom threatened to become another dreary Eastern despotism. Jezebel stamped out the prophetic protest and expelled Elijah, its leading representative. The natural result was to throw the opposition to her policy into the hands of the intransigent elements of the party, with whom Jehu was shrewd enough to ally himself. A captain in the army, Jehu, took advantage of the king's absence from the camp at Ramoth-Gilead to raise the standard of revolt, and destroyed the dynasty in a blood-bath which roused the indignant protest of the nobler among the prophets.

The political situation at this period is difficult to follow. The Hebrew sources of information are very full on Ahab's reign and the rise of Jehu. But the men who collected them were mainly interested in the religious question and everything which concerned that issue. Here and there they have preserved documents of a more secular character, which in their vividness and fullness only serve to make evident how much has been lost. And practically nothing has been preserved to throw light on Jehu's conduct and policy. It is true that the arrival of Assyria on the scene supplies the historical student with a welcome supplement to the Biblical records, and especially enables him to gain that backbone to history, an approximate system of dating. But the Assyrian annals are indifferent to minor matters in the local history of the foreigners, and, being of the nature of army bulletins, are not wholly reliable. Hence the relations between Ahab, Jehu, Damascus, and Assyria are very confusing. This, however, seems clear. Israel, torn by internal dissension, must have fallen before Damascus, had not Assyria under one of its great warrior kings risen behind the contending rivals. Damascus was forced to face Eastward and to relax its grip on Israel in order to protect its own frontier. In 842 Shalmaneser was attacking Damascus, and Jehu appears paying tribute to the Assyrian. Evidently the king of Israel was seeking support against his nearer enemy. Troubles at home prevented Shalmaneser from following up his initial successes in the West, but these had convinced the little kingdoms of Syria of the folly of devouring one another before so great a common danger. The shadow of the Euphrates eagle ended the scuffle between the Syrian kites. From this time there is nothing more heard of attack by Damascus on Samaria. Instead, when the two kingdoms are next mentioned together, they appear in league against Assyria. Pekah of Samaria and Rezon of Damascus are seeking to force Ahaz of Jerusalem into a defensive league.

The relief this advance of Assyria gave on the Eastern frontier enabled Jehu's dynasty to maintain itself to the third generation. On the death of Jeroboam II, however, the kingdom fell into utter confusion. It is impossible to trace all the factors which led to this situation ; but one can be discovered in the Book of Hosea. The prophet severely blames his people for seeking assistance, now from Egypt, again from Assyria. Evidently Egypt was intriguing for a foothold in its old frontier province and Assyria was preparing for another advance on the West, so that to other troubles in the distracted state was added the existence of a division as to its foreign policy. The result was that of the kings who followed Jeroboam II only one died a natural death, and that king followed king in bewildering succession. It is difficult to tell what the successive kings stood for, or whether some of the usurpers stood for anything more than their personal interests, which were less than nothing, and vanity.

When, therefore, Assyria began a renewed advance, there was nothing in the West to make head against it. Pekah and Rezon combined to resist Tiglath Pileser, but the conqueror captured Damascus, and made Samaria as well as almost all the surrounding kingdoms tributary. Hoshea, who succeeded Pekah, had some support from Egypt in seeking to shake off the yoke : but his intrigues only brought the end. In 722/1 Samaria, after a desperate and gallant resistance of three years, fell to Sargon, and Northern Israel became an Assyrian province. The leaders of the nation were transported into another province of the empire and new settlers were brought in and planted in Palestine. But the backbone of the inhabitants of the country remained the old Jewish peasantry, cultivating their fields and paying tribute to the conqueror. They were even permitted to re-establish a centre of worship at Bethel under charge of a priest who was sent back for the purpose from Assyria. Since these men became a factor in the later history of the nation, it is necessary to emphasize that the captivity of Northern Israel did not mean the disappearance of the Israelites from that territory. In the real sense of the words there never were any 'lost ten tribes', for those who went into captivity constituted a relatively small proportion of the inhabitants of the province.

Judah was now the sole representative of the Israelite kingdom. Its situation and its world had undergone a profound change. All the horizons had widened since the days of Omri. Assyria, secure in its frontiers, flushed with success and led by a succession of powerful kings, was moving for more than access to the Lebanon forests and a clear route to the Mediterranean. Already in practical mastery over Northern Syria, it was aiming at command of the bridge between Asia and Africa with the control of the Nile valley as the goal of its ambition. Its success would give it the empire of the Eastern world. On the other hand, Egypt was straining every nerve to maintain the buffer states of Palestine and to control their policy. The period of the world-empires had begun.

The days of Judah's isolation had come to an end, for between the two great powers, which must inevitably clash, the little state was the border province ; and the situation determined its attitude. Since it could no longer remain isolated, the real question was to which it should incline. The policy of its successive kings fluctuated continually between alliance with Egypt and with Assyria ; and with the attitude on external politics went a corresponding attitude as to religion. Political dependence on Assyria seems for some reason to have always brought with it a certain recognition of the religion of the superior power. Hence the kings who judged it prudent to submit to Nineveh were driven to tolerate the foreign worship or even to give it a place beside the national faith. But this attitude set them in opposition to the strongest elements among their people who, under the guidance of the prophets, had come to recognize their religion as the nerve of the nation's distinctive life. The result has been that all the kings who turned Eastward in their politics have received harsh judgment in the Biblical records. Instinctively Judah realized that to surrender its distinctive faith was to lose its soul, and it judged the kings who inclined to accommodation with the Eastern colossus by a more intransigent standard than the maxims of worldly prudence which are apt to guide statesmen.

The question emerged even before the fall of Samaria. Already, when Pekah of Samaria and Rezon of Damascus attempted to coerce Judah into an alliance against Assyria, Ahaz did what Jehu had done before him, preferred to submit to the more distant power. By so doing he saved his city for, when Samaria fell, Jerusalem and the dynasty of David were preserved. The price he paid was that, as an ally of Assyria, he must acknowledge also its supreme deity alongside Yahweh in the temple. This action alienated a body of his subjects who looked to Egypt as their only hope for maintaining the purity of the faith and the independence of national life. The party controlled the policy of his successor, for Hezekiah swung in the opposite direction alike in religion and in politics. He intrigued with Egypt ; and, when Babylonia under Merodach Baladan rose among the marshes at the head of the Persian Gulf to become a thorn in Assyria's side, he made advances to the new power. At home he carried through a religious reform which aimed at purifying the national faith from heathen practices.

At first Hezekiah's policy appeared to be justified by results. Assyria was compelled to take action against Egypt which had drawn several of the minor states of Palestine into a coalition. After driving out the Babylonian and securing his rear, Sennacherib marched into Syria at the head of a powerful force, and, overwhelming all opposition in his way, advanced along the coast into the Philistine territory. Here he defeated the Egyptians at Eltekeh in 701, though the victory was evidently less decisive than his bulletin sought to represent it. Before the battle a detachment of his troops had overrun the towns of Judah, broken Hezekiah's field-army and laid siege to the capital. His initial success, however, was but the prelude to a serious loss. His general was unable to capture Jerusalem and, when he himself advanced against Egypt after Eltekeh, his army suffered so signal and unexpected a disaster on the

Egyptian border that the Jews saw in it nothing less than a direct intervention of Yahweh for the defence of His city and temple. Sennacherib retired to Nineveh where he engaged in further war with Babylonia ; but he never attempted another advance on Egypt.

Hezekiah's policy at home and abroad seemed to be brilliantly vindicated. His success, however, was at best a Pyrrhic victory. With his country wasted by fire and sword and his treasury exhausted, the king was in evil plight. Assyria could better bear such a defeat than Judah could meet such a victory. The Assyrian advance was only checked, not permanently stayed, for Asarhaddon renewed the attack on Egypt and carried it to a victorious conclusion. Judah naturally fell to the conqueror. In 673 Manasseh appears among other states of Syria, paying tribute to the Assyrian, and in the campaign of 671, when Asarhaddon by his capture of Memphis made himself master of the Nile valley, a Judaean contingent is found serving in his army. Judah had become a province of the world empire. Loss of independence brought the usual consequence of adoption of Assyrian religious practices, and since the little state was now part of the empire, the measures taken to enforce this policy were more brutal. When the stricter prophetic party resisted, Manasseh was driven on to crush them by violence. How far his action was prompted by religious, and how far by political considerations, it is not easy to say. In particular, how far his persecution of the Puritans was dictated by the fact that they were not exactly submissive subjects, no one who has faced the difficulty of drawing the line between religious and political persecution in the period of Elizabeth will venture rashly to pronounce. His hesitation will be increased by his recognition that the only source of information about Manasseh comes from his convinced opponents.

Manasseh's conduct in Jerusalem may have been part of a larger policy, which was dictated by his superiors. Asarhaddon and his successor Ashurbanipal are reported to have found it necessary to settle an additional body of foreign colonists in Northern Israel. Since Samaria had not been wasted by war, the act can hardly have been prompted by a desire to increase the population. More probably the aim was to strengthen the foreign element in a province which was still obstinately Jewish in its temper. The repression of the Yahweh party in Jerusalem, combined with the increase of the heathen settlers in Ephraim, made it possible to unite the two provinces of Palestine with Manasseh as their pasha. And it is not impossible that the Judaean king was so appointed, and that the story of his exile indicates that the central authority had grown suspicious of the way in which he administered his power.

At this period Nineveh had good reason to watch the conduct of all its provincial governors. The conquest of Egypt had strained the empire beyond its power; its resources were not sufficient to hold both Asia and Africa. The Medes rebelled *c.* 650. Their defeat only drove them to seek an understanding with Babylonia which was recovering its power. The Scythians broke into the Euphrates valley from the North, and though they were finally won over to support Assyria, they shook the authority of the empire which needed to make terms with them. These troubles at home weakened the hold of Nineveh on Syria. The great empire was threatening to break up, and a breath of freedom like a spring wind passed over the lands which it had conquered. Judah could not be the last to feel that influence, and with the accession of Josiah the whole attitude of the state changed. The men who supported the young king represented the policy of greater national independence, and with that the religious policy of maintaining the distinctive national faith. Their attitude toward their northern neighbours was that of appealing to the old Israelite stock as over against the foreign settlers. In support of both aims they sought to make Jerusalem the centre of a revived Israel and the only legitimate shrine of the national worship. What aided their effort was the fact that the temple was the only shrine in the country which had never been wrecked by a foreign conqueror: Yahweh had defended His peculiar sanctuary. All sections of the people could unite in such a policy, since it made appeal to patriotism and religion alike. And Nineveh was too deeply involved in its own affairs to interfere.

But larger influences were at work which were to determine the fate of the nation, for the world was in the melting-pot. Babylonia and Media had separately rebelled against their common enemy, and been crushed. In 612 they not only combined their forces but succeeded in winning over the Scythians. Then Nineveh fell, and in 610 Harran the last refuge of the refugees was captured. Pharaoh Necho had advanced from Egypt to support his overlord, but he arrived too late. The Egyptian, recognizing that he must now deal with the conquerors, strengthened his hold on Syria. He summoned Josiah of Judah into his presence and had him executed at Megiddo, setting a nominee of his own on the throne of Jerusalem. But his power was shortlived, for at Carchemish he suffered a ruinous defeat at the hands of the victorious Babylonians. The inevitable result was that Palestine became a Babylonian, instead of an Assyrian, province. Nebuchadrezzar deposed the Pharaoh's nominee and appointed Jehoiakim in his place. As a nominee of Babylonia, the king could not be a zealous supporter of the national faith: he appears disdainfully slitting up the roll of Jeremiah's oracles and dropping the pieces into a brazier. He cannot, however, have been too deeply bound to his master, for Egypt succeeded in seducing him from his allegiance. Before Babylonia could move against him the king died, and the first captivity of Judah took place under his son Jehoiachin. As the small number of captives proves, this meant little more than the removal of the leaders of the Egyptian party in Jerusalem.

Zedekiah, appointed to be king by the Babylonian, had an uneasy task, for there was still a strong body of opinion which hated and feared Eastern influence and turned to Egypt for support. Accordingly, when Pharaoh Hophra came to the throne in 588, he did not find it difficult to draw Judah into an alliance. This time Nebuchadrezzar made clean work with the turbulent province. Marching into Syria, he set up his camp at Riblah. Thence an army advanced against Jerusalem and besieged it. The Pharaoh attempted to relieve his ally and succeeded in raising the siege. But when he was beaten back, the Babylonian general returned, captured and sacked Jerusalem, and burned the temple (587). Zedekiah, led in triumph to Riblah, was blinded in the presence of Nebuchadrezzar and, along with a large contingent of his subjects, was taken captive into Babylonia. Judah was placed under the direct control of a foreign governor with Gedaliah as intermediary between the native population and their ruler. The restless elements in the populace murdered their new head. And the curtain falls on the Jewish state. The last glimpse given of the country is the flight into Egypt of a band of voluntary exiles, terror-stricken lest the Babylonians make them responsible for this deed of criminal folly. Fortunately for the world, the state did not disappear except in its outward form. Not only the men who went into exile, but the peasants left round the ashes of their temple, were Jews, believing in a God whose character was so different from that of all the other gods that He could not become one in a Pantheon, and whose worship involved a spiritual outlook and attitude which made His people as distinct from the nations as He was from their gods.

The Babylonians had destroyed Jerusalem and deported the majority of its inhabitants. Unfortunately the number of those carried away is doubtful. But, since a wasted province could pay no tribute, the general appointed by Nebuchadrezzar to administer the country was careful to allot lands to crofters and peasant settlers. These men drew together round the ruins of their capital and made an effort to reconstitute worship on the site of the temple. But the community was weak and its attempt to renew its life would have produced little, had not Cyrus after his conquest of Babylon in 539/8 given permission to the exiled Jews to return to Palestine. Many took advantage of the permission, and in particular a strong body returned under Nehemiah with the result that in 444 the restoration of the temple was completed and the city walls rebuilt. The new-comers, however, brought much more than an accession of strength to Judah : they brought an ideal and an attitude of mind. The men who at considerable sacrifice returned to Jerusalem, did so, not merely in the interests of their national religion, but in obedience to a certain theory of that religion. To them Jerusalem with its temple and worship was essential to the true practice of their faith. They had come back to the city because only there could they rightly fulfil the demands of their religion. Already in Josiah's time the leaders of the nation had aimed at making Jerusalem the one legitimate centre of the national worship. They were prompted by political as well as religious motives in taking this step. Now the political motive was gone, but it only gave more room to the religious aim.

Hence since the new-comers, certainly in intelligence and probably in numbers, dominated the city, the community which reconstituted itself there was new in every sense of the word. It was not merely grouped round the temple : the worship there was what gave it a *raison d'être*. Since then this religion was distinct from that of all other nations, the people who practised it must separate themselves from the rest of the world. The new community segregated itself, and the lines within which it withdrew itself were religious lines. Again, since the worship of the temple had become essential to the faith, it became also necessary for every Jew to maintain himself in the condition of being capable to take part in this worship. Nationality was now identical with strict observance of religious ritual. The new community submitted itself to a law the chief aim of which was to make and preserve it in a condition of ritual purity. Its leaders were content to leave the conduct of external affairs in the power of their conquerors, if only these refrained from interference with their obedience to all religious law. Jerusalem became the centre of all Jews who thus identified religion and nationality and who remained separate from the world to concentrate their aims on the requirements of their law.

But Jerusalem did not constitute all Jewry. There remained the diaspora with its centre in Babylonia which was soon to spread through all the lands of the East. Some of these men did not return to Palestine, because they had learned through their prophets that it had been the will of Yahweh to destroy Jerusalem, i. e. that the temple was not essential to the faith. They could remain faithful Jews and yet be citizens of the new nations. They continued to pay respect to the mother city ; but their religious life was too real to support itself on what other people did in Jerusalem. It needed and received its own forms of expression. In the synagogues the prayers took the place of the sacrifices, and in their daily lives certain outward observances won new significance and content. Since, however, the ritual worship was no part of their lives and since their new observances were framed to meet the needs of a life among foreigners, it was the ethical rather than the ritual side of their faith which bulked most. There was from the beginning a somewhat wider outlook in the Jewry which lived in the Dispersion.

Thus from the period of the return from exile the life and history of the Jews begin to run in two channels. Yet both sections of the nation have one characteristic in common which concerns itself specially with the subject of this study. Properly speaking they cease to have any national or political history of their own. Alike at Jerusalem and in the Dispersion the Jews were subjects in a larger empire. In recognition of their peculiar customs and of their strong attachment to these, they were allowed certain privileges of self-government. But this was due to the fact that their rulers found it easier to delegate to men of the race the adjustment of the delicate questions where matters of administration conflicted with Jewish convictions. But there is no history of the Jewish nation after the exile; the history of the sections of which the nation was composed becomes part of the history of the several kingdoms in which these formed a constituent element.

Babylon fell and gave place to the kingdom of Cyrus. The Persian power waned before the rising star of the Greeks. Alexander the Great fell like a thunderbolt on the weakened and divided East and for a time gave it a precarious unity. Jewry passed from subjection to one kingdom into the power of its successor, and the author of the Book of Daniel writes about them all as equally mighty and equally insignificant. The people still dwelt on the ancient glories of David when Israel was a nation with control over its own destinies, but these memories began more and more to put on a religious, rather than a national colouring.

Even the Maccabee rising, which gave back for a time political life and a history proper to the Jewish people in Palestine, forms no real exception to this condition of affairs. So long as the Macedonian Empire permitted the Jew to exercise his religion in his own way, he was content to accept its domination in external matters. Its interference with the faith roused the older loyalty. When Antiochus IV succeeded to the Seleucid kingdom, 175, he attempted to discover some means of uniting the heterogeneous elements over which he had to rule.

Seeking this on the basis of a common religion in the worship of the Emperor and of a common culture in the superficial Hellenism which had followed Alexander's victories, he was driven on to prohibit the peculiar Jewish practices and to profane the temple. The nation rose and found in Judas Maccabeus a leader who had some military success. The insurrection would, however, have been shortlived but for the confusion of the Empire. There were competing rivals for the throne and watchful enemies outside. Simon who succeeded Judas was clever enough to use this situation and restore the Jewish kingdom. But the new power was in a hopeless situation. It must keep in touch with the Pharisees, the religious element in the nation which was the nerve of its strength, but which had become more intransigent through its success. Yet it must also enter the world of Eastern politics and make terms of alliance and of compromise with the foreigner. The result was the unsavoury record of the rule of the high priests in Jerusalem. In their external politics these men followed the methods of the world of their day, bribing, intriguing, murdering. In their internal politics they alternately fawned upon and bullied the religious party without whose support they could not hold the people. Jerusalem could not be at once the centre of a religion and the seat of an Oriental kingdom. The attempt to combine the two brought Herod as king, and corrupted and divided the Jewish faith.

A. C. WELCH.

THE METHODS OF HIGHER
CRITICISM

NEAR the beginning of his famous *Prolegomena* Wellhausen offers his readers a piece of spiritual autobiography. He tells us how his early interests and enthusiasms were directed towards the Books of Samuel, Kings, and the Prophets, and how he found in them inspiration. Yet all the while he was haunted by an uneasy feeling that in concentrating on these parts of the Old Testament he was trying to build the roof before laying the foundation, and that he should have begun with a thorough understanding of the Law. Eventually he turned to Exodus, Leviticus, and Numbers, hoping that there he would find the key to all that he had failed to understand and the true basis for all the later history of Israel. His hopes proved false. So far from receiving enlightenment he found himself in yet greater darkness. Instead of order, the traditional arrangement of the books of Scripture brought him only confusion, and the exposition of the whole became more uncertain than ever. Whilst in this state of unrest he casually heard of Graf's hypothesis as to the date of the Law, and even before he had the opportunity of examining the grounds on which Graf's opinion was based, he welcomed it as offering a solution of the worst of his difficulties.

Wellhausen's experience is by no means unique. Not a few earnest and faithful seekers after truth, endeavouring in all humility to trace the hand of God in revelation, have found that to begin with Genesis as it stands in our Bibles and to end the old dispensation with Malachi brings to them the feeling that they are faced by a meaningless chaos. It is true that for generations and centuries men had accepted the recognized arrangement of the material of the Old Testament, and they might well have fallen back on the authority of their predecessors; but there has been something in them which forbade an easy acceptance of a merely hereditary doctrine, and has impelled them to find God—wherever they find Him—for themselves. It has seemed to them that He who is supreme intelligence must have spoken always in intelligible language, and that He who brought the Universe out of chaos cannot, without unthinkable self-contradiction, have given to humanity a revelation of Himself in a literature where all is confusion. Without in any way reflecting on the mental powers or on the honesty of men who have failed to experience this sense of disorder, they have known that for themselves there were only two alternatives. Either this literature is not 'inspired', i. e. is not a divinely ordered message to man, or in the course of transmission the generations of human hands and minds through which it has passed have wrought such complication that in the long run the fullness of the message can be appreciated only when the tangle is unravelled and the thread may be traced along a course which is now seen to be continuous and straight.

Others have been confronted with problems not less pressing but on a smaller scale. Their search of the Scriptures has brought them face to face with contradictions in detail. At the very outset they have met with two narratives of creation which, as it seemed to them, could be harmonized only by a quibble. Again, they have in no way condemned older and better men, who have yet found it possible to accept the traditional statements; but for themselves to admit such explanations as were offered would have been a surrender of that truthfulness without which, they felt assured, God could not be embraced. Confronted with evolutionary theory they might conceivably have reconciled Gen. i with Darwin, but they could not reconcile Gen. i with Gen. ii. Other contradictions appeared. What was to be made of the repeated prophetic condemnation of sacrifice, and even of the prophetic insistence that it was not of divine ordinance, in the face of the large sections of the Law devoted to the institution? And within the Law itself how were the varying instructions as to the material and form of the Altar to be unified? At times a single narrative offered contradictions which seemed past explanation. In the story of the Flood, for instance, how many specimens of each ' clean ' animal were included by Noah—two or seven? And when Joseph was carried down to Egypt, who took him there, Midianites or Ishmaelites? There are minds which demand an answer to questions of this kind, and must have an answer if they are to continue to believe in the divine inspiration of Scripture. For they might understand that God had spoken to different ages in different terms ; that is not merely intelligible but necessary if there is to be any real validity in revelation. But that contradictions, even in details, should appear within the limits of a single chapter, and in the record of a single event is hard to reconcile with the conception of a truthful and truth-loving God.

Some years ago a group of Sunday-school teachers had met for their regular weekly discussion of the lesson for the following Sunday. Their subject was the familiar story of Gen. xxxvii, and as they studied the chapter in order to absorb it for themselves before giving it to their classes, they became conscious of the contradiction, just mentioned, between the Midianites and the Ishmaelites. It may be noted in passing that it is not wholly confined to this chapter, because whilst xxxvii. 36 speaks of the Midianites selling Joseph into Egypt, xxxix. 1 states that he was sold by Ishmaelites. Other difficulties appeared, such as the parts played by Reuben and Judah respectively, and the case seemed hopeless until the leader of the group suggested that possibly two stories were inter-twined here. At once a line of solution was offered, and in half an hour, with nothing but the English Authorized Version before them they had disentangled two narratives, each of which was in itself practically complete, and the success of the experiment seemed to justify it in their eyes.

These young people, teachers in the ' Intermediate ' section of a ' graded ' Sunday school, would probably have been much surprised if they had been told that they were doing ' higher criticism '. Yet that is exactly what they were doing. For, as distinct from ' lower ' or ' textual ' criticism, whose aim is to discover the actual words of a book at the time when it reached its present main form, higher criticism is the study of the structure, date, and authorship of any particular book or collection of books.[1] It should be carefully noted that in itself it has nothing whatever to say about the historicity or otherwise of any narrative that may be involved, still less does it attempt to pronounce on the inspiration of the subject with which it deals. These are questions for *historical criticism* and *theology* respectively. ' Higher criticism ' is simply concerned with the material as it lies before the student. If the facts seem to point to a compilation of several documents, the attempt is made to isolate them. If the work under discussion presents the appearance of being a gradual growth, the original nucleus will be sought, and, as far as possible, later accretions assigned to their proper strata. There are thus two quite distinct elements in the work, (*a*) the study of the structure, (*b*) the dating, absolute or comparative, of the whole or of the various

[1] It should, perhaps, be remarked that *any* serious study of questions of structure, date, and authorship is ' higher criticism ', and that, strictly speaking, the man who believes the Pentateuch to be a single work written by Moses is (if his belief is the result of sincere study) just as much a ' higher critic' as Wellhausen. But for the purposes of this paper the term is restricted to its popular but erroneous connotation.

portions. There may also be cases in which reasons for a definite individual authorship may be found.

By way of illustration we may follow the methods of disentanglement adopted by the Sunday-school teachers already mentioned. In Gen. xxxvii there is one clear contradiction—the Midianite-Ishmaelite question. If this contradiction is to be explained on the hypothesis of a composite narrative, then it is probable that Reuben will be the saviour of Joseph in one story and Judah in the other. Again, in the first part of the chapter two causes of Joseph's unpopularity are mentioned. One is his father's favouritism, as shown in the special coat, the other is to be found in his dreams. If, then, there are two narratives here, it is probable that they contained different reasons for the hatred of the brothers. One of these narratives we may for the time being call the ' Ishmael ' narrative, the other the ' Midian ' narrative.

We notice at once that vv. 26, 27 associate Judah with the ' Ishmael ' narrative. His plan for saving his brother is the result of chance ; the caravan passes by (v. 25) as the brothers are eating, and the idea strikes him that he may get rid of the obnoxious Joseph without incurring blood-guiltiness. So he suggests selling the lad to these traders of the desert. But as v. 28 stands, it appears that the Midianites drew Joseph out of the pit and sold him to the Ishmaelites, a statement which is directly contradicted in v. 36, where the Midianites are said to have sold Joseph, not to the Ishmaelites in Palestine but to Potiphar in Egypt. It would appear, then, on our hypothesis, that part of v. 28 belongs to the ' Midian ' narrative and part to the ' Ishmael ' story. But where does the break come ? It seems clear that the first sentence ' And there passed by Midianites, merchantmen ' belongs to one, and the last sentence ' and sold Joseph to the Ishmaelites, &c.', to the other. But to which of the two must we assign the middle clause ' and they drew and lifted up Joseph out of the pit ' ?

A clue may be found in v. 22, where Reuben tries to save his
brother by catching up a suggestion made by the others, and
accepting the plan that he should be placed in a pit, unharmed.
His purpose, then, was to return after a while without the knowledge of the rest and bring the boy back to his father. As we
have seen, we shall naturally associate Judah with the Ishmaelites
and therefore Reuben with the Midianites. So the stratagem
involving the pit and other parts of the narrative connected
with the same theme will be classed with the 'Midianite'
section. This gives us for that element in the story vv. 19–22,
28 (down to 'pit'), 29, 30, and 36. The subject to 'sold' in
v. 28 will then be 'his brethren' (v. 27), thus agreeing with
Judah's proposal in v. 27. The rest of the verses which we
have considered will belong to the 'Ishmaelite' story.

We have still to apportion those parts of the story which
deal with the hatred of the brothers and its cause. Two
are mentioned, one is his father's favouritism, exemplified by
the 'coat of many colours' (really a coat with long sleeves
which implied that Joseph was to be a 'gentleman' and do no
work), the other is the lad's habit of dreaming—and in this
matter Jacob is to all intents and purposes on the side of his
elder sons, though he does more thinking than they do. Now
vv. 19, 20, which we have already grouped with the 'Midian'
narrative, mention the dreams, and we are therefore led to
assign this cause of hatred to the same class, while references
to favouritism—possibly including the spying and tale-telling—
will naturally belong to the 'Ishmael' story. This gives us,
then, vv. 2–4 (except for the words in v. 2, 'now these are the
generations of Jacob', a kind of chapter title which appears
many times in Genesis, and indicates the original sections into
which the completed book was divided), v. 23, and vv. 31–5,
while to 'Midian' will belong vv. 5–11.

There remains now only the story of how the brothers found
their opportunity, given in vv. 12–18. There are at first sight

no signs here of a double narrative. But if any one were spinning together two threads of narrative, in the fashion which seems to be suggested by the whole of this chapter, he might quite well leave out a part of one of them if it contained nothing that was not already in the other. If, then, the two groups of stories told of the way in which Joseph came to his brothers in substantially the same terms, it is easy to understand that in this portion only one of them would be preserved. The question is, which of the two has been retained at the expense of the other? The only apparent indication is a very slight one, but it may be used in default of a better. This is the fact that in the chapter two names are used for the old father, who is called Israel in vv. 3 and 13 and Jacob in v. 34. We have already included v. 3 in the ' Ishmael ' group, and this suggests that vv. 13 ff. should also be assigned to the same class.

So far we have made only a rough analysis, and have been using the text of the English Revised Version. It will be well for us to go over the ground again with a view to correcting mistakes, and this time we will refer to the Hebrew text. We may find that our narratives are even more complete and self-consistent than we had at first been led to believe. For convenience, instead of using the full names ' Midian ' and ' Ishmael ' we will simply employ the initials M and I. As we have already noted, the narrative proper begins with the word ' Joseph ' at its first occurrence in v. 2. We may also take note of another point, cases where there are small ' doublets ', i. e. the repetition of an idea or statement in different words. Such repetition is characteristic of Hebrew poetry, and is, indeed, its primary feature, but we are here dealing not with poetry but with prose, where, though not impossible, it is far less natural.

The first point that strikes us is the phrase ' and they hated him yet the more ' at the end of v. 5. This we have seen reasons for assigning to M, and it implies that there was in this story some previous mention of hatred. Now the last two sentences of v. 4 ' and they hated him ' and ' and they ' (Hebrew rarely expresses the pronoun of the third person, and in translation it may always be inserted if there is no noun to form the subject) ' could not speak peaceably unto him ' repeat the same thought. One of these clauses may be from M, the other from I. In view of the fact that the word ' hate ' occurs at the end of v. 5, the former clause may be assigned to M and the latter to I. In that case M must have given a reason for the first hatred, and that may best be supplied from v. 2. So it is possible that we were wrong in assigning v. 2 to I, and that it ought rather to belong to M. But here another point arises. The Egyptian Jews who translated Genesis into Greek early in the second century B.C. (the translation known as the ' Septuagint ', and indicated by the sign ' LXX ') were using a Bible in which the words ' and they hated him yet the more ' did not appear. It is, then, possible that these words were originally a marginal note made in a Palestinian copy, and accidentally incorporated in the text. Our Hebrew Bibles, it should be remembered, represent this Palestinian tradition or ' Massoretic Text ', commonly indicated by the sign ' MT '. Of course it does not follow that in every case or even the majority of cases the LXX is right where it differs from the MT, but in this instance such a conclusion appears probable, and we shall still be able to assign v. 2 to I.

Vv. 5–11 awaken no further doubts, for there is nothing in them which at all suggests I. The next section of the narrative, vv. 12–18 we assigned *en bloc* to I, at the same time noting that if we were right, then M contained no account of the way in which Joseph fell into the hands of his brothers. But as we read over the passage closely, we are struck by a certain oddity in v. 14. Such a phrase as ' And he said unto him, Here am I. And he said unto him . . .' is quite common in

Biblical Hebrew. But elsewhere it usually if not always comes at the very beginning of a conversation, and not after the first words. The ordinary formula is 'And A called B; and he said unto him, Here am I. And A said unto him. . . .' May it not be that we have here the missing sentence from M, from which the phrase 'And he called him' (only a single word in Hebrew) has been omitted because it did not fit in with the rest of the composite narrative? Of course the last sentence of v. 14, 'So he sent him out of the vale of Hebron, and he came to Shechem', will be part of the longer narrative of I, and fits admirably on to the end of v. 13, the whole running 'And Israel said unto Joseph, Do not thy brethren feed the flock in Shechem? come, and I will send thee unto them. So he sent him out of the vale of Hebron, and he came to Shechem'.

An apparent doublet occurs in vv. 21 and 22, where Reuben twice exhorts his brothers not to kill the boy. But in both it is Reuben who speaks, and unless we are prepared to change the name to Judah in v. 21 (and a confusion of this kind is far from being impossible in view of the fact that Judah is not mentioned in the narrative until v. 26) we must reserve both verses intact for M. The closest examination of vv. 22–31 reveals no occasion for discussion beyond what we have already seen, but in v. 32 we are again faced with an awkwardness of expression which may find its best explanation in further analysis. This is involved in the double phrase 'and they sent the coat of many colours, and they brought it to their father'. How could they both send it and bring it? A reference to the Hebrew text shows that there was no object to 'brought'. The English translators were probably justified in putting the 'it' in to make clear the sense as they understood it, but they should have indicated the fact by the use of italics. Now the Hebrew word for 'and they brought' is *wayyābî'û*, whilst *wayyābô'û* would mean 'and they came'. Until long after the beginning of the Christian era no vowels were written in

Hebrew at all, and it is quite possible that the text here intended the word ' came ', which was misread as ' brought '. Our first glance over the passage gave us nothing of the end of the story as far as Jacob was concerned in M, for vv. 31–3 deal with the coat, and therefore belong to I. Is it not likely that in this word we have a bit of the termination of the narrative of M? The impression is strengthened by reading vv. 33 and 34 again. If we look back to v. 20, which we thought to belong to M, we find that the brothers planned to report to their father ' an evil beast hath devoured him '. These words we actually find in the middle of v. 33, though they are there put into the mouth of Jacob. It is at least possible that this phrase follows on the words we have just discussed in v. 32 ' and they came to their father and said, An evil beast hath devoured him '. (The words ' and said ' would occur in both narratives at this point, and therefore would not be repeated.) Further, in v. 34 the old father is called not Israel, as elsewhere in I, but Jacob, and this suggests that the verse belongs not to I but to M. The idea is supported by the fact that the mourning of Jacob is repeated in v. 35. This gives us the complete story in both narratives.

Our analysis, then, yields the following result : To M belong vv. 2, 5–11, 14 (down to ' bring me word again '), 19–22, 24, 28 (down to ' pit '), 29, 30, 32 (the words ' and they came to their father, and said '), 33 (the words ' an evil beast hath devoured him), 34, 36. What is left will be I. The actual texts will run, placing in brackets the two words which are required to complete the sense of M :

I. ³ Now Israel loved Joseph more than all his children, because he was the son of his old age : and he made him a coat of many colours. ⁴ And his brethren saw that their father loved him more than all his brethren ; and could not speak peaceably unto him. ¹² And his brethren went to feed their father's flock in Shechem. ¹³ And Israel said unto Joseph, Do not thy brethren feed the flock in Shechem ? come and

I will send thee unto them. **14** So he sent him out of the vale of Hebron and he came to Shechem. **15** And a certain man found him, and, behold, he was wandering in the field : and the man asked him, saying, What seekest thou ? **16** And he said, I seek my brethren : tell me, I pray thee, where they are feeding *the flock*. **17** And the man said, They are departed hence : for I heard them say, Let us go to Dothan. And Joseph went after his brethren and found them in Dothan. **23** And it came to pass, when Joseph was come unto his brethren, that they stript Joseph of his coat, the coat of many colours that was on him. **25** And they sat down to eat bread : and they lifted up their eyes and looked, and, behold, a travelling company of Ishmaelites came from Gilead, with their camels bearing spicery and balm and myrrh, going to carry it down to Egypt. **26** And Judah said unto his brethren, What profit is it if we slay our brother and conceal his blood ? **27** Come, and let us sell him to the Ishmaelites, and let not our hand be upon him ; for he is our brother, our flesh. And his brethren hearkened unto him, **28** and sold Joseph to the Ishmaelites for twenty pieces of silver. And they brought Joseph into Egypt. **31** And they took Joseph's coat, and killed a he-goat, and dipped the coat in the blood ; **32** and they sent the coat of many colours to their father ; and said, This have we found : know now whether it be thy son's coat or not. **33** And he knew it and said, It is my son's coat ; Joseph is without doubt torn in pieces. **35** And all his sons and all his daughters rose up to comfort him ; but he refused to be comforted ; and he said, For I will go down to the grave to my son mourning. And his father wept for him.

M runs as follows :

2 Joseph, being seventeen years old, was feeding the flock with his brethren and he was a lad with the sons of Bilhah, and with the sons of Zilpah, his father's wives : and Joseph brought the evil report of them unto their father, **4** and they hated him. **5** And Joseph dreamed a dream, and he told it to his brethren : and they hated him yet the more. **6** And he said unto them, Hear, I pray you, this dream which I have dreamed : **7** for, behold, we were binding sheaves in the field, and, lo, my sheaf arose, and also stood upright ; and, behold, your sheaves came round about, and made obeisance to my sheaf. **8** And his brethren said to him, Shalt thou indeed reign over us? or shalt thou indeed have dominion over us? And they hated him yet the more for his dreams, and for his words. [9] And he dreamed yet another dream, and told it to his brethren, and said, Behold, I have dreamed yet a dream ; and, behold, the sun and the moon and eleven stars made obeisance to me. [10] And he told it to his father, and to his brethren ; and his father rebuked him, and said unto him, What is this dream that thou hast dreamed? Shall I and thy mother and thy brethren indeed come to bow down ourselves to thee to the earth? [11] And his brethren envied him ; but his father kept the saying in mind. [14] (And he called him), and he said to him, Here am I. And he said to him, Go now, see whether it be well with thy brethren, and well with the flock ; and bring me word again. [18] And they saw him afar off, and before he came near unto them, they conspired against him to slay him. [19] And they said one to another, Behold, this dreamer cometh. [20] Come now therefore, and let us slay him, and cast him into one of the pits, and we will say, An evil beast hath devoured him : and we shall see what will become of his dreams. [21] And Reuben heard it, and delivered him out of their hand ; and said, Let us not take his life. [22] And Reuben said unto them, Shed no blood ; cast him into this pit that is in the wilderness, but lay no hand upon him : that he might deliver him out of their hand, to restore him to his father. [24] And they took him, and cast him into the pit : and the pit was empty, there was no water in it. [28] And there passed by Midianites, merchantmen ; and they drew and lifted up Joseph out of the pit. [29] And Reuben returned unto the pit ; and, behold, Joseph was not in the pit ; and he rent his clothes. And he returned unto his brethren, and said, The child is not ; and I, whither shall I go? [32] And they came (to their father and said), [33] An evil beast hath devoured him. [34] And Jacob rent his garments, and put sackcloth upon his loins, and mourned for his son many days. [36] And the Midianites sold him into Egypt unto Potiphar, an officer of Pharaoh's, the captain of the guard.

A comparison between these two narratives suggests two or three characteristic differences. (1) M lays a good deal of stress on dreams, their importance and their interpretation; (2) M uses the name Jacob, I the name Israel; (3) in M it is one of the northern tribes, Reuben, or rather a tribe that was associated with the northern kingdom, whose ancestor is represented as saving Joseph, in I it is Judah. This suggests that in all probability the M form of the story was that which would be more likely to circulate in northern Israel, and I in the south. These points may prove useful in studying other passages. There are many sections in Genesis where no inherent contradictions are to be noticed, which yet naturally ally themselves with one or other of these two. Thus in Gen. xii and xx we have narratives describing how Abraham lied about Sarah, saying that she was his sister, in order to save his life. There is nothing contradictory in these two narratives, and nothing to show that they are intended to refer to the same event, for the scene of the one is laid in Egypt and that of the other in Philistia. Yet there is no mention of God's method of revelation to Pharaoh, beyond the plagues, whilst the facts are brought home to Abimelech in a dream. This suggests that the latter belongs to the same group of narratives as the M element in Gen. xxxvii, i. e. to northern Israel rather than to the south. From these and other passages, simple and composite, a number of fairly safe criteria can be deduced, which enable us to distinguish between those elements in Genesis, and indeed in Exodus, Numbers, and Joshua also, which seem to have been current in the north and those which more naturally belong to the south. The most striking of these is the difference in the use of the divine names, the northern cycle preferring the general term ' God ', whilst in the southern narratives the proper name of the God of Israel ' Yahweh' (disguised in our version under the word ' LORD '— printed in small capitals), is preferred. Though this distinction is not absolute, and there are cases where variation in the LXX throws doubt on the originality of one or the other, it is the difference which has attracted most attention. In fact passages and elements belonging to the northern cycle are generally indicated by the symbol E standing either for ' Ephraim ' or for ' Elohim ', the Hebrew general term for God, whilst the southern narratives are grouped under the letter J, the initial either of ' Judah ' or of ' Jahweh ', an alternative spelling of Yahweh.

Similarly in the Flood story two narratives may be isolated, one putting *two* clean animals into the Ark and the other *seven*, separable by the same kind of process.[1] But here we have differences which not only indicate idiosyncracies that may be merely local or personal, but which point to entirely different stages in intellectual and spiritual growth. The contrast in style and vocabulary is very marked, the most obvious point being, perhaps, the fondness of the ' two ' element for exact dates and figures, but that is only one of the significant features. The ' seven ' narrative is throughout simply, homely, and comparatively primitive. Its view of God is eminently child-like. He is affected by emotions and impulses which resemble those of mankind. He ' repents ' (vi. 6) that He has made man—it was a mistake, and needs correction. He likes the smell of the sacrifice (viii. 21), and is so pleased with it that He decides never again to think of destroying beings who can give Him so much pleasure. In the note which tells of His shutting Noah in the ark (vii. 16) there is a suggestion of physical action, as though Yahweh had a material frame, not unlike that of man. The cosmology, too, is that of an unscientific and unreflecting age. The Flood is wrought by natural means, an unusual and prolonged rainfall, which does not affect the actual structure of the material universe. Indeed, there is no evidence of speculation on the form of the world ; the normal facts are accepted without further explanation or inquiry.

[1] Analysis gives to the ' seven ' narrative 6^{5-8}, 7^{1-5}, $7^{10, 12, 16b-18}$, $8^{6-12, 20-2}$, to the ' two ' narrative 6^{9-22}, $7^{6-9, 11, 13-16a, 19-22, 24}$, $8^{1-5, 13-19}$, 9^{1-17}.

In the ' two' narrative all this is altered. It is essentially the work of a ' sophisticated' age. God, though still severely personal, is pure moral reason, controlling the universe on principle, in accord with the essential characteristics of His own being. There is no hint of man-like passion, and it seems as if the suggestion of fallibility is deliberately avoided. Human iniquity does not mean a ' mistake' on His part, it is a contingency which has been foreseen and will be met by measures which are well within the normal range of divine principles of action. There is, too, a developed cosmology. The world is set in the midst of a waste of waters—the great deep (vii. 11, viii. 2)—and is apparently a hollow hemisphere. In the upper portion, the vault of the sky, there are windows, and all terrestrial waters are the overflow of the ' deep' from below. The Flood is produced by abnormal action in both directions, but the explanation is, for its age, a scientific one.

There are one or two other narratives in Genesis which resemble this last section in style and outlook, notably the description of creation in ch. i and the institution of circumcision in ch. xvii. But there are considerable sections of the Law, especially of the ecclesiastical Law, in Exodus, Leviticus, and Numbers, together with portions of Joshua, which seem to be allied to them, and to spring from the same circle of thought. On this account the whole has been called ' Priestly', and is commonly indicated by the letter P. Close affinities with the ' seven' narrative of the Flood are also frequent in Genesis, Exodus, Numbers, and Joshua. Gen. ii is an admirable illustration, and a comparison of the two accounts of creation reveals exactly the same kind of contrast as appears in the two disentangled narratives of the Flood. To this same cycle of stories belongs also the ' Ishmael' element in Gen. xxxvii.

It is commonly, though not universally, held amongst critics, that each of these three elements, to which we may now give their familiar initials, J, E, P, originally formed a complete and separate book. It seems that the same elements appear also in the Book of Joshua, and some scholars believe that one or other of them is carried as far as the end of 2 Sam. Attempts are sometimes made at further analysis, and it is, indeed, only reasonable to suppose that these three books themselves were the result of a comparatively slow growth. But the task is much more difficult and the results command a far less general agreement than is the case with the primary analysis, on which, indeed, practical unanimity has been reached. It remains to add that Deuteronomy stands apart from the three elements already noted, and has to be recognized as a fourth element in the construction of the first six books of the Bible. In addition to the actual Book of Deuteronomy, there are frequent passages from Exodus to Judges, and even later, which exhibit the same style and outlook. Their presence is generally attributed to editorial activity on the part of a Deuteronomic 'school', a class of literary men, working for successive generations, whose interests and enthusiasms—and indeed style—find their source in Deuteronomy.

Enough has been said to illustrate the methods of literary analysis employed by the critic, whether in dealing with a whole book or with a single passage. One other word may be added. In the first instance the impulse to analytic criticism is always given by an observed contrast or even contradiction. In Gen. i man is created after the animals; in Gen. ii before them. In the P narrative the Flood lasts thirteen and a half months; in the J narrative Noah is in the Ark at most for sixty-eight days. The critic did not make these contradictions—he has merely offered an explanation which satisfies him and enables him to retain his belief in the Old Testament as part of a God-given and inspired literature. No one else is bound to accept his conclusions or his explanations, but at the same time it may well be that others who have not the technical skill which is necessary for the complete analysis may have met with similar difficulties and may be satisfied by the results of the scholar's work.

The analysis, however, is only one side of the work of the critic. He has not merely to differentiate between and to disentangle the various elements, he has to rearrange the material in what he believes to have been its original order. Only so can he study the process and progress of revelation. As far as possible he must date his documents. Here there are two quite distinct elements in his work. The first is the more important, and at the same time the simpler; it is the *relative* dating of the various elements in the literature. In the case of the Hexateuch—a term which includes all the books from Genesis to Joshua—he has four main documents or rather literary groups to consider, those indicated by the letters J, E, D (Deuteronomy), and P.

A comparison between the Books of Kings and Chronicles— the latter being admittedly much later than the former, so late, indeed, that 1 and 2 Chronicles are the last two books in the Hebrew Bible—shows that whilst the tone of the former has certain resemblances to that of Deuteronomy (for instance in the judgements passed on the various kings), the main interest of the latter is in the Temple, its worship, and ritual. In other words, Chronicles has a distinctly priestly tone. This in itself suggests that the priestly interest is a comparatively late growth in Israel's sacred literature. At the same time it is possible to compare sections in all four, or in at any rate three of the four main elements, which deal with similar subjects. There are, for instance, groups of laws or legal codes in E, D, and P. When these are set side by side with one another, it becomes clear that the order just used is the correct one, for there are signs of a regular and steady development. In E (and in J) for example, sacrifice may be and is offered by laymen. In D there are no regulations as to the people who may offer sacrifice, but the functions of the priesthood are confined to the tribe of Levi. In P they have been still further narrowed down, and are now in the hands of a single family of that tribe, the family of Aaron. In other ways the same order of progress is to be observed. As we have already noticed, in E, and still more in J, the conception of God is elementary. Gen. ii, for example, is an expression of the great truth that God made the universe, adapted for a people who are still in an intellectual and spiritual nursery. Gen. i, on the other hand, with its stately and formal language, its more highly spiritualized theology and its scientific outlook, is clearly better suited to a people who have grown in both directions. No doubt it is based on very much earlier material, but that has been used and perhaps modified to meet the needs of a much more adult mind than the narratives of either J or E. And, for such reasons as have already been suggested, it seems that D is intermediate between the two. Further evidence on this point is supplied by Ezekiel, who seems to have some acquaintance with D, but not with P. His ritual laws, for instance, are an advance on anything we can find in Deuteronomy, but are far from being as elaborate as those of the Priestly Code. An example may be seen in the fact that he has no suggestion of a ritual Day of Atonement for the people as a whole, though he has two days of atonement in the year for the sanctuary. On the question of the priority of J or E the problem is far from being simple, but there are indications (which may, however, be local rather than temporal) of a slightly more developed tone in E than in J. The usual, though by no means universally accepted order, then, is J, E, D, P.

Let us now turn to the absolute dating. For this we are helpless unless we can relate one or other of the documents to events attested outside the Hexateuch. Two such have been commonly noted. One of these is the great reformation which took place under Josiah, the other is the famous reading of the Law by Ezra. If we could be certain what books were involved in these two historical events, then we should have a date by which at any rate the nucleus of the documents in question can be reached, in other words a *terminus ad quem*.

If the narrative in 2 Kings xxii–xxiii is to be trusted, there can be little doubt but that Josiah's law-book was Deuteronomy or a nucleus of it.[1] For the most striking feature of the reform was the abolition of the local sanctuaries and the concentration of sacrifice in the Jerusalem Temple. Of this there is no trace in J or E, and indeed the latter (e. g. Exod. xx. 23) seems to contemplate a large number of altars. On the other hand special stress is laid on the centralization of sacrifice in Deut. xii, and other regulations are made in that book which suggest modifications of general practice to suit the new rule. Such are the permission to eat the flesh of domestic animals at secular meals, the appointment of Cities of Refuge to take the place of the local altars as sanctuary, and the permission given to the Levites to migrate to Jerusalem and share with the priests there the emoluments of their office. 2 Kings xxiii. 9 definitely states that this was not done, and the very reference seems to imply that it was a regulation in the newly discovered law which was not carried out. One or two recent attempts to throw the date of Deuteronomy forward

[1] This paper was already in type when Prof. A. C. Welch's *Code of Deuteronomy* appeared. After a very careful study Dr. Welch comes to the conclusion that it dates from the early monarchy or even from the period of Judges. It is too soon yet to pronounce an opinion on the new theory, but the reader should be warned that as a result of Dr. Welch's work the next generation may considerably modify its view of the absolute dating of Deuteronomy and possibly of other documents. On the other hand there is a growing tendency to bring Deuteronomy down to a later date, indeed into the post-exilic period. As has been already noted, such a conclusion will involve a denial of the historicity of the narrative in 2 Kings xxii, xxiii at any rate in large part.

into post-exilic times have been shown to involve a denial of the historicity of this narrative in 2 Kings.

Of course Deuteronomy itself may have been written much earlier than 621, the date of this reform. But it is a striking fact that its main provisions do not seem to have been known at any time before this after the Conquest of Palestine. Hezekiah had initiated a reform along similar lines, but no law-book is quoted, and the suggestion of the facts is that Deuteronomy was an attempt to embody the ideals which had expressed themselves in Hezekiah's action. The tone of the book strongly reflects the moral teaching of the great prophets of the eighth century, and there are thus reasons which lead to the conclusion that the book itself (or at least a nucleus of it) was composed during the first half of the seventh century B.C.

The next occasion on which we have a record of a religious reform based on a law-book is in the case of Ezra. The story is told in Neh. viii. 1–12. In view of the fact that the reading occupied only half a day (v. 3) it is unlikely that it was the whole of our present Pentateuch. If it were a portion only, then we have to consider what part was read on this occasion. Now Ezra is throughout intensely interested in ritual, ceremonial purity, and ecclesiastical order. For the first time in the historical books (except Chronicles, which seems to be the first part of the same work as Ezra and Nehemiah) a distinction is made between priests and Levites (compare, e.g. Neh. viii. 13). This we found to be absent even from Deuteronomy, where all Levites are priests. On the other hand it is a distinction which runs throughout P, except in the case of a section of Leviticus (chs. xvii–xxvi) which seems to be earlier than the rest of the book, and may even have been used by Ezekiel. But P in the main finds its practical expression in the reforms of Ezra and Nehemiah, just as Deuteronomy appears to have been the inspiration for the reforms of Josiah. It is true that recently an opinion, to which allusion has already been made, has been springing up, to the effect that the Law on which Ezra's work was based was not P but Deuteronomy. This, however, will involve the rejection of a good deal of the detail of the Ezra narrative. The strongest argument in its favour is due to the discovery of a number of documents belonging to a Jewish community which lived near Assouan on the Nile in the fifth century B. C. They had a temple of their own, and this was destroyed by the Egyptians. In the year 404 B. C. they petitioned a number of people, amongst them the high priest at Jerusalem, for help in rebuilding it. This, it is argued, would hardly have been possible if the Deuteronomic law of the central sanctuary had been known. On the whole it seems safer to suspend judgement on these points until the new suggestions have been more fully discussed than they have been up to the present.

In the case of J and E the difficulties are even greater, because there is no historical event to which they can be related. The nearest thing we have to a clue is in the fact that some of the eighth-century prophets, e. g. Hosea and Amos, seem to be aware of the facts recorded in those collections of narratives. This suggests, though it does not definitely prove, that these collections were already in existence in their time. The character and tone of the narratives, however, tends to make us adopt as early a date as we can, and there are scholars who would throw J as far back as the time of Solomon, making E fifty to a hundred years later.

A word should be added about the process of compilation which we have to assume on the basis of what we have already seen. The closeness with which J and E are interwoven strongly suggests that they once formed a single book, i. e. that they were combined before other sections of the Hexateuch were written. The process of combination is commonly called ' redaction ', and the person or school who did the work a ' redactor ' (R). It would be almost inevitable that such a combination would involve the addition as well as the omission of occasional words, and even, perhaps, of whole sentences. Hence in critical works it is not uncommon to find a phrase or a verse attributed to a ' redactor '. There cannot be the same degree of probability attaching to this element in the analysis as that which, for instance, marks the separation of J and P. But the idea of a redactor is natural and, indeed, inevitable, and it is only to be expected that there should be some traces of his work. A second step in the combination seems to have been the union of the composite JE with Deuteronomy, and the final stage the inclusion of P in the whole. The symbols J, E, D, P, R^{JF}, R^{JED}, R^{JEDP} look alarming and perhaps fantastic at first sight, but they represent stages in a process of growth which are in themselves eminently reasonable and indeed probable in their main outline.

Problems of a rather different kind are presented by such a narrative as the story of Saul's election to the throne in 1 Sam. viii–xi. In ch. viii it is said that as the weaknesses of old age came upon him, Samuel made his sons judges, and that their misconduct led the elders of Israel to resort to Samuel and demand a king. This is resented as being not merely a slight on Samuel, but a rejection of the theocratic principle, according to which Yahweh Himself was King, acting through chosen persons. Samuel, under divine instructions, prepares to let the people have their way, but warns them of the character of the monarchy. In ch. ix for the first time the figure of Saul is introduced. He is the son of a Benjamite farmer, who has lost his drove of she-asses, and sends Saul and a servant to look for them. Their search is unsuccessful, till near an unnamed city in ' the land of Zuph ' the servant remembers that a ' seer ' of local fame may be consulted on such subjects. They find the man of God, whose name is Samuel, about to take part in a sacrificial meal, to which he invites them. They spend the night with him, and in the morning he sets them on their way, but before parting from them anoints Saul king, in accordance with Yahweh's command given two days earlier. He confirms his action by foretelling ' signs ', all of which are fulfilled. The last of these is important, for it brings Saul into contact with a company of ' prophets ' or ecstatic devotees, near his own home at Gibea. He is infected by their ecstasy, and, as a matter of fact, remains all his life subject to its access, though in later years this becomes his bane. This narrative carries us down to x. 16.

In the following verses Samuel summons all Israel to Mizpah, and Saul is elected king by lot. There are, however, people who refuse to accept his authority (x. 17–27).

Ch. xi opens with a story of the danger threatening Jabesh-Gilead from the Ammonite king Nahash. The news of their plight reaches Saul as he comes in from ploughing, an access of prophetic ecstasy falls upon him, and in its strength he gathers the forces of Israel and defeats Nahash. This confirms his sovereignty, and in the moment of victory he refuses to punish those who have previously slighted him. Samuel then gathers all the people to Gilgal and the election is finally ratified.

As this story stands there are no obvious discrepancies in the actual events. But there are none the less differences which for many students make it impossible to regard it as an original and continuous narrative. There are two totally different presentations of Samuel. In ch. viii he is the theocratic judge, the true successor of Deborah, Gideon, and Jephthah. In ix. 1–x. 16 he is a seer with a local reputation, of whom Saul has not previously heard, and whose name is possibly not known even to the servant who tells his master about him. In this same passage the monarchy is of divine ordinance, Yahweh's device for saving Israel from the Philistines (ix. 16). In ch. viii the Philistines have already been defeated and put out of action, and the demand for a king is an act of apostasy. In the one case Samuel seems to welcome the suggestion of a monarchy and heartily co-operates ; in the other he regards it as a personal affront. There are, further, differences of style so great as to make the reader who goes through the Hebrew text—if he be sufficiently at home in Hebrew to appreciate points of style—feel that he is moving in two different periods of human thought. There is no inter-weaving of the narratives, as in the case of Gen. xxxvii ; they are placed side by side in large sections, and this makes the contrast in style and presentation the more obvious. The two narratives are (*a*) viii. 1–22, x. 17–27 ; (*b*) ix. 1–x. 16, xi. 1–11 ; while the last verses of ch. xi may have been added when the two narratives were combined. If (*a*) and (*b*) be read separately, it will be seen that each gives a continuous narrative, self-consistent alike from the point of view of style and of historical presentation. It can hardly be doubted that we have here two different literary strata, dovetailed rather than interwoven.

So far our study has been one of *higher criticism*, which deals with the purely literary questions of structure, date, and authorship. But this last narrative introduces a very different study, too often confused with higher criticism, but in reality entirely distinct from it, that of *historical criticism*. This is the attempt to reconstruct the history from the conflicting materials at our disposal. Here a double process is involved. The first step is the determination of the comparative value of our sources as historical documents, and the second the determination of the actual course of events.

In the first case it goes without saying that normally of two narratives which purport to deal with the same events, the earlier will be the more reliable. A second criterion may be found in the presence or absence of a ' tendency ', theological or otherwise, which may colour the whole history. This most often appears in judgements passed on men and their actions.

Thus in 2 Kings xiv. 25–7 Jeroboam II is presented as a heaven-sent deliverer for Israel; in v. 24 he is condemned for his failure to fulfil the demands of the Deuteronomic law of the single sanctuary. But sometimes such a tendency appears to affect the general picture of the past or even the actual record. In the instance immediately before us the (*b*) passages have all the marks of being practically a contemporary record, whilst the (*a*) passages involve a theory of Israelite polity and of the position of Samuel which suggests the attitude of the eighth-century reformers or even of a later period. The result is that for the definite narrative we rely on the former, while we regard the latter as being a presentation of the facts which is intended to illustrate and enforce a special view of the dealings of God with His people. However correct this may be when the whole story of the divine guidance of Israel is considered, it is on the other that we shall rely for a sympathetic reconstruction of the history of antiquity. It is this which shows us how men felt, how they acted, what were their motives, and what their faith. The purpose of all genuine Old Testament study is to discover the process by which God led Israel to higher truth. For this end both narratives are invaluable, the one as showing us the more primitive thought and outlook of Israel's childhood, the other as giving us reflections from her adolescence and maturity. Both are necessary if we are to have that stereographic view which we most need.

Such methods as have helped men to appreciate the growth and structure of the Hexateuch and other prose books cannot be applied to such a collection as the Book of Psalms. Here for the most part internal evidence—the tone, language, and theological outlook of the individual poems—is practically the only criterion on which critical judgements can be based, and it leaves the door wide open for subjectivity. Hence there are very great differences of opinion as to the dates of various pieces. It is possible, however, to make some sort of conjecture

are, however, sections within the same book which differ widely in style and character. Nor is it possible to consider the structure of these books without some reference to the general character and methods of prophecy.

It seems that without exception the pre-exilic prophets were speakers rather than writers. Under the stress of their peculiar inspiration—and though this is in itself one of the most interesting studies in the Old Testament, a discussion of the problems involved is unnecessary to our present purpose —they gave expression, usually in public, to the truths which were committed to them for the use, instruction, and warning of their people. If they wrote them down themselves, it seems probable that they did so in calmer hours, perhaps years later than the original utterance. This at least we know to have been the case with Jeremiah, the only prophet of whose literary work we have anything like a detailed record. But in many other cases the oracles have been preserved, probably in the memory of their hearers, and written down by others than the speakers themselves.

On reading a prophetic book in Hebrew, the first feature that strikes us is that a large part if not the whole of the material is in poetry, not in prose. The study of Hebrew poetic form is still in its infancy, but sufficient progress has been made to enable us to recognize its general character, and the fact that two or three 'metrical' arrangements are commonly employed, though it seems that there is no variation in the arrangement within the same poem. This does not mean that the rhythm is identical throughout, but that certain familiar combinations of different rhythms will be used, and that other combinations are so rare as to awaken suspicion of textual corruption where they occur. At the same time it seems likely that each separate utterance was originally short, and largely confined to a single metaphor or idea. Frequently it would be introduced—this refers primarily to

oracles whose poetic form has been preserved—by the words
' Thus saith Yahweh ', and closed with the words ' Oracle of
Yahweh ', rendered in the English versions by the phrase
' saith the Lord '. These considerations enable us to determine the limits of the original oracles within a series of poetic
passages, and to recognize that we must treat each of these
sections independently of its neighbours. Thus, for instance,
if we take the first chapter of Isaiah we find it opening with
a short oracle (vv. 2–3) in the ' hexameter ' rhythm, of which
each line contains six metrical units, either divided by the sense
into two or three equal parts. Vv. 4–9, again, exhibit what is
known as a ' tetrameter ' rhythm, except for the latter part of
v. 7, and are concerned with the sufferings of Judah even more
than with her sin. Vv. 10–17 are in a rhythm which is a
combination of the ' tetrameter ' with the ' pentameter ',
and form a condemnation of sacrifice, together with an appeal
for social and personal righteousness. The same metrical form
appears again in vv. 18–20, but the verses form an appeal for
repentance and an offer of pardon. Similar analysis may be
made in the case of the poetic portions of all the prophetic books,
with the possible exception of Ezekiel and portions of Isa. xl–lxvi,
where the poems seem to be fairly long artistic productions,
very different from the emotional outbursts which meet us
in the other prophets.

A glance at the prose element in the prophetic books shows
us that this falls into two categories. Sometimes the prophet
speaks in his own person, and either tells the story of some event
in his own experience or describes a message which has been
given to him. An illustration may be found in Isa. vi, and
another in Hos. iii. In other cases the experiences of the
prophet are described by another, and the pronouns are all
in the third person. Such a passage is to be found in the story
of the conflict between Amos and Amaziah, Amos vii. 10–17.
One whole book, that of Jonah, is written in this way. It is

to be noted that narratives of this kind nearly always deal with events in the life of the Prophet, and seldom give many details of his message. Sometimes we have two accounts of the same event from these two different points of view; thus Jer. vii and xxvi appear to be concerned with the same facts, but the story in the first is told by the prophet himself and contains a fairly full account of the actual message, in the second we have a narrative by some one else, where the stress is laid on the danger to which Jeremiah was subject on this occasion, and only a slight indication is given of the words which he uttered.

Further study shows that the poetic oracles rarely stand alone, but usually occur in groups, sometimes of considerable length. It is noticeable that these groups often contain a number of passages dealing with the same or similar subjects, e. g. several of the prophetic books contain collections of oracles against foreign nations. Sometimes we find that an oracle occurs in more than one book. Thus we have the well-known case of the wonderful utterance which is found both in Isa. ii. 2-4 and in Mic. iv. 1-3. But there are others. Several of the oracles against Edom which appear in the Book of Obadiah (a good illustration of a collection of oracles dealing with a single subject, and that a foreign people) are found also in the Book of Jeremiah, and there is at least one interesting case where a book contains the same oracle twice, with minor variations—Jer. vi. 22-4 and l. 41-3—the main difference being that in the one place the oracle applies to Judah and in the other to Babylon.

Another fairly obvious feature of the longer books is the way in which they fall into longer or shorter divisions, usually comprising several chapters each. Frequently these divisions have separate headings or titles of their own. Thus in the Book of Isaiah, chs. i–xxxix, the following larger sections are clearly to be distinguished :

    Ch. i.   Introductory.

Chs. ii–v. A collection of oracles dealing in the main with Israel's sin.

Chs. vi–xii. A collection of personal narratives and oracles.

Chs. xiii–xxiii. A collection of oracles dealing with foreign nations.

Chs. xxiv–xxvii. An Apocalypse.

Chs. xxviii–xxxv. A collection of oracles, some of which deal with Israel's sin and punishment, and some with her restoration.

Chs. xxxvi–xxxix. Historical matter describing incidents in the life of Isaiah.

In the case of Jeremiah, separate superscriptions are to be found at various points, e. g. i. 1–3, iii. 6, vii. 1, xi. 1, xiv. 1, xviii. 1, xxv. 1–2, &c. The most natural explanation is that these longer sections once existed as separate collections. It is clear that some of them were not written by the prophet himself, and even amongst the oracles included in these sections there are from time to time those which awaken suspicion as to their authorship. Thus while much of the material included in the collection of oracles against foreign nations in the Book of Isaiah may be attributed to Isaiah the son of Amoz, it is very unlikely that he is responsible for the section dealing with the fall of Babylon in chs. xiii–xiv.

We are thus presented with a threefold process in the growth of a typical prophetic book. In the first place we have the actual delivery. Next we have the collection of these utterances by different people. Some may have been written and ' edited ' by the prophet himself or at his dictation, but in most cases his words would be recorded by others, possibly after years of oral tradition. Pious men, who recognized in the prophetic oracles the genuine inspired word of God would seek to gather together all that they could find. Sometimes there was a reliable tradition as to the authorship, sometimes the collector guessed, and sometimes he failed to consider the question at all, and was satisfied to group with the oracles of a known prophet other material of whose source he himself was ignorant. Such collections would grow with time, and as they grew would tend to include also such known actual writings of the prophets as might have been preserved. The third stage is reached when the collections are themselves brought together and arranged by a compiler in practically the form in which we have the books to-day. We cannot be too grateful for the process. Few would wish to confine the organs of Divine inspiration to a limited number of men whose names we know; and the methods which seem to have been adopted by these men of old have preserved for us a wealth of revelation whose human agents are for ever lost to sight and memory. It is difficult not to trace in these processes the hand of God working for the instruction, edification, and inspiration of all the ages to come.

Examples of critical method have thus been taken from the narrative books, the Psalms and the Prophets. One word may be added in conclusion. Higher criticism is an interesting and at times a fascinating study. But it is always a means to an end, never an end in itself. It must take a subordinate position as the handmaid of exegesis, and the Biblical student needs to bear in mind the fact that the final aim is more important than the method. It may well be that a later age with clearer vision and deeper insight than ours will detect our mistakes and find better solutions for our difficulties than we have reached. But for us it remains true that the attempt, imperfect and incomplete as it may be, has brought a fresh illumination. We have been able to trace the divine scheme of revelation and the divine method of training with a distinctness and a convincing continuity which would otherwise have failed us, and we look forward to yet greater achievements in generations to come. We are ' persuaded that God has yet more light and truth to break out unto us from His holy word '.

T. H. ROBINSON.

THE PRESENT POSITION OF
OLD TESTAMENT CRITICISM

It has been said that the supreme heresy is the heresy of finality. If this be so, Old Testament scholars are far enough from incurring the guilt of this heresy. Professor Welch tells us that one of his students wittily describes them as ' a band of cannibals who refreshed themselves by devouring one another '. In this amusing description there is a considerable measure of truth : whether they refresh themselves or not, they do at least devour one another. To a superficial observer the situation to-day must seem like confusion confounded. The plain man who asks for ' assured results ' may undoubtedly get them, for the indefatigable toil of the last 170 years has certainly not been in vain ; thanks to it, the old mechanical view of the Bible has gone for ever and been replaced by an intelligible and living conception of the great historical and religious movement of which the Bible is the literary deposit. The general trend of the development and its broad lines are plain enough : but when we come to detail, there is at the moment practically no unanimity anywhere. A position is no sooner established than it is challenged by plausible evidence or argument. Whether we consider the date of the component documents of the Hexateuch or the essence of prophecy or the attitude of the prophets to the law or the background and motive of individual psalms or the origin of eschatology, or questions of lesser moment such as the date of the Decalogue or the identity of the Servant in the Servant of Yahweh Songs in Deutero-Isaiah, answers of the most diverse kinds are given by scholars of equal competence. Working in the same spirit and with the same method, they may differ by five hundred years in their view of the date of a prophecy or a psalm.

This kaleidoscopic confusion would seem to discredit the critical method : in reality it does nothing of the kind. The historico-critical method is the only method we have : what we need is not less criticism, but more—more penetrating, and above all more sympathetic. The explanation of this immense and baffling diversity of opinion is very simple. It is due in the main to the paucity of the data. How immeasurably more meagre, for example, is the record left us by Hebrew historians than by the historians of Greece or Rome ! How scanty is the treatment meted out by the Book of Kings to four hundred years of crucial importance in comparison with the treatment of their chosen periods by Herodotus, Thucydides, Polybius, or by Livy, Tacitus, or Suetonius ! Where in the Old Testament—except on a tiny scale in the Book of Nehemiah—are we to look for biographical detail comparable in richness or elaboration to the material furnished by Xenophon and Plato for our picture of Socrates ? The Elephantine papyri, dealing with important aspects of Jewish life in the fifth century B.C., of which we have practically no knowledge from the Old Testament, reveal with pathetic significance the depths of our ignorance. It is because the facts are so few that they are capable of such diverse interpretation ; they have to be co-ordinated by a necessarily imaginative synthesis : if they were more numerous there would be proportionally less scope for the play of imagination in their co-ordination, and more unanimity in their interpretation. Yet, however numerous the facts, the personal equation inevitably remains. Löhr, for example, inclines to believe that the reference to *kings* in Gen. xvii. 6 implies the existence of the monarchy and stamps the passage as pre-exilic :[1] other scholars, believing the chapter to be from P and post-exilic, regard the allusion as a retrospect of the glorious

[1] *Untersuchungen zum Hexateuchproblem*, i, p. 12.

past. Similarly, Smend thinks that Exod. xxxii. 34 postulates
the fall of the northern kingdom in 721 B. C. : Eissfeldt, on the
other hand, believes that this inference is not necessary.

THE TEXT

Even in a general statement of the present position of Old
Testament criticism, a word must be said on this important
aspect of the problem, for obviously everything else depends
upon this. Infinite pains are now being exercised upon the
recovery or the restoration of the original text. Admirable
work has been done by philologists like Perles, in his *Analekten*,
Friedrich Delitzsch in his *Lese- und Schreibfehler im AT*, G. R.
Driver and others. The Versions are being studied with great
assiduity, though a vast deal remains to be done : their importance may be seen in the fact that Herrmann in his recent
commentary on Ezekiel claims for the Septuagint of this book
that it represents the ultimate textual truth more adequately
than the Massoretic text. But the point which I wish to illustrate very briefly here is that frequently in passages of crucial
importance the very slightest alteration in the traditional text
effects a radical transformation of the meaning by eliminating
ideas on which the older orthodoxy lays great stress. One of
the most important of such texts is Ps. lxxiii. 24, where the
traditional ' afterward thou wilt receive me to glory ' by the
slightest change becomes ' thou wilt take me after thee by my
hand '. The ' glory ' disappears, and with it the glimpse, or
assurance, of immortality : the clause would not be an advance
upon, but a mere parallel to the first clause of the verse, which
simply asserts the divine guidance in this life. Again, by a slight
change in the text of Isa. viii. 16, the picturesque figures of
Isaiah's disciples, who are not attested by the text of the Septuagint, would disappear. The crucial word ' flesh ' in the
famous declaration of Job xix. 26, has no support whatever in

the Septuagint, and the Greek and Hebrew texts of the still more famous Isa. liii, especially in vv. 8–11, are in the most utterly hopeless variance.   Similarly in Ps. xlv. 7 (E. V. 6) ' Thy throne, O God, is for ever and ever ', a very simple and easily defensible change in the text of the word for *O God*, transforms it into the innocent *will be*.   Illustrations of equal importance could be indefinitely multiplied.   It is not necessary to maintain that all the transformations suggested above are certain : that they are possible, sometimes even probable, is enough to show the indefeasible importance, for genuine historic study, of ascertaining the ultimate text, and with it the real mind, of the original writer.   The importance of such work is being recognized to-day more keenly perhaps than ever before.

On the other hand, there are scholars who maintain that the traditional Massoretic text is entitled to more respect than it sometimes receives.   Israel Eitan, e. g. has recently argued in his *Contribution to Biblical Lexicography* that some *hapax legomena* and some familiar words in unfamiliar senses are often quite satisfactorily explained by recourse to the corresponding root in Ethiopic, or more frequently Arabic, and that consequently the emendations in which the textual critic so freely indulges are not seldom entirely unnecessary.

The question of Hebrew metre is also being more fully explored, and this exploration has to be conducted, as Sir George Adam Smith has shown in his criticism of Duhm, in a spirit of deeper regard for the traditional text than critics have sometimes displayed.[1]

---

[1] ' I am persuaded after close study of the text that, though Jeremiah takes most readily to the specific Qinah metre, it is a gross and pedantic error to suppose that he confined himself to this, or that when it appears in our Book it is always to be read in the same exact form without irregularities.'   G. A. Smith, *Jeremiah*, p. 39.

SELLIN AND CORNILL

The most vivid and instructive illustration of the differences subsisting between critical scholars whose general methods are similar is furnished by the unhappy dispute between Cornill and Sellin which grew out of the stimulating little Introduction to the Old Testament published by the latter scholar in 1910. Cornill unfortunately took this Introduction to be a personal attack on his own views, and he replied in 1912 in *Zur Einleitung in das Alte Testament*. Sellin, naturally much aggrieved at this vexatious misunderstanding of his motive, which was of course a purely scientific one, on the part of one from whom he frankly acknowledged that he had learned much, answered the attack in another brochure of about the same length and bearing the same title as Cornill's, in which, point for point, and with great ability, he defended his original positions. It would be a liberal education in Old Testament Introduction to go carefully through these discussions, each conducted by an opponent worthy of the other's steel. We have not the space for this, but one or two illustrations typical of their deep-seated difference may be singled out, and then the broad pervasive contrast will be characterized. As illustrative of the detail may be mentioned their respective attitudes to Gen. xiv., the Book of the Covenant in Exod. xx. 22–xxiii. 33, the so-called Song of Moses (Deut. xxxii), the Blessing of Moses (Deut. xxxiii), the Epilogue of Amos, and Isa. ii. 2–4. Sellin argues for the early date and the historical value of Gen. xiv, he declines to have it dismissed as a late ' midrash ' : Cornill maintains that it is full of historical impossibilities which, in an imaginary modern analogy, he amusingly caricatures. Sellin defends the Mosaic origin of the Book of the Covenant. Cornill dates it under the monarchy : each draws a different inference from the fact that that Book contains no law to regu-late the relations of the Hebrews to the Canaanites—Sellin, that the problem had not yet arisen; Cornill, that these relations no longer required to be regulated. To Sellin's contention that the legislation of that Book was prospective, having in view the ultimate settlement in Canaan, Cornill replies that ' hypothetical legislation is a contradictio in adjecto : laws do not create conditions, but conditions laws '—a dictum which Sellin cleverly rebuts by reminding Cornill of his own excellent presentation of Ezekiel's legislative sketch as paving the way for the more elaborate P and its introduction to the post-exilic community in Jerusalem. Sellin refers the Song of Moses to the reign of Ahab, possibly to a pupil of Elijah : Cornill, after a very minute examination of its linguistic peculiarities, refers it confidently to the Babylonian exile. The oracles in the Blessing of Moses stamp it ' with certainty ', according to Sellin, as a product of the period of the Judges : to Cornill this ascription seems ' from every point of view impossible ', and he refers it to the time of Jeroboam II in the eighth century. Peculiarly instructive are Sellin's defence of and Cornill's attack upon the authenticity of the epilogue of Amos, that touch-stone of opinion on critical questions—an attack which Sellin admits to be the best thing in Cornill's book. Again, Sellin claims Isa. ii. 2–4 for Isaiah, which Cornill denies, remarking that, if this thought of the religion of Israel as a world-religion and of the conversion of all nations had been so clearly uttered by Isaiah, it is passing strange that it should then have disappeared so completely that even Jeremiah should have only once been moved to make mention of it (xvi. 19 f.). There is nothing strange, however, in such a thought to Sellin, who believes that it was inherent in Israel's religion from the beginning : ' for me,' he says, ' the thought of the world-religion is in principle contained in the religion of Israel from the days of Moses,' and he compares Gen. xii. 3, xlix. 10, Exod. xv. 11, Deut. xxxiii. 17, Amos iii. 2, ix. 7, every one of which passages Cornill could no doubt readily explain consistently with his own position.

This leads us to a broad characterization of the fundamental differences between Sellin and Cornill, which consciously or unconsciously control their interpretation of detail. Each claims the right to be regarded as an historical critic, but, speaking broadly, Cornill interprets Israel from within, and on the basis of the Old Testament as evolutionally interpreted by Wellhausen, Sellin sets Israel in the frame-work of ancient Oriental history, and, by insisting on the numerous and subtle points of contact between Egypt, and more particularly Babylon on the one hand, and Israel on the other, he can postulate a far wider range of thought, due to this cultural influence, not only for the prophetic but even for the pre-prophetic period. This indeed is one of Cornill's counts in the indictment against him, that he carries back as much as possible and nearly everything that is fundamental, to Moses: where this is impossible, he carries it back to the period of David and Solomon: and where this is impossible, then to Hezekiah. Thus the earlier period becomes the home of ideas which, to minds like Cornill's, only obscure the real course of the historical development. The discovery of the Aramaic version of the popular and widespread story of Aḥiḳar among the Elephantine papyri, opens up large vistas of the influence exercised by the nations of the ancient East upon one another, influence which was as possible in the fifteenth century B.C. as in the fifth. Apart, then, from the native genius of Israel's religion which was already embryonic in Moses, we must, it is argued, allow for far larger intellectual horizons in early Israel than was once thought, or than many still think, possible. This being so, it may be taken for granted that there were many conceptions in the mind of the Israel of all periods which have no recorded expression in the very scanty literature that survives as the Old Testament, but of which there may be hints that reveal their full significance only to the Orientalist.

The difference between Sellin and Cornill is largely to be

explained as a difference of years. The older scholars, like Wellhausen and Robertson Smith, for the most part illustrated the life and thought of Israel by analogies drawn from pre-Islamic Arabia ; but upon the younger scholars a new and entrancing world has emerged. Countless Babylonian tablets, the Tell-el-Amarna correspondence, the stele of Ḥammurapi, the Elephantine papyri, and much else, have poured upon the dark places of history, in which Israel hitherto stood, a flood of light : and it is very natural for the younger men to interpret Israel and her literature in the light cast upon her by Assyro-Babylonia and Egypt rather than by ancient Arabia. Or, as Winckler once put it, ' he who would *read* the Old Testament, must know Hebrew : but he who would *understand* the Old Testament, must know " Oriental ".'

THE HEXATEUCH

The Divine Names

We now pass from this by no means unfruitful dispute to consider the attitude of representative scholars to some of the larger questions of Old Testament Introduction. And first of all, with regard to the Hexateuch. Here the very basis of the documentary analysis has been fiercely challenged in recent years. Every one knows that the foundation of the modern view of the Hexateuch was laid in 1753 by Astruc in his epoch-making discovery of the significance of the divine names, Yahweh and Elohim, as pointing unmistakably to different literary sources—' the original memoirs ', as he describes them in his title, ' which it appears were used by Moses in the composition of the book of Genesis : ' a title, by the way, which shows pretty plainly that criticism did not originate in any bias against the Mosaic authorship. Of course, while this distinction gave the initial impulse to criticism, and is still regarded as a valuable aid to the analysis, the modern case is immeasurably strengthened by the concomitant occurrence of other phenomena, so that ' it is *untrue* to say ', as Dahse asserts or at least implies, ' that this distinction is the sole criterion, or that apart from it there would be no evidence of diversity of authorship in the Pentateuch at all '. [1] Eerdmans, however, opened his *Alttestamentliche Studien* (i. p. 5) with the challenging assertion that a renewed study of the problem of the Hexateuch had furnished him with the proof that criticism had been led by Astruc on a false track : ' the divine names Elohim and Yahweh are not reliable guides in the critical analysis.' Dahse and Wiener maintain the same position : and one of their arguments (though not the only one [2]) to discredit the documentary theory, rests on the alleged unreliability, or at any rate, insecurity of the Massoretic text, as evidenced by the frequent failure of the Septuagint to support it in its use of the divine names. Even Professor Welch argues that ' it is better to say frankly that the regnant hypo-thesis, so far as the analysis of the sources, especially in Genesis, is concerned, has been built up without sufficient attention having been given to its basis—on the one hand, to the relia-bility of the M.T. in connexion with the employment of the divine names, on the other hand, to the practice throughout the whole of Scripture in the use of the same names.' [3]

But this whole effort to discredit the Massoretic text, and with it the documentary theory, has been triumphantly, and we may say finally, defeated by Skinner in his *Divine Names in Genesis*. The textual facts of the Septuagint, he stoutly main-tains, do not justify us in throwing the whole of the textual tradition into the melting-pot (p. 58). On the contrary, the divine names ' are a remarkably stable element of the text '

[1] Skinner, *The Divine Names in Genesis*, p. 7.

[2] Dahse elaborates the view that the distribution of the names for God was influenced by the Synagogue reading.

[3] *Expositor*, May 1923, p. 352.

(p. 87) and 'have been transmitted with peculiar fidelity' (p. 88). For one thing, 'Greek translators and copyists lacked the instinctive sense of difference which was native to the Hebrew mind' (p. 176) : and apart from this, 'an immense number of cases of θεός in Isaiah for Hebrew Yahwe shows how strong was the tendency in certain later circles to avoid the Tetragrammaton' (p. 269, quoted from Kittel). Skinner further stakes his case on the extraordinary agreement between the Samaritan and the Massoretic text (p. 239), an agreement extending to over 300 cases (p. 116) with a difference in only eight or nine (p. 38)—an agreement which constitutes ' perhaps the most remarkable phenomenon in the history of the Hebrew text' (p. 116), and is all the more significant as the Samaritan is the oldest external witness to the state of that text (p. 121). We may therefore take it as settled that the documentary analysis, however difficult it may sometimes be to carry it out in detail, rests on a broad basis of unchallengeable fact. This is a point, Gressmann [1] argues, to be strenuously maintained against the caprices of recent criticism, that there is no real Old Testament science to-day which does not rest upon the hard-won results of the critical analysis of Hexateuchal sources.

The Documentary Sources

Apart from Deuteronomy, with which we shall deal later, three sources are universally recognized as yielded by the critical analysis, two prophetic and one priestly : they are known as the Yahwist (J), the Elohist (E), and the Priestly Code (P). Among scholars there are considerable and often wide differences of opinion with regard to the origin, nature, and date of these documents : but, very roughly speaking, there is general agreement that they may be approximately assigned to 850, 750, and 500–450 B. C. respectively, and that the first had its origin in Judah and the second in Israel. But many of the

[1] *Z.A.W.*, 1924, p. 2.

ablest scholars to-day dissent from one or other or all of these dates and origins. Procksch, for example, assigns the Yahwist to the period of Solomon, puts the Elohist about 800, and P at the close of the pre-exilic period. Sellin regards J as extending down to I Kings ii, and as coming from the Davidic-Solomonic period : the narrative material of the primary form of E (i. e. apart from later redaction) whose origin he places in Shechem or Bethel, was, he believes, completed before the division of the Kingdom : while with Gressmann he believes that much of the tradition embodied in the narrative material of P is as old as or older than J or E. Smend [1] argues that the home of E no less than of J is Judah, and that all doubt of this is finally removed by his placing of all three patriarchs at Beersheba in the south of Judah : further that, as the fall of the northern kingdom is implied by Exod. xxxii. 34, and as there is no adequate reason for separating the mass of E from the sections whose date is stamped on the face of them, nor, with Kuenen, for detaching particular pieces characterized by the prophetic style of thought in order to claim the remainder for the pre-prophetic period, the document was written after the fall of Samaria, probably some decades after, doubtless after the reformation of Hezekiah at the beginning of the seventh century. Hölscher assigns E to a period over a century and a quarter later still. ' With many others ', he says in his *Geschichte der israelitischen und jüdischen Religion* (pp. 101 f.), ' I am convinced that J and E are used as sources beyond the Hexateuch. It is the custom to regard these sources as ending with the reign of David, and to assume entirely new sources for the Book of Kings (annals, Temple chronicles, and prophetic legends). The result of a comprehensive examination of the source problem [2]

[1] *Die Erzählung des Hexateuch*, pp. 31–37.

[2] See his elaborate discussion of the Book of Kings in his *Das Buch der Könige, seine Quellen und seine Redaktion*, pp. 158–213 of the *Festschrift* Εὐχαριστήριον presented to Gunkel.

is, in my judgement, that J carries the story to the death
of Solomon and the division of the kingdom, E to the
destruction of Jerusalem (586) or possibly to 561. The earliest
date for J would in that case be about 900 and for E
about the middle of the sixth century.' Thus E would be
actually post-exilic and not pre-exilic, as is almost universally
believed ; and to it would belong the Elijah and Elisha cycle,
with which Hölscher maintains it has numerous affinities of
style and thought, but which are customarily, and doubtless
justly, regarded as an independent cycle ; for, as Bertholet has
pointed out,[1] Hölscher has not sufficiently reckoned with the
possibility of one writer having influenced another.

This is enough to show the extraordinary diversity of opinion
on such fundamental questions as the date and scope of the
documents underlying the Hexateuch. We include the scope,
for here too opinion has altered. It very early became evident
that the J and E which could easily be traced throughout the
Pentateuch were no less certainly present in the Book of
Joshua. But Cornill and Budde showed it to be extremely
probable that these sources extended beyond Joshua into
Judges and Samuel and as far as 1 Kings ii : and it was no doubt
this observation which pushed Hölscher on to the vastly more
precarious conclusion that one of these sources runs on to the
end of the Book of Kings and renders unnecessary the assumption of annals, Temple archives, and separate historical sources
for sections like 1 Kings xx, xxii, &c., with which most critics
have usually operated. Gressmann has entered a very necessary
caveat against this tendency to confuse the legends and early
story of Israel with her definite historical writing.[2]

Old Testament science never halts, and questions once supposed to be as good as settled are being so vigorously re-opened,
that Herrmann is thoroughly justified in saying that to-day less

---

[1] *T. L. Z.*, 17 May 1924, 196.
[2] *Z. A. W.*, 1924, p. 4.

than ever can the Pentateuchal problem be considered as closed.[1] Even the question of the number of the constituent documents of the Hexateuch has been raised and discussed with much keenness and freshness by Eissfeldt. Twenty years or so ago the era of purely literary criticism was believed to be as good as closed, and scholars began to devote their attention to the study of the relations subsisting between Hebrew literature and religion and the other literatures and religions of the ancient East. But Eissfeldt comes upon the scene maintaining in his *Hexateuch-Synopse* with elaborate argument supported by documentary evidence arranged in four parallel columns that (apart from Deuteronomy) there are in the narrative of the Hexateuch not three great documentary sources, but four—L, J, E, and P. The symbol L is used to describe what he calls the *Lay* source, the most primitive and the most secular source of all—the antipodes, whether as regards its literary or its religious spirit and outlook, of the sacerdotal P. In the Hexateuchal narrative there had always been felt to be refractory elements, which could not be readily fitted in to any of the great documentary sources, and critics were content to regard these as, in a sense, erratic blocks (e. g. Gen. vi. 1–4, Exod. iv. 24–26). Eissfeldt believes that he has detected a document which, quite as much as J, E, and P, runs through the whole historical narrative at least up to Judges ii. 2—a document in which these and other hitherto isolated fragments are found quite naturally to lie. This document is traced with immense care and thoroughness through the whole story. The general conclusion to which he comes is that L is the primitive source reflecting the nomadic ideal, belonging perhaps to the time of Elijah and embodying a protest against the Canaanizing of Hebrew life. In this connexion it is significant that this is the document which narrates the drunkenness of Noah and of Lot, in stories too, which—especially the latter—betray the rough and

---

[1] *Ezekiel*, p. xxxiii.

unsophisticated vigour of an older time. J, which dates from the prosperous first half of the eighth century, rejoices in Canaan, the land of promise, and in all the settled life of the land. E, which reflects the prophetic movement and comes from the time of Amos and Isaiah, attaches again to the nomadic ideal, regards Canaan as a peril, and, like the prophets, threatens the people with catastrophe (Exod. xxxii. 34). Eissfeldt also thinks that the place of origin of these documents is in need of further discussion, as too much has been made of the phenomena which point to Judah as the home of J and Israel of E. The spiritual unity of the kingdoms, he remarks, antedated their political separation, just as there was a spiritual unity among the various peoples of Germany long before the establishment of the German Empire, and they could and did rejoice in one another's folk-tales and legends.

This interesting argument which, if it could be substantiated, would bring with it a real enrichment of our knowledge alike of the history of Hebrew literature and Hebrew tradition, has not been allowed to pass without challenge. Against the whole meticulous method involved in studies like these Volz has recently raised an energetic protest.[1] While accepting without hesitation the existence of the four documents J, E, D and P, he confesses that for many years he has cherished a fundamental aversion to this particular kind of minute separation of the sources—an aversion which has only been confirmed by Eissfeldt's volume. In words which were later quoted with much approval by Staerk,[2] he goes on to say, ' I see in this Synopsis the culmination of the hitherto prevailing method, and I find that it proves exactly the opposite of what it is meant to prove, for the miserable fragments of narrative which for the most part the columns contain prove precisely that there were not four original narratives, and that this

---

[1] *T. L. Z.*, 22 Sept. 1923, 389 ff.
[2] *In Z. A. W.*, 1924, p. 35.

entire Pentateuchal Synopsis is nothing but the artificial creation of modern erudition'. He denies that the narrative material is continuously sustained through several sources, and in particular he objects to the rending asunder of chapters into single verses and tiny fragments of verses. Repetitions and contradictions undeniably abound ; but the critics, he argues, have been too ready to assign them to different literary sources, instead of recognizing that they may be not only just as well, but far better, explained as variants in the oral tradition, faithfully preserved by the same author and in the same document. He is prepared, he tells us, to illustrate his thesis on the basis e. g. of the story of Jacob at Bethel in Gen. xxviii. 10–22, where to most critics diversity of authorship seems undeniable : we shall await his discussion of this point with interest. In a general way he agrees with Sellin that E is a later revised edition of J, improving upon it by the ' omission or modification of anything which had become ethically or religiously unacceptable ',[1] and so adapting it for use in public worship, or, as he says, ' more probably in instruction '.

Current opinion has also been attacked from another angle by Löhr in the first of his *Untersuchungen zum Hexateuchproblem*, which deals with the Priestly Codex in Genesis. Briefly this is an attempt to prove that there never was such an independent document as most critics believe in and describe as P, that the assumption of such a source rests upon an error, and that the phenomena which have been held to prove it can be better accounted for otherwise. From the frequent repetition of the same words or phrases, e. g. ' Be fruitful and multiply ', Löhr maintains that we may have a right to infer one author, but not necessarily one continuous documentary source. We have not, he believes, anything like sufficiently reckoned with the possibility of later interpolations and glosses : the endeavour to assign practically all the material to documentary

[1] Montgomery's Translation of Sellin's *Introduction*, p. 69.

sources he regards as one of the fundamental errors of the prevalent literary criticism. The upshot of the discussion is that there never was a priestly codex composed in and brought from Babylon to Palestine by Ezra, but that essentially the Pentateuch, as we now have it, was the work of Ezra and his associates, who had before them not continuous documentary sources but smaller groups of laws and narratives of moderate compass, on which they stamped a relative unity when they put them together. This theory is practically a reversion from the prevailing documentary hypothesis to the older, and we had believed, superseded, fragmentary hypothesis in a new form.

By a piece of good fortune it fell to Eissfeldt, the champion, as we have seen, of the documentary theory in its extreme form, to review this brochure in the *Theologische Literaturzeitung* (19 April 1924). Löhr had poked fun at the ' redactor ', who here and there had inserted paltry fragments of verses from documentary sources, which Löhr thinks can be much more naturally explained as glosses or interpolations, and ironically suggested that in these interpolations he may have been guided by a feeling of sympathy with the literary critics, for whose benefit he desired, in the goodness of his heart, to set up finger-posts. Eissfeldt rejoins that we have here no occasion for mockery. He points out that we have unquestionably parallel narratives which readily arrange themselves in parallel groups, and argues that it is more natural to attempt to organize the remaining material into similar groups or documents, if it be possible (and to him his *Hexateuch-Synopse* is the proof that it is possible) than to regard its details as merely the glosses of a compiler. The whole method of Hebrew historians, he maintains, has to be reconsidered in the light of the acknowledged practice of Arabic historians. This same point has been suggestively worked out by A. A. Bevan in his essay on *Historical Methods in the Old Testament* in *Cambridge Biblical Essays*.

Deuteronomy

Of quite exceptional interest are the new attitudes—for there are two—to Deuteronomy, represented by Hölscher [1] and Welch [2] respectively. ' A revision of the whole Deuteronomic problem ', remarks Hölscher, ' is one of the most clamant needs of Old Testament science to-day.' It is of the more importance to be sure of our ground here, as the date of Deuteronomy is in a real sense the pivot of Old Testament criticism and chronology. Ever since De Wette (1805) it has been regarded as axiomatic that Deuteronomy belongs to the seventh century B. C., that it was the basis and inspiration of the reformation of Josiah, and that its chief demand was for the centralization of the worship at the Jerusalem temple. All of these statements are denied by the afore-mentioned scholars, though they differ by nearly half-a-millennium in their view of the date of the book or at least (in the case of Welch) of some of its component parts.

Hölscher sets it about 500 B. C., i. e. about half a century (in his view) after the Elohist. His indictment against the customary pre-exilic date is largely based on its ' impracticable idealism '.[3] Its author, he argues, did not make clear to himself

[1] Hölscher's view of Deuteronomy is elaborately stated in *Z. A. W.*, 1922, pp. 161–255, *Komposition und Ursprung des Deuteronomiums*, and more briefly in his *Geschichte der israelitischen und jüdischen Religion*, pp. 132–4, and incidentally, so far as it affects the Reformation of Josiah, in Gunkel's Festschrift Εὐχαριστήριον, pp. 206–11.

[2] *The Code of Deuteronomy* (James Clarke & Co., 1924).

[3] Gressmann pertinently points out (*Z. A. W.*, 1924, p. 336) that ' impracticable idealism ' may have very far-reaching consequences on the field of history. It was this that inspired Josiah to launch upon the fatal campaign which cost him his life ; and this is only one aspect of the political hopes inspired by Deut., which seem to us remote enough from reality or even probability. The historical critic has no interest in denying the idealistic strain in Deuteronomy (cf. xi. 22–5).

how impracticable his demands were, he built in the air ; and this point he illustrates thus : At the festivals the whole population of the land, men, women, sons, daughters, male and female slaves, Levites and resident aliens—before the exile that would be about 120,000 people—are to make a pilgrimage to Jerusalem, and this immense crowd is to hold its sacrifices and meals in the Temple courts. This can only be understood in the light of the fact that the legislator has mechanically, and without thinking out the consequences, transferred to Jerusalem the customs which were suitable for the local sanctuaries situated in the immediate neighbourhood of the towns or villages. The same 'impracticable idealism' appears in the general remission of debt in the seventh year, and in the general release of slaves, which is not pre-supposed by Jer. xxxiv. 8–11, but only by the redaction, xxxiv. 12. The subsequent history shows that there could not in Josiah's time have been any demand for centralization. Under his successors the high places continue to exist as before (Jer. xiii. 27, xvii. 1 f.) ; even Ezekiel [1] knows nothing of their abolition, and even much later, about 400, the cult of the Egyptian Jews at Elephantine shows that they were little influenced by the demands of Deuteronomy, which can hardly therefore have been public law for nearly two hundred years before. The reformation of Josiah consisted not in the abolition of the high places, but only in the

---

[1] Hölscher distinguishes between the real Ezekiel, who 'stands with both feet on the ground of ancient pre-exilic religion' (*Z. A. W.*, 1922, p. 243) and the *book* of Ezekiel, composed between 515 and 445 in Babylon. The prophet who regarded both Samaria and Jerusalem as wives of Yahweh (Ezek. xxiii) could not conceivably have believed, as Deuteronomy does, in the alone legitimacy of the sanctuary on Zion. It was by the fifth century writer of the book named after him that he came to be regarded as the teacher of the law and the father of the later ' nomism '. For the history of the Jewish religion, Hölscher remarks, the author of this pseudepigraph is much more significant than the Ezekiel who attracts by his imaginative poetry. (Cf. *Hesekiel, der Dichter und das Buch.*) This subversive view of the book is not shared by Herrmann in his recent commentary.

purification of the worship at Jerusalem, and has therefore nothing to do with Deuteronomy. The basis of the story of the reform in 2 Kings xxii. f., is E, which does not regard the high places as illegal. If from xxiii. 6–12 we abstract vv. 8 a, 9, we find that the reforms are all connected with the Jerusalem Temple—the destruction of the asherah, the houses of the sodomites, the high places of the satyrs, and the emblems of sun-worship : it is only these abstracted verses that extend the reform beyond Jerusalem. But, as Schmidt has pointed out,[1] these verses are not to be so easily disposed of—they are due, not to interpolation, but to accidental displacement ; and the statement in 2 Kings xxiii. 9 that the priests of the high places did not officiate at the altar in Jerusalem so distinctly implies the concession in Deut. xviii. 6 f. that they be permitted to do so that ' if Deut. xviii. 6 were not in existence, we should have to invent it as the pre-supposition of 2 Kings xxiii. 9 '. He further pointedly argues that the existence of high places so soon after Josiah's reformation is no proof that there had been no legislation against them ; for Hölscher himself admits the historicity of the purification of the worship at the Jerusalem Temple, yet Ezek. viii.–xi furnishes incontestable and pathetically eloquent proof that within less than a generation idolatry and foreign worship within the Temple itself were again in the ascendant.

It would seem, then, that Hölscher has not made out his case, but he has certainly presented it with great plausibility. Deuteronomy, he argues, is the law which is to regulate the life of the new community in Palestine after the return. To this corresponds the fictitious historical background. As long ago under Moses, so now again will Yahweh liberate His people out of heathen bondage, and give them the land which He swore to the fathers. The condition is obedience to the law. In its origin, Hölscher maintains, Deuteronomy is neither a

[1] *T. L. Z.*, 14 July 1923, 291.

prophetic book, nor does it represent a compromise between the prophet and the priest : in its recurrent emphasis on the necessity for safeguarding the interests of the Levitical priest-hood, it is thoroughly priestly.

At the other end of Deuteronomic criticism stands Welch.[1] The purpose of his book is ' to examine carefully and afresh the Deuteronomic code itself, and, on the basis of this examination, to seek to determine its aim, its composition, and its period '. The general result of his investigation is that he finds for the individual laws which he examines a relatively early date—for some of those relating to offerings, e. g., a date perhaps even in the period of the Judges, or at latest of the early monarchy. Similarly the legislation dealing with the prophets points to an early date. These are not thought of, like the literary prophets, as the councillors of kings or the defiant judges of priests ; they are of a homelier order, like the peasants who consult them, and they are coupled—as the Elohist would, but as Jeremiah would not, have coupled them—with the dreamers of dreams. The law of the monarchy also seems to him early. The king must not be a second Solomon. While ' Judah was longing for a second David, Israel was dreading a second Solomon '. That is, the law reflects the temper of the northern kingdom, and of a period not far removed from Solomon. Thus the book is

---

[1] Conclusions similar to Welch's have been reached by Oestreicher in *Das deuteronomische Grundgesetz*, and these have been still further elaborated by Staerk, who argues in *Das Problem des Deuteronomiums* that the aim of the Deuteronomic laws was not the unity, through centralization, of the Yahweh worship, but its purification; he further maintains that this argument is supported, so far as linguistic usage is concerned, by a comparison of Deut. xii. 14 with xxiii. 17, so that Deut. xii. 13 f. is not an advance upon, but essentially identical with, Exod. xx. 24 (so also Oestreicher). The linguistic argument has been fully answered by König in *Z. A. W.* 1924, p. 341 f., and the historical argument by Gressmann who, in loc. cit., pp. 313–37, ably defends, as against both Hölscher and Oestreicher, the common critical view of the date and purpose of Deuteronomy.

in the main early and of northern origin, as its affinities with Hosea would suggest.

But his most important, as it is his most radical, conclusion is that, with the solitary exception of xii. 1–7, there is no entirely unambiguous demand for the centralization of the worship. The numerous allusions to ' the place which Yahweh shall choose to cause his name to dwell there ' are allusions not to *the* alone legitimate Yahweh sanctuary at Jerusalem, but to *any* of the many Yahweh sanctuaries scattered throughout the land. What the legislators feared was the Baalization of the Yahweh worship, and this could be most effectively prevented by proscribing attendance at Canaanite sanctuaries, and peremptorily restricting it to Hebrew sanctuaries, where worship could be regulated according to the Yahweh tradition by Yahweh's own ministers in the spirit of the Yahweh religion.

It does not seem at all impossible, however, to combine this view of the relatively early origin of many of the individual laws with the prevalent opinion that the body of the book is the product of the seventh century. After the fall of Samaria the religious literature of the north would tend to drift into Judah and find its permanent home among the official representatives of Yahwism in Jerusalem : if the prophecy of the northerner Hosea was preserved and edited in Judah, there is no reason why northern legislation (assuming Deuteronomy to be in part of northern origin) should not equally have been preserved there, or why the usages of the various sanctuaries, embodying a sound Yahwism, should not have there been compiled and eventually promulgated, when the decline of Assyria offered the nobler representatives of Yahwism, supported as they were by a devout king, a unique opportunity for the assertion of the rights of Yahweh's cult, and for the exposition of those rights in terms of the best thought and usage of the past.[1]

[1] Besides the laws which account for the features of Josiah's reformation, the original Deuteronomy may well have contained a selection of such laws

There is one question to which both Hölscher and Welch owe us an answer : if the discovered law-book which constituted the basis of Josiah's reform was not Deuteronomy, what was it ? Hölscher dismisses the question with the remark that to raise it is ' to make demands upon our literary tradition which by its very nature it cannot fulfil and which therefore ought not to be made '.[1] That is not quite good enough. Until this very reasonable question is satisfactorily answered, we shall be justified in abiding by a conviction which has stood the test of 120 years.[2]

The Decalogue

Nothing reveals more decisively a scholar's attitude to the whole Old Testament movement than his view of the date of the Decalogue. The possibilities range over seven centuries. Scholars equally well equipped have contended for a Mosaic origin (of course in its brief ultimate form), for an origin in the period of Elijah, of the early literary prophets, whose teaching it is supposed [3] to summarize, and of the exile.[4] There is no space to give in detail the reasons for these so widely divergent ascriptions : and there is the less need, as the present state of opinion has been well summarized by W. E. Barnes in the *Expositor* for July 1924 (pp. 7–23).

(whether of Israel or Judah) available to the compilers as were not inconsistent with the implications of the reformation or with one another.

[1] Εὐχαριστήριον, i, p. 213.

[2] See Additional Note on p. 219.

[3] Not very justly ; for the Decalogue has no provision to protect the interests of the poor and the exploited, which was so characteristic a feature of prophecy.

[4] Steuernagel (*Einleitung*, p. 261) regards the Decalogue as an ' exilic catechism ' answering the question how Yahweh was to be served in the strange land.

Ezra-Nehemiah

The criticism of Ezra-Nehemiah presents as many intricate problems as that of the Hexateuch, but there is a growing consensus of belief that the order of the events described in these books has been disturbed by the priestly redactor who was the author of Chronicles, in order to give the priest Ezra precedence over the layman Nehemiah. Whatever the reason may be, there are many improbabilities in the story as it stands, which represents Ezra's introduction of drastic measures of social and religious reform as preceding the arrival of Nehemiah as governor of Judah. In reality Nehemiah's work has all the appearance of being tentative and preliminary to the radical reforms of Ezra, and the history certainly gains in intelligibility if we assume the priority of Nehemiah. The mistake may have arisen from a confusion between Artaxerxes I (465–424 B. C.) and Artaxerxes II (404–359). If we assume the year of Ezra's arrival in Palestine, ' the seventh year of Artaxerxes the king ' (Ezra vii. 7) to be 397, not 458, every incident in the Books of Ezra-Nehemiah, rearranged on this basis, would fall into its place.

THE PROPHETS

We now pass to the consideration of some of the problems raised by prophecy. Here also, among those who have devoted special study to the prophets, such as Sellin, Hölscher, Caspari, Duhm, Gunkel, T. H. Robinson, Joyce, &c., there are wide differences of opinion on the most fundamental questions. What, e. g., is the essence of prophecy ? is it prediction ? What is the place of ecstasy in the prophetic experience ? What is the relation of the prophet to the cult ? Were the earlier literary prophets all but exclusively messengers of doom ? Where does their eschatology, if they have any, come from ?

Prediction

It may seem absurd at this time of day to raise the question whether prediction is of the essence of prophecy.   But Gunkel has not overstated the case when he says [1] that the contents of their visions and words were almost always the future, and that even to the latest times there never arose a prophet in Israel, whose first word was not prediction (Deut. xviii. 22, Zech. ii. 13, E. V. 9).   Their primary business is not to teach the people but to declare the future.   But their highest virtue, he points out with equal emphasis, does not lie in their predictions : these have little interest for us to-day, and many of them remained unfulfilled.   Their real greatness lies in their insight into and their proclamation of God's moral government of the world.   They not only know and declare what God has said of the future, they know why He has said it, they proclaim the moral basis of the message they announce.

Ecstasy

Did their vision of the future, or their message generally, come in the form of an ecstatic experience ?   The older view was that, while at the beginning and towards the end of the prophetic movement (cf. Ezek., Zech.) this was demonstrably so, the great representatives of prophecy in the middle period were characterized by a fine sanity ; all their messages were uttered ' with the understanding also '.   But of late there has developed a tendency to regard even these prophets as, in some measure, ecstatics also, who might have claimed, in another sense than John (1 Ep. i. 1) to be declaring just what they had heard and seen, in some ecstatic experience of vision or audition.   Even the robust and clear-headed Amos had his visions, and the careers of Isaiah and Jeremiah, to whose personalities, however impressive in different ways, nothing abnormal seems

[1] *Die orientalischen Literaturen*, pp. 80 ff., cf. *Die Propheten*, p. 69.

to cling, were introduced by an experience which was anything but ordinary and which seems to deserve the name of ecstatic ; and there are occasional hints (cf. Isa. viii. 11) that this ecstasy was not confined to the initial experience. We are even told that the phrase usually rendered 'Thus saith Yahweh', is strictly and properly 'Thus said Yahweh', and that, except where it is obviously nothing but a stereotyped literary formula, it is usually to be interpreted as suggesting that the oracle which it introduces rests on ecstatic vision or audition, of something like the type so vividly reflected in the separate oracles of Isa. xxi. 'It does not follow of necessity', says T. H. Robinson, 'that all the utterances' of Amos, Isaiah, and Jeremiah, 'originated thus, yet it is at least possible.' [1] Against this Volz [2] lifts up a warning voice. 'It would not', he says, 'in my judgment be correct to consider even the majority of the prophetic words as uttered in ecstasy.' Even utterances like the famous Jer. xxxi. 15 or iv. 21 are to be understood simply as vivid poetical representations. 'Besides, the speech of the classical prophets is so polished in form, and so clear in contents, that there cannot possibly be any thought of ecstasy, glossolaly, or the like.'

The question is by no means an idle one, as with it are bound up the important questions of the length of the original oracles and of the continuity of the prophetic discourse in its present form. If the advocates of ecstasy are right, the original oracles will no doubt be short ; if they are wrong, it will be open to assume that there are relatively long and continuous passages. 'Only the great artists like Isaiah', says Gunkel, [3] 'have the power to create a longer poem constituting a real unity : as an example of this highest art of Israel's prophets is Isa. xxix. 1–7, a piece which, in finished unity and full of overwhelming

[1] *Prophecy and the Prophets in Ancient Israel*, p. 43.
[2] *Der Prophet Jeremia*, p. xxxvi.
[3] *Die Propheten*, p. 118.

force, surges past the reader like the waves of the ocean.' Even Volz allows that in its essence the prophetic word is brief—Gunkel adduces Isaiah's 'Shear-jashub', 'Maher-shalal-hash-baz', and Hosea's 'Jezreel', 'Lo-ammi' as bearing upon them the stamp of the ecstatic ejaculations of the older nebi'im : but Volz believes that recent criticism has carried this principle to inordinate lengths, and instances Jer. iv. 5 ff., xiv. 1 ff., 30 f., as glorious artistic creations whose glory is tarnished by being 'cut up into little pieces'. And the very artistic strophic arrangement of Isa. ix. 8–x. 4 with v. 26–30 is surely proof enough that ecstasy is inadequate as an explanation of at any rate the greater prophets, who were conscious and deliberate artists. But the recognition of the general principle that oracles are primarily brief in form is a valuable safe-guard against the temptation to discover consecutive thought and unity of theme in contiguous groups of verses which may, in the psychical experience of the prophet, have nothing whatever to do with one another.

Prophetic Attitude to the Cult

A question of fundamental importance is the attitude of the pre-exilic prophets to the cult, and in particular to animal sacrifice : but, so meagre is the evidence and so divergent the interpretations of it, that a categorical answer to this question is perhaps for ever impossible. The evidence is easily collated, the relevant passages are Amos v. 24 f., Hos. vi. 6, Isa. i. 11 ff., Mic. vi. 6–8 and Jer. vii. 22 f. The prophetic thesis is most succinctly and dramatically stated by Hosea in the words, 'I desire love, and not sacrifice' : with this all the passages mentioned agree. And Amos and Jeremiah go further, they deliberately assert that sacrifice had never been the divine demand, not even in the great days of the Exodus, to which doubtless the priests appealed, sheltering their practice under the august sanction of Moses. Various attempts have been made to blunt the edge of this sharp and seemingly unambiguous antithesis. It is urged that the prophets are using the language of hyperbole, it has been argued that prophets and priests were not necessarily at daggers drawn, that Isaiah and Uriah were friends (Isa. viii. 2), that the prophetess Huldah was consulted on the discovery of the Book of the Law, that the Deuteronomic movement and Ezekiel, in his own person, represent a practical compromise between prophet and priest, and that the anti-cultic psalms (xl, l, li) found a place in the Temple worship. ' A religion without ritual would have been practically inconceivable to the Hebrew mind . . . Amos was not consistently hostile to ritual. It is safer to assume that he is protesting not against ritual *per se*, but against making ritual do service for character and right conduct.' [1] Similarly Eerdmans : [2] ' the emphasis laid by the prophets on the ethical will of God by no means involves that they were representatives of an exclusively ethical religion. The cult had its significance for the prophets also ' (cf. Hos. iii. 4, viii. 12).

But there is a very formidable array of scholars on the other side—Lofthouse, Skinner, Montefiore, E. Pace, Gunkel, Balla, who says that to the older prophets the cult was ' apostasy ', Hölscher who maintains that Amos opposes the cult on principle, that his struggle was not with single Canaanitish customs, but with the cult as such—*Jahve will keinen Kult*. The case for this view has been put very forcibly by Skinner in these words : ' It is commonly held that the prophets' repudiation of sacrifice was not absolute but relative to the prevalent delusion that cultus apart from morality has an inherent value in the sight of God. That is to say, they did not reject sacrifice as such, but only as offered by a people that had lost the true knowledge of God. It seems clear, however, that the prophetic principle goes further than that. Not only is sacrifice of no

[1] J. M. P. Smith, *The Moral Life of the Hebrews*, pp. 80 f.
[2] *Das Buch Exodus*, p. 144.

avail as a substitute for righteous conduct, but a perfect religious relationship is possible without sacrifice at all . . . They never demand a purified ritual, but always and exclusively the fulfilment of the ethical commands of Yahwe.'[1]

If the prophets mean what they seem to say, they were unquestionably the implacable opponents of the cult : and if it be argued that so bold a challenge of the ritual in which they had been brought up is inconceivable, it may be answered that with men of their insight and calibre, it is precisely the inconceivable that is possible. Isaiah and his brethren in prophecy were very ' bold '. And it may well have been that their conception of animal sacrifice as an irrelevance and a futility—if that was indeed their conception—rested upon profound conceptions of the ultimate nature of God as spiritual, which they would have been prepared to defend by argument had argument been their province. The sentiment expressed in Ps. l. 13 would carry a real thinker far.

Eschatology

The last point on which I shall touch is the content of the (pre-exilic) prophetic message, and with this is intimately bound up the question of eschatology. A familiar feature of prophecy is that frequently the sternest messages of doom are immediately followed by words of hope and promises of a golden future, illustrated most signally perhaps by the epilogue of Amos. Did the original message embody both elements, or only the first, or did it vary with each prophet? Is the implicit eschatology native and original to Israel (Sellin), or has it a foreign source (Gressmann), whether Babylonian or Egyptian or other, or are the promises simply exilic or post-exilic interpolations, embodying later Israel's inextinguishable hope?

Jeremiah, in xxviii. 8, certainly leaves upon the mind the impression that the message of his predecessors was in the main

[1] *Prophecy and Religion*, p. 181.

a stern one : it will be time enough to believe in the promises when they are fulfilled (*v.* 9). The real question—and it is a vital one—comes to be whether the prophets have a gospel or not. Sellin [1] is very emphatic that they have a salvation to proclaim, involved in God's ' world-plan '—a salvation which the judgement that they also proclaim may postpone but not conceivably abrogate. He points in confirmation not only to Hosea, Isaiah, and Jeremiah, but to Amos and Micah before they have been robbed by criticism of the passages which confirm his view. Cornill [2] replies by saying that if Amos ix. 8*b*–10 is not in the most diametrical contradiction to *vv.* 1–4, he does not know what contradiction is, and that the appeal in Jer. xxvi. 18 to Mic. iii. 12 is proof that that must have been Micah's last word—any promise of salvation is categorically excluded. The contrast was put with striking force about thirty years ago, when Wellhausen characterized the epilogue of Amos as ' a weak relapse into the very illusion which the prophet had been combating', and Valeton replied by describing it as ' the triumph of faith '. In answer to Gressmann's charge that the reluctance to admit the authenticity of the prophecies of salvation is due to the mistaken isolation of Israel's literature and to defective knowledge of the other literatures of the ancient East, Cornill asks, ' What is won by their acceptance? and at what price? Won is an earlier date for a few prophetic passages than the critical school is willing to concede, but ' the price paid is that ' we have to break the back-bone of the prophets, to reduce them to weaklings who had not the courage to think their thoughts through to the end and draw from them the necessary consequences, but who, when their own people are in question, blunt the edge of their threats and " let milk and honey flow from the cup of the wrath of Yahweh " ' (Wellhausen).

[1] *Zur Einleitung*, p. 69.
[2] Ibid. pp. 79–86.

Hölscher [1] also attacks the view that early Israel had an eschatology and the hope of a redeemer. This, he says, exists only in the imagination of certain modern scholars, and it is idle to attempt to prove its antiquity by deriving it from any Egyptian prophetic ' scheme '; for the two types of prophecy are quite different, the Egyptian contemplating merely the restoration of happy political conditions in Egypt, the Jewish on the other hand contemplating the salvation at the end of all things which was to be ushered in by the triumph of the one God over the forces of the world. ' The only eschatology comparable with the Jewish is the Iranian, under whose influence, direct or indirect, the Jewish originated.' Gressmann, he thinks, has without justification made capital out of Amos v. 18–20 to prove the pre-exilic origin of eschatology. In pre-exilic prophecy ' the day of Yahweh' has nothing to do with eschatology: it signifies the expected epiphany of the god who goes forth in storm to fight his foes (cf. Judges v. 4 f.), and has its exact analogy in an Assyrian appeal to the god of fire, ' May thy dreadful day overtake thine enemies '.

Apart from Gressmann, the most fruitful recent study of eschatology is undoubtedly that of Mowinckel in his *Das Thronbesteigungsfest Jahwäs*. His study of the psalms which exalt Yahweh as King or as entering upon His reign (xlvii, xciii, xcv–c) led him to the conclusion that they were written for the New Year's festival, the feast of tabernacles, to celebrate the (annual) accession of Yahweh to His throne. His kingship is founded on His power displayed in Creation and in His victory over the primeval dragons; that accounts for the frequent allusion to these things in the relevant psalms, and many a passage in Deutero-Isaiah moves in the same circle of ideas. In time the mythical enemy over whom Yahweh triumphed became a historical enemy, first Egypt, and then, as in Ps. xlvi, the nations generally. The roots of Hebrew

[1] *Gesch. der isr. und jüd. Religion*, 154 f., cf. 105.

eschatology, Mowinckel believes, are to be found in this festival celebrating the accession of Yahweh to His throne: he was led to this highly important and suggestive conclusion by noting the extraordinary similarity between the features of the eschatological picture and those of the cult-myth underlying the accession psalms.

Of all the individual problems within the prophetic literature none is more tantalizing than those raised by the Songs of the Servant of Yahweh in Deutero-Isaiah. Who is he—an individual, the nation, or a righteous nucleus? Are the Songs organically related to their context, or are they later intrusions by another hand or even by the same hand, which perhaps in that case intended that the poems, originally written of an individual, should be, as the body of the book must be, interpreted of the nation? The individual and the national interpretations alike still find doughty champions. Of the former the most striking of recent suggestions are those of Mowinckel,[1] who argues that the Servant is none other than the prophet himself, and of Sellin [2] who, in a brilliant and skilful but not entirely convincing argument, maintains that the Servant is Moses, who, martyred in Shittim, is to be miraculously raised from the dead, to make the Torah great and glorious throughout the world.

THE HAGIOGRAPHA

We have little space to deal with the Hagiographa. Of Daniel be it only said that the learned and by no means negligible attempts of R. D. Wilson in his *Studies in the Book of Daniel* and of C. Boutflower in his *In and Around the Book of Daniel* to rehabilitate the historicity of that perplexing book can hardly be said to have succeeded in view of the damaging

---

[1] *Der Knecht Jahwäs.* The argument is sketched by Gunkel in *Ein Vorläufer Jesu.*

[2] *Mose und seine Bedeutung für die isr.-jüd. Religionsgeschichte.*

arguments, so far as they affect Belshazzar, which have recently been urged by H. H. Rowley in *The Expositor* (Sept., Oct., 1924).

Fresh light has recently been cast upon the sources of the Book of Proverbs by Wallis Budge's discovery of the Egyptian ' Teaching of Amen-em-ope '. These Egyptian proverbs happily illustrate the nature of foreign, in this case Egyptian, influence upon the literature of Israel. Erman [1] briefly, and Gressmann [2] at greater length, have shown that beyond question the third section of Proverbs (i. e. xxii. 17–xxiv. 22 or 34) is directly indebted, at any rate as far as xxiii. 11, to this Egyptian source. The coincidences, not only of thought but of language, are too precise to be accidental, and in one case (xxii. 20) a word which ought to mean *thirty*, but which in this sense is unintelligible in its present context, is readily explained on the basis of the Egyptian original, where it apparently refers to the thirty chapters of which the Egyptian book was composed.[3] Doubtless, too, Egyptian influence lies behind the figure of God as ' weighing hearts ' (xxiv. 12). Here as elsewhere, however, whatever Israel borrowed she adapted and transformed in accordance with the genius of her own religion.

Another illustration of the Hebrew power to absorb and transmute foreign material is furnished by The Song of Songs, which T. J. Meek has recently shown,[4] with some probability, to be connected with the liturgy of the Tammuz-Ishtar cult. ' The structure of the songs is the same (two lovers representing

---

[1] *Eine ägyptische Quelle der ' Sprüche Salomos '.*

[2] *Z. A. W.*, 1924, pp. 272–96, *Die neugefundene Lehre des Amen-em-ope und die vorexilische Spruchdichtung Israels.*

[3] Gressmann (loc. cit., p. 273) refers the *thirty* to the section, Prov. xxii. 17–xxiv. 22, which contains exactly thirty independent proverbs.

[4] *Amer. Journ. of Sem. Languages*, xxxix. 1–14 ; *Journal of Biblical Literature*, xliii (1924), 245–52.

god and goddess wooing each other and alternating in the praise
of each other's charms) ; the general theme is the same (love) ;
many of the phrases are quite identical. Both are liturgies of
the fertility cult.' But the Hebrew genius has successfully
effaced the original character of the poems to the eyes of all
but the Semitic scholar.

Substantial progress has been made in recent years in the
criticism of the Psalms. The possibility of a pre-exilic date for
several, perhaps even many, of the psalms is now almost universally conceded, and Wellhausen's famous dictum that ' the
question is not whether the Psalter contains any post-exilic
psalms, but whether it contains any that are pre-exilic ' is
irretrievably shattered. Kittel [1] maintains that the composition
of psalms is as old as the nation itself, going back not only to
David [2] but beyond him to Deborah and Miriam. Again with
regard to the subject of the Psalms, we have travelled a long
way from the collective interpretation, advocated so powerfully
by Smend in 1888, in the direction of an individual interpretation of at least very many of them. Babylonian and Egyptian
analogies have enormously heightened the probability of this
view. But the background of most of the psalms is as obscure
as ever, as indeed it must be, so long as the question of the
individual or collective interpretation, in specific cases, remains
unsettled. But the question has been more than ever complicated by the thesis, urged by J. P. Peters, that the psalms are
not ' occasional poems composed to celebrate some historical
event ', but ' hymns composed or used for liturgical purposes '.
Ps. 42 f. is, in that case, not the sigh of an exile for Jerusalem
and the Temple worship, but ' a festival hymn of the Dan
temple', written 'presumably for the great *haj* of Tabernacles'.[3]
For at any rate the psalms extolling Yahweh as King, Mo-

---

[1] *Die Psalmen*, p. xxxiv.

[2] So J. P. Peters, *The Psalms as Liturgies*, p. 26.

[3] Loc. cit., p. 63.

winckel[1] assumes a similar origin. Thus, in some of the greatest psalms there is the widest possible divergence of interpretation. Ps. 46 which older commentators connected with Sennacherib's menace to Jerusalem and which Gunkel treated eschatologically, is regarded by Peters as ' a liturgy to be used at the morning sacrifice ' at Dan, and by Mowinckel as one of the ' accession ' psalms. This liturgical consideration has also complicated the question of the identity of the ' enemies ' in the psalms. They are usually believed to be either influential renegade Jews or foreign oppressors : Mowinckel[2] ingeniously argues that they are frequently magicians, doers of *āwen* (i. e. M. believes, *magic*). As against the view that ' essentially the psalms are ritual hymns ',[3] Gunkel[4] maintains that, though they originated in poetry composed for the cult, most of them no longer pre-suppose any cultic action (lxix. 32) : in particular the individual psalms of lament were sung by the sick and suffering in the quiet of their homes and need not be associated, as Mowinckel would associate them, with the cult. ' Here, emancipated from cult-forms, the soul stands before her God.'

One of the most interesting contributions to the recent criticism of the Psalms is the suggestion of Peters that the Yahwistic books of the Psalter (1, 4 and 5) and the Elohistic (2 and 3) have the same origin as the Yahwist and the Elohist in the Hexateuch, the former attaching to Judah (i. e. Jerusalem) and the latter to the shrines of the north. The imagery of Ps. xlii. very plainly, but no less surely of Ps. xlvi, reflects the topography in the neighbourhood of Dan. The reference in xlvi. 5 to the streams which make glad the city of God ' surely does not describe nor apply to the Temple at Jerusalem, nor to any other sanctuary in Palestine except Dan, which it fits

---

[1] *Das Thronbesteigungsfest Jahwäs.*

[2] *Awän und die individuellen Klagepsalmen.*

[3] Peters, loc. cit., p. 24.

[4] *Die orientalischen Literaturen*, pp. 88 f.

exactly' (p. 63). He draws the conclusion that the Korahitic Psalter is a book of hymns from the Temple of Dan, coming from a period before the exile of northern Israel, and from this it is an easy inference that 'the similar Asaph Psalter had its origin in the temple of Bethel'. Naturally enough these hymns were later adapted for use in Judah and Jerusalem (p. 17).

ELEPHANTINE PAPYRI

Though they lie beyond the field of the Old Testament, a word is due to the Elephantine papyri which, like most discoveries, have raised a fresh host of problems. They give us, fifth-century documents though they be, a vivid glimpse of the popular pre-exilic religion denounced by the prophets. Of much importance for Hebrew religion is the question when monotheism was ultimately secured. W. F. Badè, of California, has made it probable that Deuteronomy is not yet monotheistic, but rather what he calls monojahvistic. Monotheism was first explicitly asserted and defended by Deutero-Isaiah. It is all the more interesting therefore to find the Jewish colony in Egypt recognizing, besides Yahu whom they fervently worshipped, other four subordinate deities, 'Anath, Ishum, Herem, and Bethel (unless Meyer [1] is right in his suggestion that essentially Bethel is identical with Yahu); and J. M. P. Smith [2] of Chicago is clearly justified in saying that 'the monotheistic view was never uncontested in Israel'. Of these deities one is certainly, and another possibly, female; and in the significant combination 'Anath-Yahu and Ishum-Bethel (if Ishum is to be equated with Ashima and Bethel with Yahu) one instinctively thinks of the two wives of Yahweh in Ezek. xxiii. In any case the general conclusion has been that the Yahu worshipped by

[1] *Der Papyrusfund von Elephantine*, p. 62.
[2] *The Moral Life of the Hebrews*, p. 234.

the Egyptian Jews had a female consort.[1] But here again we have another illustration of the provoking ambiguity that gathers round so many important texts of the Old Testament, for G. R. Driver [2] has lately argued for the possibility that by 'Anath-Yahu is meant not a consort of J., but his dwelling or abode.

CONCLUSION

To the timid this conspectus of the present position of Old Testament criticism may not seem very reassuring. Everywhere uncertainties abound, and, like the dove after the Deluge, we seem to find no solid ground anywhere for the sole of our foot. Hölscher remarks that there is hardly any department of the history of Hebrew literature or religion in which the assertions of investigators are not at complete variance with one another, and he goes the length of saying that of the work of Wellhausen and his school hardly one stone remains upon another. This is a gross exaggeration. Nothing emerges more clearly from the unresting advance of Old Testament scholarship during the last forty or fifty years than the overwhelming influence of that man of genius. The foundations he laid were well and truly laid. To him literary criticism was chiefly a means for securing an intelligible reconstruction of the history : and in their main features, still to-day his criticism and his reconstruction stand. We may consider the four great sources underlying the Hexateuch, and the date of Deuteronomy, in the seventh century—both of them discoveries older than Wellhausen—as a permanent gain, which subsequent investigation, however it may modify them in detail, is never

[1] Gressmann has suggested (*Z. A. W.*, 1924, p. 325) that the lack of a female deity among the Israelites may have tended to encourage the worship of ' the queen of heaven ' (Ishtar) which reached such a pitch in the later monarchy (Jer. xliv. 15 ff.). Ishtar may have then been regarded as the consort of Yahweh.

[2] *Journal of Theological Studies*, April 1924, p. 294.

likely to overturn ; and with so much clear, very much else follows.

From many quarters in recent years material has poured in, and we trust will continue to pour, which illustrates the social and political life and the religious thought and practice of the ancient East ; and it is within this frame-work that we must set Israel if we are to understand her. The problems of purely literary criticism will always fascinate a certain order of mind, but we must learn and are learning to pass beyond them to the larger problems raised by our growing knowledge of that ancient world of which Israel formed so supremely significant a part. Her significance lies among the things of the spirit, and especially of the spirit in its relation to God. No Old Testament science can make any pretence to adequacy which makes no attempt to recover, as Hertzberg has done in his penetrating study of Jeremiah,[1] the personalities that come to expression in the great literature of the Old Testament, and especially in the deathless pages of prophecy. For, whatever else may be uncertain, criticism has made it most radiantly certain that the prophets were incomparable interpreters of God—His servants to whom He communicated His secret.

JOHN E. MCFADYEN.

[1] *Prophet und Gott.*

Additional Note to p. 204.—Since this chapter was written, Löhr's book *Das Deuteronomium* has appeared. In it he argues that the ' Book of the Law ' is contained in specific sections of xii–xxvi, xxviii, which he singles out and discusses in detail, maintaining that there is no substantial objection to regarding them as the work of Moses. The law of centralization he also regards as certainly originating with Moses—the cultic correlate to the monotheistic tendency of the Yahweh religion. Other altars, however, he argues, of an unofficial character were also permissible ; but these were either memorial altars, or emergency altars, improvised for special occasions.

HEBREW RELIGION FROM MOSES TO SAUL

I

MANY religions point back to the authority of a Founder. Apart from Jesus, as the founder of Christianity, we have Confucius, Buddha, Mohammed, and Moses. But it is difficult to get at each of these (except perhaps the third) apart from later traditions. Moreover, there are other religions which are not provided with founders at all; we have but to think of Brahmanism, of the religions of Greece and Rome and of the ancient Teutons, to say nothing of the vast mass of animism met with all over the world. Indeed, the founder is the exception rather than the rule; and where he is discovered, careful study always reveals the fact that he has himself had a background; that if he laid the first stone, the stone had already been brought there for him by others. A generation ago there was a widespread readiness to doubt the very existence of these exalted but dim figures; more recently the tendency among scholars has been in the opposite direction. Germany in particular has produced a number of monographs—by Baentsch (1906), Volz (1907), Beer (1908), Gressmann (1913), and Sellin (1922)—in all of which, however the details of the portraits may differ, Moses is held to be a strictly historical person, and to be of cardinal importance for the religion of Israel.

But Moses too has his ' background '; that is to say, whatever conclusions we may arrive at with regard to the gifts of Moses to Hebrew religion, that religion contains a mass of elements which could not have come from Moses, since they are more or less familiar in every early religion, and lie behind all religious systems. We need not here discuss the general features of animism ; but even long after Moses we find clear traces of its characteristic beliefs in Israel ; supernatural powers or beings present in wells or springs, trees or hill-tops ; demons in the wilderness or in river-beds ; ancestors who must be remembered and served with careful ritual ; prohibitions which must be observed, and ' sacred ' places and objects which must not be approached or touched on pain of severest penalties to the whole community ; ' sin ' as a half-material pollution, divorced from considerations of morality or responsibility, but working out its consequences, like the Greek *agos*, from one generation to another, or conveniently transferable from one human being to another or to an animal. A whole significant world lay beyond the visible and beyond death ; but the power and wisdom that belonged to it might be possessed and used by diviner, priest, or king. True, later centuries both condemned and misunderstood these ideas, just as the Middle Ages, it has been suggested, misunderstood the genuine though primitive religious ideas that they condemned as witchcraft ; yet they were there, in the path of every religious teacher, and ready to influence and modify every religious reform.

But what lay behind them ? It is difficult to discuss this to-day without referring to ' the Idea of the Holy ' ; the ' mysterium tremendum et fascinosum' in which Otto has found the spring of all religion. Certainly, this sense of the ' numinous', of a God who was unapproachable and yet who insisted on being approached and on approaching His worshippers, was prominent enough in later Hebrew piety ; and in some of the quite early stories, to see God is to die, or to be in peril of death. But to say that Hebrew religion was nothing but the manifestation of this deep awe would be to neglect many striking data. God's nearness and accessibility, from the third chapter of Genesis onward, are as noteworthy as His remoteness. Hauer comes nearer to the Old Testament presentation when he finds in religion the three factors of experience, deliverance, and power. There was far more content in the early Hebrew ideas of God than is summed up in the shuddering fear of the ' numinous '. The very word for God, ' El ', suggests power and supremacy ; and from the signs and results of His power much can be told about its source. If God was at once the mighty and the mysterious, it would appear that to the Hebrews, as to the Semites in general, the might came before the mystery.

The early Semitic cultus, indeed, suggests that much could be known about the divine. There are traces, but only traces, of a totemic stage, when the fortunes and functions of god and tribe and sacred animal were closely bound together. But the tribe is throughout of vital importance. The group is often spoken of, and even thought of, as an individual ; but the individual is always bound up with his group. He must be initiated into it—there are signs that circumcision was originally performed, as with most primitive peoples, at puberty. Sacrifice, whether for the group or the individual, is the recognized means of coming into touch with God ; and the vital thing in sacrifice is the manipulation of the blood. It is the ' oneness ' of the blood, indeed, that holds the tribe together ; the tribal blood has a life of its own ; and it is respected and valued as much by God as by man. All this shows the Hebrew determined to come into relation with God ; and even if this approach has its dangers (inevitably, to his mind), it is indispensable, and he knows enough of God to be quite prepared to run the risk.

The same thing is clearly seen in the Patriarchal stories. These must be treated as ' sources ' for pre-Mosaic religion only with great care. Neglecting those which belong to the Priestly Document (5th century) we have in them a collection of ' sagas ' dating from the eighth century. In some cases they are plainly stories of tribal movements or actions ; such movements, indeed, seem to underlie the whole cycle of narrative. In others, they suggest the idealized or heroic individual; some merely hand down familiar traditions, some aim at edification. Some minister to national pride; some delight in a story for the story's sake. It is impossible to decide how far anything that is told us about Abraham or Jacob is historical, or to describe the actual religious ideas of the pre-Mosaic patriarchs. We can indeed tell much about the religion of those who collected and handed on the traditions; and since the traditions must after all have come down from antiquity, perhaps from the old days before the Hebrew migration into Egypt, they tell us of an ancient faith that held to a gracious promise from its God; of a religion whose hopes transcended the actual needs of each day's life and stretched into the distant future. The tribes had a destiny, and that destiny was ensured by God.

But what was this God's name? Did they know him, before Moses, as Yahweh? As is well known, J answers 'yes' to this question, and E 'no'. But is the question important for the student of religion? It must be, for with the name goes the consciousness of a certain character and relation to men. What evidence then is there that the name was known before Moses? Proper names containing the form YA or YAU appear to be found as early as the Babylonian first dynasty— e. g. Yaumilu, Yautum, and names with suffixes in Ya (meaning 'YA is brother', &c.). This would carry us back to the time of Hammurabi; and it suggests that Ya or Yau was originally an Amorite deity. There is also a good deal to connect the deity of the Patriarchal stories with Sin, the Moon-god. Both Ur and Harran were seats of Sin-worship; Beer-sheba, the well of the divine Seven, suggests the seven phases of the sacred moon; and the story of Jethro connects Sinai, the place of the Moon-god, with the worship of Yahweh, and the revelation of Moses.[1]

---

[1] Cf. C. F. Burney, *The Book of Judges*, where the case is conveniently summed up and the literature mentioned, pp. 243 ff.

All this, however, does not take us very far. Of the qualities of Yau or Sin we know really nothing. But we may find a little more help in proper names. Names like Yerahmeel or Ammizaduga (God is merciful, and My God (?) is just) point to the belief in ethical qualities in God, among the nomads and in Babylonia. Among the Semites only the Babylonian pantheon has a special god of justice; but the general idea of justice seems to be central for the Semitic conception of godhead as a whole. The god of the tribe or group is a sort of heavenly sheikh; and justice, as understood in the group, will naturally be thought of as flowing from him.[1]

Whatever then we finally conclude as to the origin of the Mosaic teaching about God, we can see that the name which Moses is said to have used already existed, and that it was associated with a deity tribal and yet more than tribal, who bore a patriarchal and also a moral relation to his worshippers. And whether Moses was influenced by the beliefs of his kinsmen in the desert, or of the Babylonians whose culture had permeated Palestine, the land of his ancestors, this is what would meet his thought.

II

To the later Jews Moses was, and is, the author of the whole of the Pentateuch, and the revealer of all the laws contained therein. For this, however, there is no evidence, and indeed all the evidence is against it; Moses is throughout spoken of in the Pentateuch in the third person, exactly as the other characters there; there is no suggestion of autobiography; and the laws which are contained there differ strongly from one another and point unmistakably to different periods in the nation's growth. But, as criticism has pointed out, there is more than one single tradition of Moses in the Old Testament; there are at least five. There is the Moses of the Priestly

[1] See Baudissin in Harnack's *Festgabe* (1921), pp. 1 ff.

Document, the most influential but the least historical of the
portraits; the aged legislator (he was eighty at the time of
the Exodus) who had Aaron constantly at his side, whose chief
mission was to give his people a system of ritual containing
many gaps, but elaborated in other respects down to minute
details. In E, his 'prophetic' character is emphasized; he
works miracles, as Elijah and Elisha worked them;[1] and the
Decalogue, as given in E, might be taken as the foundation
of prophetic teaching. In J, Moses is a national leader;
Yahweh's representative and agent rather than His spokesman—
and his Decalogue, as given in J, deals with cultus rather than
morals. Deuteronomy takes up E and may be said to prepare
the way for P. Moses is there the great religious teacher;
interested in cultus, but also in the whole national life. The
Decalogue in Deuteronomy is practically identical with that
of E; and if Moses must die before he enters Canaan, it is not
for his own sin but for the sin of his people; 'Yahweh was
angry with me for your sakes'. Finally, there is the tradition
of Moses which seems implied in the prophets. The prophets
say very little of Moses (though Sellin thinks that they say
more than appears on the surface); but they point back to the
sojourn in the desert as a time of ideal obedience to Yahweh;
and this obedience rests on morality and unwavering trust on
the part of Israel, and protection and the demand for Israel's
undivided worship in Yahweh Himself. And if the prophets
do not quote the Decalogue, it is the prohibitions of E's
Decalogue to which they are constantly referring.

But the distinction between these traditions, and the fact
that in reading the Pentateuch we have often to pass from one
to the other with bewildering rapidity, must not blind us to
their common elements. Even to-day, the composite character
of the Pentateuch strikes only the minority of its more culti-
vated readers; and this could never have been the case if the

---

[1] Cf. Exod. xvii. 8; Num. xii.

same elements had not been at least implied in its component parts. There are at least six definite factors in the Mosaic conception of Yahweh as we find it in every part of the Pentateuch. He is the deliverer, both at the Red Sea, in the Wilderness, and, afterwards, in Canaan.[1] He is the self-revealer; this is prominent in E (Exod. iii); but it lies behind the accounts of the different ' covenants ' in P; and it is constantly implied by J; for what Yahweh *does* shows what He *is*. He is also moral, or rather, He is regarded as the source of morality and law; the laws of the altar and the feasts (what there are of them in E and J) are given through Moses from Yahweh, just as Shamash gives his great code to Hammurabi.[2]

Yahweh too is clearly the source of the moral ideas of the Torah; these may be summed up under the two heads of honesty and kindliness, the two great tribal virtues and perhaps, at least in Oriental society, as rare to-day as in the time of Moses. It is true that the morality of acts attributed to Yahweh is not always the same as ours. Pharaoh was undoubtedly deceived by Moses' demand for a three days' journey into the wilderness (Exod. v. 3); and the borrowing from the Egyptians was not much better than Auncient Pistol's ' conveying '. Nor, to our mind, could destruction by an earthquake be regarded as ' appropriate punishment for inadequate ideas about public worship '. But these criticisms are beside the mark. In dealing with moral commands we have always to distinguish between the form and the content. As to what must or must not be done, ages, like individuals, may differ; that certain kinds of conduct are right because God wills them was the conviction of the best minds in ancient Israel; but in how few early religions beside!

[1] This is quite clear when we remember that the Book of Joshua belongs to the Pentateuch, forming with it what is known as the Hexateuch.

[2] Contrast the mass of cults in the Mediterranean basin, whose origins are attributed vaguely to some god or hero, or never so much as considered.

Yahweh's morality, however, is perhaps seen most clearly in the conception of the Covenant. This appears in every section of the Pentateuch. The Covenant at its lowest is a pact or bargain between two individuals, which one or other of them, especially in the absence of policemen and law-courts, is likely to break, and which must therefore be fortified with the sanctions of religion. At its highest, it is a promise by God, as one of the two parties, to act in a certain way, if Israel, the other party, fulfils, or even neglects, its corresponding obligations.[1] The force of morality can go no farther than this in primitive society—nor, perhaps, in advanced civilization.

Fourthly, Yahweh is ' jealous ' or passionate. He feels and wills, and does both strongly. He reacts violently against ' sin ', whether the sin is a wrong moral relation or the infraction of some tabu. He reacts against any meddling with Israel, His chosen people ; but with equal vigour against any ' flirting ', in Israel, with other deities. He also exhibits a number of other human or personal feelings. He is indeed supreme over nature. He sends the tempest, the quails, the manna, pestilence, and drought ; He opens or closes the womb ; He stays the sun and moon in the heavens. Yet He may be disappointed, surprised, angry, or even thwarted. He can ' repent ' or change his mind ; He may forgive or He may reject the prayer of His servant. And there is an element in Him of the capricious or, as we might say, the incalculable, far more puzzling indeed to us than to those whose thoughts travelled easily from the earthly potentate to the heavenly. Lastly, if we may borrow Otto's word, He is the ' numinous ' ; He is known in the fire, the storm, or the blinding light of noonday. His dwelling is among the mountain-tops, or in the mysterious seclusion of the desert ; and His glory overwhelms the beholder.

Now in all this there are many similarities to what we have

[1] For Yahweh as presiding over covenants see Judges ix. 4, and 2 Sam. xxi. 1–14.

observed in the pre-Mosaic stage of religion ; the ' numen ', the ' El ' who is supreme over nature, the deliverer, and the importance of tabu and of sin. In the details of P's legislation, indeed, we find other similarities. These, however, are not found in J or E, and only very occasionally in Deuteronomy.

But the differences are more striking than the likenesses, whether we contrast the Mosaic literature with the animistic ideas which we have noticed in the Old Testament, or with the earlier elements in the Patriarchal stories. When we reach Moses, Yahweh's character or personality is something new. Caprice or liability to change may be found in it ; but on the whole it is steadfast and actuated by a definite purpose. It reacts, as the psychologist might say, in a uniform way to its environment ; in other words, Yahweh is ' righteous ' or ' straightforward '. And His name has a meaning. The famous passage in Exod. iii. 14 may be interpreted in different ways ; and we must not suppose that the etymology there suggested is necessarily correct. But the Yahweh who thus reveals His nature through His name is much more than a mere ' Baal ' or ' Adon ', a lord or master. He is a God of *grace*. This word (Hebrew, *ḥesed*) demands a further consideration. It is as hard to translate adequately as the Greek *charis*. It is commoner, indeed, in the later literature ; particularly common (not unnaturally) in the Psalms ; but we meet it in both J and E applied to God, as well as to human beings ; and when we put together all the various instances of its use, we are led to think of the attractiveness or beauty, half physical and half psychical, of a kindly or (as we say) gracious smile, eloquent of resentment and self-seeking banished, and the presence of the eager desire to gratify and delight. There is indeed an aesthetic as well as a psychological and moral element in the word, just as there is in the word for the unclean, which suggests the ugly and repulsive as well as the merely forbidden. When, however, intercourse between God and man moves in an atmosphere of

' grace ' (and God does not only show grace, He looks for it), there is evidently no place in religion for demons or for ' mana ', for witch-doctors or for magic. The world becomes for us a friendly world ; and if we do not find its friendliness, it is our own fault.

Again, when we turn to consider Torah, there is relatively but little stress on cultus in J and E ; even in Deuteronomy morality is at least on a level with cultus ; and when we add that morality, like cultus, is regarded as a definite command of Yahweh, and an integral part of His worship, we feel at once the different level on which we stand, a level from which religion will pass to what we call monotheism. The writers had not made up their minds as to the exact meaning of existence when applied to the deities worshipped by other nations ; just as St. Paul had not made up his mind as to whether the pagan gods of his time were sheer illusions or demons. But, for them, there was only one god with whom Israel had to do. This ' monolatry ' was not the metaphysical belief of the thinker ; it was the conviction of the reformer and the patriot. We might perhaps best express the truth by saying that Israel could no more have dealings with another nation's god than an individual could have dealings with another man's wife. Theoretical belief is of very little importance without practical conviction ; the thing that really mattered Israel possessed. And Yahweh was so different from other gods in His character, as well as in His relation to His people, that time alone was needed for the further discovery that other gods could be no gods at all. It was but a step from ' Thou shalt have none other gods but me ' to ' beside me there is no god '. And the step was inevitable, because, for the Hebrew, Yahweh and Yahweh alone made and kept a covenant.

Thus far we are led by our analysis of the traditions current in the eighth and perhaps we may add the ninth centuries. Here are certain definite and striking ideas about God, connected with and attributed to Moses, not found outside Israel, except where Israel's influence has reached, and separable from the traditions of the patriarchs. What then was their source? Either tradition is right, and they came to Israel through Moses; or they came through some one else, and were attached by tradition wrongly to Moses; or they slowly took shape as the result of the movement of what may be called the common mind.

The last hypothesis must be ruled out. There is nothing in what we have seen of the pre-Mosaic religion to suggest the earlier stages of Mosaism. And great religious ideas appear to need great religious personalities to set them on their career. Once started, they may spread by a multitude of unknown missionary agencies; but, like a great artistic achievement, they need the genius to bring them into the world. The second hypothesis is equally difficult. Who else was there but Moses? Samuel, or one of the Judges? We can hardly conceive of a character earlier than the Exodus who could serve. Or shall we imagine some ' great unknown '? In that case, why should his name be lost and his work handed over to Moses? It would seem that, as Bohl put it, if Moses had not been mentioned, it would have been necessary to invent him. But characters like the Moses of our records are not invented. And if we attribute his work to some one else, there is still that some one else to be accounted for.

If then what we have called Mosaism entered the world through the mind and heart of Moses, how did it find its way there? It is manifestly no explanation to say that Yahweh was a storm or fire or volcano god. The God of Moses, as we have come to understand Him, was nothing of the sort. A man may be specially conscious of his god as he watches a storm, or he may see the signs of his god's power in the volcano; but that is not to identify or associate his god with a natural phenomenon. We must insist that the god who is thought to speak out of the whirlwind is not thought to be the whirlwind itself. Some mighty drama of wind and tempest may have roused daring thoughts in the mind of Moses, as they did in the author of the eighteenth Psalm, and in Ezekiel ; but the God was not the storm, nor was He even ' in ' the storm, in the sense that He could not get out of it.

Nor do we find much help in the suggestion that Moses learnt his Yahweh-worship from Midian and his father-in-law Jethro or Reuel (Exod. xviii. 5–12). Moses may have found a simple desert-faith in Midian, or some belief that the moon (possibly connected with the name YAU) was the one deity to be worshipped. But this gives us very little to go upon ; and if Zipporah was a Midianite woman, so was Cozbi ! [1]

The religion of Israel has generally been thought to be peculiarly free from Egyptian influence. But it has been urged that both Akhenaten's famous hymn, and the code of morals enforced by Osiris in the Book of the Dead, have left their mark on Hebrew thought. Did Moses draw his religion, or his morality, from Egypt ? Not his religion ; for the ' monotheism ' of Akhenaten was cosmic and speculative, and had no connexion with the fiery enthusiasms of the worship of the ' jealous ' Yahweh ; the only Hebrew literature which could be supposed to show traces of its spirit (like Ps. civ) is much later ; and Akhenaten's heresy was swept away long before the time of Moses. On the other hand, the resemblances between the morality of early Israel and the Osiris morality are too vague and general to allow us to build any conclusions upon them.

That the name ' Yahweh ' may have been known to the Hebrews in Canaan before Moses, and, therefore, to Moses himself, we have seen to be quite possible. But that any one before him ever meant by it what Moses meant by it, and taught to

[1] The use that Sellin makes of these two names, however fanciful, is striking (*Mose*, 1922).

Israel, there seems nothing to suggest. It was, in fact, a revelation. It may have come to Moses as a result of long brooding ; or in a flash of light, like the revelation to Saul of Tarsus on the road to Damascus, or to Jesus, as many have supposed, at His Baptism. He may have imagined that he heard a voice, as the prophets and Joan of Arc (to take a single more modern instance out of scores) appear to have done. However that may be, he became convinced that his God was a mighty deliverer, making passionate demands upon His people's obedience, and ruling all their social life.

And here we seem to come upon what religion really is, as we understand it ; equally advanced beyond religion in Athens in the time of Socrates and beyond the religion of the India of the Brahmins. For Christianity too is faith in a deliverer rather than in mere deliverance ; Christianity knows the meaning of jealousy—the warm personal relation which shows itself in anger as well as love ; and Christianity, like the Hebrew prophets, claims that religion should rule the whole sphere of conduct, and that through conduct rather than ceremonial will a man be accepted or rejected by God.

If we are right so far, we can see how Jesus is the fulfilment of Moses ; but we raise another difficulty. The main significance of Moses would seem to be his teaching about God. But was he not pre-eminently a legislator? What was the relation of Moses to the Torah ? [1] The Torah exists for us in the documents known as J, E, D, and P. But the authors of these documents did not invent the laws contained in them. Laws far older than the documents are embedded in each of them. There is every sign of growth, here as in the legal institutions of other countries. Law stretches back to the

---

[1] The word Torah means properly 'instruction'. It was applied by the Jews to the whole body of laws, ritual and moral, that they possessed— commonly called by them the Torah of Moses : and, more widely, to any official instruction or information given by priest or prophet.

earlier days of custom.[1] The civil sections of the Torah, both in Exod. xxi–xxiii and in Deuteronomy, point to the arbitrator rather than to the magistrate. How much then of this Torah is actually due to Moses? Have we at least his work in the Decalogue?

It is well known that the Decalogue exists in two somewhat different recensions, in Exod. xx and in Deut. v, and the divergencies, coupled with the further divergencies in the text of the Decalogue in the ' Nash Papyrus ', suggest that its original form must have consisted of ten short sentences—perhaps all of them prohibitions. There are really, however, two separate questions before us. First, did Moses originate these commands? In the case of V–IX the answer must be ' no '. For Moses was legislating for a community, and no community could have existed for a day which was unaware of these laws. If it be replied that the Hebrews before Moses had only thought of them as being applicable within the group, there is nothing to show that Moses would have thought of them in any different way ; certainly, most of the Hebrews for generations did not. As to I, if our previous contentions are accepted, he either did originate it, or poured into it a conception of God which made it new. II has often been thought to be post-Mosaic, since images are constantly referred to as existing among the Hebrews in Canaan. But this proves nothing. At best, images were tolerated on sufferance ; an imageless worship was the ideal. A law that is disobeyed is not necessarily unknown, or non-existent. And it is difficult to see whence the revolt against images could have sprung, if not from Moses. III apparently follows from I, whatever precise meaning we attach to the prohibition. The idea of a periodical rest in IV is certainly older than Moses. The Babylonians had a ' day of rest for the heart ', though whether this was a seventh day or a fifth is still doubtful. The Hebrews too had their new moons ;

---

[1] Compare the reference to tribal custom rather than law in 2 Sam. xiii. 12.

and it has been suggested that the Sabbath was at the first a full-moon festival, to correspond to that of the new moon so often mentioned with it. The true originality of IV consists in the stress laid, in both versions, on the transition from merely ceasing from work to resting ; from the ritual tabu to the moral and social provision. Whether this can be attributed to Moses it is impossible to be sure. But, in the main, the Decalogue appears to be a list of commands either Mosaic or anterior to Moses.[1]

Then, secondly, did Moses himself select the commands? 'No', many would answer ; 'no more than he can be supposed to have written the rest of the Torah'. Or, 'there are other collections of Ten Words, notably that in Exod. xxxiv (belonging to J) ; why should one alone be from Moses?' In the first place, it is impossible to argue that Moses could not have written the Ten Words, unlikely as it might appear. In the second, it is noteworthy that the little code omits all mention of sacrifices and feasts and of circumcision ; nor does it make any reference to patriotism and the religion of war. Had the code been written later, or by a mere compiler, these omissions would have been hard to understand. But it seems clear that Moses himself laid no emphasis on the ritual side of religion, and the earlier prophets speak as if sacrifices were no part of the religion revealed in the desert. As it is not likely that one of the prophets could be regarded as the author of the Decalogue, we seem to have strong ground for attributing it to Moses. If any Hebrew leader were likely to hold the specific commands in this compendium to be particularly important, it would be Moses. The question cannot, and need not, be finally decided. The Decalogue at all events contains the spirit of Mosaism, with no mixture of what was to come later in Canaan.

How much else is from Moses? It is impossible to say. The

---

[1] See the suggestive but rather venturesome discussion of the Decalogue by H. Schmidt in *Eucharisterion H. Gunkel gewidmet*, Bd. i, 1923.

rest of the laws—for a simple agricultural community ('Book of the Covenant', Exod. xxi–xxiii) ; for a monarchy (Deuteronomy) ; for a community which has passed from being a state to a church (P)—can hardly have come from Moses as they stand ; it is easier to associate with him the stress laid in the earlier codes on the laws of honesty and kindliness, not in their present form (where they are often exemplified in agricultural life, as in gleaning) but in their spirit. And the belief that all law is derived from Yahweh, and that therefore conduct between man and man is Yahweh's concern, as the English theory is that the king is the fount of law, is so distinctive and deep-rooted that it must in all probability be traced to him.[1]

We can thus arrive at what we may call the religion of the desert, or of Moses, the desert leader. All the points which have been noted hitherto as connected with Moses are appropriate to the desert environment. Religion is a personal and practical response to a god who redeems and rules his people ; the law is mainly confined to the simple provisions of the Decalogue. Such a religion has no need of shrines, priests, or ritual. On these, indeed, Moses appears to have been silent.

But did they exist ? Probably ; they had existed previously in Canaan. And in the course of a long stay, as at Kadesh, there would be room in the nomads' life for the shrine. If there were no harvests and vintages, there were the firstfruits of the flocks to offer ; the Passover was probably far older than Moses.[2] And the initiation of all the children of the stock, or

[1] We have already referred to Hammurabi and Shamash. But the connexion between law and the deity was in the ancient world for the most part conventional. In Palestine it was as vivid as the belief of many primitive peoples that the violation of sexual tabus is visited by some specially dreadful divine punishment.

[2] The story of the institution of the Passover (Exod. xii. 11 ff.) just before the Exodus is aetiological : a fact which will bring relief to those who have found it difficult to see how the Heavenly Father could act with the blunt and cruel favouritism of that narrative.

its survival in circumcision (a practice much wider than Israel), is pre-Mosaic also.

But what was his attitude to them? Did he command or adopt them? Later thought, which carries back to Moses everything in the established religion of the country (except circumcision), of course regards the whole sacrificial system as having been instituted by Moses, including those ceremonies which (like that of the scapegoat or the curious rite in Deut. xxi. 1–9, esp. v. 5) have their parallel in most primitive tribes.[1] But if we are right in regarding Moses as pre-eminently the revealer of God's personal relation to Israel, and if in addition we assign any worth to the consistent prophetic tradition, he will at best have tolerated them. They were aliens, though they could not be actually expelled.

Was then Moses a priest? In a later age, this question would be half answered by saying that he was of the tribe of Levi. But there is confusion in the earlier, and indeed in the later narratives, where Aaron, Moses' brother, is a priest, but not Moses himself. Originally, Levi was a tribe like the rest; but it was almost wiped out, like Simeon; it then became a kind of clerical caste or guild, perhaps making its head-quarters with Judah in the south, its members employed not necessarily to conduct sacrifices—any one could do that, at all events till the later monarchy—but, as specialists in such matters, to direct the worshippers' approach to Yahweh, whether at the altar or with the oracle. In Deuteronomy Priests and Levites are identified; in P, the Priests form a species, the Levites are the genus. If Moses then belonged to the tribe of Levi, he is not brought for that reason any more closely into contact with distinctively sacrificial religion.

Few things reveal Moses to the student of religion more than a comparison with Mohammad. Mohammad turned a collection

[1] See Frazer, *Folk-lore in the Old Testament*, though the zeal there exemplified for accumulating parallels may easily grow uncritical.

of insignificant desert tribes into a world-conquering power, as Moses turned a horde of slaves into a nation of freemen. But Mohammad stressed the future, and its promise; Moses the present and its duty. The gaze of Islam (in spite of its name) was really manward—to what man might receive and enjoy; the gaze of Mosaism was Godward—to what God required of man. Mohammad preached an unchanging destiny coupled with the constant assertion of superiority over unbelievers. The heart of Moses' teaching was that God, demanding all from His worshippers, and ready to give all to them, looked for their co-operation in the fulfilment of the pact or covenant which He had formed with and for them.

III

We have now to pass to the fortunes of the religion given to Israel by Moses when Israel reached Canaan. It is clear that in Canaan a new chapter was begun; and the effects of the new life there in transforming Mosaism must now be traced. Here, the only documents at our disposal are the books of Judges and Samuel. These, to a careful student, are packed with information; but, like the Pentateuch, they were written by men who understood little of the religion of the time of which they wrote, and cared less. It is necessary, however, to begin by considering the new environment in which the Hebrew religion of the desert found itself. This was, in the first place, if we may be forgiven the anachronism, founded on the principle of ' cujus regio, ejus religio '; that is, the inhabitant of Canaan conceived his god, or gods, as bound more or less to a definite locality. Palestine, as Sir G. Adam Smith has pointed out, is little more than a large oasis on the edge of the desert; and the invaders had but a very little way to go before they found themselves in the heart of their new country. But Palestine contains all the differences of the ' sown ' from the ' desert '. The ' religio loci ', as we may call it, is different; for men's desires and fears are one thing in the desert, another in a settled country of farms and fields. In the latter they are more concrete, as the forces that surround men there are more numerous. The farmer gives many more hostages to fortune than the Bedouin. His satisfactions, too, are more numerous ; and life is more sensuous and more furnished. Naturally, therefore, he will have a different conception of God, and different ways of approaching Him.

Properly speaking, there was nothing that could be called ' the religion of Canaan '. There was, and to a certain extent there still is, a general similarity in the culture of the countries lying round the eastern end of the Mediterranean ; and recent investigation points to the existence of what must rather be called Mediterranean religion ; a mass of diffused religious ideas underlying the specific cults of Crete, Greece, Italy, and Asia Minor.

Prominent in all these countries we find sacrifice as the recognized means of approaching the god, with constant traces, and survivals, of human sacrifice. Trees, along with wells and springs, are regarded as sacred, that is, as connected with the presence of a divinity. The reproductive processes of nature are half or more than half personified, as male or female or both ; the god has his consort, or the goddess has hers ; and there are stories or rites of the young god who dies with the dying year, and is mourned or brought back to life by his wife or his mother. At such seasons, religion grows excitable and orgiastic, as the worshippers, priests and people, join in wild laments or rejoicings. It would be an error to call such a religion simply licentious, even in its phallic manifestations. In the presence of the changes, the opulence, and the catastrophes of nature, the devotees imitate and try to induce the processes that fill their universe of desire ; and if that may entail acute sensual satisfactions, it may also rouse gloom and fear and horror.

Of these various elements some are more noticeable in one

place, others elsewhere ; but nowhere do we find any religious authority, books, creeds, or even morals. A priestly caste, as we understand it, can hardly be said to exist. The rites belong to the community ; the religion is spectacular and emotional ; it rests on the ' dromenon ' or even the ' opus operatum ' ; and the beliefs which originally shaped the rites have in most cases, as regards historical times, long been forgotten.

We find all its elements, however, in Canaan. On old Canaanite sites, Gezer, Taanach, and the rest, are the places of sacrifice, with the altars, standing stones, sockets for the sacred poles, and even the remains of infant human victims. The Old Testament books contain clear references to sacred stones and trees—perhaps also to the sacred birds associated with the trees and shrines. The local fertility-god has his consort Ashtart (written in our texts as Ashtoreth), who is identical with the Babylonian Ishtar, herself recalling the myths of Isis or Ceres or the ' Berecyntia mater '. Tammuz, or Adonis, we know, was lamented in a later century ; and it may be that the story of Jephthah's daughter carries the rite back to Israel's early years in Canaan. The solemn presentation of the ' firstfruits ' of corn, wine, and oil shows the awe with which these divine gifts were regarded ; and the presence of the lamp and bowl in the foundations of so many ancient buildings points to the ever-present mystery of death and life, and the ensurance of stability by human blood.[1] The prominence of the orgiastic element in religion is made clear by the number of words in the Hebrew language for ritual dancing, and the stories of Saul, David, and Michal, and the prophets on Mount Carmel.

The rites were far more important than the character of the god to whom they were offered. Of this very little was or could be known. If the crops failed in the drought or were swept away by storm or flood, doubtless the god was angry ; and the defeat of an enemy would be a sign of his good-will.

[1] Cf. 1 Kings xvi. 34.

What meets us, it seems, is chiefly a simple peasant faith in ' them above ', which often made great demands, which could afford keen pleasures, but which could never touch the soul.

On the other hand, though we may think of the Canaanites as simple peasants, they had felt the influences of the ancient civilizations of Babylon and Egypt. These influences indeed are easier to see in social life than in religion. The cuneiform contract tablets found at Gezer, the similarities between the laws in the ' Book of the Covenant ' and the code of Hammurabi, the prevalence of Assyrian as the official language in Canaan even among the vassals of Egypt in the ' Amarna ' period, and the echoes of Babylonian religious stories in Genesis and perhaps in the hero-tales of Samson, show how completely Babylon had penetrated to the Mediterranean.[1]

The influence of Egypt appears to have been political more than distinctly social. The Amarna tablets point to the un-questioned predominance of Egypt in the preceding century (in the XVIIIth Dynasty) ; and the story of Sinuhe (at latest *c.* 1950 B. C.) carries us back to the time of Hammurabi himself. A cylinder found at Taanach is curiously typical ; half the characters on it, like the object itself, are Babylonian, and half Egyptian. Traces of the greater Egyptian gods are absent ; but the popular divinity Bes has left many signs of his presence in Palestine ; and the knowledge of Egyptian antiquity in the Joseph stories of Genesis (8th century) is as unscholarly, and as shrewd, as that of Herodotus four centuries later, or an English traveller's knowledge of Indian religion before the epoch-making studies of Sir William Jones.

Now, what would be the effect of all this upon the Hebrews, entering the great oasis from the desert ? First of all, they would feel the social and economic differences ; they could not

[1] Traces of Babylonian religion among the ancient Hebrews have been already noticed (p. 224 f.). These were probably assimilated in Canaan.

but admire what would seem to them plenty, wealth, and even luxury. Imitation would naturally follow;[1] though, as we know from the actual remains at Gezer and elsewhere, imitation was awkward and clumsy at the best. They would build their houses and fashion their pottery on the models they saw around them. In their agriculture they were bound to be imitative; and with the farmer's lore, they would naturally learn the farmer's religion. The shrines and altars, the dolmens and poles, the feasts and sacrifices, were all waiting for the incomers. The house of their religion, as we may say, was swept and garnished. Moses had left them with no ritual tradition. They were not disobeying any word of his. Faced by new opportunities and needs, they accepted new means and duties.

But it was not a matter of imitation merely; it was assimilation. The rites might be the rites of Canaan; they could not well be anything else. The God was the God of Moses. If they learnt to sacrifice, they sacrificed to Yahweh. The sacred places they found were the places where Yahweh was to be met. They even used the dangerous term Baal (after all, the word only meant ' lord '), but they used it of Yahweh. Similarly, as they became a settled community, they needed some law or ' instruction ' for settling quarrels and disputes; the customs of their new home they would take over as readily as its worship. The ' Book of the Covenant ' and J's ' decalogue ' in Exod. xxxiv can hardly be anything but Palestinian in their main provisions. But the Hebrews, who had learnt from Moses to think of all their law as being the will and direction and gift of Yahweh, understood this as Yahweh's will also.[2]

---

[1] Cf. the story of Achan (Josh. vi).

[2] It may be suggested that the humanitarian provisions and exhortations—they can hardly be called laws in our modern sense—in Exod. xxii. 21 ff., or xxiii. 1 ff., sprang from the impulse that added the tenth commandment to the old Hebrew code: note also Exod. xxii. 20—' sacrifice, but unto Yahweh only!'—and contrast Exod. xxii. 11 (Yahweh) with Exod. xxii. 28 (El or God).

This predominance of Yahweh is the more noteworthy witness to the influence of Moses because life in Canaan meant intermarriage and much common social life. The story of Abimelech as ' tyrant ' of Shechem is of special importance.[1] At other times, the relations were reversed. But whether the Hebrews or the Canaanites were uppermost, it is the religion of the country, like its language, which generally has the advantage. Yahweh, however, did not cease for a moment to be Israel's God. Other factors may have helped in this conflict with Canaanism. Some Hebrew tribes the incomers found when they arrived; but these had probably not known Yahweh before; the very names of Asher and Gad appear to be divine, and pagan; the tribes were called after their deities. On the other hand, the incomers were themselves descended from men who had lived in Palestine, and they may have revived old traditions on their arrival, besides learning new ones.[2]

In spite of all this, the danger was very serious. For if Yahweh was worshipped like the Baals, what was there to prevent His coming to be thought of as if he were a Baal— a fertility-god, who demanded sacrifices, who punished the violation of tabus, and whose function was simply to provide His people with what they wanted? Only one thing could prevent this: the perpetual call to war. That aspect of Old Testament religion which most surprises and even shocks the modern reader was, paradoxically enough, in these early days, its surest preservative. ' The land which Yahweh gave to your fathers '; the phrase is current coin in Deuteronomy; but it is also used in the story of Jephthah; it is implied in the other

[1] Judges ix. Another act in the drama of Israel in Shechem is alluded to in Gen. xxxiv.

[2] The old sacred sites of Palestine are connected not only with the patriarchs, but with Yahweh—and with the Yahweh of whom Israel had learnt from Moses.

narratives of Judges—Barak, and Gideon, as also in the earliest parts of Joshua. Yahweh, Israel knew, had led them out from Egypt, and had destined Canaan for them. If they had to fight for it—as they clearly had—it was with His help and under His guidance. Constantly tending to settle down in virtual isolation from one another, it was the stern necessity of war which flung the tribes together, and forced them to emphasize the one thing which they had in common, the lordship of Yahweh.[1]

This sense of separateness, so necessary at the time, was aided by another institution, to us still more distasteful—the ' ban ', or military extermination. The word exists in other Semitic languages to denote what must not be used for common purposes; but it is only known in this restricted sense among the Hebrews and their kinsmen the Moabites. Whether Mosaic or pre-Mosaic we can hardly tell; it was probably not post-Mosaic ; it may have originated in the wild life of the desert ; but it was, like other Israelite institutions, connected firmly with Yahweh ; and, as such, unlike the borrowings from Canaan, it made for national purity.

It was thus by war that the dangers of assimilation, though by no means annihilated, were countered ; and when, later on, Israel had to meet the Philistines, a far more resolute and formidable foe than the indigenous Canaanite tribes, Yahweh became firmly established, in the land of the Baals, as God of Israel and God of Hosts.

If, however, Yahweh was still God of Israel, He was now very different from Moses' God of the desert. For better or worse, He had become a god of shrines and altars. We have seen that the sacrifice had no place in the Mosaic teaching. It may have

---

[1] This effect of war on the Hebrews finds an interesting parallel among more modern Jews : orthodoxy and (in the last two generations) Zionism have been strongest when anti-semitism and persecution have been doing their worst.

been tolerated ; it was not enforced. But in Palestine, with the Canaanite practice constantly before their eyes, and perhaps the memory of sacrifices and shrines before the descent into Egypt, the incomers made sacrifice an essential of their religion. No one was to ' appear before Yahweh empty '. Even the Canaanite practice of the sacrifice of the first-born child appears to have been followed, at least at times ; [1] the story of Abraham's interrupted sacrifice of Isaac (Gen. xxii) may be the descendant of a protest against the importation of the rite into Yahweh's worship ; but the rite broke out in later ages. Sacrifices indeed became intimately connected with social life ; they were the natural accompaniment of all family and communal festivities (1 Sam. i. 3, xvi. 5, xx. 29). Indeed, since blood was sacred, it could only be properly or safely shed at a holy place and with due rites ; [2] that is, every killing of an animal for food—a luxury that would be reserved for special occasions—was necessarily a sacred operation, a sacrifice. At the same time, it was the natural and prescribed method of approach to Yahweh. Whatever else the sacrificial system did, it bound Yahweh to the social life of His people. In the peace or ' quits ' offering, the ' shelem ', Yahweh and His worshippers shared the meal together, the choicest parts being reserved for Him ; and the ' whole burnt-offering ', the ' olah ', which they did not share with Him, was yet the appropriate expression of prayer or gratitude.[3]

Now, too, that Yahweh had His shrines, there followed a large extension of the sphere of the ' holy '. As is well known, the two apparently contradictory ideas of the holy and the unclean

---

[1] Whatever was the actual practice in Canaan, we cannot suppose that the custom alluded to in Exod. xiii. 12 was ever literally carried out at the altar : see Driver, ad. loc. (C.B.S.).

[2] Cf. Deut. xii. 23 f., and G. A. Smith, ad loc. (C.B.S.).

[3] Deuteronomy, the ' Holiness Code ', and Ezekiel show clear signs of the resolve, while preserving sacrifice as a religious institution, to purify it from its unsavoury associations.

are both rooted in the primitive idea of the untouchable, as likely to convey some danger if meddled with. The holy becomes distinct from the unclean, when the danger is thought of as arising from the God with whom the holy is believed to be specially connected. But the danger can be avoided if proper measures are taken. There is every reason to trace back this idea to Mosaic times ; indeed, it must have existed long before ; but now it can attach itself to everything at the shrine ; and by its side grows the category of the unclean objects (i. e. things regarded as distasteful or abhorrent to Yahweh) which, as we now say, are regarded as ' tabu '.

With the shrine comes the priest or ' kohen '. The priest is the natural guardian of the shrine. He may have been originally in Israel, like the ' kahin ' among the Arabs, the soothsayer or giver of oracles ; and this, as we shall see, was long one of his recognized functions ; but he was chiefly needed as instructor in the difficult and dangerous business of drawing near to the holy Yahweh, and of acting as intermediary between Yahweh and the worshipper. There were certain things that the worshipper might be shown how to do ; he always killed his sacrifice himself ; but certain other things, such as the manipulation of the blood, were too sacred or dangerous for him, and were best left to the priest. Was the office tribal or hereditary ? Not necessarily. Micah was glad to have a ' levite from Bethlehem ' as his priest—apparently the name here denotes a guild rather than a tribe (see above), and David appointed some of his sons as priests.[1] But the shrines were at this time the most stable things in Israelite life ; and the priests were, therefore, the most stable functionaries. They would naturally exalt their office ; and they would as naturally be resorted and looked up to in times of uncertainty or even war. In particular,

[1] It must be remembered that when we read of Gideon, Elkanah, Saul, or Solomon as sacrificing, we cannot assume that no priest was present to perform what would have been dangerous for a ' layman ' or non-priest.

the guardians of the shrine at Shiloh became for a time the centre of national life ; and like many a medieval ecclesiastic endowed with force of character, they were expected to lead in war. The city or the fortified post would grow up round the shrine, as in medieval Europe the town or the castle would often appear by the side of the Abbey.

Shiloh was regarded as peculiarly sacred because of its possession of the ark. Much speculation has recently been devoted to the ark.[1] Was it a box, or a car, or both? We cannot decide ; nor is the point material for Hebrew religion. The ark may well have owed its origin to Moses, or the desert ; it was certainly portable ; and, as the symbol of Yahweh's presence, when it was, very daringly, taken to the battle-field, the highest hopes were entertained from its influence. So far as we know, it was never itself worshipped ; but it was charged with Yahweh's holiness, and this made its neighbourhood very perilous, both for foes and friends.

Another sacred, and, to us, obscure object, was the Ephod. It is supposed to have been a bag, in which were kept the sacred or oracular stones for casting lots—or, perhaps, it was some kind of image. Gideon ' made ' an ephod, which certainly seems to have been, from the context, an image and not a bag (Judges viii. 27 : cf. Judges xvii. 5 and 1 Sam. xxi. 9). But the priest wore the ephod when he proposed to divine. Perhaps the word was used both for the oracular bag and the divine figure on which it might be placed. Divination, when practised by others than persons consecrated to Yahweh, was strictly forbidden ; but to ' inquire of Yahweh ', especially before a military undertaking, was as natural and praiseworthy as it was prudent. Here again, connexion with Yahweh was the touchstone of right and wrong.

In a famous passage of Hosea (iii. 4) the ephod is mentioned in the same breath with Teraphim. These apparently were

[1] For the latest discussion see H. Schmidt, op. cit., p. 120.

life-size figures, connected with worship, not held to be actually unorthodox, and yet suspected by the stricter Hebrews.
They were anti-Mosaic (see p. 236) but not necessarily anti-
Yahwistic.   Michal, Saul's daughter, possessed one (1 Sam.
xix. 13 : cf. Judges xvii. 5).   We know no details as to their
being definitely worshipped ; but they were perhaps objects
of devotion like the icons of the Greek church.   The soil of
Palestine has yielded a number of small figurines, chiefly female,
and used, it would seem, in private rather than public worship ;
the teraphim,[1] if larger, appear to have discharged the same
function.

In the more public rites, at the shrines, we find Yahweh
worshipped as a calf or a bull.   This, of course, is an even more
flagrant violation of the Mosaic Decalogue ; and the traditions
regard it as originating in the desert, and hotly attacked by
Moses.   The bull was connected with the deity in Egypt,
in Crete, in Greece, in India, and elsewhere.   It is not
strange that this identification should be seen in Canaan also—
if it was an actual identification, and not a representation ;
but since the bull was connected at the Israelite shrines with
Yahweh, and not with some other deity, the general sense of
Israel could support it, and even the earlier prophets, as it
would seem, did not protest.

Other objects were also worshipped, under the name or the
aegis of Yahweh : notably, the serpent, which was regarded
by some as legitimate till the time of Hezekiah.   The story in
Numbers (xxi. 9, E) is evidently intended to explain how the
serpent came into this honour ; and it shows as clearly that
the writer responsible for the story, although he did not attack
the practice, had no sympathy with it, and did not himself
regard it as an object of worship, or as an image of Yahweh ;
nor must we conclude, because we have no actual protest
against a particular rite or cult, that the protest was not or

[1] The word is used even for a single figure (1 Sam. xix. 13).

would not on occasion have been made. Indeed, for the circles which welcomed the narratives of J and E, idolatry was as alien as were human sacrifices to the public of Homer.

But we can now understand the transformation of Mosaism in Canaan. The change has sometimes been called syncretism. But that is an error. Two religions did not coalesce. But one of them, Mosaism, in a new environment, received a number of alien rites into its bosom, as the Christian church, from its early ages, received a number of rites and offices of which the Apostolic age knew nothing. By this process, the spirit of Mosaism might have been swamped. Much of it was in danger of being lost. But one element at least was preserved ; that Yahweh was Israel's God ; everything, therefore, that was, or could be, connected with Yahweh was legitimized or, as we might say, ' circumcised ' ; everything else was rejected and forbidden. In this way, Hebrew religion passed from being the religion of the promise and the code of conduct to being the religion of the priest and the altar. But it was the religion of Yahweh still.

We have spoken of Hebrew religion as having become the religion of the priest. To most sympathetic students to-day it is the religion of the prophet. In the period covered by this essay we find only the beginnings of prophecy ; but they must not be omitted. The outstanding figures are Deborah and Samuel ; though most can be learnt on the subject from the two sets of traditions about Saul. Prophets seem at the beginning to have been known only in Northern Israel ; at least, there is at first no mention of them in the rather pathetically isolated Judah. Some of the Saul stories suggest that the prophets were devotees mastered by a kind of religious madness or ecstasy, like the flagellants of the Middle Ages, or the dancing dervishes of modern Islam. As such, it has been urged that their origin is to be sought outside Israel, in Canaan, or in the frenzy of the wilder types of Mediterranean religion. On the

other hand, there is no trace of frenzy in the representation of
Samuel; indeed, we have an interesting notice to the effect
that the prophet used to be called a seer, i. e. that he was
originally one who by second-sight or in dreams could receive
messages from Yahweh; and this does not imply the appearance
of madness. That these messages were from Yahweh was apparently never doubted; [1] and this placed the prophet by the
side of the priest. The priest, however, was, as we may say,
' established '; he could always be found at a certain place, and
could be relied on to do what was wanted; and naturally he
was a supporter of the settled order of things. The prophet
had no local ties; he might appear at one place or another; he
spoke as he was moved, and his message was often disturbing or
even revolutionary. But in so far as he was the bearer of a
message from Yahweh, the prophet came forward as an extreme
nationalist; he was a separatist and a ' Puritan '. He and the
priest thus represent opposing tendencies in Israel. Psychologically, his excitement may resemble the Canaanite or ' Mediterranean ' ecstasy; religiously, he is a fierce opponent of all
assimilation. Samuel, we read, organized the prophets into
guilds; and the perils of such institutionalism were abundantly
exemplified later on; but from Samuel himself onwards there
was a succession of prophets who preserved their independence
and individuality, and, with a unique combination of saneness,
enthusiasm, and religious insight, form perhaps the most remarkable group of religious teachers the world has ever known.

We may thus see in the prophets, as they saw in themselves,
the centre of conservatism in Hebrew religion. But there were
other conservative elements, more particularly in the South.
We have already noticed the comparative isolation of Judah.
Nearer to the desert in social economy and in habit of mind,

[1] Only at a later period did some of the prophets, or their adherents,
accuse others of being prophets of Baal. Jeremiah and Ezekiel simply
called their opponents false prophets whom Yahweh had not sent.

Judah was, even in the later monarchy, less infected by image-worship than the northern kingdom. As a tribe, it appears to have been closely connected with other distinctively desert tribes, the Kenites (Judges i. 16, iv. 11), Jerahmeel, and the like. Probably (see p. 126 f.) it had reached Palestine from the south, and not with the central force. And these desert tribes long retained their simpler ideals of life. The clearest example is that of the Rechabites (Jer. xxxv. 6 ff.), who shunned the settled life of houses and farms, lived on as nomads on the borders of the ' sown ', and refused to touch the distinctive product of Canaanite culture, wine. We may see in them the champions of the earlier and simpler Mosaic religion ; and when, later on, the prophets formulated their own opposition to the Yahwism of Canaan, and protested that sacrifice had nothing to do with the genuine religion of Yahweh, these conservatives, like so many ' Protestants before the Reformation ', were ready with their welcome.

The second part of our period, therefore, brings us to what may be called the two religions of Israel. We must not think of opposing the orthodoxy of Judah and David to the orthodoxy of Israel and Jeroboam ; nor of the true as opposed to the false ; nor of Yahweh as opposed to Baal. There was no apostasy from Yahweh, even in the worst times of the northern kingdom, any more than there was apostasy under ' Bloody Mary ' or Charles II.[1] The real opposition, at least in our period, was between the religion of the desert and the religion of the field and the vineyard—between the religion of milk and honey, on the one hand, and the religion of corn and wine on the other. The differences were not based on creed or authority, but on the presence or absence of cults. Yet the question of cults was really a question of morals. First, because the Yahweh who demanded sacrifices was the opposite of the

---

[1] Neither Ahab nor Manasseh resolved to expel Yahweh, but to set up the cults of foreign deities, mainly for political purposes, at His side.

Yahweh who demanded obedience and fervour, honesty and kindliness ; and secondly, because the recognized cults themselves were the direct incentives to immorality and vice. The Yahweh who was enshrined at Shiloh or Bethel or Jerusalem had Himself, like His worshippers, become dependent on a place; the Yahweh who did not dwell in houses made with hands was as austere as His dwelling in remote desert fastnesses, as spiritual as His abode in the prayers and praises of His people. The opposition is seen at its clearest under the monarchs and in the prophets of the eighth century ; but its early stages, however little understood later, are to be watched in the first generations in Canaan.

The struggle is in its essence perennial. All the great conflicts between two religious ideals have reproduced it. But we must remember that to the Hebrews themselves the issues at stake were for the most part confused. We must never think of two distinct churches ; seldom of two distinct programmes. All recognize Yahweh as supreme in Israel ; but some look to a continuous appropriation of existing customs and cults, the possession of a kind of religious promised land which will bring prosperity and satisfaction ; others to the blessings of a stern devotion to the God who made Himself known to their fathers in the wilderness ; whose rule is ' hold up and hold off ', ἀνέχου καὶ ἀπέχου ; as implacable to His foes as He is gracious to His servants, and revealing His goodness, not so much in the gifts of a bounteous earth, as in the happiness of men joined in mutual loyalty to their God and to one another, when the solitary are set in families and when brethren dwell together in unity.

Ages of struggle with new forms of danger were necessary to bring out the true significance of the hidden forces at work in the thirteenth and eleventh centuries in Palestine ; but when we pass from the Old Testament to the New, and meet the blessing of the poor in spirit and the pure in heart, when we read of the ideal of the life for which few things are necessary or even one, of the better part which cannot be taken away, and the heart of all false worship in which covetousness and idolatry are to be regarded as the same thing (Col. iii. 5), we can appreciate the immense importance of the issues which were beginning to call for decision in the centuries between Moses and Saul.

W. F. Lofthouse.

THE RELIGION OF ISRAEL
FROM DAVID TO THE RETURN
FROM EXILE

OF the period in the history of Israel's religion, which opens with Moses and closes with the Maccabees, the central section, stretching from the accession of David to the collapse of the Babylonian Empire, is the most fully known. The historical records provide us with much ampler detail and a scheme of chronology which, while it is only roughly accurate, yet enables us to arrange the chief events in their true sequence and determine their approximate date. The preoccupation of the historians with religious and ecclesiastical interests has indeed left long stretches of the history in obscurity, even when they were periods of momentous development. This would not be so serious a drawback to the student of the religion, if the secular and the sacred, politics and religion, had not been so inseparably associated. For since revelation is a process in history and through experience, the course of national development was in no small measure the medium through which the religion expanded and attained loftier heights. And therefore it is not merely the student of Israel's history who is handicapped by the slenderness of our information. A similar disability is felt by the student of the religion. But here, as so often elsewhere, the question is not whether we have what will content our desires, but whether our knowledge is enough for our bare necessities. Many of the problems which vex us would not have existed at all if the historical records had satisfied the most elementary requirements of modern scientific history.

This is familiar enough both in the earlier and the later periods. The long and at present unsettled debate as to the date of Moses and the Exodus could never have arisen if the historian had taken care to identify the Pharaohs of whom he speaks. And a similar vagueness is responsible for the doubt as to the chronological position of Ezra's activity. But even in our more richly documented period the disproportion of the Biblical narrative is very obvious and the substitution of vague and conventional generalizations for exact and adequate accounts of periods, when new forces were released and revolutionary changes occurred, is acutely felt by all students who desire to uncover the roots and to trace the growth of significant historical developments. And even where it is individual experience, rather than movements on the national scale, which supplies the medium of revelation, we may have to lament our ignorance. How much controversy, for example, would have been avoided if the biography of Hosea had not left the crucial points in obscurity !

We may nevertheless be thankful that the period in which Old Testament religion touched its loftiest point and fashioned its most splendid achievement is that in which the history is most fully known. The Hebrew records themselves answer more completely, though still very imperfectly, to the demands of scientific history. We are also fortunate in possessing invaluable contemporary sources in the prophetic literature, while the records of other nations furnish us with welcome illumination. It is true that the historical narratives must run the gauntlet of critical inquiry and that the prophetic writings themselves must be sifted that later insertions may be detected. Nevertheless we are fortunate in the possession of contemporary documents of indisputable authenticity and records which preserve a wealth of historical information.

The accession of David to the sovereignty of a united Israel marks a new epoch in the national development the significance of which is discussed elsewhere (p. 133 f.). Inevitably it had a reaction on the religion. The military successes of David and his creation of a small empire lifted the prestige of Israel's God. The sense of national unity, created in the first instance by the religion, now gave that religion a stronger hold upon the people and a loftier place in their esteem. With solemn ceremonial and Corybantic enthusiasm the ark was brought into Jerusalem. Thus David's new capital, round which no tribal jealousies had gathered, gained at one stroke a unique consecration in that it became, as Shiloh had previously been, the shrine of Israel's most sacred and most precious possession. We cannot speak in this connexion of any centralization of the cultus at Jerusalem ; the customary worship at the high places or local sanctuaries went on as before, unchallenged and unrebuked. The shrine of the ark, in other words, had no monopoly ; but it inevitably acquired a unique prestige. For the ark was not simply the most sacred relic of Israel's wilderness wanderings, of that creative epoch in which the religion and the nation came at once to birth. It was so instinct with holiness, so filled with the ' numinous ' Presence of Yahweh that it inspired the Hebrews now with triumphant courage and now with abject terror, and always with that solemn and shrinking awe which the worshipper must feel most intensely where the Presence of the Divine is most intensely concentrated. A later generation felt that David's failure to build a temple for the ark needed explanation, and found it in the fact that the blood-stained hands of the warrior were unfitted for this sacred task. But it was really the conservatism of the religious instinct which controlled his action. For Yahweh was a wilderness God, and He who shared the wanderings of His people, had to dwell, not in a fixed building, but in a movable tent. The true spirit of the ancient religion breathes in Yahweh's protest, communicated by Nathan to David, against the king's proposal to build a house of cedar for his God (2 Sam. vii.

5–7). But Solomon, who was less enamoured of ancient ways
than his father and whose policy was directed to the creation
of a typical oriental despotism, broke with tradition in this as
in other respects. His block of royal buildings included not
only his palace but a temple. And in its innermost shrine,
not as yet perhaps screened from public view by the curtain
which later separated the Holy Place from the Holy of Holies,
the ark was placed. Hither the pious Hebrew, who normally
offered his sacrifice at the local sanctuary, might come at some
high festival to ' see the face of God ', that is to behold the
ark, which mediated, as no other object on earth could mediate
it, the Presence of his Deity.

Since the arts and crafts had made but little progress in
Israel, Solomon had recourse to Phoenicia. The temple would
accordingly bear marks of Phoenician design. But presumably
the models followed by his craftsmen had themselves been
affected by various influences, Babylonian, Hittite, and
Egyptian. The temple was true to the best Hebrew tradition,
however, in that it contained no image of Yahweh. That
Solomon provided sanctuaries wherein his foreign wives could
practise their native worship may be taken as certain ; that
he systematically practised these worships himself is highly
improbable, though occasional conformity is not out of the
question. But naturally the presence of these sanctuaries,
which would be attended by the numerous foreign traders as
well as by the foreigners attached to the Court, would famili-
arize the Hebrews with the rites of various types of heathenism.
They were not suppressed till the reign of Josiah (2 Kings
xxiii. 13). If matters had pursued their natural course, the
history of the religion would have been very different. Canaan
held a strategic position between the rival powers on the Nile
and on the Euphrates or the Tigris. A strong Hebrew monarch
would have been in a position to exact ample recompense for
support extended to either of the competitors for supremacy.

To the possibilities of the position David and Solomon were, we may well believe, fully alive. But these bright secular prospects were ruined by the disruption of the kingdom.

The deep discontent, which had been held down by the strong hand of Solomon, might have been assuaged by Rehoboam had he proved more conciliatory. But at his arrogant and menacing reply the smouldering fire leapt into flame. The northern tribes renounced their allegiance to the dynasty of David and established a kingdom under Jeroboam, while Rehoboam was left with his own tribe of Judah. The reaction of the political development on the religion was profound. Had Solomon's successor been as strong and as capable a personality as himself, he might have cowed the rebels into submission; or, having met them with fair words, might have waited his opportunity to rivet the fetters more firmly upon them. And thus the Hebrew State might have developed into a richer and mightier kingdom, after the common oriental pattern; and possibly taken its place among the powerful empires of the Nearer East. Under an established despotism the religion would have been stifled. There would have been one more commonplace religion, splendid in its ceremonial, but dominated by the Court, served by a sycophant priesthood and divorced from morality. The disruption of the kingdom averted this fatal development. The temple, which might well have been deeply infected by Canaanite tendencies, was not entirely immune, but yet was a stronghold of the purer worship. For in Judah the tendency to Canaanite heathenism had always been slighter than in northern Israel, since proportionately the mode of life had been more pastoral and less agricultural. But in the northern kingdom, though probably less on the East of Jordan than on the West, the division of the kingdom accelerated the corruption of the religion. For here the land was more fertile and the heathen rites, designed to promote the fruitfulness of the corn-land, the vineyard, and the olive-yard, had already gained a stronger hold. The religion was now further degraded by Jeroboam, who instituted the worship of the calves. It is true that this involved no intentional apostasy from the national God, for Yahweh was the object of worship. But the religion was inevitably coarsened when images, and animal images at that, were used to represent Him. And while in Judah there were movements for reform, such movements, except for the extirpation of the worship of the Tyrian Baal, seem to have been entirely absent in the northern kingdom. Yet it was in it, rather than in Judah, that the main stream of religious development was to be found. This was specially associated with the work of the great prophets from Elijah onwards.

The earlier history of prophecy is touched upon elsewhere (p. 249 f.). The problem of the prophetic consciousness is investigated (pp. 371–5) and the attitude of the prophets to the cult, the element of prediction in their message and their eschatology are examined (pp. 205–13). It is accordingly possible for us to go forward with the history without delaying over the preliminary and very important problems which would otherwise demand discussion at this point.[1] The crisis which forced Elijah into action was of the gravest kind. Hitherto the right of Yahweh to the sole allegiance of His people had apparently been generally recognized in principle. The cult of the local Baalim or of the household deities was not conceived to be any infringement of His monopoly; they stood on another and much lower plane. The worship of the calves was regarded as offered to Yahweh. Even if Solomon on occasion paid homage to the deities of his foreign wives, and that is by no means certain, there was nothing in this parallel to the action of Ahab. For the essence of this was that the solitary position of Yahweh in the religion was now definitely

---

[1] I have dealt with them in my *Roots of Hebrew Prophecy and Jewish Apocalyptic.*

challenged. Jezebel, the consort of Ahab, promoted with resolute fanaticism the cult of Melkart, the god of Tyre, her native city. The alliance of Israel and Tyre was to find its proper expression in the friendly union of Yahweh and Melkart. Yahweh was worshipped with as much zeal as ever. There was widespread apostasy from the monolatry which characterized the genuine religion ; but the foreign cult, though practised on a large scale, was apparently not deeply rooted. The prophets, true to the tradition of their order, offered active opposition, which Jezebel met by an attempt to exterminate them. Not a few of the people quietly stood aloof.

The story of Elijah presents historical difficulties which cannot be here discussed. In particular his utter despondency in the wilderness and at Horeb follows strangely on his miraculous triumph on Carmel. Yet we need some event of colossal character to justify the tremendous, the unparalleled, impression he made on the people. On the significance of the scene on Carmel it is not necessary to dwell. But a right understanding of the experience at Horeb is essential to the right appreciation of the personality and work of the prophet. He goes to ' the mount of God ' that in His original earthly home he may find the Deity who had revealed Himself to Moses. There at the original springs of the religion he seeks to renew his courage and his strength. He too, like his great predecessor (Exod. xxxiii. 18–23) will stand in the cleft of the rock as Yahweh proclaims His name, and His goodness and His glory pass before him. The cave in which he lodged may well have been identified in tradition with the cleft of the rock in which Moses had stood. It is only in the light of this attempt to experience for himself what Moses had experienced, that the significance of the narrative becomes clear. For Israel's God to appear in hurricane, earthquake, and fire, was in strict accordance with the ancient precedent. But the historian emphasizes the novel fact that Yahweh was in none of these, they were but the forerunners of Him ' who maketh his angels winds and his ministers a flame of fire '. It is only when they have passed and the prophet's ear just catches the whisper, so soft that it is just heard in the hush which has followed the roar of nature's most stupendous forces, that his sensitive spirit, attuned to the voice of God, realizes that God Himself has come.

It has often been supposed that the theophany is intended as a rebuke to Elijah for his violence in exterminating the prophets of Melkart. But this cannot be the meaning. The assurance which cheers the lonely and despondent prophet is that the forces he is to set in motion by the threefold act of anointing will bring a judgement on the apostate people so terrible and complete that only the seven thousand who have paid no homage to the Phoenician god will escape. So far from implying a rebuke for the use of methods which God cannot approve, the Divine voice assures him that the good work he has already begun in cutting off the prophets of Baal will be consummated in a judgement on the devotees of the foreign god from which no survivor will be left. The lesson which the theophany conveys to the prophet is that he should not seek to recapture the ancient experience, to galvanize the dead past into an artificial life. He had come to Horeb that he might touch for himself the elemental forces in which the religion had its birth. But centuries have elapsed, the methods suited to the primitive period have been outgrown; the God of Moses now finds in the gentle human voice, rather than in the titanic forces of nature, the fittest medium for His self-disclosure. The prophet ought never to have come to Horeb ('What doest thou *here*, Elijah ? '). Let him remain at his post in Palestine, with his face turned toward the future.

The question whether Elijah was a monotheist cannot be answered with certainty. If monotheism can be rightly attributed to Moses it might with probability be attributed also to Elijah. But we are perhaps safer if we limit ourselves to the claim that both were champions of monolatry. This was, in fact, the vital issue. Whether other gods existed or not, Israel was the people of Yahweh and should serve Him alone. Such a service included morality as well as religion. In Elijah's denunciation of the murder of Naboth this side of the prophetic message comes to expression. And in his combination of zeal for righteousness with zeal for Israel's undivided allegiance to Yahweh, we have that blending and interpenetration of religion and morality which were so characteristic of his successors. Nor can we doubt that the nation sympathized with the prophet's vindication of its ancient and inalienable rights and of the eternal principles of justice and truth. Perhaps the shock to the public conscience given by Jezebel's foul blow at the immemorial privileges of the citizen did more than her fanatical religious propaganda to prepare the way for the revolution of Jehu.

The incident of Micaiah and the courtier prophets of Ahab is far less important in itself, yet most instructive for the light it throws on the conception of prophecy. He recognizes no distinction in the source of their prophecy and his own, he allows the genuineness of their inspiration. Yet admitting this and not disputing the reality of their conviction that God was speaking the truth through them, he asserts without misgiving, his parallel conviction that his own message is true. He does not permit himself to be overborne by the prestige of numbers and professional position or shaken by the Divine origin of the optimistic prediction. The temptation to prophesy smooth things was great, especially to a king who did not bear patiently with prophets of evil. They, too, were under the sway of patriotic feeling. Micaiah's own certainty was more convincing to him than the certainty of another could be; and his estimate of the prophets had presumably been formed already. On earlier occasions he had probably been in collision with them. He felt that they had deserved nothing better at the hands of God than to be chosen as the victims of Divine deception. He had known them as time-servers and flatterers, cowards who shrank from speaking the unpalatable truth. So they were appropriately condemned to be the victims of real Divine inspiration and to utter a lie in the name of Yahweh, sincerely believing it to be a Divinely revealed truth. For ourselves the moral difficulty involved in attributing such action to God remains unremoved; but as least we can understand how Micaiah was driven to the strange belief that Yahweh Himself had inspired the prophets to utter in good faith a lie which would prove fatal to the king.

The narrative is of special interest since it brings before us the first example of the distinction between the false prophets and the true, which in later times became very prominent. We need not assume that the false prophets were, as a rule, conscious impostors. But they yielded to the temptation to speak smooth things, to flatter the pride or pander to the prejudices of their hearers, to gain money or popularity for themselves. The true prophets spoke the word of Yahweh with unflinching fidelity, even though it affronted the cherished prejudices of their people. Probably the official prophets largely degenerated as time went on, not merely through self-seeking but through a narrow patriotism or a mistaken loyalty to obsolete convictions. The future of religion was entrusted to those who declared with undaunted boldness the truths they had learnt in long wrestlings through the darkness till the truth came with the coming of the dawn, or which suddenly flashed upon them in some moment of radiant insight.

When, with oriental thoroughness, Jehu had massacred the whole family of Ahab, he butchered the adherents of Melkart. Since these could all be accommodated in a single temple, the number of avowed Baal worshippers seems not to have been large. Some will have been too wary to attend the celebration ; and indeed a usurper, who had ordered Jezebel to be put to death and had ostentatiously taken Jonadab the Rechabite into his chariot, that he might see his zeal for Yahweh, could hardly have expected his protestations of devotion to Melkart to be accepted with implicit confidence. Those who were simple enough to believe him and to act on this belief paid for their credulity with their lives. Thus the foreign worship was rooted out of Israel, though in the southern kingdom it was maintained by Athaliah, the daughter of Ahab and Jezebel, who seized the throne and massacred the royal family, herself to perish by a counter-revolution a few years later. From the first it had been recognized that Yahweh was intolerant of rival or companion. Ahab and Jezebel had weakened Israel's hold on this truth ; Elijah restored it to its dominant position in the religion.

Under the new dynasty the Syrian war continued. But when Israel's fortunes seemed desperate, the strength of her antagonist was drained by Assyria ; and thus Joash and Jeroboam II won back from Damascus the territory the Hebrews had been forced to yield and expanded the kingdom to an extent unprecedented since the days of Solomon. Wealth poured into the country, the rich became richer while the poor sank into still more abject poverty. The small owners of land had largely disappeared. Lavish expenditure on luxury, pitiless pressure on the poor, costly religious ceremonial, barefaced robbery of the weak by the strong, scandalous maladministration of justice—such were the characteristics of Hebrew society when the great canonical prophets began their work. And though conditions may have been somewhat better in the southern kingdom, it is doubtful if essentially there was much to choose between Judah and Israel.

At the time when Amos appeared at Bethel there seems to have been no anticipation in Israel that any reverse of national prosperity was near. With Syria laid low and the great empire of Assyria quiescent, the fortunes of the northern kingdom had never seemed brighter. But Amos is assured that an annihilating judgement already threatens the guilty people. His own conviction is that this assurance rests on direct revelation. ' Yahweh doeth nothing but he revealeth his secret to his servants the prophets.' But what precise train of thought led to his conclusion is not clear. Was it an inference from the moral and social conditions in Israel, a certainty resting on the ethical postulate that the righteous Ruler of the world could not suffer such sins to pass unpunished ? Or was it the sensitiveness to approaching change, a presentiment that Yahweh was going to intervene in history with a drastic judgement upon His people ? Undoubtedly Amos felt that his appearance as a prophet was a portent which in itself ought to have wakened light-hearted optimists to a foreboding of approaching doom. It is not unlikely that both causes were at work, the psychical sensitiveness to atmospheric change, the moral postulate that sin so flagrant as Israel's demanded exemplary chastisement. And keen political foresight should be taken into account. Amos probably began his career several years before the accession of Tiglath Pileser in 745 inaugurated the renewed movement of Assyria towards the West. But he would recognize that the inactivity of the great military power was likely to be only temporary and, since judgement was inevitable, Assyria would seem to him its natural instrument. He does not limit the scope of judgement to Israel. He believes that it will embrace the surrounding peoples. They are not judged for religious but for moral offences, they are punished not for idolatry but for sins against our common humanity. Still more significant is it that the same standard is applied to the conduct of Israel. Sin for him lies in the ethical not in the religious domain, though their punctilious and costly ceremonial is hateful to Yahweh as the service of evil doers, and the vice which was foul in

itself became all the fouler when it was practised in the domain
of religion.   Their copious sacrifices, their punctual tithes,
their thrilling, sensuous music in the worship inspire in Yahweh
only hatred and disgust.

·The prophet does not deny the election of Israel.   He
represents Yahweh as saying, ' You only have I known of all
the families of the earth '.   True to the fundamental thought
that the religion of Israel was a covenant religion, he recognized that all nations were at Yahweh's disposal and that the
choice of Israel to be His own was a free act of grace and
dictated by no natural compulsion.   Free to choose any
people, He had chosen Israel.   With this description of Israel
as a chosen people the prophet's hearers would be in cordial
agreement.   But they drew from it the inference that Yahweh
would stand by them, would deal leniently with their failings
and never, for His own sake and for theirs, contemplate their
destruction.   But the inference Amos drew was unwelcome
and incredible.   Not energetic support against their foes nor
leniency to their shortcomings was to be expected, but a far
stricter retribution.   ' You only have I known of all the
families of the earth—therefore I will visit upon you all your
iniquities.'   Their blindness to the inevitable future was
inexcusable, for the judgements they had already endured
were clear tokens of God's attitude and intention.   Famine,
drought, blight, and mildew, the locust and the plague, should
already have taught them that the worst was in store.   Foolishly
they yearned for the Day of Yahweh, the day of triumph over
all their enemies.   That Day was indeed coming, but it would
be a day of unrelieved darkness and irretrievable ruin.

Behind all this hot denunciation of cruelty and injustice
and this inflexible proclamation of judgement to come, there
lies an exalted conception of God.   It is not formulated in
the terms of systematic theology or the philosophy of religion,
but expressed in that vivid, concrete language congenial to

Hebrew thought and imagination. Yahweh is inexorably righteous, and there is no prospect for the obstinate evil-doer save a fearful expectation of judgement. And what stirs His deepest anger is not any ritual offence, it is injustice, oppression, and cruelty. Wherever on earth or by whomsoever practised, such offences are certain of punishment. But the unique privileges of Israel have made its sin the darker, its punishment the more severe. For Yahweh is no sentimentalist swayed from the path of rectitude by weak indulgence. And the will to smite is not thwarted by lack of power, for He is the Creator, the Lord of Nature, the controller of history. The destinies of all nations are in His hands. He moves them on the chess-board of history as He will, they are the instruments of His purpose. We do not indeed get any formal assertion of monotheism, but it ought not to be denied that, whatever view be taken as to his predecessors, in Amos at least no term short of ethical monotheism can do justice to his conception of Yahweh. It is disputed whether he so far modified his prediction of the absolute destruction of Israel as to predict the preservation of a righteous remnant. The answer depends on the view taken as to the authenticity of the closing verses of the book. It seems highly improbable that a forecast, so contradictory to what he has elsewhere depicted and so exclusively preoccupied with material felicity, should have been entertained by one so inflexible in his insistence on God's inexorable judgements, so austerely ethical in his conception of the highest good.

The other great prophet who laboured in northern Israel was Hosea. The problems presented by the Book of Hosea are difficult, and interpretations which seemed securely established have in recent years been vigorously challenged. At the outset we are confronted by the question how the biographical sections in the book are to be explained. It was not unusual for the older expositors to treat the narrative as purely allegorical. This had to encounter the weighty opposition of Ewald : and the arguments of Wellhausen in the fourth edition of Bleek's *Einleitung* (reproduced and expanded in *Die Kleinen Propheten*) made a decisive impression. To British readers his view was admirably expounded by Robertson Smith in his *Prophets of Israel*. In his article on Hosea, contributed to Hastings's *Dictionary of the Bible*, A. B. Davidson leaves the matter in suspense, but apparently with a leaning to the allegorical interpretation. This has been revived in recent days by Gressmann. Not only, however, does the actual language strongly favour the alternative view, but no successful, or even plausible, allegorical explanation of the name of Hosea's wife, Gomer bath Diblaim, has been given. Most interpreters probably still hold that Hosea recognized only some time after the event that his marriage was due to a Divine impulse. In that case the unpleasant description of Gomer (Hos. i. 2) is proleptic, representing her, not as she was at the time, but as she subsequently became. Or it may indicate an innate tendency which was later to find its expression in her conduct. The usual reconstruction of the history is then as follows. Hosea married Gomer, a woman at the time unstained by vice. He was already a prophet of judgement when his first child was born, and it was not till after his birth, or the birth of his second child, that he discovered the infidelity of his wife. The names of the second and third children may disclose Hosea's knowledge of Gomer's guilt. Whether she left him or whether he sent her away is not clear ; but they were separated, and she pursued with less restraint than ever her evil course. Later Hosea experiences what, either then or subsequently, he traced to the Divine prompting, the impulse to purchase Gomer when, forsaken by her lovers and sunk in destitution, she is to be sold as a slave. He takes her home and keeps her in seclusion, hoping that she will be cured of her wayward passions and that the old relations between them may ultimately be resumed. In this dark experience he sees reflected the relations between Yahweh and Israel and attains the conviction that God's inmost nature is love ; that He can never therefore abandon Israel to herself, but will lead her through discipline and penitence to a renewal of the ancient ties between them.

A number of recent scholars have asserted that this is a mere romance created by modern interpreters, and that, however beautiful, scientific scholarship should break with it. It may be granted that it has been ' constructed ' ; but it is questionable whether the substitutes proposed by its critics are as acceptable, and it must not be forgotten that they differ much from each other.[1]   To the objection that the story

---

[1] Marti believes that the woman whom Hosea is bidden to marry in the third chapter is another woman than Gomer ; but he takes the whole chapter to be a much later insertion and quite unhistorical. Duhm also supposes that the wife of ch. iii is to be distinguished from Gomer ; but he regards the second marriage as historical, both were women of unclean life when he married them, the first marriage represented the shameful disloyalty of the land to God, the second the punishment which God would inflict upon it. Hölscher, like Marti, deletes the third chapter but strikes out i. 2 and thus gets rid of the shameful designation of Gomer altogether. In this way he eliminates the representation of Gomer on which the current interpretation is based and takes the point of the story of his marriage to lie simply in the symbolical names given to the children. Steuernagel argues that ch. iii is not a continuation of i. 2–9 but a parallel narrative to i. 2 f. The story of Hosea's marriage with Gomer is accordingly told twice over, once in the first person and once in the third. On this view Hosea contracted one marriage only, with a woman whom he knew to be unchaste, but whom he had nevertheless to love ; for long he avoided all intercourse with her, and only after she had reformed begot the three children to whom he gave the symbolical names. Sellin's view is not dissimilar, but he supposes that the editor divided Hosea's autobiography into two parts, leaving ch. iii standing as it was, but transforming i. 2–9 into an introductory narrative about Hosea. In this way the error of two marriages of Hosea and Gomer's adultery originated. When Hosea first received the Divine command he shrank from it, and so the command had

has been reconstructed by a combination of elements derived from the second chapter with the biographical sections, it may justly be retorted that it is the unwarrantable refusal to employ the data in chapter ii which has led to the rival theories, all mutually exclusive and all intrinsically unsatisfactory, not to speak of the violence to the text which some at least of them involve. Since the prophet finds a Divinely intended meaning in his experience and suggests the parallelism between his relations with Gomer and those of Yahweh with Israel, we are not entitled to neglect the illumination which one side of the parallel may cast upon the other. It is here as with the parallel and contrast which Paul institutes between Christ and Adam, where also it would be a wanton neglect of the clues placed in our hands, to draw no light from one side of the parallel for our interpretation of the other. It is sometimes asserted that it makes little difference whether we reconstruct Hosea's experience in this way or that, or even if we suppose that the biographical sections are not a record of fact but a mere allegory. It is true that Hosea's doctrine is the same, by whatever way he came to it; but the criticism completely misses the vital point that it is not by any means indifferent that he reached his central conviction through his own tragic experience.

We are then to think of Hosea as at first, like Amos, a prophet of judgement. It is possible that all three of his children received their ominous names while he was still unaware of his wife's unfaithfulness. But it is more probable that the third name, Lo-ammi (' no kin of mine '), means that Hosea disclaims paternity. Since relations with Gomer were not

to come to him a second time (iii. 1). Gomer was not unfaithful to Hosea ; the three children were his own ; and he did not divorce her. It may be added that the transposition of iii. 1–5 to follow immediately on i. 9, which had been previously suggested, is skilfully defended by Melville Scott in *The Message of Hosea.*

broken off till long after the birth of Lo-Ruhamah, it is probable that his tragic discovery was not made till later. And
when it came, it would intensify the severity of his denunciations and make him more keenly sensitive to the prevalence
of the sin from which he had suffered and of kindred sins.
But his preaching would take on a more distinctively religious
colouring ; for he would realize that what he had suffered
on the individual, God was suffering on the national scale.
Israel was Yahweh's Gomer. She had been led by the pursuit
of agriculture into illicit relations with the Baalim, to whom
she attributed the gift of the corn and the wine, the oil and
the flax. The prophet denounces also the worship of the
calves. He finds the root of Israel's flagrant immorality in
her lack of right knowledge, an ignorance for which the official
leaders of religion are responsible.

During all this time Gomer was sinking deeper in the mire.
All relations with Hosea were presumably broken off. But in
leaving him she had left behind her an aching heart in an
empty home. His love for her remained unabated, and when
her paramours had deserted her and slavery stared her in the
face, he took, at Yahweh's instigation, the opportunity thus
offered him and purchased her. Legally she became his
property and was wholly at his disposal. To the discipline of
adversity there was now added the discipline of isolation from
evil companions and renunciation of the pleasures of sin. And
as the prophet meditated on the motives of his action he saw
into the heart of God. He found there a love for Israel deeper,
purer, and diviner than his own love for Gomer ; and he looked
forward with confidence to the reunion of Israel with the
bridegroom of her youth. She, too, must know the bitterness
of desertion by the false gods and the loss of her worldly
resources. Then, like the prodigal in the far country, she would
yearn for her proper home and make the great resolve, ' I will
return and go unto my first husband, for then was it better

with me than now '. Back to the wilderness, where of old they had plighted their troth, Yahweh would allure her and speak to her heart. He would restore the penitent nation, healing all her backslidings and giving His love full scope. Restored to her fruitful land she would know that it was He, and not her lovers, who had so bountifully bestowed upon her the corn, the wine, and the oil.

Thus while Amos is the prophet of God's strict, and indeed implacable, righteousness, Hosea is the prophet of His imperishable love which can never abandon His people to ruin but must lead them back through repentance to His full favour again. If the appropriate motto for Amos is, ' You only have I known of all the nations of the earth, therefore I will visit upon you all your iniquities ', a motto for Hosea might be, ' How shall I give thee up, Ephraim ? . . . mine heart is turned within me, my compassions are kindled together '.[1]

The fall of the northern kingdom left Judah as practically the sole representative of the religion of Israel. So far as that religion was of the lower type, it would not long survive the collapse of the State and exile of the people to a foreign land. The loftier religion represented by Amos and Hosea was as yet too feebly rooted, long to survive the shock of transplantation. The preservation of the religion when, more than a century later, Jerusalem fell and Judah followed Israel into exile, was due to the work done by prophet and reformer in nursing the frail plant into a lustier growth. Already Isaiah had been at work for nearly a score of years. He like Micah and Ezekiel stood in the succession of Amos, while Jeremiah and the Second Isaiah were the spiritual heirs of Hosea. The characteristic teaching of Isaiah is contained, explicitly or implicitly, in the vision in which he became conscious of his

[1] I cannot assent to the view taken by many of the most eminent critics that the closing section of the second chapter (ii. 14–23) or xiv. 1–9 should be regarded as additions to Hosea's genuine work.

call. As from the temple threshold he looks towards the ark he falls into an ecstasy and with clairvoyant gaze sees Yahweh, who was thought by the Hebrews to be enthroned on the cherubim, which spread their wings above the ark. The attendant seraphim express in their demeanour their utter abasement in God's presence and their readiness for instant service. Their antiphonal chant proclaims His holiness and His glory. Nature trembles at their proclamation and the temple is filled with smoke, the reaction of the Holy God to the presence of the unclean man. That God was the thrice holy, that mortal man was too impure to look upon Him and live, all this was dogma well known to Isaiah. Now he knew it as a soul-shattering experience, confessing himself to be worthy of death that he, a man of unclean lips and implicated in the uncleanness of his people, should have seen the King in His majesty. The seraph touches his lips with the glowing coal, cleansing him from his impurity and his sin. Now at last he can hear God in consultation with His heavenly court, and offers himself for whatever mission it may be of which they speak. His offer is accepted, accompanied by the warning that his message will serve only to harden his people in their unbelief, their ignorance and their sin. And it will have for its sequel a judgement so devastating that but a tenth of the people will be left, as the stump of a tree remains when the tree itself is cut down. Then this also will be rooted up and doomed to the flames.[1]

The supreme thing in this vision is the overwhelming sense of God, His unapproachable Divinity, His awful purity, His

---

[1] The view that the record of the vision has been deeply coloured by the prophet's disillusion in the early years of his ministry is, I believe, quite incorrect. Even if we had to reckon with an experience created entirely out of his own mental and emotional state, such an explanation would probably be unnecessary. But if we are dealing with a real revelation, there is no warrant for it.

sublime majesty. Isaiah feels in the depths of his being the shock of contrast between the Divine and the human, the holy and the unclean. Utterly broken, he faces the King of Terrors, aware that instant death is the penalty if a mortal, though without intention, surprises the secret, reserved for the immortals and closely guarded by them, and looks on the face of God. He learns the goodness and the grace of God to the man of lowly and contrite heart ; he learns also that the mission which he has accepted will prove a failure, and that judgement is to come on the sinful people to the uttermost. Yet, although it does not seem to be expressed in his vision, either then, or at most a little later, he is so assured that a remnant will turn to God and be spared that he embodies his conviction in the name of his son, Shear-jashub. For Zion is Yahweh's earthly home, therefore it will not be overthrown ; and since a city implies inhabitants, some of the people must be spared. He had himself been pardoned and others might share his experience. It is possible indeed that at the outset he thought of the northern kingdom as doomed to destruction and identified Judah with the remnant to be spared. But if so, he found reason ere long to correct this application of his doctrine. For when Ahaz refused, in his panic at the coalition of Syria and Ephraim, to trust in God and refrain from invoking the aid of Assyria, the prophet recognized that the king and the people as a whole were too disloyal to be spared. Judgement must come not on Israel alone but on Judah. Of this judgement Assyria was to be the instrument, to be checked by no human power till all the Divine purpose had been fulfilled. Then for its arrogance and blasphemy the mighty empire, which is as nothing in comparison with Almighty God, would be broken and thrown aside. Hence the prophet discourages all attempts of Judah to throw off the irksome weight of Assyria which, against his counsel, it had invited. For Assyria could not be overthrown by any combination of her restive subjects, even when these were supported by Egypt. Yahweh reserved it for Himself to deal the annihilating blow. Then the age of blessedness will begin under its Messianic King, a ruler of Davidic stock who, after crushing his foes in sanguinary battle, will reign as Prince of Peace.

A junior contemporary of Isaiah was Micah. He was a man of the people belonging, unlike Isaiah, to the country districts ; and his denunciations of the oppression of the poor by the rich is more scathing than Isaiah's, in that it is the fruit not simply of observation but of bitter experience. The critical problems of the book are difficult, and not a little in the last four chapters probably belongs to a later period. The most notable passage (vi. 1–8) may plausibly be assigned to the reign of Manasseh and may be the utterance of Micah himself.[1] It closes with the noble words, ' He hath shown thee, O man, what is good : and what doth Yahweh require of thee but to do justly, to love mercy, and to walk humbly with thy God ? '

We are told (2 Kings xviii. 4) that Hezekiah carried through a reformation of the cultus, which included the abolition of the high places or local sanctuaries, the destruction of the Asherah, and the obelisks, and in particular the breaking up of the brazen serpent made by Moses, to which incense was offered. The historicity of this reformation has been questioned, though it finds support in the reference which the Rabshakeh is reported to have made to it (v. 22). It has even been thought

---

[1] The tendency of critical opinion on the whole has been to leave Micah little beyond the first three chapters. Wellhausen is not disinclined to recognize his authorship of vi. 1–8 ; and Duhm (*Anmerkungen* [1911], p. 52, *Israels Propheten* [1916], p. 103 f.) is disposed to favour his authorship of vi. 1–vii. 7, and to regard these four poems as written in Micah's old age. He still leaves the alternative open that they are the work of an important prophet, otherwise unknown, of the time of Manasseh. He assigns chs. iv and v to the second century, and regards vii. 8–20 as also very late.

that some form of the Deuteronomic Code may have been at the basis of the reformation. But the absence of any reference to a Law Book in this connexion does not favour the hypothesis. It is more probable that the reformation was due to the inspiration of Isaiah. The delivery of Jerusalem, when its capture by Sennacherib seemed certain, and the withdrawal of the Assyrian army nobly vindicated the faith of Isaiah. But the terrible losses which had been inflicted on the country in men, money, and material probably created a reaction against the higher teaching of the prophets, of which advantage was taken by the religious reactionaries when Hezekiah was succeeded by Manasseh. During his long reign the old religious abuses came back and new ones were added. The local sanctuaries were restored, astral worship was introduced on a large scale, child sacrifice became terribly prevalent, divination and occult arts were practised. The chronicler informs us that Manasseh was taken captive to Babylon by the king of Assyria, that he repented in exile and was restored (2 Chron. xxxiii. 11–13), whereupon he instituted a religious reformation (vv. 15–17). In view of the silence of Kings this statement, in all its parts, is very questionable. It is possible that the captivity may be historical; but if Manasseh repented and carried through a reformation, the author of Kings, in representing his career as one of unrelieved wickedness and as deciding the fate of Judah (2 Kings xxi. 1–16, xxiii. 26 f., xxiv. 3 f.; cf. Jer. xv. 4), has done a grave injustice to his memory, all the more remarkable that the repentance of Ahab and the consequent postponement of retribution are carefully recorded (1 Kings xxi. 27–9).

During all this period the ground gained by the great prophets and their followers seemed to have been lost. The historian does not explicitly say, but his language suggests, that the representatives of the true religion, who opposed the revival of old disloyalties and the introduction of new abominations, were the victims of a sanguinary persecution. But the good work could be continued in concealment, and it is not improbable that during this time the Law Book, which was discovered in the eighteenth year of Josiah, was compiled. Into the tangled problems connected with the sources employed in its composition, and the relation in which it stood to the Book of Deuteronomy as we know it, it is not necessary for our purpose to enter (pp. 199–204). Nor yet is it necessary to examine the theories, stated in their most extreme form by Hölscher, which would bring the composition of Deuteronomy down to a much later period (pp. 199–202). It is here assumed that the generally accepted view is correct, that the Deuteronomic Code in some form or other was the Law Book, the discovery of which led to Josiah's Reformation.

In view of the great prominence given in modern critical discussions to the centralization of the worship at Jerusalem, it may be as well to point out that the supreme aim of the reformers was to extirpate idolatry. The record of the actual course of the reform (2 Kings xxiii) contains far more about the suppression of idolatry than about the abolition of the high places. The Deuteronomic Code itself strongly emphasizes the necessity for taking drastic steps against idolatry; and its opening command, requiring the destruction of the high places of the Canaanites, is connected with the idolatry which has been practised there (Deut. xii. 2 f.). But on this follows the command that in an unnamed place, to be subsequently chosen by God, the Hebrew cultus is to be concentrated (vv. 5–27). And certainly as the Book now stands this injunction is intended to be the dominant feature of the legislation. But it was presumably dominant as a means rather than an end in itself. The suppression of the local sanctuaries cut off at a stroke the rank growths of idolatrous worship outside Jerusalem, while with a single sanctuary the purity of the cultus could be easily controlled. It also secured the unity of Yahweh, which had been endangered by the differentiation of Yahweh into the Yahweh of this shrine and the Yahweh of that. Its principle was, ' Yahweh our God, Yahweh is one ', that is one and not a multitude of Yahwehs. If on the one side the Code was the creation of lawyer and priest, it had behind it also the work of the great prophets. Its ethical quality was high, it stood for justice and humanitarianism, and showed a special care for the poor and defenceless. The reform, it is true, did not go deep enough, and it introduced into religion a legalistic temper which was to grow stronger till in course of time it became supreme. But its practical reforms were largely on the right lines, and if they had been faithfully carried out social and religious life would have been greatly elevated and enriched.

The advance made by Jeremiah was not so much in the formulation of new doctrine as in the fundamental transformation of the very conception of religion. Since he was himself the great contribution he made to religion, and his supreme doctrine was rooted in his experience, we can estimate the advance he made only through a sympathetic study of his personality. This was of a very rare and exquisite type. Nature seemed to have fitted him but ill for the stern life of conflict to which his vocation condemned him. He was sensitive and high-strung, timid and shrinking, not self-reliant, not marked out for leadership, not a dominant personality. He did not love the limelight but courted obscurity. Almost morbidly conscious of his natural deficiencies, a public career was terrifying to him. Acutely distressed by strife and bitterness, he longed above all for quiet, untroubled days in peaceful retirement. Yet the victory of his courage is the more amazing that it triumphed again and again over his timidity. In unfaltering tones he rebukes the sins and follies of his countrymen, outrages their cherished prejudices, risks his life again and again, and is indeed more than once doomed to apparently inevitable execution. He possessed in an exceptional degree the more feminine qualities—sympathy, intuition, delicacy of feeling. He was in his measure ' a man of sorrows ', overwhelmed with immeasurable grief for the sins, the follies, and the calamities of his people. This richness of the emotional nature was accompanied by an unusual gift of psychological analysis. Beyond his predecessors he was versed in man's inner motives, he understood the windings of the human heart because he had so often explored his own. No prophet reveals to us so fully his inmost thoughts and emotions. Out of these experiences his great contribution to theology was created. If in other respects he does not add much to his predecessors, yet he is the greatest of the prophets, since all that he inherited was deepened and made more inward, and since in his anticipation of the New Covenant (xxxi. 31–4) he made the supreme advance by which the individual rather than the nation became the unit of religion. We can hardly over-estimate the greatness of this conception or the revolution it involved. It marked an epoch-making change in the very conception of religion. For religion had been conceived as primarily a relation between the people and its God. This relation, it is true, is to continue, for the New Covenant will be made with the nation. But it is of such a character that the individual comes to full recognition. His relation to God is not secondary and indirect, mediated through the nation; it is direct and primary. Each man is for himself the object of God's renewing grace and spiritual illumination. Thus Jeremiah became the prophet of individualism in religion.

It was in his own experience that this doctrine had its birth. His writings reveal to us an intimacy with God for which we have no earlier parallel. He was driven to it by the failure of human fellowship, by the derision and persecution which his faithfulness brought upon him. Lonely and misunderstood, despised, forsaken, and hated, he was driven to cast himself and all the weight of his cares and sorrows upon God. In such intimacy of personal fellowship he realizes that he has discovered the religious ideal. He looks forward to a time when what has come to be a necessity for himself will be an experience shared by all the people of God.

The downfall of the Jewish State and the destruction of the temple had not the disastrous consequences to the religion which attended the parallel experience of the northern kingdom. The work of the great prophets and reformers had strengthened the hold and raised the quality of the religion to such an extent that the exile proved its opportunity rather than its doom. Detached from the cramping connexion with a tiny country and a material structure, it was thrown on its own inner resources and forced to develop the more immaterial forms of worship. The fascinations of the familiar cult at the local sanctuaries could no longer ensnare the exiles, and thus one great incentive to heathen worship was removed. In a foreign land confronted by a magnificent cult, beside which that of their own temple seemed mean, if they resisted the temptation to abandon their faith and to become devotees of the gods by whom Yahweh seemed to have been worsted, they would inevitably be thrown much more on the defensive and be forced to accentuate their racial and religious peculiarities. Thus circumcision and the Sabbath gained a new prominence at this time. Pious hands collected the relics of the past—history, prophecy, legislation, wisdom, and sacred song. The law of the single sanctuary had a better chance of acceptance when the exiles returned, because the majority of them, born in Babylonia, had never felt the spell of the local sanctuaries in Canaan which had meant so much to their fathers.

It has been usual to emphasize the affinities of Ezekiel with Jeremiah ; and it is true that they took a similar view of the actual situation and its inevitable sequel. But while the affinities lie on the surface, the differences are fundamental.

Jeremiah was of priestly lineage, probably an heir to the great traditions of the family of Abiathar, and to the deep resentment his descendants must have felt that he had been forced to resign the custody of the ark to Zadok. But he was essentially a layman in his temper and outlook and, so far from nursing resentment at the downfall of his family, he incurred its deadly hostility by advocating the reform of Josiah (Jer. xi. 1–8, 18–23, xii. 5 f.) [1] which gave a monopoly in privilege to the rival house of Zadok. Not indeed that sanctuary and ceremonial were of vital importance to him ; but the reform was a blow struck against idolatry and for social righteousness. Ezekiel belonged to the family of Zadok, the temple was central for his ideal of religion. He took sides with his own family against the disestablished priests of the local sanctuaries (Ezek. xliv. 10–16). Both prophets were individualists. But the difference between them is here acute. Jeremiah puts the stress on personal religion, Ezekiel on personal responsibility. And this is significant of a distinction more radical still—their conception of God and attitude to Him. Jeremiah confronts God face to face, he is daring in his language to Him, not shrinking from expostulation, from disappointment, or even embittered reproach. But he knows also the intimacy of close, personal fellowship with Him. Ezekiel is overwhelmed by the greatness of God. He never forgets the infinite distance which separates the creature from his Creator, the weak and perishable ' son of man ' [2] from the Holy, the Omnipotent, and the ever-living God. The vision of God, in which his

[1] This is denied by Marti, whose view has been accepted by several scholars. My reasons for the view taken in the text are given in my commentary on Jeremiah, and I am glad that I can now refer to Skinner, *Prophecy and Religion* (chs. vi, vii), and G. A. Smith, *Jeremiah*, pp. 134–61.

[2] So Ezekiel is constantly addressed. Since the term has gained quite other associations, its sense might be better conveyed by some such paraphrase as ' child of earth ' or ' frail mortal ' as I have suggested in *The Messiah and the Son of Man*, p. 20.

call came to him, burnt deep into his soul the sense of the sovereignty and the holiness of God. Yahweh is for him a self-centred egoist who bends the whole course of history to His own glory. One of the strangest features in the prophet's representation of God is the sensitiveness of Yahweh to His reputation among the heathen. It is tender regard for His own holy name, even ' pity ' for it when it has been compromised, that is the driving force in His dealing alike with Israel and the heathen. Israel's history from first to last has been one of ingratitude and rebellion. The expression of Yahweh's resentment has again and again been curbed by the thought that the heathen would attribute the downfall of His people to the weakness of her God, and He shrinks from this slur upon His Divinity. But when her persistent misconduct at length casts its shadow on His own moral reputation, He realizes that in one way or the other His honour is bound to suffer. So He resolves to give the wrath, which has been so long accumulating and craving for expression, its unhindered course ; and with this discharge of His tormenting emotions He will be ' comforted ', will regain the inward harmony of which Israel has robbed Him. But now the other side of His dilemma must receive attention. Though He has satisfied His holiness, He has, in doing it, incurred the stigma of feebleness. Hence Israel must be restored from exile that the heathen may recognize the true cause of its calamity. But Yahweh has still to repay the heathen who have slandered Him. Hence He entices Gog to come with his vast hordes from the ends of the earth, tempted by her apparent defencelessness to fall upon Israel. Then He will finally settle His account with the heathen world, overwhelming the invaders with appalling destruction. And if it be thought that the motive for Yahweh's action lies outside Himself, and that loving pity for His people prompts their signal deliverance, first from exile and then from annihilation, the utmost pains are taken to guard against such a misconstruction. ' I do not this for your sake, O house of Israel, but for mine holy name, which ye have profaned among the nations, whither ye went.' And when the restoration is accomplished and Yahweh dwells in the temple on Zion, His holiness is elaborately insulated from all that would profane it. The temple, the city, and the land are holy. A belt of consecrated priests encircles His presence. Beyond that, with diminishing holiness, are the Levites and then the laity.

Ezekiel's individualism also is rooted in his concern for the fair fame of Yahweh. The people complained, not indeed without the warrant of Holy Writ, that the fathers had eaten sour grapes and that the children's teeth were set on edge. To this intolerable denial of the Divine equity Ezekiel replies with the emphatic repudiation of the belief that punishment could be transferred from the guilty to the innocent. The sinner is crushed by no burden of guilt incurred by his race, his ancestors, or his family. He is answerable for his own sin alone. But not only is he freed from all responsibility for others, he is free also from the burden of his own past. Not by his total record is his fate decided, but by the moral condition in which he is found when the crisis arrives. Hence no transgressor need despair, his will is free to repent. The repentance of a moment will wipe out the sins of a lifetime. But the transgression of a moment may also wipe out the righteousness of a lifetime ; and if the critical hour surprises a man in a state of sin, he shall die in his iniquity. So the prophet's commission is widened to embrace the individual. He becomes a watchman to the house of Israel, warning the righteous not to presume on his record and indulge in sin ; admonishing the wicked to turn from his evil way, with the assurance that repentance and reform will be his security when the hour of destiny strikes.

However little we are attracted by the systematic theology

of Ezekiel, we must pay him the tribute that he did more than any man to create the Judaism which, by its rigid legalism and its closely articulated organization, preserved the higher religion of Israel for the world. And not in this alone is he the father of Judaism. If the lawyer and the ecclesiastic find in him their great exemplar, some elements in apocalyptic are also to be traced in his work.

A far more winning figure appeared about twenty-five or thirty years later. This was the author of Isaiah 40–55, commonly known to us as the Second Isaiah. Zion was still in ruins and Judah was still in captivity. Babylon was still seated on her imperial throne. Yahweh, it would seem, had forgotten His people and His city. Had He indeed done anything to prove that He was a match for the triumphant deities of the oppressor ? Yes, the prophet replies, for Cyrus has already begun his career of conquest, which is to be crowned by the capture of Babylon and the return of the exiles to their home. And it is this which demonstrates the supremacy of Yahweh. For it is His prophets who have announced it before it came to pass ; and therefore Yahweh knows the future and can predict it with certainty. But, if so, He must be the controller of history, who can bring His own predictions to pass, since no higher power can thwart their fulfilment. The heathen deities are confidently challenged to competition, but they are nonentities who can achieve nothing and predict nothing. But Yahweh is the incomparable one, the Lord of Nature as well as of history, the mighty, tireless Creator, in whose sight man and the cosmic forces are insignificant, and whose imperious word the stars in their courses must punctually obey. He is the eternal God, the Everlasting One. The monotheistic faith which was implicit in the utterances of his great predecessors now becomes explicit, and all the more impressive that it is proclaimed, not in the technical language of the schools, but in picturesque and concrete description.

But the Sovereign of the universe is no such self-centred egoist as He is in the theology of Ezekiel. He is the gentle and the gracious God, the good shepherd of His people. Israel is ever in His mind, never to be forgotten. The hard period of captivity is drawing to its close, the downfall of Babylon is at hand. Already the angelic powers have received their commission to construct a highway across the desert, straight and level, bountifully supplied with fountains and with the grateful shade of trees; that thus, without fatigue or privation, the chosen people may return with songs to Zion. For, in spite of present appearances, Israel is still Yahweh's chosen, other nations will be sacrificed for her deliverance and will serve as her menials.

Yet the nations have their place in the gracious purpose of God. They are not, as with Ezekiel, the victims of His vindictive resentment; they are to be delivered from their heathen darkness by the missionary activity of Israel. For Israel is the Servant of Yahweh, to whom the knowledge of the true God has been disclosed.[1] He is the Divinely trained

---

[1] I must assume here, since there is no room for discussion, that the Servant of Yahweh in the four Servant poems is to be identified not with an individual but with Israel. My reasons may be seen in *The Problem of Suffering in the Old Testament* (1904). The discussion has, of course, not stood still during the interval, and within the present decade it has passed into new and interesting developments. If confident assertion that the collective interpretation has been refuted could secure its refutation the matter would now be definitely settled in favour of identification with some individual. This, however, is not the case, and I must continue to hold, as at present advised, that the grave objections to any form of this interpretation have not been adequately met. Mowinckel's attempt to show that the Servant is no other than the Second Isaiah himself is of exceptional interest; and so, too, is the identification with Moses proposed by Sellin and defended with his usual resourcefulness and skill. The latter theory involves the view that Moses met his death by martyrdom, and was expected by the prophet to be raised from the dead and fulfil the functions assigned to the Servant.

teacher, patient and sympathetic, waiting to coax into flame whatever spark of truth he may find among the heathen. Selected for this mission before his birth, he is tempted to despond at his failure. But he throws himself and his cause upon God, receiving the assurance that he shall bring light and salvation to the Gentiles. But his mission involves persecution, which he has borne with courage and resolution. And this persecution has culminated in death. The national existence has been destroyed, the people are in exile. But, as Ezekiel had already prophesied, the nation is to have a glorious resurrection. Then the heathen nations which had looked on Israel with contempt, or looked away from it with loathing, will be filled with amazement at their misjudgement. They will plead indeed the excuse that there was nothing in Israel's earlier career to prepare them for so dramatic a reversal of fortune. And as they meditate more deeply, amazement will pass into penitence, remorse, and gratitude. For they will be arrested by the strange course of history, that Israel, which has been loyal to the one true God, should have suffered persecution and national death, while they who had gone astray into idolatry have escaped. It would have been fitting if Israel's fate had been theirs. And now, no longer in their heathen blindness and with a great revulsion of feeling, they advance to the thought that the penalties they ought them-

The view that the Servant is the ideal Israel has secured very eminent support ; the best defence of it may be seen in the revised edition of Dr. Skinner's Commentary on Isaiah, 40–66, in the Cambridge Bible (1917). I should like to call special attention to the reply he has made to my statement of the view that the Servant is the empirical Israel, given in the *Problem of Suffering*. Difficulties may be urged against every theory. I do not think that the Servant is an ideal Israel which is distinct from the actual nation. It is the nation itself which had died in the exile and is to be raised to life at the restoration. But it is the nation regarded from an ideal point of view, the nation, not in its sordid and unworthy aspects, but contemplated in the light of its function in God's plan for the world.

selves to have suffered have been endured by Israel, on whom Yahweh has laid the iniquity of them all. Thus the author rises to the profound interpretation of suffering as borne vicariously by the innocent for the redemption of the guilty. A splendid triumph is reserved for the martyr. Israel will not only be a missionary nation. It will be elevated to lofty rank among the great powers of the world.

With the Second Isaiah the golden age of Hebrew religion comes to an end. Prophecy dwindles in quality after the return from captivity and is gradually transformed into apocalyptic. Legalism is more and more in the ascendant. The sweet singers of Israel touch the depths and heights of religious experience, but for their ideas they are indebted to the great prophets. The coiners of pithy aphorisms move for the most part in the region of conventional and prudential morality. The post-exilic period has indeed stars of greater magnitude, such as the poet to whom we owe the Book of Job, or the large-hearted prophet of God's boundless grace who gave us the incomparable Book of Jonah. But where shall we find in the literature of religion a galaxy comparable with the series of great prophets, which opens with Amos and closes with the Second Isaiah ?

ARTHUR S. PEAKE.

THE DEVELOPMENT OF THE RELIGION OF ISRAEL FROM THE RETURN TO THE DEATH OF SIMON THE MACCABEE

(A) *The Historical Background*

In ' the first year of Cyrus king of Persia ', i. e. probably in 538 B. C., Cyrus the conqueror of Babylon and master now of the empire of Nebuchadrezzar issued a ' firman ' allowing the Jews to rebuild the Temple at Jerusalem. To give effect to this decree he permitted and encouraged any of the Jewish captives in Babylon who desired to help in the work to return to Judaea. Thus the rebuilding of the Temple was his first care, the Return of the Captives was secondary. Indeed it is conceivable that some Jews who returned to Jerusalem to forward the work on the Temple would, when they were satisfied with the progress of the building, return again to the land of their adoption. For the truth must be told that for many of the ' Captives ' Babylon had ceased to be a land of captivity. They had built houses, married wives, and begotten children ; they were more truly ' at home ' by the rivers of Babylon than on the barren hills of Judaea.

Babylon had become a scene of Jewish prosperity, while Jerusalem remained the faded picture of a long-lost glory. So we may understand the appeal with which Deutero-Isaiah opens his prophecy,

> ' Bring ye comfort, bring ye comfort to my People,
> Speak ye to the [stricken] heart of Jerusalem.'

Isa. xl. 1, 2.

The ' Exiles ' are addressed. They in their new-found ease

and wealth alone had power to bring comfort to their desolate brethren in Jerusalem. It is the remnant which still clung to the Holy city and the Holy land whom JEHOVAH honours here with the title of 'My People'. The prosperous Exiles are bidden to go and comfort the afflicted people which still dwelt round Zion.

So we must think of the Return not on its Quantitative but on its Qualitative side. It was not a whole Nation that returned in answer to the decree (or permission) of Cyrus, but—a more significant fact—some of the noblest of the Nation went back to share in the affliction of Judaea, and to comfort their brethren. So the Temple was rebuilt through the efforts of Zerubbabel the prince, Joshua the priest, and Haggai the prophet in 516 B. C., and so again seventy years later the national and religious life of Judah received a great uplift through the coming of an able and courageous leader in the person of Nehemiah (' JEHOVAH hath brought comfort '). He rebuilt the walls of Jerusalem in 444 B. C. and thereby made Judah practically independent of Samaria. In 432 in his zeal for the purity of the priestly race he widened still more the breach between Samaritan and Jew.

Unfortunately the long half-century which followed the rebuilding of the Temple is all but blank in the records of Israel. Darius Hystaspis who sanctioned the rebuilding on appeal (Ezra vi) died in 485. Xerxes (' Ahasuerus ') his successor, so far as we know, did neither good nor evil to the Jews in his reign (485–465 B. C.). Artaxerxes I (465–425) on the other hand was the patron of Nehemiah, and two events in Nehemiah's life are dated respectively in the twentieth and thirty-second years of this monarch.

The work of Nehemiah might be summarily described by the Hebrew word, *Habdālāh*, ' Separation '. The conviction of exiles like Nehemiah and Ezra who returned to the ' Holy Land ' was that the land was ' defiled ' by the heathen strangers

(Ezra ix. 11) who had intruded into Israel's territory since the fall of the Northern kingdom in 722 and of the Southern in 586. No doubt heathen forms of worship were being regularly practised in Palestine by such strangers in conjunction with some Jewish sympathizers. Nehemiah's belief was that the only way to break with idolatry was to break with idolaters. He was a statesman, and statesmanlike he used material means for the execution of his policy.

But the man who takes strong measures must have a strong vantage-ground on which to stand. In the ancient world this was supplied by a well-fortified city (πτολίεθρον ἐϋτείχεον) like Troy or Tyre or Athens. But Jerusalem was worse than an unwalled town ; it had imposing walls that were of no use. Great breaches yawned in the circuit, and the gates had no strong doors and bars to close them. No man could speak and hope to be listened to, who spoke from a city thus humiliated. So the first word of leading which Nehemiah uttered on his arrival in Judaea was, ' Come, and let us build up the wall of Jerusalem, that we be no more a reproach ' (Neh. ii. 17).

It was no easy task to which Nehemiah invited his country-men. It was certain to be opposed both from within and from without. Sanballat, governor of Samaria under the king of Persia, would feel his own power and influence towards the south limited by the rise of Jerusalem under a strong governor like Nehemiah. He did in fact oppose the work by threats and insinuations and by an attempt at treacherous negotiations (Neh. iv. 7–11, vi. 1–14). Perhaps the difficulties were not less from within. Some of the Jews asserted that the site of the walls was overlaid with too much ' rubbish ', and the task of removing this was too great for the strength of the ' burden bearers '. ' We (builders) shall not be able to build.' Worst of all was the nervous dread that the building of the walls would actually bring down upon the Jews the wrath of the Persian king.

But Nehemiah was undaunted. He was a strong godly man confident that he himself was an instrument chosen of God to seek the welfare of the children of Israel. He was God-confident rather than self-confident. When he persuaded Arta-xerxes to his will, he declared that it was ' according to the good hand of my God upon me ', and when the walls of Jerusalem were finished, he testified ' This work was wrought of our God ' (Neh. ii. 8, vi. 16).

The man who built the walls of Jerusalem had the courage to attempt the Separation (*Habdālāb*) of his own small people from the heathen who encompassed them on every side. The task was great indeed. Not only did Jew and heathen live side by side, but they had intermarried. Even some of the priests had taken foreign wives. ' In those days ', writes Nehemiah, ' I went to see the Jews who had brought home women of Ashdod . . . and as for their children half of them spake in the speech of Ashdod ' (Neh. xiii. 23 f.). Against such Jews he took violent measures, violent in tongue in some cases, violent in act in others. Of the former he says, ' I contended with them and reviled them ' ; of the latter ' And some of them (the more conspicuous offenders) I smote [1] and plucked off their hair '. Cutting off the hair was a sign of mourning, so that it may be said that Nehemiah put them violently into mourning for their fault. Then he adjured them not to marry their daughters to foreigners nor take foreign wives for themselves or for their sons. A threat of punishment lurks in this adjuration. More-over Nehemiah was not content to deal with obscure and nameless people. Tobiah the Ammonite had a chamber in the Temple assigned him by his kin by marriage in the high priestly family. In this case Nehemiah used his power as Governor to the utmost. He cast forth all Tobiah's stuff from the sacred chamber, and then proceeded to banish from his presence the high priestly scion who had married into the Ammonite's

---

[1] Did his satellites actually wound them ?

family. Nehemiah was ' thorough ' in his plans, but success in action fell (it is probable) to his successor. Who was this successor?

The view taken in this Essay is that Ezra followed Nehemiah after an interval of about forty years and that he took up part of Nehemiah's work and carried it to success. But the older view of the history is quite different. According to it Ezra arrived in Jerusalem in the seventh year of Artaxerxes I, i. e. in 458 B. C., struggled hard to put an end to mixt marriages before the arrival of Nehemiah, and finally, with the aid of Nehemiah who arrived in Jerusalem in 445 or 444 B. C., promulgated the Law (probably the complete Pentateuch) and made it authoritative for the Jewish community. In this Law intermarriage was entirely forbidden (Deut. vii. 3 ; cp. xxiii. 3). This reading of the history has its chief support in the fact that in the present text of Neh. viii. 9 Nehemiah is associated with Ezra in the story of the promulgation of the Law.

But in spite of this it is more probable that Nehemiah preceded Ezra (as was said above) by a long generation of over forty years. The mention of Nehemiah in Neh. viii. 9 seems to be an interpolation inserted by a scribe whose mind was full of Nehemiah and who could not conceive that he was absent on such an occasion. But it must be observed (1) that Neh. viii does not form part of the Memoirs of Nehemiah ; (2) that Nehemiah is not mentioned again in connexion with this incident, though Ezra's name is mentioned no less than six times ; (3) that in Esdras (1 E. ix. 49) Nehemiah's name is absent from the passage which corresponds with Neh. viii. 9 ; (4) that only once in Nehemiah's Memoirs, viz. in Neh. xii. 36, is ' Ezra the scribe ' referred to, and again the reading is doubtful. If the two were contemporaries and fellow-workers, is it at all probable that no certain reference by the one to the other would be found in the compound work Ezra-Nehemiah?

We therefore adopt the conclusion that Ezra went up from

Babylon to Jerusalem in the seventh year (not of Artaxerxes I, but) of Artaxerxes II. This monarch is he whom Cyrus the Younger and Xenophon with the Ten Thousand Greeks strove in vain to dethrone. He became king in 404 B. C., and the mission of Ezra falls thus in 397 B. C. Nehemiah and Ezra never met. Ezra's promulgation of the Law may be dated soon after 397 B. C., for this promulgation was the chief business of Ezra ' the Scribe '. If this dating be accepted the introduction of full Pentateuchal strictness happened some fifty years later than 445–4, the date which used to be given. Ezra with the newly promulgated Pentateuch behind him was able to take strong measures against mixt marriages and to carry a reform further than Nehemiah. Ezra, himself a priest, ' dealt faithfully ' with his fellow priests who had taken foreign wives (Ezra x).

But Judaism was not confined to Jerusalem and Babylon. Documents written in Aramaic recently discovered at Elephantine show that there was a strong colony of Jews and a much venerated Jewish Temple in Upper Egypt during the days of Darius II (424–404 B. C.). This temple was destroyed by the Egyptians in 410 B. C. with the connivance of the local Persian authorities, but it was rebuilt by permission of the higher authorities a few years later. Here the Egyptian Jews desired to establish a full cultus of animal sacrifice, but the feeling of Jerusalem in favour of the single sanctuary was too strong for them. Permission to offer incense and the meal offering was obtained, but the right to practise the full cultus was reserved for the Temple on Mount Zion.

After 397 B. C., the presumed date of Ezra, comes a long period of Jewish history for which we have hardly any historical documents. It seems probable however that the reign of Artaxerxes III (' Ochus ', 358–339 B. C.) brought serious troubles upon Israel, for Phoenicia and Egypt revolted, and the forces of the Persian king must have passed through Palestine

in suppressing the revolt. Again in 332 B. C. Alexander the
Great captured Tyre and marched along the sea coast to the
conquest of Egypt. At the break-up of Alexander's empire
Jerusalem after some vicissitudes was taken by Ptolemy, King
of Egypt, *c.* 301. Whether the Jews made any resistance to
these successive passages of armies we do not know. Possibly
Judaea

> . . . bow'd low before the blast
> In patient, deep disdain ;
> She let the legions thunder past,
> And plunged in thought again.

Fortunately the second century B. C. is illuminated for the
history of the Jewish people by native and other documents,
and the great Jewish struggle for faith and freedom is a well-
known episode in the World's story. In 198–197 B. C. Antiochus
III of Syria took Jerusalem and annexed Judaea. The country
was unhappy under Syrian rule. Under Seleucus IV, the
successor of Antiochus, a struggle for the High priesthood
began. Moreover the kings of Syria were short of money, and
an attempt was made to seize the Temple treasures. But more
serious trouble began in the sphere in which politics and
religion meet. Antiochus IV, Epiphanes, the successor of
Seleucus, strove to weld his far-flung ill-compacted empire
together by setting up an imperial cultus which should
embrace all his dominions. It should be noted, however, that
he did not wish to suppress local cults, provided that they could
be fitted into the general scheme of the State religion. But
this arrangement could not be accepted by Jews who had
inherited the tradition of *Habdālāh* established by Nehemiah
and Ezra. A deadlock ensued. Antiochus Epiphanes forbade
the practice of circumcision which distinguished the Jew from
the heathen, and further sought to destroy all copies of the
Pentateuch, because it enjoined religious isolation on Israel.
The Jews had no option but to revolt, and in 167 B. C.

Mattathias the priest and Judas 'Maccabaeus' his son and their followers took to the hills and appealed to the sword against the overwhelming power of Syria. Mattathias fought and died, and Maccabaeus fought and died, but Jonathan his brother was chosen 'prince and leader' in his stead, and by hard fighting secured a breathing-time for his people. About the year 157 B. C. it was possible to write:

'And the sword ceased from Israel. And Jonathan dwelt at Michmash and . . . began to judge the people.'[1]

From this time onwards there were rival claimants to the throne of Seleucus, and Judah enjoyed peace and a qualified independence owing to the dissensions of Syria.

'In the hundred and seventieth year (*c.* 143 B. C.) was the yoke of the heathen taken away from Israel.'[2]

And the land had rest all the days of Simon.[3] This was the brother and successor of Jonathan.

(B) *Authorities*

From *c.* 520 to 136 B. C., the date of the murder of Simon the Maccabee, the authorities for the history of the religion of Israel (as distinguished from the external history of the people) are fairly full and numerous. First are to be reckoned Haggai and Zech. i–viii., documents of primary importance. Next we place 'Trito-Isaiah', i. e. Isa. lvi–lxvi. The dating and indeed the coherence of this section of the book is doubtful, but critics are generally agreed that at least part of it was composed in the Holy Land and not (like Deutero-Isaiah) in Babylon or in one of the other lands of exile. When we try, however, to fix a more particular date within the limits of the 400 years between Deutero-Isaiah and Simon the Maccabee, the great uncertainty of the critical problem must be borne in mind. Some would assign the section to the lifetime and (perhaps) to the author-

[1] 1 Macc. ix. 73.   [2] 1 Macc. xiii. 41.   [3] 1 Macc. xiv. 4.

ship of Deutero-Isaiah. Others would make ' Trito-Isaiah '
a contemporary of Nehemiah. But a few passages remain
difficult of interpretation on either dating.

Next to be reckoned is Malachi which is somewhat earlier
than the reforms of Nehemiah, i. e. earlier than 444 B. C. Ezra-
Nehemiah, one continuous book in the old Hebrew reckoning,
has valuable hints for the fifty years following 444 B. C. Joel
is later than Malachi, but earlier than the ' Greek ' period.
(Cp. Sellin, *Introduction*, p. 164.)

Important light is thrown on the Hebrew religion from
520 B. C. onward by the Psalter, though the book was not completed for at least a couple of centuries after this date. But
Psalms must be used with special caution. Their language is
poetic, and formal doctrine must not be wrung out of it. Again,
though the Psalter as a book certainly falls within our period,
and late enough perhaps to include Maccabean Psalms, yet the
dating of a particular Psalm remains a very difficult task.
Further, some particular Psalms have borrowed material from
earlier sources, so that passages of different dates stand side by
side in one Psalm. Thus Ps. lxviii seems to borrow an ancient
war cry for its opening note, ' Let God (JEHOVAH) arise, let his
enemies be scattered ', and Ps. xix unites (perhaps) an earlier
nature poem on the Heavens with a later liturgical composition
on the excellence of the Torah. Thus the use of the Psalter leads
the student between Scylla and Charybdis. On the one hand
it is easy to misdate a Psalm or a Psalm-passage and so to draw
from it a wrong conclusion as to the development of religious
belief; on the other hand to neglect the Psalter for fear of mis-
using it is to give up a great deal of potentially valuable material.

The book of Job again is a tantalizing witness. It is a sym-
posium of older views and ' modern ' speculations, and its date
as a book is uncertain. ' The most we can do is to place the
author between Jeremiah and Malachi, between 600 and
450 B. C.' (Sellin, p. 222). ' It was perhaps as the fifth century

was slipping into the past that the poet . . . wrote his mighty
work ' (A. S. Peake, *Problem of Suffering in O. T.*, p. 83).

Finally it must be said that though Isa. xxiv–xxvii is
confidently dated by Duhm in the late Maccabean era, i.e. as
late as *c.* 100 B.C., his confidence is ill-grounded. Sounder is
the verdict of Sellin, ' [This] Apocalypse gives no clue whatever
to the more exact determination of its date ' (Sellin, p. 138).
This Apocalypse contains, it is true, some very interesting
theological ideas, but great caution is needed in attempting to
date them. In short Isa. xxiv–xxvii ministers questions rather
than information to the investigator.

The strange book Koheleth (Ecclesiastes) falls within our
period. Grätz puts it as late as the reign of Herod the Great,
but it is more likely that it was written about 200 B.C. Ecclesiasticus (soon after 200 B.C.) had the whole book before him.[1]
It should be used cautiously (if at all) as an authority, for it
gives the speculations of a recluse, and not any generally
accepted doctrine.

The latest authority is the book of Daniel, which as a complete book dates from *c.* 167 B.C. But again some caution is
needed in the use of the book. There are elements in it which
must be far older than the beginning of the Maccabean era ;
e. g. chs. ii–vi are too general in the nature of their contents :
they could not have been composed *ad hoc*, though they may
have been adapted by slight changes to the Maccabean crisis.
They were written by a great story-teller, whereas the rest of
the book was composed by a ' painful ' preacher.

(C) *Preliminary Considerations*

It is necessary to be careful in applying the principle of
Development to the history of Hebrew religion. Development
whether in Nature or History is never tied to one line. Certainly in the history of the religion of Israel from the Return

[1] Sellin, p. 228–9· cp. Peake, *Problem of Suffering*, p. 125.

onwards two widely divergent lines of development are to be traced. It would be a serious mistake to suppose that we get an adequate description of this development simply by tracing Legalism from Ezekiel and from Ezra down to the Pharisees and the Rabboth. There was very much beside Legalism in the religion of Israel in the post-Exilic period.

Some one has indeed written that the Legalism of later Judaism began with Ezekiel and grew strong during the Exile and onwards. The statement (whatever truth there be in it) must not be allowed to convey the impression that the development of the Jewish religion from 520 B. C. to the Maccabees was of the nature of a dreary decline into Formalism and Legalism. In the first place it must be said that the story is on the contrary a varied and interesting one. There was a conflict of ideals and a clash of thought and feeling which brought great men to the fore. If it be said that there was no Moses, no David, no Isaiah in this later period, the whole of the truth is not told. Haggai and Zechariah, through whose prophesying the building of the Temple 'prospered', were men of force to meet a great crisis. Trito-Isaiah (if he be distinct from Deutero-Isaiah) can sometimes speak words as moving as those of his predecessor. Malachi is a prophet on fire with God. Nehemiah, if not as meek as Moses, was for his own day as great a leader. Both Zechariah and Nehemiah could stand up for righteousness and against oppression with a zeal like that of Elijah or of Isaiah. The post-exilic prophets carried on their work in a spirit not unworthy of their great predecessors of the eighth century B. C. They prevented the religion of Israel from becoming a mere routine of ritual actions. The prophets did indeed ' prophesy unto John '.

In the Gospels there are signs that still in our Lord's time the *Haggādāh* (teaching drawn from the Prophets) maintained itself as a power beside the *Halāchāh* (legal decisions founded on the Pentateuch). The scribe who publicly agreed with our

Lord that love of God and the neighbour was ' much more than all whole burnt offerings and sacrifices '[1] was a faithful inheritor of the old prophetic teaching.

Another important axiom to be borne in mind is that religious ideas are sometimes mixt almost inextricably with political ones, so that the hasty student fails to detect the religious element. Particularly is this the case with eschatological passages, such as Isa. lx–lxii. Such promises as ' All that despised thee shall bow themselves down at the soles of thy feet ', and again, ' Thou shalt suck the milk of the nations and shalt suck the breast of kings ' have a strongly political colouring, and the whole passage to which they belong has to be carefully scanned before its underlying religious character can be perceived.

Again, in forming our estimate of the religion of this period it is necessary to take full account of the background which is supplied by the Psalter. What eminent leaders thought and taught may be gathered from great prophetical passages and from the memoirs of Nehemiah and Ezra and the like, but the religion of the people at large also needs its chroniclers and its interpreters. These are to be found in the Psalms. It does not take from the honour of the Psalter to say that it expresses the everyday reflections and aspirations of the common people. It is thus that we see the religion of a nation in action, and we discern the faith and works of those who were ' quiet in the land ' (Ps. xxxv. 20). The nation which produced the Psalter possessed a religion which gave men faith in God, stedfastness in purpose, love of the brethren, and humility towards God. If this religion was sometimes narrow, it was on the other hand deep. If it was fierce against the Gentiles and the oppressor, it was tender towards the poor and the afflicted of Israel. It was personal and internal. It was not put on and off like a garment.

[1] Mark xii. 33.

(D) *Religion in Israel* 520–136 B. C.

The generation which built the Temple to the prophesying of Haggai and Zechariah inherited from their fathers the sublime doctrine of the nature of JEHOVAH, which Deutero-Isaiah had impressed upon his contemporaries. The God of Israel was, so he taught, far above all the heathen and their gods. Deutero-Isaiah is in fact the first prophet to preach unmistakable monotheism. There is nowhere a more telling (short) statement of the doctrine of God, than in Isa. xl. There is nowhere a more daring (short) description of the work of God than in Isa. xlv. 6, 7, 'I am JEHOVAH, and there is none else. I form the light, and create darkness ; I make peace, and create evil ; I am JEHOVAH, that doeth all these things.' JEHOVAH is Creator of heaven and earth by His own wisdom ; He alone knows the Future ; His providence rules and guides all events. JEHOVAH is one and solitary : no other being shares His throne or His secrets. There is no room for angel or spirit, good or bad, in the Theology of Deutero-Isaiah.

Trito-Isaiah, the post-Exilic prophet, takes up the doctrine which Deutero-Isaiah delivered. Some of his utterances are equal in life and force to those of his predecessor : ' Heaven is my throne and earth is my footstool : what manner of house will ye build unto me ? . . . For all these things hath mine hand made.'[1] And yet he sometimes flinches from the austere consistency of Deutero-Isaiah. He suggests the existence of a lesser spirit dwelling by the side of JEHOVAH, when he writes, ' And the angel of his presence saved them ', words which might denote some secondary Being who was occasionally deputed to act for the heavenly king.

Teaching similar to this is given by Zechariah. His monotheism is beyond suspicion. He describes JEHOVAH as the Lord of the whole earth (iv. 14, vi. 5), and again and again he gives

[1] Isa. lxvi. 1, 2.

Him the title of *Ṣĕbāoth*, which we may paraphrase, 'Lord of the hosts of heaven'. There is no place in Zechariah's scheme for heathen gods, and he makes no mention of them.

But the exalted view of the nature of JEHOVAH, as Zechariah and Deutero- and Trito-Isaiah held it, was accompanied by certain drawbacks. From it men deduced the conclusion that so great a God as JEHOVAH must be transcendent and beyond all contact with this earth and its inhabitants. And so Imagination evolved an ' Angel (or Messenger) of JEHOVAH ', a projection of JEHOVAH into the sphere of the world. This ' Angel ' was not thought to be a being distinct from JEHOVAH, yet he was conceived as acting and speaking for JEHOVAH as though he were rather His Minister. The conception marks the bank-ruptcy of human language when it is used to describe the Divine nature.

A good illustration of this conception is seen in the first vision of Zechariah (i. 7–13). The prophet sees the Angel of JEHOVAH as a man riding on a horse. (He would never have seen JEHOVAH thus, not even in vision.) Behind this Angel are other horses. Zechariah asks the meaning of what he sees. An angel who speaks within him promises to ' show ' him the answer. So the prophet is enabled to hear the Angel of JEHOVAH declare that these horses are JEHOVAH's scouts, who report to Him the state of the world. So again Zechariah is enabled to hear the Angel of JEHOVAH appealing to JEHOVAH-Ṣĕbāoth for mercy on Jerusalem, and also JEHOVAH's answer to the Angel in comforting words.[1]

Thus though Zechariah is a prophet, his access to JEHOVAH is not direct; it is rather doubly mediated. First, JEHOVAH communicates His will to the Angel of JEHOVAH, and then another angel, the ' familiar spirit ', we might almost call him,

---

[1] The Angel of ver. 13 I take to be the Angel of JEHOVAH. The qualifying words, ' that talked with me,' are probably a gloss, which has been intruded from ver. 14.

of the prophet interprets to Zechariah the Divine answer given to the Angel of JEHOVAH, and commissions him to prophesy to the people, ' Cry aloud, saying . . .' Thus the Divine word reaches Israel through three intermediaries. Its course runs from JEHOVAH through the Angel of JEHOVAH, through the angel who is the prophet's familiar, and finally through the prophet himself to Israel. When even a Prophet's thought places JEHOVAH at such a distance from His people, it is easy to imagine that the people generally put God too far from them. The spontaneity of religious service must have been checked. The Warrior-God of Israel, so anthropomorphically conceived in older times, was losing His characteristic form, and becoming merely an abstract idea. There was great loss here. It is true that anthropomorphisms accepted and unguardedly used tend to debase our thoughts of God ; but anthropomorphisms are necessary to help the imagination to realize that God is accessible to man. Zechariah in his desire to exalt JEHOVAH above the earth was unwittingly suggesting to men that their God was beyond all human reach. But what then had man to do with God ?

Babylonian Theology was pictorially represented to Hebrew eyes by many graven images and especially by the colossal gilded statue of Bel (Marduk), which according to Herodotus,[1] ' adorned or defiled '[2] the splendid city of Babylon. How could unlettered folk have or retain spiritual thoughts of God with this man-made colossus dominating the view ? This objection, or something like this, was in the mind of Zechariah ; certainly the words of his predecessor, Deutero-Isaiah, suggest it.[3]

The doctrine of the majesty of JEHOVAH, the doctrine that He is exalted almost to the extent of remoteness, was taken up and pushed to extremes by at least one school of Hebrew

[1] Herod. I. c. 183. [2] Gibbon's phrase.
[3] Isa. xlvi. 1–13.

thought. Men became afraid even to use the name JEHOVAH,
for it seemed to them too sacred to repeat. Thus while
in the books of Kings the Tetragrammaton alone is freely
used, it is frequently replaced in the Chronicles by the colourless ELOHIM, 'God'. In the Memoirs of Nehemiah we meet
Lord (Adōnai), *my God*, *our God*, but only rarely JEHOVAH. In
the text of many Psalms [1] ELOHIM prevails almost to the
exclusion of JEHOVAH. The latter is reserved for passages of
special emphasis, e. g. lxxxiii. 18.

A still more extraordinary phenomenon, due to the same
form of thought, meets us in 1 Macc. No mention of the
name of God, neither *God* nor *Lord*, occurs in the correct text
of the book. Allusion is made to the Temple, the Temple-
vessels, Sabbaths, sacrifices, circumcision, and the book of the
Covenant (the Pentateuch), but the God of Israel is only
named obscurely as 'Heaven' (iii. 18, iv. 10, 24, ix. 46; cp.
vii. 40–2). This attitude was surely further removed from
true religion than the 'infantine, familiar clasp of things
Divine' which so many Psalmists show. Indeed we may say
that the Psalms testify to a different development of the doctrine
of the nature of God. The latest Psalms show but little trace
of the fear of anthropomorphism : they rest upon the belief
that ' JEHOVAH is *nigh* unto all them that call upon Him '.
Thanks to the Psalmists, thoughts of His transcendence did not
extinguish thoughts of His interest in His people, even of His
loving care of them. This double aspect of Theology is a most
important fact in the history of Hebrew religion.

The tendency to exalt JEHOVAH almost beyond any possibility of contact with the world left room for the imagination
to create lesser beings to act as His agents between Heaven and
Earth. Deutero-Isaiah had not hesitated to put into JEHOVAH's
mouth the words : ' I ... create darkness ; I ... create evil.' [2]

---

[1] See Pss. xliv–lxxxiii.
[2] 'physical (not moral) evil,' as it appears from the context.

But later generations did not repeat His words. Yet plainly there was evil in the World; whence came it? The theory of the Satan (' the adversary ') was the answer given by later Hebrew theologians (Zechariah, Job, 1 Chron. xxi. 1). This Hebrew Satan was not the Devil of popular Christian theology, he was not the enemy, still less the rival of God. The Satan [1] was one of the ' sons of God ', one attached to the court of JEHOVAH, entrusted with the task of an inspector of JEHOVAH's subjects. He did not exist to persuade or entrap men into evil by his own wicked will, but simply to test men's sincerity by the permission of the Almighty. Similarly in Zech. iii. 1–5 ' the Satan ' is only the prosecuting counsel, who points to Joshua's filthy garments. Joshua, until acquitted by the Angel of JEHOVAH, is rightly accused.

JEHOVAH was the source of all the good that comes to man: how were His benefits to be conveyed to Israel? Above all, how was Israel to be saved from extinction in the clash of great powers, Syria and Egypt, and again from the unknown barbarians, Gog and his associates, who again and again were found waiting to overwhelm civilization with a flood of savage horsemen? [2] When the book of Daniel was written an answer was ready.: Israel had a spirit guardian, Michael ' the great prince ', ' one of the chief princes ' to act as patron saint and defender (Dan. x. 13, 21, xii. 1 ; cp. viii. 25). Since the name of ' the great prince ' was Mi-cha-el (' Who is like God? '), it is clear that this Being was a subordinate agent, and no rival to the God of Israel, but rather the minister of His will.

We have already noticed that an angel was the intermediary in the first vision of Zechariah : in Daniel (viii. 16) the same conception recurs, only the ' angel ' bears a name, *Gabriel*, ' man *or* servant of God ', a name denoting a close dependence upon God. From an angel in attendance on a prophet it is an easy

---

[1] The word has the article prefixed in Job and Zechariah.
[2] Ezek. xxxviii. 2–4.

transition to an angel guardian appointed for a limited time and for a private person, such as we find Raphael in the book of Tobit.[1]

But it is the book of Tobit which first sets forth quite clearly the doctrine that angels exist as an order of beings. 'I am Raphael,' says the angel to Tobit,[2] 'one of the seven holy angels, which present the prayers of the saints, and go in before the glory of the Holy One.' Here we seem to see the doctrine of angels revealing its 'make'. Semites looked upon God as a 'king'; *the* king of ancient story was the king of Persia; and the king of Persia had 'seven princes . . . which saw the king's face, sitting first in the kingdom'.[3] So Imagination figured for the King of all kings seven 'angels', who had the right of entry before Him. In the light of this passage of Tobit we may identify the Michael and the Gabriel of the book of Daniel as also angels, i. e. as belonging to an order of beings intermediate between God and Man, though Michael is not called 'angel' in the book of Daniel, and Gabriel is expressly styled a 'man'. In short the clear picture of the Unity and Solitude of JEHOVAH, as Deutero-Isaiah had painted it, became somewhat dim in the books of Daniel and Tobit—in the second century B. C., let us say.

But in the meantime Poetry preserved a different angelology. In the Psalms and in Job angels are rather personifications of the powers of Nature, which serve JEHOVAH as Lord. So Ps. civ. 4 should be rendered :

> Who maketh winds his messengers (angels),
> Flaming fire (i. e. the lightnings) his ministers.

The same representation is found in Job xxxviii. 35 :

> Canst thou send forth lightnings that they go,
> And say unto thee, Here we are ?

---

[1] v. 4 ; *al.* The date of this book is uncertain ; it may be as early as the Maccabean period (Sellin, p. 243).

[2] xii. 15.   [3] Esther i. 14.

This poetic view survived in the dictum of later Judaism that every angel is created for a special purpose, and comes to an end when that purpose is fulfilled.

* * * * * * * * *

Next to the doctrine of God, the doctrine of Redemption has to be considered. It attaches itself especially to the story of the Return from Babylon. Redemption was seen in a double aspect by Deutero-Isaiah. In ch. xliii it means the delivery of the exiled and scattered nation of Israel from its Babylonian captivity and oppression; in ver. 3 JEHOVAH seems to say that he will pay a ' ransom ' to Cyrus who frees the Jews by granting Egypt and Ethiopia to his conquering arms. From one aspect Redemption was an event of external history.

But from another aspect Deutero-Isaiah saw Redemption as a religious process. In xl. 2 Redemption is represented as following on the expiation of the sin for which Israel was sent into captivity. And here it is to be noticed that the Prophet does not call upon his people to repent; rather he calls upon the more prosperous exiles around him to carry comfort to Israel in Jerusalem.[1] The first duty of Deutero-Isaiah was to hearten, not to cast down. The sins of Israel might be more seasonably urged against the people after they had enjoyed the goodness of God in the rebuilding of the Temple and in the growth of prosperity in the home-land. So when Deutero-Isaiah does refer to these sins, it is only to remind Israel that JEHOVAH has blotted out his transgressions. The sign of this forgiveness is that JEHOVAH has already ' sent to Babylon ', and the judgment on Babylon has begun.[2]

But when the Return had been accomplished and Zerubbabel and Joshua were successfully rebuilding the Temple, the time came for a fresh reasoning with Israel. The old pre-Exilic sins had reappeared in the restored community, and troubled the

---

[1] See above, p. 289. [2] Isa. xliii. 14 and 25.

heart of Zechariah.[1]   Zechariah hoped for a supernatural cleansing of the nation; first he figured the destruction of the wicked in Israel by means of a huge ' flying roll ', which carried a destroying curse to the house of the sinner ; and next he had a vision of ' Wickedness ' being carried off from the land of Israel to a permanent home in Babylon. But he left the tale of cleansing half-told.

The fuller story is given in Isa. lii. 13–liii. 12. This passage is unfortunately marred by some false readings, but the general sense is clear. A mediator, a Servant of JEHOVAH like Moses or one of the old prophets, has borne Israel's sins, and will continue to bear them :

' Surely he hath borne our griefs and carried our sorrows ; . . . By his acknowledging them shall my servant justify many : and he shall bear their iniquities.' [2]

The true religious note is struck here. It is not enough to have a Zerubbabel to lead the Exiles back to Judah ; it is not enough to have a Temple-builder ; One is needed who will deal with the sin of Israel, and such a one (the Prophet says) has lived recently in obscurity unnoticed, yet he has died for Israel's sin, and still, though dead, will intercede for the transgressors. His sufferings borne in silence and submission plead for Israel with God. The Prophet gives us here something very near to the doctrine of the Cross.[3]

*   *   *   *   *   *   *   *   *

Was Redemption to be for Israel only ? Or were the Gentiles to share in those benefits which Israel looked to obtain from JEHOVAH ? Was indeed JEHOVAH to be the God also of the Nations of the World ? It was not easy for Israel in early post-exilic days to answer in the affirmative. His sufferings had been too great. The roll of the Nations was the roll of Israel's

---

[1] Zech. vii. 8–14.   [2] Isa. liii. 4 and 11.

[3] I assume throughout that Isa. lii. 13–liii. 12 is twenty or thirty years later in date than Isa. xl–xlv.

oppressors—'Edom and the Ishmaelites . . . Moab . . . Ammon and Amalek . . . the Philistines with them of Tyre '.[1] The Jewish natural man prayed 'Remember, O JEHOVAH, the children of Edom in the day of Jerusalem ', or he cried aloud, ' O daughter of Babylon, happy shall he be that rewardeth thee, as thou hast served us '.[2]

But Israel now had a faith which must be communicated to the rest of the Peoples, since otherwise it would wither into nothingness. Deutero-Isaiah had taught clearly and fully that JEHOVAH was Creator and Governor of the whole earth.[3] In different forms this doctrine was taken up and enforced by other prophets. Trito-Isaiah welcomed proselytes into the congregation of Israel, and even declared in JEHOVAH's name, ' My house shall be called an house of prayer for all peoples '.[4] So too the last prophecy of Zechariah was that ten men out of all the languages of the nations should take hold of the skirt of a Jew saying, ' We will go with you, for we have heard that God is with you ' (Zech. viii. 23).

But these large and generous terms were severely modified in the course of a century or so by the action of Nehemiah and Ezra. Their policy of *Habdālāh* [5] was based on experience of the dangerous relaxation of restraints which resulted from any large influx of proselytes. Nay, even commercial intercourse with heathen carried danger with it. To trade with the Tyrians brought to the inhabitants of Jerusalem temptation to buy fish and general merchandise on the Sabbath. This profanation of the Sabbath was (as we shall see presently) a more serious matter than the twentieth-century English critic would suppose. Thus it may be said that during the period we are considering there was a double development ; on the one side to greater freedom in admitting Gentiles to the Congregation,

[1] Ps. lxxxiii. 6, 7.   [2] Ps. cxxxvii. 7, 8.
[3] Isa. xlii. 5, xliv. 24–8, xlv. 12, 14.
[4] Isa. lvi. 3–7.   [5] See above, p. 290 f.

but on the other side to greater strictness in maintaining outward observances.

*   *   *   *   *   *   *   *   *

The particular subject of the Sabbath introduces the general subject of the strictness of the Jewish religion. Almost all ancient religions laid taboos on the course of daily life, and promulgated minute rules for worship. Judaism was no exception, and it would be easy by carefully selecting our authorities to represent the Judaism of the post-exilic period as a specially burdensome system of ritual regulations. Nehemiah and Ezra stood for strictness, and the people at the instance of the great Scribe accepted the rules that were given them as from ' the book of the law of Moses ' (*nomen venerabile*), or ' the book of the law of God '.[1] The enforcement of the distinction between ' clean ' and ' unclean ' put the daily life of men at the mercy of the priest. The minute regulations as to sacrifice made for ' priestcraft '. The taboo of the Sabbath seemed to lay a very heavy burden on daily life :

' They found a man gathering sticks upon the sabbath day . . . And JEHOVAH said unto Moses, The man shall surely be put to death . . . And all the congregation brought him without the camp, and stoned him with stones and he died.' [2]

But this incident stands by itself ; its significance must not be exaggerated. When on the other hand the stern Nehemiah saw the Sabbath broken on a large scale he ' testified ' to the small men, and he ' contended with ' the nobles.[3] There was no stoning. A broader view of our authorities shows us that the Sabbath was a gift rather than a restriction. Our Lord did not say in vain, ' The sabbath was made for man '.[4] The object of the institution according to Deuteronomy was, ' That thy manservant and thy maidservant may rest as well as thou '.[5]

[1] Neh. viii. 1 and 18.
[2] Num. xv. 32–6 ; cp. Exod. xxxv. 3 (no fire to be kindled).
[3] Neh. xiii. 15–18.   [4] Mark ii. 27.   [5] Deut. v. 14.

Hard fieldwork (very hard in Palestine) was especially for-bidden : ' On the seventh day thou shalt rest : in plowing time and in harvest thou shalt rest.' Not even the master's anxiety to make the best of the season is to be allowed to abridge the servant's rest. God took thought for the servant. The Sabbath was a large, simple, and effective piece of social legislation (Exod. xxxiv. 21).

But on the other hand the Sabbath was a ' positive ' institu-tion by which Judaism was distinguished from other religions,[1] by which indeed JEHOVAH was served, as no other deity was served. The Sabbath was a special badge of loyalty to JEHOVAH, as the LORD himself declares to Ezekiel, ' Also I gave them my sabbaths to be a sign between me and them '. The Sabbath was, as it were, a royal standard under which the Jew served his Divine king.

The double aspect, ' positive ' and ' moral ' of this institution, should serve as a warning against an arbitrary division of the elements of the Jewish religion into ' ethical ' (or ' moral ') and ' ritual ' (or ' positive '). In the Judaism of post-exilic times the ' moral ' and the ' positive ' elements are often closely interwoven. In particular the fervour of the post-exilic prophets for righteousness should not be ignored or minimized. Trito-Isaiah is a champion of the Sabbath,[2] but he is none the less valiant for judgment and righteousness. Not Isaiah himself could denounce more trenchantly the rigorous fast of a hard taskmaster. JEHOVAH's chosen fast is ' to deal thy bread to the hungry, to cover the naked with a garment, and not to hide thyself from thine own flesh '.[3] Zechariah is not so eloquent, but he is equally peremptory :

' When ye fasted and mourned in the fifth and in the seventh month, . . . did ye at all fast unto me, even to me ? . . . Execute true judgment

---

[1] The Babylonian ' Sabbath ' seems to have had a very different range and meaning.   [2] Isa. lvi. 2–6.   [3] Isa. lviii. 2–7.

and show mercy and compassion every man to his brother : and oppress not the widow.' [1]

So Malachi again announces that JEHOVAH's coming judgment will turn on moral issues :

' I will be a swift witness against the sorcerers and against the adulterers and against those that swear falsely, and against those who oppress the hireling in his wages . . . and that turn aside the stranger from his right.'

To these prophetic utterances we may add the example of Nehemiah who forbore to exact a revenue for himself as governor, and further exerted himself vigorously on behalf of the poorer Jews who had fallen into the hands of merciless usurers.[2] These facts (and others) point to the conclusion that there was a much larger moral element in the Judaism of the sixth and fifth centuries B. C. than is commonly allowed. And again, as we have said before, where the later prophets are keen about what seems to be an external matter, the matter is found to have a moral side. Thus if Malachi pleads fervently for the payment of tithe, he is thinking of Levites ' separated ' to JEHOVAH, and yet left to starve. Again, if he denounces mixt marriages, he is thinking of the wrong done to Jewish wives who have been put away to make room for alien women. Even the Chronicler (*c.* 300 B. C. ?) could rise above merely ritual interests. Does he not narrate that some eat of Hezekiah's Passover in a state of uncleanness, yet JEHOVAH accepted them on Hezekiah's prayer ? [3] Our conclusion must be that even if legalism and externalism grew in Judaism in the centuries which followed the Return, yet Judaism remained a strong moral force in the World. It remained in particular the religion of sympathy and pity, the religion of the book of Ruth and of the book of Tobit, and (in part) of the book of Jonah. The ideal Jew of the post-exilic period is described in Job's attempted portrait of himself :

[1] Zech. vii. 5–10 ; cp. viii. 16, 17.   [2] Neh. v. 1–15.

[3] 2 Chron. xxx. 18–20.

I delivered the afflicted when he cried,
The orphan and him that had no helper.
The blessing of him that was ready to perish came upon me,
And I caused the widow's heart to sing for joy.
I put on righteousness, and it clothed me ;
My justice was as a robe and a turban for me.
I was eyes to the blind, and feet to the lame.
I was a father to the needy, and the cause of him I knew not I searched out.
And I brake the jaws of the unrighteous,
And plucked the prey out of his teeth.[1]

Further it must not be forgotten that it was in the period of which we are treating that the Decalogue came to its own. The Pentateuch was now complete, and its contents were published and known abroad, thanks to the action and example of Ezra. In what written context the Ten Commandments originally stood is not known, but in the completed Pentateuch they stood at the head of the whole of the legislation given on Sinai (Horeb).[2] Such is the position they occupy in Exodus, a position emphasized in Deuteronomy, where their text is again given in full.[3] The great influence of Deuteronomy has often been remarked. It has been traced in the activity of Josiah,[4] in the work of Nehemiah and Ezra,[5] and throughout the book of Malachi. It was a far-reaching influence, for Deuteronomy is written with persuasive eloquence as a book addressed to the masses. Now Israel's great day, the Deuteronomist tells his people, was ' the day that thou stoodest before JEHOVAH thy God in Horeb '. After he has reproduced the text of the Decalogue he adds :

' These words Jehovah spake unto all your assembly in the mount out of the midst of the fire, of the cloud, and of the thick darkness with a great voice : and he added no more. And he wrote them upon two tables of stone, and gave them unto me.' [6]

[1] Job xxix. 12–17.   [2] Exod. xx. 1.   [3] Deut. v. 6–21.
[4] 2 Kings xxii., xxiii.   [5] Neh. viii. 1, xiii. 1.   [6] Deut. v. 22.

Could Israel have been told more plainly that the chief element in his religion was the moral law? There is no merely ceremonial element in the Decalogue. We have already seen that the Sabbath commandment was a social charter and not a mere ritual restriction. When we consider this prominence of the moral law coupled with the testimony which the Psalms give to the inwardness of the religion of those who wrote and used them, we must confess that the Religion of the post-exilic period was far above the religions (as we know them) of the surrounding peoples, for it was a mighty moral force. The Pharisees whom our Lord rebuked for setting the ritual above the moral were not merely blind to the True Light; they were false to the best teaching of Judaism.

*   *   *   *   *   *   *   *   *

This survey would not be complete without some reference to Eschatology: what expectations had the Jews after the Return from Babylon as to their own future? Careful statement is needed, for the political element mingles here with the religious. The newly restored Jewish state was a sickly plant; the second temple was a poor substitute for Solomon's splendid range of buildings. The Jews were bound either to fear much or to hope much for their struggling commonwealth. Hope predicted that the kingdom would be restored to the descendants of David;[1] fear expected that a flood of barbarians would overwhelm the small newly restored state.[2] After this renewed judgment Israel would be saved; Judah would dwell safely purified from ' blood '; and ' strangers ' would no more pass through Jerusalem. JEHOVAH would dwell in Zion:[3] and JEHOVAH would become king over all the earth.[4] This means that all the earth is to worship JEHOVAH, yet the distinction between Israel and the nations is to be preserved. They are to come once a year, for the feast of Booths,[5] whereas

---

[1] Zech. iii. 8–iv. 14.   [2] Zech. xiv. 1, 2 ; cp. Joel iii. 9–15.
[3] Joel iii. 21.   [4] Zech. xiv. 9.   [5] Zech. xiv. 16.

Israel was bound by ancient law to appear three times a year before JEHOVAH.[1]   These expectations are expressed again in somewhat different form by Trito-Isaiah :

' For as the new heavens and the new earth which I will make, shall remain before me . . . so shall your seed and your name remain. And it shall come to pass, that from one new moon to another, and from one sabbath to another, shall all flesh come to worship before me, saith JEHOVAH.' [2]

It is especially to be remarked that the figure of a personal Messiah is generally absent from these prophetic visions of the future. It may be (as many scholars have suggested) that when Zerubbabel failed to answer the expectations of Zechariah, the figure of Messiah faded from the Jewish consciousness for two or three centuries. But after the successes of the Maccabees it became easier for the Jews to imagine how much one hero or leader might effect for them. It is significant that the Jews made Simon the Maccabee ' their leader and high priest for ever, until there should arise a faithful prophet '.[3]   Moreover the book of Enoch in its Maccabean section expects a personal Messiah. On the other hand, in the seventh chapter of Daniel the ' one like unto a son of man ', who was ' brought near before the Ancient of days ' is generally taken to be a personification of Israel. Perhaps, however, he represents rather the Guardian Angel of Israel. In any case the hope for a personal Messiah survived among the ' common people '. They indeed were false to their inmost hope when they allowed themselves at the bidding of the priests to cry in the presence of the Christ Himself, ' We have no king but Caesar '.[4]

*   *   *   *   *   *   *   *   *

The aspect of Jewish religion represented by Koheleth (Ecclesiastes) need not detain us long. The book is the record

---

[1] Exod. xxiii. 14–17.   [2] Isa. lxvi. 22, 23.
[3] 1 Macc. xiv. 41 ; cp. Deut. xviii. 18.   [4] John xix. 15.

of a discussion imaginary in form, but real in matter. The names of the interlocutors are not given. The pessimist is allowed to speak at length and with entire frankness. He declares that there is no ' good ' (no ' profit ') in life. No distinction is made between the lot of the ' righteous ' and the lot of the ' wicked '.[1] All is vanity. Men perish utterly when they die : ' A living dog is better than a dead lion.' Men are told to ' fear God ', but they are not helped on their way by this book. Indeed it seems to have been preserved to us chiefly for the sake of the confutation given in the last verses :

' Fear God and keep his commandments, for this is every man's concern. For God shall bring every work into judgment with every hidden thing, whether it be good or whether it be evil.'

Pessimism could not maintain itself within Judaism in spite of the darkness of the days through which Israel passed from Ezra to the Maccabees. The last word of Judaism is not ' Vanity of vanities ', but ' Rest in JEHOVAH, wait patiently for him ', and ' Wait on JEHOVAH, and keep his way '.[2]

* * * * * * * * *

An important matter still to be noticed is the position of the Individual in Judaism during this period. What were his responsibilities ? What were his hopes and fears ?

Now in the ancient world, and not least among the Semites, the individual tended to be merged and lost in the family. The Head of the family was important as representing the family, but the rest were individually of small account. Herein lies the explanation of many strange, even repulsive deeds of early Hebrew history or saga. Isaac about to be sacrificed has no appeal against Abraham, nor Jephthah's daughter against Jephthah. Abraham surrenders Sarah to Pharaoh in order to save his own life, and that it might ' be well ' with him. Achan the head of a house commits a trespass, and he and all his family

---

[1] Eccles. viii. 14, ix. 2.   [2] Ps. xxxvii. 7 and 34.

with him suffer death for it. These incidents may be grouped together; they combine to illustrate the ancient view that the ' rights ' (and the ' wrongs ') of the individual are lost in those of the family.

But it was the merit of the religion of Israel that it went more and more as time went on against corrupt Semitic custom. If the kernel of Deuteronomy (i. e. chs. xii–xxvi) be pre-exilic (as we believe), then even before the Exile Hebrew law had improved the position of the individual in one most important case.

' The fathers shall not be put to death for the children, neither shall the children be put to death for the fathers : every man shall be put to death for his own sin.' [1]

It is even said that Amaziah of Judah (9th century B. C.) obeyed this law when he punished the assassins of his father.[2] In any case this law was well known during the early half of the Exile. What the Deuteronomist had put into one corner of his book, Ezekiel proclaimed at large. There is no more impressive passage in the Old Testament than that which elaborates the text : ' All souls are mine : ' (saith the Lord JEHOVAH) ' as the soul of the father, so also the soul of the son is mine : the soul that sinneth, it shall die.' [3]

Perhaps the Exile hastened the process of the recognition of the individual. Families were broken up by removal, foreigners (themselves perhaps exiles) joined themselves to Israel. New conditions required new decisions. Trito-Isaiah addressed himself to the proselytes and also to those Israelites who had been made eunuchs by their foreign masters :

' Unto the eunuchs that hold fast by my covenant will I give in mine house a name better than of sons and daughters.[4] . . . Also the strangers that join themselves to JEHOVAH will I bring to my holy mountain, and make them joyful in my house of prayer.' [5]

[1] Deut. xxiv. 16.   [2] 2 Kings xiv. 6.   [3] Ezek. xviii. 4.
[4] Isa. lvi. 4, 5.   [5] vv. 6, 7 ; cp. Zech. viii. 23.

When the prophets prophesied thus, Judaism could not remain a merely national or family religion. The individual had been recognized.

But an important question remains : Had the individual any future, any life after death? Of the future of the nation almost every prophet spoke. Zechariah in particular conveys the promise that Jerusalem shall ' be inhabited as villages without walls' in perfect peace and security.[1] In earlier days Ezekiel had seen Israel raised from the sepulchres, quickened from the dead, and standing up ' an exceeding great army '. Such a resurrection was a metaphor as far as the individuals were concerned ; there was no promise for them ; it was only for the continued existence of the nation. The Hebrew could be happy in the thought of living on in his descendants.[2]

But when the existence of the individual as such came to be acknowledged after the Return, the question of his survival after death began to be seriously asked. Job, it seems, longed to answer the question in the affirmative, but could not.[3]

At this point must be noticed the passage Job xix. 25-7. It is understood in the Authorized Version as Job's expectation of a bodily resurrection, ' And though after my skin [worms] destroy this [body], yet in my flesh shall I see God'. This interpretation, however, greatly strains the Hebrew, and does not suit the context. There is no such triumphant tone in what precedes and follows, neither can this interpretation be reconciled with xiv. 7-12. A closer translation of the Hebrew is as follows :

> But I know that my Redeemer liveth,
> And that he shall stand up over [my] dust at the last.
> Yea, after my skin has thus been destroyed,
> From my flesh I can behold God,
> Whom I used to behold for myself,
> And my own eyes saw, and not another's.[4]

[1] Zech. ii. 4.   [2] 2 Sam. vii. 12, 13 ; cp. 16 and 19 ; Ps. ciii. 15-17.
[3] Job xiv. 7-12.   [4] Cp. Job xxix. 2-5.

Job for all his sufferings has confidence in God. He is sure that
God who has so wonderfully created his flesh, will not fail
ultimately to justify him in the spirit. And so, sooner or later,
even if it be put off until Job is dead, the intervention will
come. He will have a champion against his 'friends', who
have assailed his integrity so vehemently. Let them fear the
champion's sword (ver. 29).

It is the Maccabean book of Daniel which gives the clearest
announcement of the resurrection of individuals. The fact
fits the time. No doubt the Jews as a nation, and also individual
Jews, suffered for their religion in greater or less degree long
before Antiochus Epiphanes began to persecute. But 168 B.C.
and the next few years were distinguished by several martyr-
doms in the full sense of the word. Jews deliberately suffered
for their faith, when they had the choice of escaping suffering
and even of earning favour by compliance with the demands
of their persecutor. The scribe Eleazar, ninety years old, deliberately preferred torture and death to eating swine's flesh.
The Seven Brethren with their mother likewise suffered
voluntarily ' for the laws of our fathers '.[1] So again 1,000 men,
women, and children allowed themselves to be massacred rather
than defend themselves by entrenching and fighting on the
Sabbath day.[2] Inevitably the question arose, What recognition
were such Jews to receive of their eminent faithfulness? No
reward in this life was possible. But the martyrs themselves
were confident. 'The king of the world', said the second of the
Seven Brethren, ' shall raise up us, who have died for his laws,
unto an eternal renewal of life.'

The writer of the book of Daniel went further. The faithful
were to be rewarded with eternal life, others were to wake
to shame and eternal abhorrence. The latter we may suppose
are the apostates. But it is interesting to note that no

---

[1] 2 Macc. vi. 18–vii. 41.   [2] 1 Macc. ii. 29–38.

general resurrection is announced. It is a special resurrection to meet the case of the specially faithful and the specially guilty :

' Many of them that sleep in the dust of the earth shall awake, some to eternal life, and some to shame and eternal abhorrence. And they that be wise shall shine as the brightness of the firmament, and they that turn many to righteousness as the stars for ever and ever.' [1]

*   *   *   *   *   *   *   *   *

EPILOGUE

We have approached so near to the time of our Lord that we are bound to add by way of Epilogue a few remarks on the next period of Jewish religious history. We must ask especially, What at that time was the Future Hope of Israel? The answer could not be given better than in the words of Dr. Sanday :

' Many of the Jews in the time of our Lord (I do not say all, and perhaps not a majority, but at least a large minority) fully expected that the world-age in which they lived was soon about to come to an end ; and that it would end with a complete break-up of the existing order of things, through a direct divine interposition. The interposition was to be essentially supernatural. It was to take the form of a visible establishment of God's kingdom upon earth. The agent through whom the kingdom was to be established was the Messiah. There was to be a great crash and collapse of all human kingdoms, and the divine kingdom alone was to be left standing.' [2]

Such doctrine as this could indeed be held by Quietists subject to the gloss, ' The LORD shall fight for you, and ye shall hold your peace '. It is probable that our Lord himself accepted it—in this sense. But a very different application of doctrine could be made as the history of the Zealots (Cananaeans) [3] shows. These men expected to fight in the

---

[1] Dan. xii. 2, 3.   [2] *Life of Christ in recent research*, p. 77.
[3] Mark iii. 18.

army of Messiah. Hence the prayer in the (so-called) Psalms of Solomon (xvii. 23 ff.) :

Raise up the son of David. . .
That thy servant may reign over Israel. . .
Gird him with strength to break in pieces the unjust rulers.
Purge Jerusalem from the nations which tread her down.

The kingdom for which the Zealot looked was as much political as spiritual. Under the teaching of Jesus, Simon the Cananaean had to eschew the political passion of his sect. For the Christ the Roman was not ' the Enemy '.

Our Lord brought Life and Incorruption to light through the Gospel. Before this the subject was dark. Between the Pharisees and Sadducees there was a division of opinion as to a Future Life. Unfortunately Josephus our chief authority hurries over the subject, and does not give us precise information. According to him the Pharisees taught that the soul is incorruptible (ἄφθαρτον), and that only the soul of the good passes into another (ἕτερον) body, while the soul of the bad is chastised with eternal (ἀιδίῳ) punishment. On the other hand, the Sadducees, he says, refute (ἀναιροῦσι) the doctrine of the permanence (διαμονήν) of the soul and of punishments and rewards in Hades (Josephus, B. J. II. viii. 14). Did the Sadducees do more than reject the Pharisaic doctrine ?

The statements in the New Testament are briefer even than those of Josephus. ' The Sadducees say that there is no resurrection (Matt. xxii. 23 ; Luke xx. 27), neither angel nor spirit ' (Acts xxiii. 8). But was this indeed the view of the Sadducees generally ? The critical question was put to our Lord by ' Sadducees ' (Matt., not by ' *the* Sadducees '), or (as St. Luke says) by ' certain of the Sadducees '. Probably there was a variation of opinion among the Sadducees themselves.

We learn further from Josephus that Pharisees and Sadducees were divided on the questions of Free Will and (as it seems) of

Moral Responsibility. Was the Pharaoh of Moses' day a free agent,[1] or was he held in the grip of fate ($\epsilon\dot{\iota}\mu\alpha\rho\mu\dot{\epsilon}\nu\eta$)? The Sadducees favoured the first, the Pharisees the second of these alternatives. The subject is glanced at more than once in the Fourth Gospel : ' Rabbi, who did sin, this man or his parents ? ' —' No man can come to me, except the Father draw him.' [2] Our Lord gave no formal decision on the great question, but his use of the word ' Father ' suggests perhaps that sooner or later every man is ' drawn '.

W. EMERY BARNES.

[1] Exod. ix. 16.   [2] John ix. 2 and vi. 44.

WORSHIP AND RITUAL

In its origin the Hebrew religion, together with its forms of worship, comes from the common Semitic stock. So that both religious conceptions and religious rites in their earlier stages among the Hebrews find their analogies and parallels in those of other Semitic nations. This fact often enables us to explain, on the one hand, and to supplement on the other, the paucity of detail which the Old Testament gives concerning the earlier stages of Hebrew religious belief and practice.

I

The earliest period during which we have any definite knowledge of Hebrew forms of worship is that comprising the centuries immediately preceding what is often called the 'Egyptian bondage'. And in this pre-Mosaic period the Hebrews were in the polytheistic stage; the beings they worshipped were called *Elim* (' gods '). But stages in religious development are never clearly marked off from those which precede them ; earlier conceptions, with their outward expression in ritual acts of worship, persist even when their meaning is not realized. And, therefore, in that stage of Polytheism which we make our starting-point, the influence and remnants of what preceded—Animism, Polydaemonism, Ancestor-worship, together with such more or less primitive institutions as Totemism, Magic, and Taboo—are to be discerned, though in some respects only faintly.

The *sacred tree*, for example, which in this pre-Mosaic period constituted a sanctuary, was regarded as the spot to which an *El* or ' god ' came when called upon ; but this was only the development of an earlier belief that a daemon dwelt there permanently ; and this, in its turn, developed from the animistic conception that the tree itself was animated by a life and will like those of a human being.

Though worked over in the interests of later Yahweh belief, the passage Gen. xii. 6 ff., e. g. is instructive as reflecting the conditions of the period of which we are thinking. The oak, or better ' terebinth,' of Moreh (' Oracle terebinth ') is represented as the first spot to which Abram came on entering the land of Canaan. Although the text does not say so, it was presumably with the intention of consulting the *El* who gave the oracle that the patriarch came here : he desired guidance. He therefore calls upon the name of the *El*, which in this case has not been preserved, as it has in Gen. xvi. 13, 14, xxi. 33, xxxv. 7 (cp. also xxxi. 42, 53 ; Judges ix. 46), and waits for the sign that the *El* has come. Judging from 2 Sam. v. 23–5, which records a very old-world idea of the deity announcing his presence in the tree-tops by the sound of marching, i. e. by the wind swaying the branches, we may justifiably conclude that the *El* made his presence known by the wind rustling in the tree. After the oracle has been given, Abram erects an altar and offers a sacrifice, as we must assume, since there would be no point in an altar without a sacrifice.

Another instance is given in Gen. xiii. 18, where Abram is said to have built an altar by the terebinths (it should probably be ' terebinth ') of Mamre ; it is the presence of the deity in the oak, or terebinth, which makes the tree holy, and for which reason an altar is erected by it.

Various other sacred trees are referred to (e. g. Gen. xxi. 33 ; Joshua xxiv. 26 ; Judges vi. 11, ix. 6, &c.). During the period with which we are dealing the worship consisted in calling upon the name of the *El* of the locality, and offering him a sacrifice.

But another ritual act in connexion with sacred trees, though not mentioned in the Old Testament, may be referred to ; for there is evidence of its practice in ancient times, and it is, moreover, in vogue among the Arabs of Syria and Arabia at the present day. They call certain trees *manâhil*, i. e. dwelling-places of supernatural beings ; to these sacrifices are offered, and pieces of flesh are hung on the branches.[1] Hanging things on a sacred tree was, and is, done with one of three purposes ; they are either gifts to the deity who owns the shrine, and his good-will is thus secured ; or they are offerings of thanksgiving in recognition of a request that has been granted ; or else, when as often happens, a worshipper hangs a piece of his or her clothing on it, it is a token of attachment to the deity.[2]

As with sacred trees so with *sacred stones*, or pillars. Jacob, according to Gen. xxviii. 18, 22, sets up a pillar (*Maṣṣēbah*) and pours oil on the top of it (cp. Gen. xxxi. 13) ; that this pillar is called ' the house of *El* ' shows that the *El* was believed to take up his abode in it. As Gunkel, however, rightly points out, ' in antique religion the symbol and the god are often *naïvely* identified ', hence in Gen. xlii. 24 the ' stone of Israel ' has become a name for the god of Bethel.[3] The anointing of the stone with oil shows how close is the identification between the symbol and the god.

We are probably justified in believing that another ritual act was that of kissing the pillar as a token of affection and honour, and therefore of worship ; this is suggested by the usage referred to in such passages as 1 Kings xix. 18 ; Hos. xiii. 2, which speak of kissing an idol.

The presence of the *El* in a holy stone is further illustrated in Gen. xxxi. 45 ff., which tells of a covenant being made of which the stone, i. e. the *El* within it, is a witness (cp. *El-Berith*, ' the covenant *El* ', Judges ix. 46).

---

[1] Doughty, *Arabia Deserta*, i. 448 ff. (1888).

[2] For examples see Robertson Smith, *The Religion of the Semites*, pp. 185 ff. (1894) ; Curtiss, *Primitive Semitic Religion To-day*, pp. 91 ff. (1902).

[3] *Genesis*, p. 290 (1901).

The special importance of the sacred stone, or *Maṣṣēbah*, of which there are many other instances mentioned in the Old Testament, is that the altar, in the ordinary sense, developed from it. This can be gathered, e. g. from 1 Sam. xiv. 33 ff., where it is evident that the sacred stone was a stone for slaughtering, i. e. a *Mizbēach*, 'altar' (from the root meaning to 'slaughter'), as among the ancient Arabs.[1] The pillar was always of unhewn stone, hence the prohibition, echoing very ancient usage, in Exod. xx. 25 : 'If thou make me an altar of stone, thou shalt not build it of hewn stones; for if thou lift up thy tool upon it, thou hast polluted it,' cp. Deut. xxvii. 5, 6. To hew a sacred stone would result in driving the *El* out of it. The prohibition, therefore, shows that it was the sacred pillar, in which the *El* dwelt, which became the altar. But to avoid misunderstanding it is well to point out here that the sacred stone, as Robertson Smith says,

'is more than an altar, for in Hebrew and Canaanite sanctuaries the altar, in its developed form as a table or hearth, does not supersede the pillar, the two are found side by side at the same sanctuary, the altar as a piece of sacrificial apparatus, and the pillar as a visible symbol or embodiment of the presence of the deity, which in course of time comes to be fashioned and carved in various ways, till ultimately it becomes a statue or anthropomorphic idol of stone, just as the sacred tree or post was ultimately developed into an image of wood.'[2]

In addition to sacred trees and sacred stones the ancient Hebrews had their *sacred wells*. As the abode of an *El* the sacred spring or well would naturally be regarded as his property; so that it is probable that the first act on the part of any who came to draw water would be to ask the *El*'s permission. The Old Testament, it is true, says nothing of this; but it is an interesting fact that in Palestine—in that 'unchangeable East' as it was, at any rate, until recent years—it is believed

[1] See Goldziher, *Muhammedanische Studien*, i. 232 ff. (1888–90).
[2] Op. cit., p. 204.

that all springs are the dwelling-places of spirits, and the peasant women ask their permission before they would think of drawing water.[1]

Among the sacred wells mentioned in the Old Testament there is one the name of which suggests that it served a purpose somewhat similar to that of the ' Oracle terebinth '. This is *'En-mishpaṭ* in Kadesh, referred to quite incidentally in Gen. xiv. 7. The name means the ' spring of judgement ', from which it must be inferred that it was used as a final resort when a decision on some point of tribal law could not be reached in the ordinary way. That it served such purpose as this is the opinion also of Robertson Smith, who says that ' the principle underlying the administration of justice at the sanctuary is that cases too hard for man are referred to the decision of God. Among the Hebrews in Canaan this was ordinarily done by an appeal to the sacred lot, but the survival of even one case of ordeal by holy water leaves no doubt as to the sense of the ' fountain of judgement ' (*'En Mishpaṭ*) or ' waters of controversy '. And he cites the case, mentioned in Num. v. 11 ff., of the ordeal of drinking holy water (it is in reference to a wife suspected of infidelity) ; the belief being that the ' holy water, which was mingled with the dust of the sanctuary, and administered with an oath, produced dropsy or wasting ', in the event of the woman being guilty. That the ceremony must be ancient is evident ' not only from its whole character, but because the expression "holy water" (Num. v. 17) is unique in the language of Hebrew ritual, and must be taken as an isolated survival of an obsolete expression '.[2]

Another interesting point of ritual in connexion with the sacred well occurs in the narrative of Abraham and Abimelech

---

[1] See *Zeitschrift des Deutschen Pal. Ver.* x. 180, and compare also Curtiss, op. cit., pp. 88 ff. For parallels among other Semites see Baudissin, *Studien zur Semitischen Religionsgeschichte*, ii. 153 ff. (1878).

[2] Op. cit., p. 180 f.

at Beersheba (Gen. xxi. 22 ff.), a place which received its name from the sanctuary of the ' seven wells '. Seven was, of course, the sacred number among the Hebrews, as indeed among all Semites ; and the Hebrew verb ' to swear ' means literally ' to come under the influence of seven things '.[1] This appears clearly in Gen. xxi. 27 ff., where it is told how Abraham made a covenant with Abimelech at Beersheba with an oath ; seven ewe lambs of the flock are given to Abimelech as a special pledge and witness (v. 30) ; they are not part of the covenant sacrifice, but the seven things under the influence of which the oath is made.

One other instance may be given of the ritual connected with the cult of sacred springs. In Num. xxi. 17, 18, there is preserved a song to a well at a place called Bĕēr (=' well ') :

> Then sang Israel this song,
> Spring up, O well ; sing ye unto it :
> The well which the princes digged,
> Which the nobles of the people delved,
> With the wand and with the staves.

This is an ancient fragment sung probably, in its original form, to the *El* who owned the spring when the water failed in the dry weather. To judge from other parallels the song accompanied a sacred dance in honour of the divine owner. Nilus relates that when the nomadic Arabs found a well they danced by it and sang songs to it ;[2] and Kazwini says that ' when the water (of the wells of Ilabistan) failed, a feast was held at the source, with music and dancing, to induce it to flow again.[3] In each case it is an act of homage to the divine owner of the well. The Old Testament omits to mention another ritual act which is instructive as showing how real the belief was in the presence of a divine being in the well. This was the throwing

[1] Robertson Smith, op. cit., p. 182.

[2] Migne, *Patr. Gr.*, lxxix, col. 648.

[3] i. 89 : quoted by Buchanan Gray, *Numbers*, p. 288 f. (1903).

into it of votive offerings, a custom prevalent at the present day in Palestine.

There are also records, belonging to later times, however, of worshippers bathing in the sacred spring ; possibly this was believed to be a means of union with the god. Whether these acts of worship were practised by the ancient Hebrews cannot be stated with certainty ; but the performance of them by other Semites makes it probable.

The most important of the sanctuaries mentioned were those marked by the sacred stone or pillar, for it is probable that the earliest form of sacrifice was performed in them, i. e., the pouring out of the blood of the victim at the base of the stone pillar ; and sacrifices constituted the central act of worship. The altars set up by a sacred tree were of earth, or else they consisted of a heap of stones, but these were extensions of the idea of an altar, i. e. the stone pillar or *Maṣṣēbah*.

The details of the sacrificial system given in the Old Testament belong to much later times ; in these are embodied rites of immemorial antiquity, together with those which religious development brought into existence subsequently. To distinguish between these is not always easy, and one must survey the general field of Semitic belief and practice, especially of the ancient nomadic Arabs, to reach definite and reliable conclusions as to what obtained among the Hebrews of pre-Mosaic times.

There can be no doubt that the essence of worship among these ancient Hebrews centred in the sacrifice known as *Zébach* (lit. ' slaughter '). This consisted of two parts ; the pouring out of the blood of the slaughtered victim upon, or at the base of, the *Maṣṣēbah*, and the subsequent feasting on its flesh at a sacred banquet. The former was the actual offering to the god ; the latter was the sacrificial meal of which the god was believed to partake with the worshippers. The conceptions underlying these acts were, firstly, the gift of a life to the god, for the blood poured out contained the life (Lev. xvii. 11, 14) ; and secondly, union with the god through partaking with him of the holy sacrificial food ; this was the most important part, indeed, the essence of the rite.

Sacrifices could be offered by any one, so that in this early period there was no priesthood.

The element of prayer which is naturally associated with worship does not come into consideration here, at all events in the ordinary acceptation of the term. The idea of the relationship between the worshipper and his god, from this point of view, is reflected in Gen. xxviii. 20 ff. : ' And Jacob vowed a vow, saying, If God will be with me, and will keep me in this way that I go, and will give me bread to eat, and raiment to put on, so that I come again to my father's house in peace,[1] this stone that I have set up as a maṣṣēbah shall be a house of God ; and of all that thou shalt give me I will surely render thee a tithe.'

The only feasts which can with reasonable certainty be assigned to this early period are *Pésach* (Passover) [2] and the new moon. It is probable that at the former the firstling males of the flocks and herds were offered. How the new moon festivals were celebrated at this time cannot be said ; but they evidently originated among nomads.

The Sabbath is often mentioned together with the new moon festival ; but whether it was observed in nomadic times is a question regarding which much diversity of opinion exists. The subject is too large to enter upon here [3] (a further reference is made to it in the next section).

---

[1] The words ' Then shall Yahweh be my God ' are the redactor's insertion.

[2] It was only in later times that the feast of unleavened bread (*Maṣṣôth*) became connected with *Pésach*. The name *Pésach* does not occur in Genesis : but the sacrifice of the firstlings implies it.

[3] The intricacy of the subject will be realized by consulting, e. g., Nielsen's *Die altarabische Mondreligion und die mosaische Ueberlieferung* (1904), and Meinhold's *Sabbat und Woche im alten Testament* (1905).

These brief details, then, of the cult of the Hebrews in pre-Mosaic times sufficiently indicate the general character of the religious conditions with which Moses was faced when he undertook the task of introducing a new religion among his people. It must be recognized that, so far, the worship and ritual of the Hebrews is at one with those of other Semites of the nomadic stage, and they offer nothing that is distinctive in Hebrew cult.

II

It was Moses who brought to the Hebrews the knowledge of Yahweh, and thus originated among them a new religion with, in some respects, a new mode of worship.[1] But, as is always the case with the introduction of a new religion, the old ideas and the traditional forms of ritual are not wholly obliterated; points of attachment between the new and the old emerge, so that in various particulars the familiar cult continues in essence even though forms and names change. Therefore, although there is real distinctiveness in the religion that owed its foundation among the Hebrews to Moses, we must be prepared to see signs of the older *El* religion continuing to assert themselves.

The various traditions (there are at least three) which have been embodied and intertwined in the Old Testament make it difficult and sometimes perhaps impossible to get at the actual facts; and when the facts are ascertained they are in many cases differently interpreted by scholars. This, however, must be expected. The chief points may be thus enumerated: while in the pre-Mosaic period there were, as we have seen, multitudes of sanctuaries—sacred trees, wells, and stones, each the abode of a different *El*, we have now one central shrine, the Ark in the

---

[1] With the question of how Moses first came to the knowledge of Yahweh, and the reason for the introduction of the new religion, we are not concerned here: see pp. 224–33; Budde, *Die Religion des Volkes Israel bis zur Verbannung*, pp. 1 ff. (1900); Gressmann, *Mose und seine Zeit*, pp. 161 ff. (1913).

Tabernacle; and in place of many *Elim*, one God, Yahweh. Not that the *Elim* were regarded as non-existent, but only that Yahweh was acknowledged as superior to them. The words put into the mouth of Jethro reflect this belief: ' Now I know that Yahweh is greater than all gods ' (Exod. xviii. 11 ; cp. xxiii. 13).

The Ark [1] (*'Arôn*) was not only the symbol of Yahweh, but was actually identified with Him. In Num. x. 35, 36, for example, it is said : ' And it came to pass, when the ark set forward, that Moses said, Rise up, Yahweh, and let thine enemies be scattered, and let them that hate thee flee before thee. And when it rested, he said, Return, Yahweh, unto the ten thousands of the thousands of Israel.' The adaptation of these words to circumstances of later times does not obscure the old-world conception that Yahweh took up His abode in the ark, which could thus be identified with Him. We have here, then, an illustration of how the traditional belief of the presence of a deity in a shrine persists, though a development regarding the deity has taken place.

The resting-place of the ark was in the tent, or tabernacle ; [2] it was for this reason that every one who sought Yahweh ' went out unto the tent of meeting ' (Exod. xxxiii. 7), i. e. they went to consult the oracle there; and it is probable that a medium for declaring the oracle to the inquirer was always present.[3]

The ark was carried about or driven on a cart, see Num. x. 35, 36; 1 Sam. iv. 3 ff. ; 2 Sam. vi. 3 ff., 13 ff., xv. 24 ; that is

---

[1] Hölscher doubts whether the Ark belongs to the Mosaic period : he regards it as Canaanite in origin (*Geschichte der israelitischen und jüdischen Religion*, p. 22 (1922).

[2] This is not explicitly stated in the Old Testament, but a sacred shrine must have been kept somewhere : and an empty tent would have been meaningless.

[3] ' Joshua the son of Nun, a young man, departed not out of the tent ' (Exod. xxxiii. 11). Another way of consulting the oracle was by means of Urim and Thummim (Deut. xxxiii. 8).

to say, the deity is not tied to any particular locality, whatever might be the case with the inferior *Elim*.

Belonging to the early Yahweh cult was the brazen serpent which was introduced by Moses, and to which incense was burned as late as the time of Hezekiah (2 Kings xviii. 4). Gressmann [1] identifies the rod of Moses with the brazen serpent. Moses received this rod from Yahweh on Mount Sinai (Exod. iv. 17), and it was kept in the tabernacle ' before Yahweh ' (Num. xvii. 7) ; it therefore belonged to the implements of the cult. According to the tradition it could be turned into a serpent (Exod. iv. 3), could bring thunder, hail, and fire from the skies (Exod. ix. 23), and could bring forth water from a rock (Exod. xvii. 5, 6). But the most significant thing about Moses's rod was that, as in the case of the ark, it was not only a symbol of Yahweh, but was identified with Him ; this, at any rate, seems to underlie the story in Exod. xvii. 9–16. [2]

The question of sacrifices during this period must be to some extent a matter of conjecture, because the ideas and customs of far separated times appear in the sources. It would be very precarious to base anything regarding their number and frequency upon what obtained after the settlement in Canaan, for new conditions of life, and the adoption of other cults resulted in a considerable development of the sacrificial system. What may be stated with certainty, however, is that the comparatively primitive conditions of life in the wilderness necessitated simple modes of worship, and, therefore, a sacrificial system of a simple character. It is probably safe to say that it did not differ in form or substance from what had hitherto obtained, excepting that sacrifices were offered to Yahweh, and to Him alone.

The offering of incense belongs to the Yahweh cult as to the

---

[1] *Mose und seine Zeit*, p. 456 (1913).
[2] See further on this Gressmann, op. cit., p. 457.

earlier ritual; it is represented as having, on special occasions, miraculous powers (see Num. xvi. 41 ff. = xvii. 6 ff. in the Hebrew).

A new element, so far as the Hebrews were concerned, was introduced by Moses through the inauguration of the Levitical priesthood. The new religion demanded priests initiated into the proper mode of offering sacrifices to the new God, to look after and minister before the new sanctuary, the ark, and to declare oracles, which were now inspired by Yahweh (cp. Deut. xxxiii. 8).

While in the matter of sacrifices the form continued as hitherto, in the other great essential of worship, prayer, there is reason to believe that a real development began to take place. Confessedly it is by inference rather than by concrete examples that we are guided in making this statement; and it is recognized that the accounts of the lifting up of Moses's staff to bring the plagues (Exod. vii. 14 ff.), and to effect the victory over the Amalekites (Exod. xvii. 8 ff.), which may be regarded as in some sense prayer in action, partake of the character of magic, and in so far do not suggest development of earlier practice. But there are other facts which must be taken into consideration here. What clearly impressed Moses and his people about Yahweh more than anything else was His power, manifested above all in the overthrow of the Egyptians [1] and the deliverance of the Hebrews. The God who could accomplish this must be more powerful than all other gods, hence the allegiance offered to Him alone. Now it lies in the nature of things that prayer addressed to a God who has proved Himself more powerful than any other God, and who is, therefore, alone acknowledged as the God of a people, will be more trustful and more concentrated than that offered first to one and then to another of a multiplicity of gods, whose power is confined to

[1] That some historical fact underlies the narrative in Exod. xiv. 26, 27 seems certain.

small things for individuals, not to any manifestation of awe-inspiring might on behalf of the whole people.

The assertion, therefore, seems justified that together with belief in Yahweh a real development in the nature of prayer took place, and with it a tendency to more spiritual worship.

The *Pésach* festival, together with the sabbaths and new moons, continued as heretofore, excepting that they were celebrated in honour of Yahweh. With regard to the sabbath, it is well to point out that Gressmann argues with much cogency that its introduction among the Hebrews was due to Moses. He believes that it was a specifically Yahweh weekly festival, emphasizing the significant fact that in the Decalogue this only, among the rites and festivals observed, is enjoined. Its inauguration is ascribed to Moses in Exod. xvi, a combination of the two oldest sources (JE).[1]

The rite of circumcision, whatever its origin, was adopted by Moses as a mark of dedication to Yahweh.[2] It was performed on men; but in later times infants of eight days old were circumcised (Gen. xvii. 12, P : cp. Lev. xii. 3).

It is difficult to over-estimate the importance of the work of Moses in the domain of ritual and worship (his ethical teaching is dealt with elsewhere, see pp. 227–36); for while in some respects one cannot fail to recognize the persistence of antique conceptions, the advance he made in the great essentials was epoch-making, and of abiding influence. It was Moses who first created real distinctiveness in Hebrew religion. The acceptation of *one God only* to whom worship was due, even though the existence of other gods was not denied, resulted in the *centralization of worship*, a conception which was destined to have a profound influence upon the religion of the people both at the time and at a much later period. It is true that Moses

[1] Op. cit., pp. 461 ff.
[2] Gen. xvii. 10 ff., which connects the origin of the rite with Abraham, belongs to the latest source (P).

did not originate a monotheistic worship, but the monolatry which he taught was the biggest step in the direction of monotheism which the world had yet known.[1] And what is so significant about the religion of Moses is that, although the time came soon after his death when his teaching and influence seem to have been almost obliterated, the seed which he had sown was there, and in due time bore fruit.

III

It is natural enough that however many points of contact a new religion may have with that which it is designed to supersede, it will meet with opposition on the part of many who are attached to the old beliefs and customs. The Old Testament has preserved some clear indications that this was the case during the lifetime of Moses (see, e. g., Exod. xxxii. 1 ff.; Num. xvi. 1 ff.). As long as he was alive he was able to combat and to silence this opposition; but when his dominating personality was withdrawn, and when, with the gradual penetration into Palestine, the people came more and more into contact with the higher culture but lower cults of the Canaanites, a great change for the worse took place, and the religion of Yahweh became little more than a name among the bulk of the people for many years.

Canaanite rites and religion were in the main those of the Semites in general, though some extraneous elements had been absorbed. Common to all the Semites were goddess cults, the influence of which upon the Israelites has not always been recognized; but as this type of worship had a baneful effect upon Israelite cult, it demands some attention. There is, however, a more important reason for devoting a little space to the subject. We shall see that, together with the worship of

[1] The monotheistic conception of Ikhnaton (if it was earlier in date than Mosaism, which is by no means certain) was ephemeral and influenced nobody.

Yahweh, goddess cults were prevalent in Israel up to the eve of the Exile ; indeed, there is evidence pointing to a combination of the name of Yahweh with that of a goddess among the Jews of the Dispersion. But though the Israelites, together with all the peoples of antiquity, worshipped goddesses, they were the one and only nation to abolish these cults ; and in spite of the higher culture of Babylonians, Persians, Greeks, &c., Israel had for centuries discarded this type of worship while it continued among all other nations. This point of superiority in Israelite religion, which showed itself for centuries before the Christian era, needs emphasis, for the history of religion shows that there is an extraordinary fascination in the worship of a woman type of deity, a fascination against which even Christianity has not always been proof.

There are *a priori* reasons for believing that among the *Elim* worshipped by the Hebrews in pre-Mosaic times the female *El* was not unknown. The Hebrew name for God, *El*, has in origin nothing specifically masculine about its formation or conception, whatever may have been the case later. Though generally used of God, it is also found in connexion with a goddess, e. g. in 1 Kings xi. 5, 33, where the Canaanite goddess, Ashtoreth, is spoken of as *Elohim*. As nomads, with flocks and herds, the early Hebrews must, on the analogy of ancient Arab belief, have worshipped a goddess of fertility. Indeed, the existence of this belief among them is reflected in a striking way in the Old Testament; for in Deut. vii. 13, it is said : ' He (i. e. Yahweh thy God) . . . will also bless the fruit of thy body, and the fruit of thy ground, thy corn and thy wine and thine oil, the increase of thy kine and the young of thy flock.' The literal rendering of these last words, ' the young of thy flock ' is ' the *'ashtārôth* of thy flocks ' ; and that is very significant, for what it originally meant was that the fertility of the flocks was conceived to be due to the power of Astarte, the goddess of fertility ; so much so that the young of the flocks came to be known by her name. And this expression became so ingrained in the language as to be used in later times without any thought of what it originally meant, and without any idea of its being inconsistent when used by monotheistic believers in Yahweh. A phrase like this, *the 'ashtārôth of the flocks,* ' which has descended from religion into ordinary life ', says Robertson Smith, ' is very old evidence for the association of Astarte with the sheep ; and it is impossible to explain it except by frankly admitting that Astarte, in one of her types, had originally the form of a sheep, and was a sheep herself, just as in other types she was a dove or a fish '.[1]

Of course, it does not necessarily follow that the Hebrews in pre-Mosaic times knew a goddess under the name of Astarte ; it is quite likely that among the female *Elim* one rose to special eminence to whom this name was applied after it was met with in Canaan. At any rate if, as seems certain, the pre-Mosaic Hebrew nomads worshipped a fertility goddess, Canaanite influence would have been more strongly exercised in this direction when the settlement in Canaan began.

The adoption of a goddess cult by the Israelites in Canaan has within recent years been proved by excavations in Palestine. On the site of ancient Gezer Mr. Stewart Macalister found within the temple area a small bronze statuette, $4\frac{1}{2}$ inches in length, representing an undraped female, from the head of which, ' just above the ears, spring two slender horns, coiled like those of a ram, and trending downwards'. There can be no doubt that this must be regarded as ' a representation of the 'Ashtārôth Karnáim, or two-horned Astarte ' (cp. Gen. xiv. 5), and that it points to the worship of this goddess as a sheep or cow divinity ' of which traces, in the shape of small heads of cattle modelled in pottery, come to light almost every day in the excavations '.[2] It is worth adding that Sellin, in excavating

[1] Op. cit., p. 477.
[2] Pal. Explor. Fund, *Quarterly Statement,* 1903, pp. 225 ff.

on the site of the ancient Taanach, also found a statuette of the two-horned Astarte ; [1] this belonged to the Canaanite, i. e. pre-Israelite, stratum ; but the Macalister finds lay in the sixth stratum which dates from 1000–600 B. C.

A further fact in this connexion should be noted. Just as there were in the Palestine to which the Israelites came, place-names compounded with Baal, denoting ownership of the locality (such as Baal-hazor, ' lord of the enclosure ', 2 Sam. xiii. 23 ; Baal-hermon, ' lord of the sacred [mount] ', Judges iii. 3 ; Baal-tamar, ' lord of palms ', Judges xx. 33 ; Baal-shalishah, meaning uncertain, 2 Kings iv. 42 ; and others), so there were also place-names, though their mention is rarer, compounded with Baalah, the feminine form of Baal, viz. : Baaläth-bĕēr, ' mistress of the well ', Joshua xix. 8 ; Baalah, ' mistress ', a place a little to the west of Jerusalem, Joshua xv. 9 ff., 29 ; 1 Chron. xiii. 6 ; Baalath, ' mistress ', a city in Dan, Joshua xix. 44 ; 1 Kings ix. 18 ; Bĕâlôth, ' mistresses ', in the south of Judah, Joshua xv. 24 ; 1 Kings iv. 16. As the Israelites assimilated the worship of Yahweh to that of the local baals, the presumption is justified that they did the same in the case of the local bĕâlôth, or female baals.

The name of another ancient goddess is Anath ; this is the name of a man, Judges iii. 31, but the form is feminine ; it is also contained in Anathoth, near Jerusalem (1 Kings ii. 26, and elsewhere). This name is mentioned in the Tell el-Amarna tablets as that of a goddess worshipped by the Syrians and Phoenicians. It appears also in the Elephantine papyri.[2] Dr. S. A. Cook, in writing about the Hyksos and their gods, says : ' An interesting name contains Anath, the Syrian goddess of war and love, and apparently the same as the Babylonian Antum, wife of Anu, God of heaven ; and it combines Anath and El, just as, among the Jews of Elephantine in the fifth

---

[1] *Tell Ta'anek*, pp. 50, 106 (1904).

[2] Ed. Meyer, *Der Papyrusfund von Elephantine*, p. 39 (1912).

century B. C., the same goddess is combined with Yahweh in the name Anath-Yahu.' [1]

There are thus good grounds for the belief in the existence of a goddess cult among the Israelites. Of the details of this worship the Old Testament has very little to say; but that little is significant; it must suffice to point out that rites of an impure character were connected with these cults.

Turning now to the sanctuaries of the Israelites in the land of Canaan, we find that though the mass of them were taken over from the Canaanites, a centre here and there was devoted to the true worship of Yahweh. The sacred ark is Yahweh's dwelling-place and is identified with Him (1 Sam. iv. 3–8); it is no more housed in a tent, but in a temple (1 Sam. iii. 15) in Shiloh. Other sanctuaries in which Yahweh-worship in its original character was preserved were in all probability Gilgal and Sichem, among others. But these were exceptions. The nature of the general type of sanctuary, and the kind of worship offered there is plainly indicated by the prohibitions in Deut. xii. 2, 3 :

'Ye shall surely destroy all the places wherein the nations which ye shall possess served their gods, upon the high mountains, and upon the hills, and under every green tree : and ye shall break down their altars, and dash in pieces their pillars (*Maṣṣēbôth*) and burn their Asherim with fire : and ye shall hew down the graven images of their gods ; and ye shall destroy their name out of that place.'

This passage, though centuries later than the time with which we are dealing, records the type of cult which the Israelites had learned from the Canaanites. The places on mountains and hills were the 'high places', or *bâmôth* (sing. *bâmah*), so often denounced, though in this immediate post-Mosaic period they had no such evil connotation as attached to them in subsequent ages ; this is clear from, e. g., 1 Sam. ix. 12–14. Here sacrifices were offered and incense was burned (1 Kings iii. 3), the name

[1] *The Cambridge Ancient History*, 233. (1923).

Yahweh being substituted for the traditional baal of the
sanctuary. By the side of the altar stood the *Maṣṣēbah*, the
stone pillar, and the *Ashērah*, the wooden pole, representing the
ancient sacred stone and sacred tree (cp. Hos. iii. 4, x. 1),
symbols of the divine presence; sometimes the sacred tree
itself stood in the *bāmah* (1 Sam. xxii. 6). After the sacrifice
had been offered, a sacrificial feast was held (1 Sam. ix. 22).
The idols (*pĕsīlim*) spoken of in the Deuteronomy passage
quoted above were of stone or wood (Judges iii. 19, 26; Hos.
iv. 17, x. 5; Mic. i. 7; Deut. vii. 5, 25, &c.); they were in the
form of calves in Bethel and Dan (1 Kings xii. 28, 29); what
other form they took cannot be said with certainty; but in
view of what has come to light during the Gezer and Taanach
excavations the possibility of goddess figures can scarcely be
ruled out. Ritual acts of worship accorded to idols consisted
of bowing the knee to them and kissing them (1 Kings xix. 18;
Hos. xiii. 2), and there was also the sacred dance performed in
their honour (e. g. Exod. xxxii. 6 [see Samaritan Pentateuch and
Septuagint], Judges xxi. 21; 2 Sam. vi. 5, and probably 1 Sam.
xvi. 11).[1] In the larger sanctuaries the idol had its shrine and
even its temple; thus, Gideon seems to have set up an idol of
some kind in Ophrah,[2] and from the fact that ' all Israel ' came
to worship it, one must assume that it stood in a temple (Judges
viii. 26, 27). So also in Nob (1 Sam. xxi. 9), Bethel (Amos vii.
13, ix. 1), and in Jerusalem (1 Kings vi. 1 ff.).

The mention of the idol in Ophrah raises the question of the
Ephod which had its place in the cult of the Israelites. The
earliest references to this object make it plain that it was an
idol. In Judges viii. 26, 27 it is said that Gideon required
1,700 shekels of gold in the construction of an Ephod; the
word used in verse 27, ' he set it up (not ' put it ' as in the

---

[1] See the writer's *The Sacred Dance*, p. 91 (1923).
[2] But see Burney's full note on *Ephod* in his *The Book of Judges*, pp. 236 ff.
(1918).

Revised Version) in his city', shows that it was something in the nature of an image. From 1 Sam. xxiii. 9–11, xxx. 7, 8, it can be seen that the *Ephod* was used for obtaining oracles ; that it was something which stood upright is implied in 1 Sam. xxi. 10 (9 in Revised Version), according to which the sword of Goliath was kept behind it. From these passages it is to be concluded that the *Ephod* was an idol to which worship was offered (cp. Judges viii. 27, ' All Israel went wantonly astray after it '), and that it was especially connected with the giving of oracles. It was, therefore, something entirely distinct from the priest's vestment called ' the linen ephod ' (1 Sam. ii. 18, xxii. 18 ; 2 Sam. vi. 14).

Other cult objects were the *Těrâphim*, ' Nourishers ', or ' Maintainers '. These images are spoken of as gods (Gen. xxxi. 30 ; Judges xviii. 24), and as being kept in houses (Gen. xxxi. 19 ; Judges xvii. 5 ; 1 Sam. xix. 13, 16), which points to the family being under their care ; and it is the father of the family who seems to have the special charge of them (Gen. xxxi. 19 ; Judges xvii, where Micah, the head of the family, owns them ; cp. 1 Sam. xix. 11–17). It is to be gathered, therefore, that the *Těrâphim* were household gods, and were a remnant of ancestor-worship.

Inasmuch as the nomadic life of the desert had now given place to that of agriculture, the purpose as well as the material of sacrifices underwent some modification and development. This was due not only to the change in mode of life, but also to a somewhat different conception of Yahweh, who took the place of the local baals of the Canaanite sanctuaries.

Animal sacrifices continued to be the most important part of worship : *Zébach* the ' sacrifice ' *par excellence*, and *'ôlah* the ' burnt-offering ', when the victim was wholly burnt on the altar ; with the latter the *shélem*-offering is often combined. This word is translated by ' peace-offering ' in the English Bible, but, as Robertson Smith says, it is not a plausible rendering, and ' can hardly be separated from the verb *shillem*, to pay or discharge, e. g. a vow '. *Zébach* is the more general term, ' including all animals slain for food, agreeably with the fact that in old times all slaughter was sacrificial. In later times, when slaughter and sacrifice were no longer identical, *zébach* was not precise enough to be used as a technical term of ritual, and so the term *shelâmim* came to be more largely used than in the early literature.' [1] The ritual was the same as heretofore, viz. the blood of the victim was poured out at the base of the altar or smeared upon it. Portions of the fat were burned upon the altar, and the flesh boiled and eaten by worshippers at the sacrificial banquet (see 1 Sam. ii. 15, 16, ix. 22 ff.).

But in addition to the animal sacrifices were the vegetable oblations, the first-fruits of the soil : meal, wine, and oil. These were mostly offered together with the animal sacrifices, though not invariably. The general term for vegetable oblations is *minchah*, ' gift ', or ' tribute ', which consisted of the first-fruits (' the first of the first-fruits of thy ground thou shalt bring into the house of Yahweh thy God ', Exod. xxiii. 19, xxxiv. 26), consisting of a small portion of the produce of the soil made over entirely to the deity. In Lev. xxiii. 11 the mode of presenting this is described, a sheaf is to be ' waved ' before Yahweh ; the word denotes that it is to be thrown down ; and in Deut. xxvi. 2 ff., it is prescribed that first of all the fruits shall be presented to the priest in a basket which is set down before the altar.

Belonging to the cereal oblations was the shewbread ; this was ' holy bread ' set on a table in the sanctuary (1 Sam. xxi. 4–7 [3–6 in E.V.]).

Finally, there were the drink-offerings (*nẹsek*), libations of wine, which did not, however, occupy an important place ; they were merely the accompaniment to sacrifices.

In general, the sacrifices mentioned came under the category

[1] Op. cit., p. 237.

of those which were obligatory ; they belonged of right to the deity. In addition to these there were free-will offerings, called *nedabôth*, and those offered in fulfilment of vows, called *nedārim* ; these were voluntary, and of a private character.

Of these sacrifices all those which were connected with agriculture were taken over from the Canaanites ; the animal sacrifices were the Israelites' heritage from their forefathers.

Prayer is spoken of in connexion with sacrifice (1 Sam. i. 3), and doubtless the efficacy of prayer was believed to be greater when offered in the sanctuary (cp. 1 Sam. i. 10). It is noticeable that prayer in the ordinary sense tends to occupy a more important place ; this is to be explained by the fact that, in spite of the predominant Baal cult, there were those among the people whose belief in Yahweh was unimpaired ; and with the conviction of His solicitude for the welfare both of His people and of individuals grew the natural desire of offering prayer to Him. Thus Hannah prays for a child (1 Sam. i. 10) ; when Samuel is asked to give the people a king he prays to Yahweh for guidance (1 Sam. viii. 6) ; David prays to Yahweh concerning the building of the Temple (2 Sam. vii. 27), he prays to Him also for his child (2 Sam. xii. 16) ; and there is the prayer of Solomon, doubtless an elaborated form, in 1 Kings viii. 22 ff.

Although the evidence is uncertain, there is some justification for believing that songs of praise began to be part of the regular worship in the time of David.

The subject of the priesthood, as this existed among the Israelites in Canaan well into the period of the monarchy, offers some points of interest. The chief of the priests' duties was undoubtedly in connexion with the giving of oracles ; they also had charge of the sanctuaries. As to the priesthood being a sacrificing ministry, it is to be noted that sacrifices were by no means necessarily offered by the priests. For example, sacrifices are offered by Gideon at Yahweh's command (Judges vi. 23 ff.), the men of Beth-shemesh offered burnt-offerings

(1 Sam. vi. 14) ; Saul (1 Sam. xiv. 33–5), David (2 Sam. vi. 17), Solomon (1 Kings iii. 4 ff., ix. 25), and Elijah (1 Kings xviii. 30 ff.), all sacrifice, and this is regarded as the right and proper thing. Indeed, a sacrificing priesthood comes into existence only in the reign of David and especially with the building of the Temple in Jerusalem ; and even then it is not an independent body like the earlier Shiloh or Nob priesthood, but the priests are officials whom the king appoints or dismisses according to his will (see 2 Sam. viii. 17, xx. 25, 26 ; 1 Kings iv. 1 ff., ii. 26, 27, 35). These conditions did not, however, last long ; with the development of the sacrificial system a special body of ministers, experts in the ritual, became a necessity ; [1] and the power of the priesthood grew with its indispensability.

With the agricultural life of the Israelites arose some new feasts in addition to those handed down. Foremost among these were the feast of unleavened bread (*Maṣṣôth*), combined with Passover (Deut. xvi. 1–8), the harvest festival (*Ḳāṣîr*, Exod. xxxiv. 22 ; Deut. xvi. 9–12), and the feast of ingathering at the end of the year (*Asîph*, Exod. xxxiv. 22 ; Deut. xvi. 13–15, where it is called by the more familiar name *Sukkôth*, or the feast of tabernacles). In their origin these feasts were Canaanite which the Israelites celebrated in honour of the baals of the land, but which subsequently they held in honour of Yahweh. Their chief note was one of joyousness (cp. Lev. xxiii. 40 ; Deut. xii. 18 : ' Ye shall rejoice before Yahweh your God '). The due sacrifices having been offered, there was the feeling of security for the future, and feasting and dancing followed.

From the time of the entry of the Israelites into Canaan, then, up to about the beginning of the ninth century there was a gradual assimilation of the religion of Yahweh to the Canaanite

---

[1] Regarding the intricate and controverted question of the Levites we must content ourselves with referring to the convincing argument of Gressmann, op. cit., i. 211 ff., 275 ff., 463 ff. : see also Hölscher, op. cit., pp. 64 ff.

vegetation cults. Not that adherents of the original Yahweh
religion as instituted by Moses were wanting, the subsequent
history proves that there were such; but for centuries they
were unable to assert themselves. A crisis was reached when
Ahab (876 B.C. is probably the year of his accession) having
married Jezebel, the daughter of Ethbaal king of Tyre and
priest of Astarte, built a temple in Samaria for the worship of
Melkarth, the Tyrian Baal (1 Kings xvi. 31–2); and in the
southern kingdom Athaliah, the daughter of Jezebel, likewise
introduced the worship of the Tyrian Baal in Jerusalem
(2 Kings xi. 18). This produced a reaction, and a stern struggle
ensued between the upholders of the religion of Yahweh and the
champions of the Baal cults. But the fact must be recognized
that, in spite of reforms which took place at different times,
the influence of Canaanite worship was not eradicated during
the whole period of the monarchy, and this in spite of the co-
operation of certain of the kings with the priests and the
prophets. Our knowledge of the worship and ritual during
these centuries is gained largely from the denunciations of the
prophets, though by no means exclusively.

The first attempt at reform took place under Asa, king of
Judah, who 'put away the sodomites out of the land, and removed
all the idols which his fathers had made; and also Maacah his
mother he removed from being queen-mother because she had
made a shocking thing [1] for the Asherah; and Asa cut down
her image, and burnt it at the brook Kidron. But the high
places were not taken away . . .' (1 Kings xv. 12–14). One sees
from this the existence of a goddess cult; it is also noteworthy
that the high places were clearly not considered incompatible
with the worship of Yahweh. That Asa was only partially
successful is seen from 1 Kings xxii. 46; 2 Kings xii. 3. As to
the northern kingdom, Jehu, in the middle of the ninth century,

---

[1] The word comes from the root 'to shudder': the reference is probably
to some obscenity.

undertakes vigorous action on behalf of Yahweh worship; but the brief notice in 2 Kings x. 26 ff. is very instructive as showing how deeply the Canaanite cults had taken root; the temple of Baal in Samaria is, indeed, destroyed; but the golden calves are still worshipped. And so it continues. The eighth century prophets bear ominous witness to the prevalence of cults incompatible with true Yahweh worship (see Amos v. 4 ff., 26, viii. 14; Hos. iv. 10–19, vii. 13 ff., viii. 4, 11, ix. 9, xii. 11, xiii. 1, 2; Mic. i. 5 ff.; Isa. x. 10, 11, and many other passages), and it is the same with the prophets of later centuries.

But it is not only the influence of Canaanite cults on the worship of Yahweh during these centuries which is met with. Towards the end of the eighth century the southern kingdom came under the suzerainty of Assyria, and this had a marked effect upon the cult in Jerusalem. From Zeph. i. 4–9 it is seen that foreign, i. e. Assyrian, customs had been introduced. How this affected the worship is seen in 2 Kings xxi. 3 ff., cp. xxiii. 5 ff., 11 ff., for, in addition to the Canaanite cults, we find that the worship of the sun, moon, and stars is introduced; incense is burned to these as well as to the ‘ twelve signs ’ (the Zodiac), and all the host of heaven; horses are dedicated to the sun; and altars are erected in the courts of the temple and on the roof of the upper chamber of Ahaz on which sacrifices were offered to the celestial bodies.

Nevertheless, the worshippers of Yahweh, headed by priests as well as prophets, held their own, and gained ascendency in course of time. The cult reform of Josiah in 621 B. C. was inspired by the high-priest Hilkiah; Assyrian and Canaanite forms of worship were abolished; and it looked as though the final victory for Yahweh had been gained. But this lay still in the future. The death of Josiah and the ascendency of Egypt at the battle of Megiddo reduced Judah to a vassal state of Pharaoh Necho; he in his turn was conquered by Nebuchadnezzar at the battle of Carchemish a few years later; and Judah, together with the whole of Syria, came under the power of Babylonia, with the result that foreign cults were once more adopted; the worship of the queen of heaven, Sun worship, Tammuz worship, and animal cults are enumerated (see Jer. xliv. 15–19; Ezek. viii). Then followed the downfall of the kingdom of Judah.

The picture is a melancholy one. But it is painted by those who were the true followers of Yahweh. Their work was going on throughout these centuries, and was ultimately to bear fruit. So that although much that was extraneous flourished in the religion and worship of Israel, there is another side to the picture; for there was also much that was specifically Israelite. This, however, only appears later, when during and after the Exile the spiritual descendants of the true Yahweh worshippers were offered, through the circumstances of the times, the opportunity of consolidating and developing what had been handed down.

IV

The post-exilic period presents us with some perplexing questions; a new state of affairs regarding worship and ritual has arisen, but it is the final phase of a process that had been going on long before the exile. It is by no means all new: we see the result of co-ordination and consolidation as well as of development; old and new are combined; but since the records do not give us much information as to the when and how of much which exists before the exile, we cannot always know for certain what belongs to the earlier periods and what was developed during the post-exilic period. Dr. S. A. Cook expresses precisely what, doubtless, many investigators have experienced when he says that ' the fundamental problem of Israelite history is that of the relation between the Judaism of Ezra's time and the earlier Mosaism, and of determining how much is Mosaic, how much exclusively post-exilic, and what historical development intervenes '.[1] This applies also to the restricted area of worship and ritual.

The priesthood, whose power and influence had been exercised on behalf of Yahweh worship during the period of the Judaean monarchy, has now risen to the height of power, and has taken the place of the monarchy as the ruling body. Whereas in pre-exilic times priests and Levites expressed the same idea, we find now a difference of rank among them ; priests are only those among the Levites who are ' the sons of Zadok ', the rest being ministers in the Temple of an inferior order (cp. Ezek. xliv. 10 ff.). Not only so, but there is now a high-priest who stands at the head of the priesthood ; he differs from the high-priest of earlier times in that he is not a *primus inter pares*, but the spiritual head of the Jewish people.[2]

Whether the Mosaic ideal of the centralization of worship in a single sanctuary was held and striven for before or after the exile turns upon the difficult and complicated question of the date of Deuteronomy ;[3] but, in any case, the ideal was not attained until late in the post-exilic period ; for it is clear that Ezra's polemic against his people was not confined to the mixed marriages ; this can be seen, e. g., by what is said in Ezra ix. 1 : ' The people of Israel, and the priests and the Levites, have not separated themselves from the peoples of the lands, doing according to their abominations, even of the Canaanites . . .' (see the whole chapter). Hölscher points out that even as late as Roman times the cults in the ancient sanctuaries were still practised, viz. at Mamre, Gilgal, at the well of Enaim, on Carmel, and in Dan.[4] It must, therefore, be recognized that

[1] Op. cit., i. 221.   [2] See further, Hölscher, op. cit., p. 144.
[3] See Hölscher's important essay in the *Z. A. T. W.* for 1922, pp. 161–255, and the equally important volume by A. C. Welch, *The Code of Deuteronomy ; A new theory of its origin* (1924).
[4] Hölscher, *Geschichte* . . ., p. 139, where the references are given.

the ideal of a central sanctuary at Jerusalem was not altogether realized, though there can be no doubt that the bulk of the people adhered to it.

One of the most important witnesses to the development of religious ideas is to be seen in the sacrificial system as it appears in post-exilic times. Although, as already pointed out, it is not always possible to indicate precisely when particular developments arose, there is no doubt that the daily morning and evening burnt-offerings, the various sin and trespass offerings, culminating in the ceremonies of the Day of Atonement, ' the keystone of the sacrificial system of post-exilic Judaism ',[1] all belong to this period. Hölscher, following Bertholet, points out that the public obligatory sacrifices alone required annually 1,093 lambs, 113 bullocks, 37 rams, 32 goats, 150·6 ephahs of fine flour, 342·08 hin of wine, and an equal quantity of oil; besides these there were the innumerable private offerings.[2]

The great increase of sacrifices which arose during the post-exilic period was due to the developed sense of sin, which was one of the consequences of the exile.

While liturgical music, both instrumental and vocal, formed part of the worship in earlier times, a great and increasing development took place during the post-exilic period; hymns of thanksgiving were sung in procession round the altar during the sacrificial offering (Ps. xxvi. 6, 7), and frequent reference is made in the Psalms to the songs of praise and thanksgiving, accompanied by various musical instruments, in the worship of the temple.

Notable and significant for the growth of spiritual religion was the character and frequency of prayer. It occupies now a far more definite place in worship than hitherto; regular times for prayer are fixed; and the subjects of prayer correspond to the fuller and more spiritual conceptions of God. It is in

---

[1] Margolis, in the *Jewish Encycl.* ii. 286 *a*.   [2] Op. cit., p. 145.

a high degree probable that the oldest prayers in the Jewish Liturgy trace their origin to the earliest centuries of the post-exilic period.[1]

The concentration on worship and religious observances as prescribed and enjoined in the Law, which was characteristic of the great bulk of the Jewish people, had as one of its consequences an exaggerated punctiliousness in regard to ritual. The method of keeping the Sabbath grew stricter both as to abstention from work and in religious observances, and the same applies to the great festivals. Circumcision became the distinguishing mark of a Jew. But things also of minor importance came to be regarded as essential, such as the wearing of fringes (Num. xv. 37 ff.), the ' binding ' of God's commands on the hand and forehead (phylacteries), and the door-post symbol (Deut. vi. 6–9) ; all very ancient objects used as safe-guards against evil spirits, but now impressed into Yahweh worship with the object and intention of honouring His commands.

The ancient practice of fasting, which in pre-exilic times, however, was only undertaken on special occasions, e. g. as a mourning custom (1 Sam. xxxi. 13 ; 2 Sam. i. 12), or when the divine wrath had been provoked (Judges xx. 26), or for national sin (1 Sam. vii. 6), or in preparation for some important undertaking (Jer. xxxvi. 6, 9)—became in post-exilic times a regular institution ; indeed, periodic fasts in memory of the tragic fate of Jerusalem were, according to Zech. vii. 3, 5, viii. 19, observed during the exile itself.[2] These continued in post-exilic times and culminated in the great fast on the Day of Atonement (Lev. xvi. 29). Other lesser fasts, though not obligatory, were observed in later days.

W. O. E. OESTERLEY.

---

[1] See the present writer's *The Jewish Background of the Christian Liturgy*, chap. iii (1925).

[2] These were the fasts of the fourth month (Tammuz), the fifth month (Ab), the seventh month (Tishri), and the tenth month (Tebet).

HEBREW PSYCHOLOGY

THE modern study of anthropology has done as much for
the elucidation of the Old Testament as that of archaeology.
Just as we re-date the fall of Nineveh from 606 B.C. to 612 B.C.,
on the evidence of a Babylonian tablet, so we interpret the
Hebrew idea of 'soul' from parallel ideas about the breath-
soul amongst primitive peoples. The evidence is less easy to
gather and to apply, for we are moving in the realm of *ideas*
with less support from material facts. But it can be gathered
from a very wide field, and tested by a not less wide application,
since (with our modern methods and outlook) there is little
that psychology does not affect. We must, of course, remember
that ancient 'psychology' does not mean an ordered and
scientific account of consciousness; it means rather that
branch of anthropology which interprets the ideas held about
human personality, and in this interest must often throw
a wide net. The well-known anthropological works of Tylor
and Frazer will illustrate the proper scientific approach to the
psychological terms and ideas of the Old Testament, with
which we are here concerned.

The primitive Semitic idea of man seems to have been very
much like that which we find amongst other primitive peoples,
of the ancient or of the modern world. There is no distinction
of the psychical and ethical from the physical, so that the actual
breath of man can be thought of as his 'soul', and the reek of
hot blood identified with this breath-soul. Psychical and
ethical functions are considered to be just as appropriate to the
bodily organs as the physiological, with the result that there
can be ascribed to the heart everything which popular thought

to-day ascribes to the brain, a quite neglected organ in Semitic thought. Though there was entire ignorance of the nervous system, man's consciousness, with its ethical qualities, was thought to be so diffused through the whole body that the flesh and bones, as well as the mouth, eye, ear, hand, had a quasi-consciousness of their own. Man's organism is in fact a ' United States ', rather than a monarchic or imperialistic realm. The usage of psychological terms in the Old Testament is not systematic, but syncretistic ; a number of originally independent explanations, such as blood-soul, breath-soul, heart, &c., have been brought together by popular use, and have settled down into a sort of working agreement and division of labour, though with much over-lapping. Further, there is the constant idea of the self as easily accessible to all kinds of outside influences, as in the elaborate Babylonian demonology, though in the Old Testament these are largely unified through control by the Spirit of Yahweh. There is the idea of a ghost or double (not necessarily to be identified with the soul), a faint and shadowy replica of the self, such as the ghost of Samuel described by the ' witch of Endor ' (1 Sam. xxviii. 14)— an old man, wrapped in the familiar cloak of life (ib. xv. 27), or rather its ghostly counterpart. This fainter self, or ' shade ', as the Hebrew calls it, can be detached even from the living, and is seen by others in their dreams, whilst after death it passes to some underground cave. This is the general outline of Semitic, as of other primitive realms of belief, and from such general beliefs the particular terms of the Old Testament have emerged.

These terms fall into three main classes, according as they relate to : (1) the breath-soul or blood-soul, pervading the body ; (2) obviously important central organs, such as the heart, liver, kidneys, bowels ; (3) peripheral organs, such as the tongue or ear or eye. The three most important terms are *néphesh*, *rūach*, and *lēb*, usually rendered ' soul ', ' spirit ', and 'heart', though it will save us from some misconceptions to use the original terms. The first of these, *néphesh*, is not at all adequately rendered by 'soul'. Literary usage shows that there are three more or less distinct meanings covered by the word, which include respectively 282, 249 and 223 out of the 754 instances. The first group relates to the principle of life, without any emphasis on what *we* should call its psychical side. Thus the Israelite captain, threatened with destruction, says to Elijah, 'let my *néphesh* and the *néphesh* of these fifty thy servants be precious in thy sight' (2 Kings i. 13). Here the proper rendering is 'life', as in the Revised Version, though in Jer. xxxviii. 16, the Revised Version has 'As the Lord liveth, that made us this soul', where 'life' should be the rendering. A falsely spiritual tone is given to many of the psalms, for example, by the rendering 'soul', instead of 'life'; 'deliver my *néphesh*' (Ps. vi. 4) means simply 'save me from physical death', as the context shows. In the third group, again, the meaning is usually quite plain, for it denotes 'self', or the personal pronoun, as in Ps. iii. 2, 'Many are saying of my *néphesh*, there is no deliverance for him in God'. Here there is no reference to the Psalmist's inner life as distinct from his outer, and 'soul' is a wrong translation. That which is meant is the man as a whole, threatened by physical peril. One curious and late usage belonging to this group makes *néphesh* actually mean 'corpse', as in Num. v. 2, 'unclean in respect of a *néphesh*', i. e. a dead man, as is shown by xix. 13. The corpse is now all that is left of the once living personality, and, therefore, inherits its name as the tombstone does in Syriac (*naphsha*). Incidentally, we may notice that this use of *néphesh* for a body suggests that the body is the predominant partner in the Hebrew idea of personality, a suggestion confirmed by the other evidence. There remains the second group of usages, the only one that can be called psychical in the proper sense (though, for the Hebrew, 'psychical' includes much that we should call simply physiological; they simply did not distinguish the two). In this group, *néphesh* denotes the human consciousness in its full extent, as in Job xvi. 4 : ' I also could speak like you, if your *néphesh* were instead of my *néphesh*.' In actual usage, however, the psychical functions ascribed to *néphesh* are usually what we should call emotional, and include even physical appetite : e. g., ' thou mayst kill and eat flesh within all thy gates, after all the desire of thy *néphesh* ' (Deut. xii. 15) ; ' we saw the distress of his *néphesh* ' (Gen. xlii. 21). This predominance of the emotional connotation must not be taken to mean that the Hebrews formally distinguished *néphesh* from other terms in this respect ; it is to be explained by the development of other terms of like generality, such as *lēb* (heart), which appropriated in course of time the more intellectual or conational psychoses. *Néphesh* could be used even of these, as when Abraham says, ' if it be your *néphesh* that I should bury my dead ' (Gen. xxiii. 7), where the meaning is ' will ' or ' mind ', as the Authorized Version and Revised Version properly render.

Such is the evidence of actual usage, with which it is always advisable to begin. There is no reason to doubt that the primary meaning of *néphesh* was ' breath', like that of the Arabic *nafsun* = soul (*nafasun* = breath), though there is but one instance in the Old Testament in which ' breath ' is the most natural rendering. It is found in that passage of Job (xli. 19, 20) which describes the rising of the crocodile from underneath the water, the breath from its nostrils expelling the water which flashes in the sunlight like fire :

> From his nostrils there goes out smoke
> As (of) a pot boiling, and rushes,
> His *néphesh* sets coals ablaze
> And a flame from his mouth goes out.

One of the most widely spread ideas of general anthropology is to identify the life-principle, and ultimately all the phenomena of consciousness, with the breath, for while there is breath there is life. But in Hebrew usage another word (*nĕshâmah*) came to denote ' breath ', and *néphesh* was reserved for those psychical uses already described, though always with the thought of ' breath ' as the life-principle, underlying the usage. This breath-soul is conceived as the animating principle of man's life, its essential constituent, though as much dependent on bodily organs for its activity as these are dependent on it for life itself. This virtual identification with the breath shows that the ' soul ' is quasi-materialistically conceived. Death is properly explained as the going out of the breath-soul from the body ; Rachel's breath ' goes out ', in naming her child ' Ben-oni ', and this is explained by the remark, ' for she died ' (Gen. xxxv. 18). Even temporary unconsciousness is explained in the same way, as when the Shulammite swoons : ' my *néphesh* had gone out when he spoke ' (Cant. v. 6). Elijah prays that the *néphesh* of the widow's son may return *into* him (1 Kings xvii. 21), and when it does, he lives. In similar circumstances, Elisha not only stretches himself on the body, but is said to put his mouth to the dead boy's mouth, doubtless to breathe into it, and help the return of the *néphesh* (2 Kings iv. 34—the ancient equivalent to our ' artificial respiration '). The mortally wounded Saul, longing for death, cries, ' all my *néphesh* is still in me ' (2 Sam. i. 9).

The *néphesh* is also brought into relation with another, and originally independent, idea of the soul as connected with the blood. This also is a widespread idea of primitive thought, which obviously springs from death as the result of bleeding wounds, the life seeming to go out with the blood. Many usages, such as abstinence from blood (Gen. ix. 4), blood-revenge (Gen. iv. 10), the offering of blood to the deity (Lev. xvii. 11), show this idea of the mystery of life indwelling in the blood. In one late passage, the breath-soul and the blood-soul (easily identified by the primitive mind because of the reek of newly shed blood) are correlated to form a theory of sacrifice :

' the *néphesh* of the flesh is in the blood : and I have given it to you upon the altar to make atonement for your *něphâshoth* (the plural of *néphesh*) ; for it is the blood that makes atonement by reason of the *néphesh*.' (Lev. xvii. 11.)

The second of the three principal terms, viz. *rūach*, is of the greatest importance and interest, both for psychology and theology, though it occurs only about half as many times (378) as does *néphesh*. There are four main groups of its use in the Old Testament. In the first, it denotes ' wind ' in either a natural or figurative sense. But when we say ' natural ', we must remember that there was no such distinction of natural and supernatural amongst the Hebrews as we often make. The wind was due to the direct causation of God, and poetry retains the primitive belief that the wind is actually the breath of God :

' The east wind (*sirocco*)—the *rūach* of Yahweh—shall come, coming up from the desert, and his spring shall be dry, and his fountain shall be dried up.' (Hos. xiii. 15.)

' By the breath (*něshâmah*) of God they perish, and by the *rūach* of His anger (nostril) they are consumed ' (to describe the destruction of a figurative harvest, Job iv. 9).

' By the *rūach* of thy nostrils the waters were heaped up.' (Exod. xv. 8.)

' By the breath (*něshâmah*) of the *rūach* of His nostrils ' (description of storm, 2 Sam. xxii. 16 ; Ps. xviii. 15).

' As a stream pent in, which the *rūach* of Yahweh drives on.' (Isa. lix. 19.)

' His *rūach* (is) as an overflowing wady ' (rainstorm, Isa. xxx. 28).

Such examples, in which an earlier ' science ' has become a later poetry, show us how difficult, indeed how impossible it is, to distinguish the wind in what we should call a natural sense from the wind as the energy of Yahweh, His angry breath.

They also serve to remind us that there was no very clear line
of demarcation between this first group and the second, which
we may call 'inspirational'. Here we have some 134 instances
of *rūach* used as 'the spirit' of Yahweh, to explain some
unusual phenomenon of human conduct or character, or
occasionally some other energy or activity traced back to
Yahweh. The unusual feature may be the strength of Samson
(Judges xiv. 6, 19, xv. 14), the ecstasy of primitive prophecy
(I Sam. x. 6, 10), both the anger (I Sam. xi. 6) and the madness
(I Sam. xvi. 15) of Saul, the wisdom of a ruling prince (Isa.
xi. 2) or of a clever craftsman (Exod. xxviii. 3), the divine energy
that gives new physical and psychical life to the dry bones of
the valley in Ezekiel's vision (xxxvii. *passim*) and so recreates
the nation. This last example may be regarded as transitional
to the next group, in which *rūach* denotes the principle of life
in both human beings and animals (Gen. vi. 17, vii. 15), usually
in parallelism, explicit or implicit, with *nĕshâmah*, the word for
'breath', and, therefore, suggesting identification with the
breath-soul, which was also denoted, as we have already seen,
by the term *néphesh*. The most instructive passage in this
connexion is Ps. civ. 27 f., where it is said of God's creatures :

> All of them to thee look hopefully,
>> To give their food at its time ;
> Thou givest to them, they gather,
>> Thou openest thine hand, they are satisfied with good ;
> Thou hidest thy face, they are dismayed,
>> Thou gatherest their *rūach*, they expire,
>> And unto their dust they return.
> Thou sendest thy *rūach*, they are created,
>> And thou renewest the face of the ground.

This clearly shows that (in the post-exilic period) the divine
rūach is held to be the principle of life in man and beast,
exactly the same as the 'breath' (*nĕshâmah*) of life, blown into
the clay figure of man by Yahweh in the primitive creation

story, with which this psalm is clearly connected. The term has changed, the idea remains the same. At an earlier period, *rūach* denoted the energy of life (as distinct from mere existence) as when it is said of the wearied Samson, thirsting unto death, that when he drank, ' his *rūach* returned and he revived ' (Judges xv. 19). The overwhelming effect of Solomon's wealth and wisdom on the queen of Sheba is described by saying that ' there was no more *rūach* (life-energy) in her ' (1 Kings x. 5). But an important distinction should here be made. The instances in which *rūach* is clearly identified with the breath are not pre-exilic, e. g. Job ix. 18 : ' He will not suffer me to take my breath ' (*rūach*). A still more suggestive fact emerges when we turn to the fourth class of instances, in which *rūach* is used psychically, i. e., not as the wind of God, not as the spirit of God producing unusual results in men, not simply as the principle of energy or life in man (traced back to God), but as the permanent substratum or entity of man's own consciousness, with varied psychical predicates—like *néphesh*, in fact, though with a range less wide. Now, out of the 74 instances which belong to this group, there is no clear or well-supported example in pre-exilic usage. The inference from this fact, taken in conjunction with the closely related fact that *rūach* is not used of breath-soul (as distinct from life-energy) before the exile, is that in *rūach* we are not dealing with a term originally parallel with *néphesh*, a mere synonym of it, still less with a constituent of human personality, making a third with body and ' soul ', but with a term that has had a very different history. The original meaning seems to be ' wind ' ; the wind, conceived as a divine breathing, on the analogy of man's, is also conceived as the energy which enters a man (at Yahweh's will) and enables him to do unusual things. As the emphasis fell increasingly on God in the prophetic religion, and especially in Ezekiel (the most ' supranaturalistic ' of the prophets), the energy of normal life is ascribed to a divine inbreathing—

parallel with the primitive idea of a breath-soul (*néphesh*), but with the higher associations brought by the new term, *rūach*. Thus man's life, with all its phenomena of consciousness, can be described by the term *rūach* which did not originally mean ' breath-soul ' at all. Something of its higher origin as the wind or spirit of God always clings to it, however difficult it is to express this in translation. This view of the development is confirmed by the fact that even when we reach these psychical usages (*in the post-exilic period, and not before*), the emphasis falls on the stronger and stormier emotions in the use of the term, e. g. ' Be not hasty in thy *rūach* to be angry ' (Eccles. vii. 9), or when Esau's Hittite wives were bitterness of *rūach* to Isaac and Rebekah (Gen. xxvi. 35, P.). In the latest usage, *rūach* is almost indistinguishable from *néphesh* and *lēb* (heart), except of course for the implication carried on by its association with divine energy :

' Create in me a clean heart, O God,
  And renew a steadfast *rūach* within me.' (Ps. li. 10.)
' Into thine hand I commend my *rūach* . . .
  Thou hast known the adversities of my *néphesh.*' (Ps. xxxi. 5, 7.)

If the full significance of this development of usage has been grasped, it will be seen that it solves one of the crucial problems of Hebrew psychology, still often misunderstood and mis-represented, viz. the relation of ' soul ' and ' spirit ' (*néphesh* and *rūach*). Underneath the double usage there lies no mystery of subtle distinction consciously made. ' Soul ' and ' spirit ' eventually denote the same thing, viz. the conscious life of man, associated with the breath as the vital principle. But because ' spirit ' originally denoted an energy acting on man from with-out, a divine energy, it naturally suggests a higher conception of the life of man, *as drawn from God.* (It is of interest to note that Aristotle distinguishes the inborn *pneuma*, or air, of the body from that which is inhaled ; cf. Burton, *Spirit, Soul, and*

Flesh, p. 21.) This conception of inbreathed air does not
belong to the term *néphesh* at all, in its own right, but only
through the quite arbitrary association of the creation story.
Thus there is no trichotomy in Hebrew psychology, no triple
division of human personality into ' body, soul, and spirit '.
An exhaustive description of human personality was given by
saying ' body and soul ' (*bâsar*, flesh, and *néphesh*, as in Isa.
x. 18). But even the phrase ' body and soul ' would mislead
a modern reader, influenced far more than he realizes by Greek
and modern psychology. There is not even a dichotomy in any
strict sense. We shall see this when we come to the ' flesh '
and the physical organs of the body, which are conceived
psychically just as much as ' soul ' or ' spirit ' are conceived
(in connexion with the breath) quasi-physically. The Hebrew
idea of personality is an animated body, and not an incarnated
soul.

We pass to the second class of psychological terms, those
which consist in the names of central physical organs to which
the Hebrews ascribed psychical functions. This, it will be seen,
affords a quite independent line of approach to the problems
of man's life and consciousness. The body was a strange and
wonderful complex of parts (Ps. cxxxix. 14), of which the
functioning was known only vaguely, if at all, so far as central
organs were concerned. Any one of these parts could be
regarded as a centre of consciousness, since the psychical and
the physical (physiological) were not distinguished. The organs
thus entering into Hebrew psychology are chiefly the heart,
the liver, the kidneys, and the bowels, the first being by far the
most important. The term for heart (*lēb*, *lēbāb*) occurs 851
times in the Old Testament ; about a third of the instances
denote the personality as a whole, the inner life, the character ;
a considerably smaller number (166) the more emotional side
of conscious life, much like *néphesh* ; almost half the instances
denote either the intellectual (204) or the volitional (195)

functioning of conscious life. Thus, for the Hebrew, ' heart ' suggested the mental rather than the emotional activities of consciousness, the very opposite of its (figurative) use amongst ourselves, by which ' heart ' is often contrasted with ' brain '. When Ephraim is called ' heartless ' by Hosea (vii. 11), the meaning is that Ephraim is wanting in intelligence, that he is stupid—not that he is wanting in sympathy. The heart is naturally regarded by primitive thought (quite ignorant of the circulation of the blood) as a centre of physical life ; when Nabal was (apparently) smitten by a stroke of paralysis, the explanation is that ' his heart died within him and he became stone ' (1 Sam. xxv. 37), though physical life as a whole did not cease until ten days later. The use of the term to denote the personality generally, or the inner life in contrast with the outer, or the character of a man, hardly needs illustration, for it resembles our own use of ' heart ' ; e.g. ' this people approaches me with its mouth and honours me with its lips, but its heart is far from me ' (Isa. xxix. 13). The heart is conceived as the seat of sensations, as when strengthened by food (Gen. xviii. 5), or of emotions, as of happiness at the prospect of advancement (Judges xviii. 20). But this usage, found in the earlier rather than in the later phase of the use of the term, and corresponding with what ultimately came to be the predominant use of *néphesh*, is not the distinctive and characteristic use. As *néphesh* came in syncretistic usage to denote chiefly the emotional side of consciousness, so ' heart ' came to denote chiefly the intellectual and volitional—though there was nothing in the original meaning of either term to lead to this, for both ' breath-soul ' and ' heart ' obviously cover potentially the whole of consciousness. As an example of the intellectual use of ' heart ' (in the special psychosis of attention), we may take Prov. xxiv. 32 : ' I beheld and applied my heart, I saw and received instruction.' The most important and characteristic use is for volition. Yahweh speaks of Israel's idolatrous practices as that which ' I have not commanded, and have not spoken, nor has it come up upon my heart ' (Jer. xix. 5), i.e. as a purpose. The will is primary in Hebrew ethics, and it is natural that this central organ should predominantly, though not exclusively (since the use of the term covers so long a period of development), be devoted to the volitional aspects of conscience.

The liver, so important for Babylonian psychology, takes little place in the Hebrew. It is named twice (Lam. ii. 11, Prov. vii. 23) as a life-centre, and should probably be read as the original meaning of the Hebrew consonants in three places where we now read the rather meaningless ' my glory ' (*kĕbēdī* for *kĕbōdī*), viz. Gen. xlix. 6 (so LXX) ; Ps. vii. 5 and xvi. 9. The kidneys are named more frequently (31 times), and in the ten instances of psychical use they locate some form of emotion, as in Prov. xxiii. 16, ' my kidneys shall rejoice, when thy lips speak right things '. The Rabbinical distinction made (Talmud B. *Bĕrâchoth* 61a) between kidneys and heart is substantially that of the later Old Testament usage : ' the kidneys advise,' i. e. urge to action by the emotion aroused, ' the heart examines ', and discerns the material so presented to it. In the same place we read ' The Rabbis taught, Two kidneys are in man, the one advises him to good, the other advises him to evil ', but this is a speculation beyond the stage of Old Testament inquiry, however much a plausible development of it, and an explanation of man's divided nature. The ' bowels ', used psychically in nine passages, are also used emotionally, and specially for sexual love or sympathy in general ; thus, when the love-sick Shulammite sees her lover's hand at the latch, the resultant emotion (or sensation) is located in the bowels (Cant. v. 4).

This attribution of psychical function to parts of the body which to us seem to be purely physiological is not confined to the central organs. It operates also in regard to the peripheral organs, such as eye and ear and mouth and hand, though the modern reader of the Old Testament is apt to dismiss the relevant phrases as mere metaphors. Comparative study, however, will show that these phrases cover a real attribution of psychical function to these organs. The eye is co-ordinated with recognized psychical centres as one of them (Deut. xxviii. 65); it has the ethical qualities of pride (Ps. cxxxi. 1) or humility (Job xxii. 29, see Revised Version, marg.) associated with it, amongst many others. It will be remembered that Elisha put his eyes on the dead child's eyes to communicate local life to them (2 Kings iv. 34), and the opening of the eyes marked the return of that life, just as the sneezing of the child marked the return of the *néphesh* into it. The widespread belief in the evil eye or in the location of the soul in the eye amongst a number of peoples further illustrates this localization of function. So the ear has the power of the palate (Job xii. 11, xxxiv. 3) in respect of testing what it hears, and has ethical qualities ascribed to it like the eye. A careful examination of the usages would convince the reader, in the light of the very copious anthropological evidence, that all the peripheral organs are regarded psychically, and that this attribution was the almost inevitable consequence of ancient ignorance of the nervous system, which has enabled us to centralize the psychical functions in the brain, to the psychical and ethical impoverishment of the peripheral organs. But what we centralize, the Hebrews (like other peoples) distributed, and their linguistic usage shows this, even when the phrases were used in current speech without explicit thought about their meaning.

We are compelled to carry this principle further still. Not only the special organs on the surface of the body, but the more general bodily parts, the flesh, bones, belly, breast, loins, and thighs, in greater or less degree, are conceived psychically as well as physically. It is not possible or necessary to give the

366 Hebrew Psychology

full evidence here, but we can see its significance in such a phrase as that of Ps. lxiii. 1 :

> ' My *néphesh* thirsteth for thee,
> My " flesh " longeth for thee '

where the ' flesh ' is functioning psychically just as much as is the *néphesh*. We can reach an adequate idea of Hebrew psychology only by constantly bearing this in mind. If we are inclined to dismiss as a superstition the idea that contact with Elisha's bones could restore a dead man to life, we must not ignore the underlying psychology which made the bones and other parts the centres of psychical power in their own right, and apart from central control. It implies much more than a metaphor when a Hebrew says, not only : ' My *néphesh* shall rejoice in Yahweh,' but also : ' All my bones shall say, Yahweh, who is like thee ? ' (Ps. xxxv. 9, 10).

If then we ask again the old question, ' What is man ? ' and try to answer it, not in the old theological, but in the new psychological fashion, we shall say that for the Hebrew, man is a unity, and that that unity is the body as a complex of parts, drawing their life and activity from a breath-soul, which has no existence apart from the body. Hebrew has no proper word for that body ; it never needed one so long as the body was the man ; definition and nomenclature come in only when there is some conscious antithesis. That antithesis is not reached in the Old Testament, nor could it be reached along native lines of Hebrew thought. The ghosts or ' shades ' of Sheol are no part of man's personality ; they are no more than much fainter replicas of what it was *as a whole*. The most important aspect of this personality is its constant accessibility to ' spiritual ' influence from without ; in that fact lay the germ both of the Old Testament prophetic consciousness and of its sequel in the New Testament doctrine of the Spirit of God. Without these, what would the Bible be?—or rather, there would have been no Bible.

It will serve to bring out the fuller meaning of these results, if we apply them to certain conceptions of the Old Testament which must obviously be affected by the psychology. The most natural starting-point is the idea of God, and of His relation to man. When Isaiah is protesting against the pro-Egyptian policy, based on the material resources of Egypt in cavalry and chariots, he makes an illuminating contrast between God and man : ' the Egyptians are men and not God, and their horses flesh and not spirit' (xxxi. 3 : cf. Jer. xvii. 5 ; 2 Chron. xxxii. 8). The whole realm of spiritual energies belongs to Yahweh, here identified with *rūach*, and over against Him stands all material existence, including man himself, here virtually identified with *bâsar*, ' flesh '. But to speak of God as ' spirit ' does not mean that Yahweh is formless. In the more primitive creation story, He walks in the garden in the cool of the day. In the chariot vision of Ezekiel (i. 26) the prophet's glimpse of God is of a manlike form upon the throne. Even so late as the Book of Daniel (vii. 9) God is seen as a very old man (the ' ancient of days '), His raiment white as snow, and the hair of His head like pure wool. Moses is told that he cannot see Yahweh's face and live, but that when the ' glory ' of Yahweh has passed, he shall see Yahweh's back (Exod. xxxiii. 20–3). The majestic figure seen by Isaiah in the temple is in human form, though endowed with superhuman qualities. If we ask for further definition, we shall find that the ' glory ' of Yahweh, His full visible manifestation, is conceived in terms of dazzling and unbearable light. Yahweh's body is shaped like man's, but its substance is not flesh but ' spirit ', and spirit seen as a blaze of light. It is true that the imageless worship of prophetic religion repudiates the making of any likeness of God, and no form was seen in the storm-theophany of Sinai (Deut. iv. 12). But it is one thing to shrink from the vision of the form, and another to deny that a form exists, though a form wrought out of *rūach*-substance.

In the earlier creation-story (Gen. ii) Yahweh creates man
before the plants and animals, moulding him essentially of clay,
as a potter does his vessels, and then blowing into the nostrils
of this clay figure, so that man becomes a living *néphesh*,
a term which must here denote the man as a whole, body and
soul, i. e. ' a living creature ', as the same phrase is properly
translated in regard to the animals (ii. 19). It is not said that
Yahweh blows His own breath into them, and they are
distinctly created for man's sake. When they prove inadequate
companions, woman is created on a new method, not from man's
' soul ' but from his body, with the result that the awakened
man instinctively recognizes the kinship of this new companion
—' Bone of my bone, and flesh of my flesh '. This confirms the
view given above that the body, not the ' soul ', is the essential
man. In the later creation story the cruder anthropomorphisms
of the earlier are eliminated. Elohim speaks, and it is done, and
man is the crowning work of creation. It is on the sixth day only
that Elohim says, ' Let us make man in our image, after our
likeness' (i. 26). How are we to understand this historic phrase ?

The word *tsélem*, rendered ' image ', meant originally something cut out, as in Ezek. xvi. 17 (' male images '), or a painted
figure (Ezek. xxiii. 14), ' men pourtrayed upon the wall, the
images of the Chaldeans pourtrayed with vermilion '. The
word may denote a ' semblance ' as distinct from a reality
(Ps. xxxix. 6, lxxiii. 20). Midway between this physical and
this figurative meaning, we have the usage found in Genesis and
elsewhere in the Priestly Code, but nowhere else. Besides the
three occurrences in Gen. i. 26, 27, it occurs in Gen. v. 3, ix. 6 :
' Adam lived an hundred and thirty years and begat in his own
likeness, after his image ' ; ' whoso sheddeth man's blood, by
man shall his blood be shed : for in the image of God made
he man.' The parallel word, ' likeness ' (*dĕmūth*), is a more
general word to denote similarity, used, e. g., of the pattern of
the altar sent by Ahaz to Urijah (2 Kings xvi. 10). There is,

therefore, no suggestion in these words of anything more than external and visible likeness. The natural meaning of the sentence, ' God created man in his own image and after his likeness ' is that the bodily form of man was made after the pattern of the bodily form of God (the substance being different). With this agrees the statement that Adam's son, Seth, from birth bore the same pattern as his father, where the suggestion is certainly that of bodily form, not of spiritual qualities as yet unrevealed in the babe. (There are Babylonian parallels confirming this interpretation ; cf. Skinner, *Genesis*, p. 31.) No doubt, writers so late as those of the Priestly Code thought not only of man's bodily shape and erect posture as distinguishing him from the animals, but also of his obvious mental and spiritual differentiæ from the animal world. But this was not expressed by the words ' image ' and ' likeness ' ; it was implied in the psychology which did not divorce body and soul, but conceived the body psychically. Man's unique body carried with it a unique psychical quality, and it was made after the actual pattern of God's, though of the inferior substance called ' flesh ' (which of course includes all the physical organs, animated by the breath-soul).

Each human birth was a new miracle of creation to the devout Hebrew mind. There was no modern thought of germ-plasm, evolution, the continuance of life from one generation to the other by its own inherent energies. The mystery of the phenomena of conception and birth was proverbial—' thou knowest not what is the way of the wind, nor how the bones grow in the womb of her that is with child ' (Eccles. xi. 5 : cf. Prov. xxx. 19 ; 2 Macc. vii. 22). God is thought of as operating directly in the conception and birth of each child :

Didst thou not pour me out like milk, and curdle me like cheese ?

With skin and flesh thou didst clothe me, and with bones and sinews thou didst weave me together. (Job x. 10, 11.)

The impregnating principle is here supposed to coagulate in

the womb, where it forms the nucleus of the framework of bone and sinew which is to be covered with ' flesh '. So in Ps. cxxxix. 13–16 :

> For thou didst create my kidneys,
> Thou didst weave me together in my mother's belly . . .
> Not hidden was my bony frame from thee,
> When I was made in secret,
> I was embroidered in the lowest parts of the earth,
> My unformed mass thine eyes saw.

The birth-stories of the Old Testament are remarkable for the light they throw upon this direct dependence on Yahweh, from Eve, who is represented as seeing the direct intervention of Yahweh in the birth of Cain (Gen. iv. 1), onwards, especially in the narratives of the births of Isaac, Samson, and Samuel. The prophetic calls of Jeremiah and the Servant of Yahweh are carried back to the womb, which was regarded as a peculiar avenue of divine approach and operation, not less wonderful than the way of the first creation of man.

The continuance of man's life is not less directly dependent upon God (cf. Pss. viii, civ). ' He giveth breath unto the people upon it (the earth), and *rūach* to them that walk therein ' (Isa. xlii. 5) ; ' if he were to cause his *rūach* to return unto himself, and were to gather unto himself his breath, all flesh would expire together ' (Job xxxiv. 14, *em.* ; cf. Isa. ii. 22). So in the late Book of Ecclesiastes, death means that the dust returns to the earth as it was, and the *rūach* (the divine energy) returns unto God who gave it (xii. 7), exactly reversing the process of creation. It no more tells of man's survival after death than Gen. ii. 7 implies his pre-existence (cf. Eccles. iii. 20, 21). Not only man's physical existence but also his psychical consciousness is directly dependent on God, as we should expect from the Hebrew unity of outlook :

> Yahweh's lamp is man's breath (*něshâmah*),
> Searching all the chambers of the body (*béṭen*). (Prov. xx. 27.)

It is this deep sense of physical and psychical dependence that gives such force to the cry, ' With thee is the fountain of life ' (Ps. xxxvi. 9). God *is* life, the living God by whom men swear the oath, ' As God liveth ', the life that endures whilst the generations come and go (Ps. xc), needing not like man to slumber and sleep (Ps. cxxi). The Hebrew idea of God is that of activity rather than passive enjoyment, and the *rūach* of God, His energy at work, becomes a real expression of His being, delivered from being a mere nature-force, because ethicized by the prophets.

The prophetic consciousness is itself a specialized form of this direct and fundamental dependence of man on God, and Hebrew psychology throws much light on its *modus operandi*. The prophet shared with his non-prophetic contemporaries their general idea of human personality, which has already been outlined. He thought of himself as an animated body with many parts, which could function in quasi-independence of one another, every physical organ having psychical and ethical attributes of its own. He believed in invasive influences, good and bad, which might take possession of any one of these organs, so that a man might become the agent and instrument of such influences in word or deed. He analysed his consciousness (so far as he did analyse it) not into general faculties or abstract ideas, but into the more or less detached working of these different organs, so that Jeremiah, for example, could say, ' Upon me my heart is sick ' (viii. 18). It was, therefore, much easier for him to detach himself from any of his psychoses, and to objectify them over against the sense of personal identity. It would probably not be misleading to compare such an explanation of psychical phenomena with our own use of the subconsciousness. The difference would be that the Hebrew reference to concrete, physical organs, subject to invasive influences from without, made the whole proceeding much more definite and vivid, and more easily enabled the

Hebrew mind to regard itself as the vehicle of divine revelation.

When, however, we advance from predisposition to actuality, we must reckon with something more than the contemporary psychology of normal consciousness and experience. The whole history of prophecy shows that a prophet was the subject of an abnormal experience which separated him from other men, and warranted him in the belief that he was called of God. This experience is usually called ' ecstatic ', though the term is not very appropriate, since it is drawn from a different psychology, that of the Greeks. The familiar examples from the primitive ' prophecy ' are such as that of Saul, infected with the ' enthusiasm ' of a dervish band, carrying instruments of music (1 Sam. x. 6 ff.) ; later on (xix. 20 ff.) we find him stripping off his clothes, and lying down naked, in the course of his ' prophesying '. It is clear that a primitive prophet could be called a ' madman ' (2 Kings ix. 11), whilst it was possible for the contemporaries of Jeremiah himself to class him with ' every man that is mad and maketh himself a prophet ' (Jer. xxix. 26, 27). No one, of course, would contend that this is the whole, or the essential thing, in the experience of the classical Old Testament prophets. But the frequent references to (abnormal) vision and audition imply much more than an inner consciousness of truth ; they describe an experience accepted by the prophet as ' objective '. Amos says, ' the Lord Yahweh shewed me ' (vii–ix), Zechariah, ' I saw in the night ' (i. 8 ff.). Isaiah, ' Yahweh of Hosts revealed himself *in my ears* ' (xxii. 14). There is significant reference to the compelling power of the revelation, as a force acting irresistibly from without : ' Yahweh spake thus to me *with strength of hand* ' (Isa. viii. 11). Jeremiah struggles in vain against the divine commission, which is as a burning fire shut up within him (xx. 9). ' The Lord Yahweh hath spoken,' Amos says, ' who can but prophesy ? ' (iii. 8). In Ezekiel, this abnormal element is exhibited more than in any other of the greater prophets, and sometimes seems to take the special form of the trance state. All this does not mean necessarily that every message received and recorded in the Old Testament was given through these abnormal experiences (which have so many ethnic and modern parallels). There is clear evidence (as in the controversy of Jeremiah with the ' false ' prophets of his time, xxiii. 9 ff.) that there were many different kinds of experience which mediated the prophetic message. In Jeremiah we doubtless reach the point of greatest freedom from abnormalities and greatest use of conscious and normal experience of fellowship with God. Yet Jeremiah sees visions, has to wait for the coming of a message beyond his own control, performs symbolic acts, and could be plausibly described as a madman. At some point or points in every prophet's ' inspiration ', it is reasonable to assume that there was an experience of abnormal contact with God, which in itself separated him from his fellows. In any attempt to understand the prophetic consciousness we should carefully distinguish the prophet's own account from such an explanation as we should give in the light of modern psychology, whilst neither the ancient nor the modern explanation affects the ultimate question (lying beyond our subject) as to the truth or divine origin of the prophecy itself.

The story about the relation of Aaron to Moses admirably illustrates the objectivity of the experience from the prophet's standpoint. ' See ', says Yahweh to Moses, ' I have made thee a god to Pharaoh : and Aaron thy brother shall be thy prophet ' . . .' thou shalt speak unto him, and put the words in his mouth . . . and he shall be thy spokesman unto the people, and it shall come to pass that he shall be to thee a mouth, and thou shalt be to him as God ' (Exod. vii. 1, iv. 15, 16). Moses was to supply the ideas, Aaron was to clothe them in fitting speech ; this Aaronic function we may take to describe the ordinary relation of the prophet to God, giving him scope for the elucidation and expansion of the original message, yet with the provision of some original message as the nucleus, perhaps due to the sudden leaping into consciousness of some word or phrase, vivid as the writing on the wall at Belshazzar's feast. It is just here that the idea of a diffused or localized consciousness would greatly affect the form of the explanation. Each of the prophet's organs was at the service of Yahweh who made them, who was greater in mystery and power than His work :

He that planted the ear, shall he not hear ?
He that formed the eye, shall he not see ? (Ps. xciv. 9.)

So it is that the inaugural visions of both Isaiah and Jeremiah record the touching of the prophet's mouth, since the mouth was the local organ which needed to be purged or equipped for speech in Yahweh's name. When the prophet spoke, he would be intensely conscious that his mouth was speaking by such a power directly given, and that his own volition was, so to speak, ' short-circuited ', and out of the current. It would not be possible for a modern man, to whom the mouth is simply a physiological organ, to hold this belief in the same way.

When we turn from the outer utterance of the message, including all its conscious or unconscious expansion or application by the prophet, to its inner history, we find the same sense of ' objectivity '. A remarkable example of this is seen in the record of ' dual personality ' in Isa. xxi, where an anonymous prophet reports his vision of the coming fall of Babylon. After describing his own physical sensations in the trance or ' ecstatic ' state, he says that he was bidden, ' Go, set a watchman '. He detaches part of himself, a sort of second self, to watch for the cavalcade marching on the doomed city, and this watchman announces the vision to him. Frequent parallels to such experiences may be found amongst the seers of other peoples, and we must not forget the remarkable possibilities of telepathy, clairvoyance, &c. As an example of the experience on a more normal level, we may take the dialogue between Jeremiah and Yahweh recorded in Jer. xv. 10 ff. Here the prophet rebels against his hard lot, and reproaches Yahweh with infidelity to him. Yahweh answers in words which are of the utmost importance for understanding the nature of Hebrew prophecy at its highest : ' if thou take forth the precious from the common, thou shalt be as my mouth ' (19). Here we come as nearly as possible to what a modern would call a ' value-judgement '. In the last resort, this is what prophecy means. Into the complex organism of the prophetic consciousness, with its many avenues of approach from without, not limited to the peripheral organs, or to their physiological aspect, there came some impulse that was transformed into, or expressed by, a phrase or a picture, and often projected into the outer world. As the selenium bar can translate a light-ray into terms of an electric current, so the prophet's consciousness translates into terms of his own experience this original impulse. But in the very process he is constrained to refer it to the seeing eye or the hearing ear, and to give it an other-than-self quality. Many such visions and auditions came to him, as they come to a man amongst ourselves between the waking and sleeping state ; the genuine prophet was he who knew how to distinguish the precious from the common, to exercise a moral judgement, and to advance to the faith that that moral judgement was true for God. When we come to his experience through the psychology of his times, we are better able to understand his manner of speech, to sympathize with its sincerity, and to realize the intensity of conviction with which he was able to speak, as the obedient servant of a higher authority.

The close and sympathetic identification of the prophet with his people, as well as with his God, forms another important branch of Hebrew psychology (in the large sense in which the term must be used), viz. corporate personality. The social psychology of the Hebrews differs as much from that of our own times as does the individual. The Apostle is true to Hebrew tradition and sentiment in his parable of the human body as a figure of the community (1 Cor. xii. 12 f.), though there are Stoic elements in his use of the term *pneuma*. As in the human body, so in the community, there is mutual inter-dependence of each of the parts upon the rest, and yet each of the parts functions in quasi-independence of the others. But the relation of the individual to the society is much closer than it seems to-day to our more individualized assumptions. There is such a thing as ' corporate personality ' in the ancient world generally, and in the Hebrew thought in particular. Modern psychology sometimes speaks of it under the name of the ' herd instinct ', which goes back to the wolf pack or the bee swarm. Corporate personality means for us in this place the treatment of the family, the clan, or the nation, as the unit in place of the individual. It does not mean that no individual life is recog-nized, but simply that in a number of realms in which we have come to think individualistically, and to treat the single man as the unit, e. g. for punishment or reward, ancient thought envisaged the whole group of which he was part. This sense of corporate personality has taken many strange forms, as that of cannibalism, where fellow-clansmen are eaten to keep the life of the clan within itself, or of the marriage practices of Australian aborigines, where there are two groups in a tribe which may intermarry, but each group is forbidden to marry within itself; there are even instances of group-marriage, where a number of women have marital relations with a group of men, the group being treated as a unit. In particular the whole practice of ancestral cults, as in China, will illustrate the sense of corporate personality, as, in another way, does the familiar story of Oedipus. In many respects, the centre of gravity for ancient law, ethics, religion, and custom lay not in the individual but in the group.

To enumerate all the Old Testament examples is impossible. When Achan had personally broken the taboo laid on the spoil of Jericho, not he only but his family and his possessions also were stoned and burned (Joshua vii. 25). In regard to a famine in the time of David, Yahweh gives an oracle that it is due to a slaughter of the Gibeonites by Saul in the past, and to the fact that their blood has not been avenged. The Gibeonites ask for seven of Saul's sons to atone, and David gives up to them to be hanged before Yahweh two sons and five grandsons of Saul (2 Sam. xxi. 8). In the declaration made by Yahweh to Moses, He speaks of Himself as ' visiting the iniquity of the fathers upon the children, and upon the children's children, upon the third and upon the fourth generation' (Exod. xxxiv. 7). The other side of retribution is also true, though naturally less noticeable : when the ark remains for three months in the house of Obed-edom, ' Yahweh blessed Obed-edom and all his house' (2 Sam. vi. 11). The custom of Levirate marriage, by which the widow of a childless man is married by his brother, to raise an heir to his name, ultimately rests on the sense of the unity of kinship, springing from corporate personality. The sense of ancestral unity, perhaps linked with ancestor worship in the remote past, underlies the striking words of Jeremiah, ' A voice is heard in Ramah (near to Rachel's grave, 1 Sam. x. 2), lamentation and bitter weeping, Rachel weeping for her children ' (Jer. xxxi. 15). But it is not the family only that possesses corporate personality ; a city also has a unity of its own, and if there is in it the worship of other gods, the Deuteronomic law directs that the city is to be wholly devoted to destruction (Deut. xiii. 15). The largest unity of all, which takes so great a part in the religion of the Old Testament, is that of Israel as a nation. So speaks Amos in the name of Yahweh, ' You only have I known of all the families of the earth : therefore I will visit upon you all your iniquities ' (iii. 2). Again and again, as in the Psalms, when the modern reader is apt to individualize the ' I ' and the ' thou ', the reference is to the unity of the nation, conceived not simply by what we should call a personification, but according to the ancient principle of corporate personality, which gives a difference of tone and atmosphere to almost every page of the Old Testament. We must not attempt to decide whether the figure drawn in Isa. liii is individual or national, before we have taken into account the remarkable lengths to which the principle of corporate personality can go. Similarly, when the experience of a direct personal fellowship with God makes Jeremiah the pioneer of a new individualism, we see how that experience entails the separation from his village home and the worship of Anathoth, from the city and the temple, from the nation and the state—all of them increasing and concentric circles of the idea of corporate personality. Except for the doctrine of corporate personality, there would have been no doctrine of original sin, the doctrine that Adam's sin condemned the race to death, because he was the corporate representative of the race, and they must share in his condemnation (a very different idea from that of the biological inheritance of tendencies to evil, with which it is sometimes confused). Again, the idea of corporate personality has largely influenced the emphasis of Hebrew ethics on social morality, the chief content of the prophetic message. It is owing to this idea, also, that the doctrine of righteous retribution could be maintained as a fact for so long without a belief in life after death. To think nationally, or even in terms of the family, is to escape from the pressure of the problems of individual fortune, so often apparently unjust.

In regard to the life after death, it has already been said that the inhabitants of Sheol are ' shades ' or ghosts, not ' souls ' or ' spirits ' in the Old Testament, and that the only life man has or can have is here on earth, since it is bound up with an earthly body. Numerous peoples have distinguished the soul or life-

principle from the double, the man's wraith, e. g. the Babylonians, the Egyptians, the Karens of Burmah. But in any
case, the life of Sheol affords formal and not real continuity
of life. The Israelites seem to have been content with this
shadowy ' life after death ' that was no life, so long as the idea
of corporate personality enabled them to think of themselves
as living on in their children or their nation. But the rise of
the new individualism with Jeremiah and Ezekiel gave birth
to an acute sense of the problem of innocent suffering and the
injustices of this life. In the Book of Job and some of the
Psalms (e. g. lxxiii), we see the struggle towards the hope of
a new life that was life beyond death, but the faith is never
explicitly reached. The only two passages in the Old Testament
which explicitly declare a life after death are found in Isa.
xxvi. 19, part of an apocalyptic book of about 300 B. C., and in
Dan. xii. 2 (165 B. C.) :

> Thy dead shall live,
>> Their corpses shall arise ;
> They that dwell in the dust
>> Shall awake and give a ringing cry.
> For the dew of lights is thy dew,
>> And the earth shall give birth to shades. (Gray's trans.)

' And many of them that sleep in the dust of the earth shall awake,
some to everlasting life and some to shame and everlasting contempt.'

The former passage declares that Yahweh will re-people the
desolated land by bringing back to life those who had given up
their lives for their religion, i. e. the martyred saints. It will
be seen that this declares a partial and special resurrection to
renewed life upon this earth, a resurrection of the good alone.
The latter passage also declares a partial and special resurrection,
though here including the very bad (for punishment) as well
as the very good (for reward). But in both instances, these
beginnings of the Apocalyptic doctrine of life after death,

which were destined to have so wide a development in Jewish and Christian literature, take the form of a ' resurrection ', a bringing back to the life of the body, the only real life which the Hebrew could conceive. Hebrew psychology is of value here in helping us to realize why the belief in life after death took this form. It was because the Hebrew had never thought of a disembodied soul, and could not or did not conceive it, whilst the surviving ' ghost ' offered no sufficient basis in itself for real continuity of life. The Pauline doctrine retains this faith in the form of resurrection ; for Paul is too much a Hebrew to be able to conceive a naked spirit. But Paul has learnt to regard the present body of flesh as defective for the purpose of man's ' spirit ', even when yielded to the control of God. He, therefore, looks for a ' spiritual ' body, a body corresponding to man's real needs as the *rūach* body of God to His activity.

Out of many other possible applications of Hebrew psychology to the interpretation of the Old Testament which cannot here be developed, two should at least be mentioned, viz. the psychology of grammar and vocabulary, and the psychology of sacrifice. The first is a delicate and difficult study, and generalizations are apt to be as misleading as they are easy. But both the vocabulary and the syntax of Hebrew show that attention to concrete detail, rather than to abstract completeness, which characterizes the Hebrew psychology. The style is the man. A Hebrew sentence is like the Hebrew idea of personality ; its parts are vividly and picturesquely set before us, but they are co-ordinated, rather than subordinated to one central idea, and the nature of the co-ordination is often implicit, rather than explicit. The relatively large number of synonyms in particular cases, which perpetuate different single qualities of an object, may be illustrated by Burton's remark about a cognate language : ' Generalization is not the forte of the Arabic language . . . the Badawin will have names for each separate part, but no single one to express the whole.'[1] The peculiar nature and usage of the Hebrew tenses shows both weakness in the sense of time, and graphic 'externality' (cf. Driver, *Hebrew Tenses*, p. 5).

The psychology of sacrifice would involve consideration of two main ideas which have already emerged—the mystery of the blood-soul, and the idea of corporate personality seen in the identification of the offerer with the sacrifice, which is quite different from the idea of any transference of penalty. The most primitive Hebrew sacrifice seems to be the pouring out of the blood of the slain animal on a sacred stone (1 Sam. xiv. 33 ff.). The taboo on the consumption of blood is due to the peril attaching to its mysterious life-principle.

There is much in modern psychology that suggests interesting comparisons with the Hebrew. The central problem of the relation of body and soul has been greatly modified in form by the discovery of the function of the heart in the circulation of the blood by Harvey (1628), and especially by the discovery of the nervous system through the physiological work of the eighteenth and nineteenth centuries. Yet the old problem remains as to the relation of 'soul' and 'body', and it could be fairly argued that the drift away from the Greek idea of an incarnated soul is towards the Hebrew emphasis on the physical organism, however different the detail. The Hebrew idea of the accessibility of man's personality to outside influences has a parallel in the growing recognition of telepathy as a well-ascertained fact; the movement away from the 'closed' psychology of Locke and his successors brings our position nearer to that of the Hebrew. Indeed the Christian man who accepts the New Testament doctrine of the Holy Spirit as the basis of the life of faith is working with Hebrew conceptions. The modern stress on the sub-consciousness and the interest in psycho-analysis have their parallel in the idea of different

[1] *A Pilgrimage to Al-Madinah and Meccah*, i. 250 n.

bodily parts functioning in quasi-independence of the self, though constantly exerting an influence upon it. Finally, the corporate personality of the Hebrews has more than one point of contact with what is called ' social psychology ' in our time. As Hebrew myth and legend often enshrine permanent truths about God, so the Hebrew ideas about man seem to have anticipated by intuition some of our modern science.

H. WHEELER ROBINSON.

THE CONTRIBUTION OF THE OLD
TESTAMENT TO THE RELIGIOUS
DEVELOPMENT OF MANKIND

UNTIL recent times the teaching of the Christian Church, in the widest acceptation of the term, took it for granted that the Old Testament was the oldest book extant, that it contained a true history of the creation of the world and of all subsequent events in it recorded, that the story of the Garden of Eden explained the presence in the world of sin and suffering, and that in the Old Testament it was possible to trace from the earliest days of mankind the development of God's purpose in ' the redemption of the world through our Lord Jesus Christ '. Such at least was the teaching which the present writer received in his boyhood, and such is the belief still cherished by not a few Christians who unquestionably have a zeal for God, even if it be not according to knowledge.

It is true that the belief in the infallibility and antiquity of the Old Testament did not in the past go altogether unchallenged. As early as the second century Marcion declared the Old Testament to be incompatible with the teaching of Christ, and in the middle ages Rabbi Ibn Ezra (1088–1167) hinted at the difficulties in the way of accepting the theory of the Mosaic authorship of the Pentateuch ; while in later days astronomers, geologists, and exponents of the various branches of Natural Science shewed that the account of the creation of the world contained in the book of Genesis could not be accepted as true—at least in the natural sense of the words. Nevertheless, the old ideas about the Old Testament held their ground, and few clergy or teachers ventured openly and explicitly to contradict them.

But a theory which may be maintained against isolated and unconnected attacks upon it must give way, when the various facts on which such attacks are based have themselves been correlated and combined into a consistent whole; and what neither science nor literary criticism nor archaeology could effect, when appealed to independently, has been brought about by their combination. This generation in general reads the Old Testament without the prepossessions with which our fathers approached the study of it. Whereas they took it for granted that the Old Testament was absolutely free from error, we know that in historical matters it is often untrustworthy and inconsistent with itself, and that its account of creation is irreconcilable with science. Again, arguing from the assumed infallibility of the Old Testament, our fathers inferred that where a commandment ascribed to God, or an action represented as approved by Him, seems contrary to what we feel to be morally just, there must have been special circumstances, unknown to us, which justified such a commandment or action. The present generation on the other hand, since it frankly acknowledges that the Old Testament is not free from error, for the most part approaches the study of it with a critical attitude of mind of which our fathers, from the circumstances of their education, were incapable; and it can, therefore, perceive that much which our fathers justified simply on the ground that it is ascribed to God in a book which they regarded as infallible, is really opposed to what our moral sense, rectified by the teaching of Christ, feels to be right. Accordingly it needs no great boldness on our part, having admitted that the story of Genesis ii and iii for example is irreconcilable with the received facts of science, to maintain that if the story were true Jehovah would be flagrantly unjust.

But the critical faculty, that is, the power of discrimination, develops with its exercise. The more we subject the Old Testament to critical investigation, the more we find it to contain passages at variance with what as Christians we believe to be true and right. Not only in regard to history and science, but also—what is far more important—in connexion with morality and Theology we feel that much of it is untenable : and this being the case, it is inevitable that the question should be asked, What has the Old Testament to do with the Christian faith ?

From another side also the Old Testament is disparaged. There is in these days ' a murmuring of the Grecians against the Hebrews ', and what we may call constitutional antisemitism is inclined, not always justly, to belittle the Old Testament, and to insist upon the inferiority of Israel to Greece. It is obviously unfair to compare the Old Testament as a whole— that is to say, its lowest as well as its highest utterances—only with carefully selected masterpieces of Greek thought. And if in mere art the Greek surpassed the Hebrew, it is but just to remember with what base, foul, and morbid ideas some of the Greek masterpieces were connected. What Christian, or indeed Jewish, father, for example, would willingly put into his boy's hands unexpurgated stories of the gods and heroes on whose representation Greek artists lavished their utmost skill ? Of no ancient Jewish community could Saint Paul have given such a description as he has given of some members of the Corinthian Church before their conversion (1 Cor. vi. 9 f.).

Moreover those who exalt the Greek against the Hebrew and are impatient with the Hebrew element in the Christian religion are apt to forget that in the Christian Church ' there can be neither Jew nor Greek ' ; and that it is as contrary to the spirit of Christianity to force all Christian thought into Greek channels as it is to insist that all Christian devotion must conform to Hebrew models.

If then we are to give a satisfactory answer to the question,

What has the Old Testament to do with the Christian faith? we must endeavour to approach it with an impartial mind. Above all our study of the Old Testament must be *critical.* Every part of its teaching must be scrutinized in the light of what our Lord has taught. The result of such a scrutiny will be that we shall find ourselves compelled to classify the teaching of the Old Testament under various categories. Thus, for example, we must recognize that some of its elements are mere survivals of primitive heathenism, and are, except by violent and arbitrary perversion of their obvious meaning, incapable of adaptation to the needs of a higher religion; some other survivals of heathenism, whether by way of being allegorized or as possessing, irrespective of the ideas in which they originated, some practical utility, have been made subservient to genuine spirituality; we must recognize also teaching of an infinitely higher order which has to a great extent transformed the heathenish elements of which it was unable wholly to get rid. Such teaching in its various stages may be compared to the development of a bud into the ripe fruit, in the process of which that which has only temporary utility falls away and decays.

Among the survivals of heathenism we may class those folk tales of which the book of Genesis furnishes the greatest number of examples, and which, in their original form, are scarcely superior to the tales told by Hesiod; such as the story of the creation of Adam and Eve, and the temptation by the serpent in the Garden of Eden; the marriage of gods with human women; the Flood; the destruction of the Cities of the Plain and the transmutation of Lot's wife into a pillar of salt; Jacob's wrestling with a divine being at the ford of the Jabbok; Samson's supernatural strength, which is conditional, not on his godliness, but upon his remaining unshorn. Similarly, survivals of primitive thought are found in many of the ritual ordinances; such as the propitiation of Jehovah by the warm

blood or by the savour of sacrificial smoke; the means prescribed for getting rid of infection (Lev. xiii. f.); the trial by
ordeal (Num. v. 11–31); the means employed to rid the land
of the consequences of the Gibeonites' curse (2 Sam. xxi). Of
a different kind, though equally pagan in character, is the book
of Esther, which we should not consider inappropriately placed,
if it were bound up with the *Arabian Nights*.

In the above instances we can see modes of thought to which
parallels can be found among those races which we regard as
both barbarous and heathen; but some of them at least,
heathenish though they are in origin, have been adapted by,
and made subservient to, a much higher form of religion. It
would be difficult to find a story which in itself is more absolutely heathenish than the account of Jacob's wrestling at the
ford of the Jabbok. But if, as is probable, we have in Hosea
xii. 3 f. not indeed an interpretation of the *written* account of
Gen. xxxii. 24 ff., but an adaptation of a story which in its
more primitive form is there found, we have a clue to enable
us to account for the retention of some of these early folk tales.
And although it is impossible reasonably to allegorize every
feature of such primitive stories, useful illustrations of important truth could frequently be found in some of their
details.[1] Thus Gen. iii. 7, in which a primitive teacher has
tried to tell the first effect of an increase of knowledge, finds
an illustration in Saint Paul's words in Rom. vii. 9.

It must, however, be admitted that the adaptability of some

[1] In this connexion it will not be out of place to call attention to a remarkable difference between the methods of a Jewish teacher and of a modern
Englishman. The latter, being somewhat matter of fact, is beset by a dread
of mixing his metaphors or of saying that which will be characterized as
ridiculous. The former cares little about the form of his illustrations, if
that which he desires to teach is thereby made plain. The book of Jonah,
for example, sets forth a great and noble truth; but what modern *English*
allegory writer would venture to let his hero be swallowed by a fish in the
sea and after three days be vomited up unhurt on to dry land?

of the Hebrew legends to use as allegory or parable does not in itself differentiate the Old Testament from pagan literature, since many a pagan myth exhibits a like adaptability. The allegorizing of such Old Testament stories was not the cause, but the outcome of a higher spiritual development.

Nor can a hard and fast distinction be drawn between the morality of the Old Testament and that of pagan systems. It is true that, taken as a whole, the morality of the Old Testament is far in advance of pagan morality ; but it must also be admitted that the latter at its highest is in advance of the former at its lowest. Similarly we find certain religious ideas, held by pagan races, which are superior to those which find expression in the greater part of the Old Testament. Whereas, for example, the ancient Egyptians looked forward to a judgement after death and a separation of the righteous from the unrighteous, the crudest ideas of retribution, which, it was thought, must take place in this life, are found in almost all the Old Testament. It is indeed arguable that it does not contain a single passage which definitely contemplates any sort of resurrection from the dead : in any case the passages which are supposed to indicate such a belief are of late date, and are very few in number, particularly in regard of the numerous passages which imply, or even assert, that after death there is nothing worthy of being called life.

It may well be asked therefore, What is the unique value of the Old Testament as a whole, that the race which produced it should have been chosen to prepare the way for Christ ? To such a question the answer is clear. The uncompromising monotheism of the Old Testament, as distinct not only from polytheism but also from henotheism or monolatry, has given to Israel, and through Israel to the world, a sense of undivided allegiance to a Higher Power, without which there could have been no true development of Theology, that is to say, of the idea of God. Classical paganism ascribed to its gods all the weaknesses and vices displayed in human nature at its worst. The gods and goddesses are jealous of one another ; they try to thwart one another, and are unscrupulous and reckless in the means which they employ to accomplish the ends which they have in view. It is impossible to be loyal to the whole pantheon ; the votaries of one god appeal to him for protection from the spite or jealousy of another ; the gods themselves are lawless, and thus religion and morality are divorced to the detriment of each.

In the religion of Israel, however, there can be no thought of playing off one god against another : Jehovah alone can answer men's prayers and grant that which they need. To Him belongs the earth and the fullness thereof, the habitable world and they that dwell therein. Jehovah alone is King, and therefore He alone is Judge. The Israelite felt that he had to deal not with conflicting supernatural wills, but with one Will and one law—one standard of righteousness to which he must conform. The conception of that righteousness differed in different ages and among various sections of the nation— but though men might differ in their idea of what Jehovah required, they were all alike convinced that whatsoever was the form of service which Jehovah required, this they were bound to render, and what Jehovah abhorred they must eschew.

And thus the conviction that Jehovah's people must be assimilated to Him—' Ye shall be holy : for I the Lord your God am holy ' (Lev. xix. 2 f., xi. 45)—has produced an ever developing ideal of righteousness. As the idea of God is perpetually rectified and developed, so the idea of what God requires of man undergoes a corresponding rectification and development. Theology has acted on morality, and morality has reacted on Theology. Whereas polytheistic peoples ascribe to this deity one moral quality and to that another, Israelite thinkers, believing Jehovah alone to be God, and also to be righteous, ascribed to Him all that was of value in the beliefs of other nations concerning their gods. Moreover the prohibition of any idol in Israel helped to purge Israelite religion from the gross associations of the gods of heathenism. In Jehovah's superiority to mere human passions the prophet Hosea finds the assurance of His pardoning love—' I will not execute the fierceness of mine anger, I will not return to destroy Ephraim : for I am God, and not man ; the Holy One in the midst of thee ' (Hos. xi. 9).

Further, the Old Testament, in maintaining the coexistence in Jehovah of qualities, which in men might seem incompatible one with another, has led the way to a truer appreciation of those qualities. Justice and mercy are not antagonistic, for neither can have its perfect work unless it be combined with the other. Jehovah is judge to punish the wicked and to vindicate the righteous : yet He is not extreme to mark what is done amiss : for in Him truth can never be severed from mercy, but might and gentleness, holiness and compassion meet together. He is infinitely great, infinitely powerful : ' He fainteth not, neither is weary : there is no searching of his understanding ' ; nevertheless He is touched by the feeling of His creatures' infirmities. He tells the number of the stars, and calls them all by their names ; heaven is His throne, and earth His footstool ; the nations before Him are as a drop of a bucket or like the fine dust which has no effect on the balance ; and yet He feeds His flock like a shepherd, gathering the lambs with His arm, and carrying them in His bosom, and gently leading those that give suck. He is a father of the fatherless, and defends the cause of the widows ; He takes thought for the brute creation, and feeds the young ravens that call to Him. He has no pleasure in the death or sorrow of His creatures, but in their life and happiness. It is His will to remove the mourning veil cast over the nations, and to wipe away the tears from off all faces. His love of His people is described in terms of the tenderest, most sacred human affection. He comforts His

own as a mother comforts her son ; and the rapturous love of
the bridegroom for his bride is for all time glorified and sanctified, in that it has been made a figure of Jehovah's love of Israel,
and thus of Christ's love of the Church.

It is evident that those who had this conception of God could
scarcely fail to see that He must desire like qualities in His
worshippers. If in His hatred of oppression and wrong He had
delivered Israel from the Egyptian taskmaster, He could not
hide His eyes from similar oppression when the offenders were
Israelites. It is the belief that Jehovah's mercy is the result
of no caprice, but is founded in truth and justice, that gives
force to the prophets' vehement denunciation of Israel's sins.
Amos's teaching is indeed a foreshadowing of our Lord's as
given for example in the parable of the two servants (Matt.
xviii. 23 ff.). As Jehovah has dealt with His people, so He
desires that His people should deal one with another. Those to
whom much is given, of them shall much be required. Jehovah
has known (i. e. has entered into close relations with) Israel
alone of all the families of the earth ; therefore He will visit
upon them all their iniquities (Amos iii. 2). He cannot be
bribed or propitiated by costly offerings ; and such offerings,
when the wealth which makes them possible has been amassed
by violence and robbery, are abominable in His sight. As He
heard the sighing of His oppressed people in Egypt, so He hears
the cry of the hapless debtor crushed and enslaved by a re-
morseless creditor (Amos ii. 6 ff. ; Exod. xxii. 21–27 ; Deut.
xxiv. 10–13). He will not tolerate the withholding of the
hireling's wage, nor the cruel seizure of the land from which
the peasants should gain their livelihood (Isa. v. 8). Those who
look to Him for justice must themselves be just. It is not the
least glory of the Old Testament that it sets forth an ideal of
justice far superior to the ordinary morals of those who profess
and call themselves Christians. There must be no swerving
from strict honesty ; no plea of expediency, not even a pretext

of mercy, however specious, can warrant any tampering with justice. The lost property of an enemy must be restored as punctiliously as that of a friend (Exod. xxiii. 4 f.). There must be no shiftiness in trade dealings, no making of the ephah small and of the shekel great (Amos viii. 5).—' Thou shalt not have in thy bag divers weights, a great and a small. Thou shalt not have in thine house divers measures, a great and a small. A perfect and just weight shalt thou have ; a perfect and just measure shalt thou have : that thy days may be long upon the land which the Lord thy God giveth thee ' (Deut. xxv. 13–15 ; cf. Lev. xix. 35 f.). ' Thou shalt not take up a false report : put not thine hand with the wicked to be an unrighteous witness. Thou shalt not follow a multitude to do evil ; neither shalt thou speak in a cause to turn aside after a multitude to wrest judgment ; neither shalt thou favour a poor man in his cause ' [1] (Exod. xxiii. 1–3 ; cf. Lev. xix. 15).

It may perhaps be objected, however, that the Israelite conception of justice is directly responsible for no small amount of judicial cruelty and injustice, as well as of diabolical persecution in the name of religion ; and no doubt those who have been guilty of such evils have often appealed to the Old Testament to justify their actions. But this charge against the Old Testament rests on a misapprehension of the political, social, and economic conditions of the times in which the laws and stories of the Old Testament took shape. Freedom of every kind is really possible only in a law-respecting community. If the law of Deut. xiii. 12–18 is by its intolerance appalling to modern ideas, it at least discourages trumped up charges of

---

[1] This injunction is so remarkable in the age which produced the law, that it has been supposed that ' poor man ' is a mistake for ' great man ', the difference in the Hebrew being merely of one letter. But the mistake, if mistake it be, occurs also in Lev. xix. 15, which is perhaps influenced by this passage ; and since it is anterior to the Septuagint, the Jewish Church must have the credit of recognizing that it is not inconsistent with its context, but completes the ideal of justice there set forth.

apostasy by insisting that those who engage in a holy war shall gain absolutely no profit to themselves by their enterprise. Those who are loyal to the principles of the law cannot make their abhorrence of idols a pretext for the robbing of temples. And indeed those who approach the study of the law with some knowledge of the customs not only of primitive man but also of races which have made considerable progress in art and culture will at once recognize that the law of Israel, even when in these modern times it seems barbarous and unjust, was designed to correct that which was still more barbarous, and to put a stop to far greater injustice. The injunction, ' Thou shalt give life for life, eye for eye, tooth for tooth, hand for hand, foot for foot, burning for burning, wound for wound, stripe for stripe ' (Exod. xxi. 24 f., Deut. xix. 21), was not intended to justify private retaliation out of personal spite ; but it was designed on the one hand to insure that those who were guilty of the same offence should not receive punishments of unequal severity according to the caprice of individual judges, and on the other to fix a limit to the extent of the punishment judicially inflicted. Moreover in the Deuteronomic legislation a principle is enunciated in connexion with punishment which even as late as the days of our grandfathers was ignored in English criminal law :—' Forty stripes he may give him, he shall not exceed : lest if he should exceed, and beat him above these with many stripes, *then thy brother should seem vile unto thee* ' (Deut. xxv. 3).

Further, no estimate of the debt which the world owes to the Old Testament can be just, which does not take full account of the high standard of sexual morality which is found in it. It is true that in this respect the books of the Old Testament do not all attain the same high level. Those who have given accounts, for example, of the amours of Samson and of the *régime* in the harem of Ahasuerus, shew no horror of the gross animalism which they describe. Moreover it must be recognized that some of the ordinances which on the whole have tended to promote a higher ideal of matrimony and of personal purity had their origin not in any sense of the sanctity of the body such as S. Paul insists on, but rather in primitive man's dread of that which was beyond his comprehension. But though it would be worse than folly to refuse to recognize these obvious facts, full justice must be done to the other side of the picture. The Old Testament as a whole, its lowest with its highest, is infinitely superior to the literature of ancient Greece or ancient Rome. If in some parts of it we find polygamy and concubinage taken for granted, this is not true of the whole. There is not one of the utterances of the prophets which would justify the conclusion that they accepted polygamy, whereas there are several which imply monogamy, and inculcate loving faithfulness to the wife married in youth. Here again the prophet's teaching of man's duty is based on their conception of what Jehovah is. He has not repudiated Israel whom He betrothed to Himself in Egypt, and He would have His people imitate His stedfastness :—' Take heed to your spirit, and let none deal treacherously against the wife of his youth. For I hate putting away saith the Lord' (Mal. ii. 15 f.).

The teachers of Israel were convinced that there was no relationship or activity of life unaffected by the revelation of Jehovah, and it is not their fault that those who substituted rules for principles sometimes reduced the religion of Jehovah to a puerile hair-splitting casuistry. A belief in the inspiration of a book, when divorced from all understanding of historical exegesis, is pretty certain to lead to distortion of the truth ; and of this the Christian Church not less than the Jewish affords many instances. Laws and injunctions must be studied in their historical setting ; and then it will commonly be found that things which to unintelligent literal interpretation are an occasion of stumbling, embody a principle which should be for our spiritual and moral wealth.

It was inevitable that the teachers of Israel, inasmuch as they were convinced that true allegiance to Jehovah affected their whole life, should look to Him to reward righteousness and to punish sin. Accustomed as they were to take their metaphors from the legal procedure with which they were familiar, Hebrew prophets insisted on a time of judgement when the righteous would be vindicated and the wicked would suffer the penalty of their misdeeds. This conviction of a coming judgement produced those earnest vehement calls to repentance which are indeed ' as a hammer that breaketh the rock in pieces ' ; and it is remarkable that so unshakable was the faith in Jehovah's executing judgement, that it held its ground even in an age when it was believed that retribution must come in this life. We who approach the problem of retribution from a different angle perhaps feel that the prophet Ezekiel, in attempting to vindicate Jehovah's justice to every individual while limiting the sphere of the Divine activity to this life, has set himself an impossible task. Science and experience alike, teach us that in this life, when ' the fathers have eaten sour grapes ' . . . ' the children's teeth are set on edge ' ; and indeed this fact is plainly recognized in the familiar words of the Second Commandment ; nevertheless we must not shut our eyes to Ezekiel's faith which, in spite of appearances to the contrary, maintains unwaveringly Jehovah's absolute justice. ' Clouds and darkness are round about him ; righteousness and judgment are the habitation of his seat.' ' The waves of the sea '— human misery and human wickedness—' are mighty and rage horribly, but yet the Lord who dwelleth on high is mightier.'

The Old Testament is not a compendium of moral rules, but a record of God's revelation to Israel. That revelation is unique—not that God has left Himself without witness in any nation, or that other races have contributed nothing to the intellectual and religious wealth of mankind—but because the revelation of God to Israel, regarded as a whole, possesses a unity and a completeness not found elsewhere. This fact becomes apparent at once, if we try to imagine any other nation in which our Lord Jesus Christ could have proclaimed His Gospel with equal immediate effect. Jerusalem, it is true, crucified Him, but Athens, far worse, would have smothered His preaching in ridicule. It must be remembered to the credit of the Jew that, with all his exclusiveness, he was willing to admit on terms of equality the Gentile proselyte to Judaism, and that even slavery as it was regulated by the law of Israel was little more than indentured labour. Jewish Pharisaism was therefore a more fertile soil than Athenian snobbishness in which to plant the gospel of the Fatherhood of God and the brotherhood of man. No reasonable person will deny the beauty and the truth of the utterances of many a Greek thinker; but such utterances are scattered gems which were never combined in one harmonious setting for the good even of a single nation. Such a unity could be achieved only in a nation which, like Israel, believed in one God working out His purpose yesterday, to-day, and for ever.

The Old Testament then is a record of a continuous revelation of God. That revelation, as the author of the Epistle to the Hebrews has told us, was given ' by divers portions and in divers manners '—here a little, there a little, as the exigencies of each age demanded, or else by a great forward movement of thought, itself the outcome of some historical crisis affecting the whole nation. It is impossible to understand the Old Testament without a study of the history of the people among whom it took shape; for the teachers of Israel were interpreters of the national history in the light of their belief in Jehovah. They were for the most part primarily concerned with what was in their time altogether modern history; that is to say, with the events which had just taken place, and with the clouds, big with possibilities of good or evil, which were then rising above the horizon. But it was not only of what was just past, present, or in prospect that they sought to discover the explanation and the cause. In their scrutiny of the signs of the times, and in their efforts to interpret them for their people, they learned to look to the distant past as well as forward into the future. If, as they believed, Jehovah's mind could be known from what was then happening, it was evident that it must have been revealed also in the events of the past. And since in the thought of the older portions of the Old Testament the nation or tribe was the unit rather than the individual, the interpretation of past history became naturally the interpretation of Israel's history. Israel, which had been in bondage in Egypt, had been led by Jehovah through the wilderness into a land flowing with milk and honey. Why was such a blessing granted to Israel rather than for example to Edom, which, though militarily more powerful than Israel at the exodus, had become possessed of a territory less desirable than the land of Canaan? Why had Jehovah helped Israel and not Canaan? Such were the questions that presented themselves to the minds of Hebrew thinkers. They were not always answered in the same way ; for the religious and political condition of the nation might suggest now one answer, now another. To some of Israel's teachers, who were only too well acquainted with the evils which had existed in Canaan and were not yet eradicated from the land, it seemed that the downfall of the Canaanites and the dominance of Israel had been due to Jehovah's just indignation with the former and to His desire that in Israel He would find a people more capable of serving Him in righteousness : ' Speak not thou in thine heart, after that the Lord thy God hath thrust them out from before thee, saying, For my righteousness the Lord hath brought me in to possess this land : whereas for the wickedness of these nations the Lord doth drive them out from before thee. Not for thy righteousness, or for the uprightness of thine heart, dost thou go in to possess their land : but for the wickedness of these nations the Lord thy God doth drive them out from before thee ' (Deut. ix. 4 f.).

Jehovah had desired a people for His own possession that should serve Him with unswerving loyalty ; and He had selected Israel from all the nations of the earth, not because Israel was already perfect, for it was ' a stiffnecked people ', but because it possessed a capacity for a higher religion than Canaan had ever known. From the beginning Jehovah had been disciplining Israel for communion with Himself : ' Thou shalt remember all the way which the Lord thy God hath led thee these forty years in the wilderness, that he might humble thee, to prove thee, to know what was in thine heart, whether thou wouldest keep his commandments or no. And he humbled thee, and suffered thee to hunger, and fed thee with manna, which thou knewest not, neither did thy fathers know : that he might make thee know that man doth not live by bread only, but by every thing that proceedeth out of the mouth of the Lord doth man live ' (Deut. viii. 2 f.).

The belief that Jehovah had chosen Israel, and in so doing had conferred innumerable benefits upon Israel compelled the prophets to insist upon the principle *noblesse oblige* :—' You only have I known of all the families of the earth : therefore I will visit upon you all your iniquities ' (Amos iii. 2). But insistence upon this principle involved the tracing out of all Jehovah's dealings with Israel. Not only since the deliverance from Egyptian bondage, but even in the age of those whom the Israelites regarded as their earliest ancestors, Jehovah had been working out His purpose for Israel. Israel was His chosen ; but since Israel had so often proved unworthy of its destiny, Jehovah's choice of Israel must be due not to any arbitrariness but to a settled purpose. If earlier Israelite thinkers regarded their nation simply as called to be Jehovah's servant to minister to Him in His own house, later ages perceived that the Lord of such a servant might employ him also as a messenger beyond His house. As we might expect, such teaching is not apparent everywhere in the Old Testament. In times when Israel seemed in danger of being utterly crushed by the great empires which overpowered it, it was not easy for the chosen people to remember that they had obligations even to their oppressors. 'Consume them in thy wrath, consume them that they may perish,' is the prayer which most readily rises to our lips, when we are the victims of oppression and wrong; and the Old Testament furnishes not a few examples of such prayers. But it also contains promises of free forgiveness to those who have been in the wrong, if they will but turn and seek Jehovah: 'Let the wicked forsake his way, and the unrighteous man his thoughts: and let him return unto the Lord, and he will have mercy upon him; and to our God, for he will abundantly pardon' (Isa. lv. 7). It will perhaps be objected, however, that the prophets' assurances of Jehovah's forgiveness and compassion are limited to Israel, and to those of the Gentiles who are willing to acknowledge Israel's superiority and to throw in their lot with Israel. This is to a great extent true, but it is not the whole truth. In the development of real monotheism there arose also the germ of universalism. The book of Jonah makes it abundantly clear that Israel has a mission to the kingdom of the world, and that Jehovah's compassion is not limited to Israel, but extends also to the heathen city, 'wherein are more than sixscore thousand persons that cannot discern between their right hand and their left hand, and also much cattle'. It is not necessary to be an Israelite by descent to receive the favour of Jehovah. Rahab the Canaanite harlot and Ruth the Moabitess are honoured among the 'mothers in Israel'. The poet of Ps. lxxxvii believes that the time is coming when Jehovah, in taking a census of the peoples, will count them all as true-born Israelites. The noblest sons of Israel pray for the new era when Jehovah's way will be known upon earth, and His saving health among all nations; when the light with which

He has illumined Israel will lighten also the Gentiles, and all the peoples will praise Him.

There are indeed two conceptions of Israel in the Old Testament, one as a nation, the other as a church. They are not always distinguishable, and some Old Testament writers, especially when smarting under heathen oppressors, or in the first flush of victory over them, have confounded the latter with the former, and have drawn pictures of a nationalist Jewish monarch shepherding the Gentiles with a rod of iron, and dashing them in pieces like a potter's vessel ; but we shall not do justice to the Old Testament unless we recognize also the conception of Israel as a church, and the aspiration that Jehovah's house may become a house of prayer for all peoples.

But not only do we find in the Old Testament the germ of universalism, but, what is of equal importance, the germ of individualism. Jehovah, being just, will not tolerate that the fathers should be put to death for the children, or the children for the fathers (Deut. xxiv. 16). Ezekiel, who shepherded Israel in exile, felt the responsibility which rested upon him, of warning individual men (Ezek. iii. 16–21). The poet of Ps. cxxxix describes God's infinite knowledge of him personally. Another psalmist (xxvii. 10), forsaken by his father and mother, trusts in Jehovah to take him up. Jehovah is a father of the fatherless, and defends the cause of the widow ; He helps those to right who suffer wrong, and feeds the hungry. And thus the way is prepared for the teaching of Israel's greatest Prophet : ' Are not two sparrows sold for a farthing ? And not one of them shall fall on the ground without your Father : but the very hairs of your head are all numbered. Fear not therefore ; ye are of more value than many sparrows.'

It is almost superfluous to say that the development of this individualism among a monotheistic people has produced a faith which can move mountains. The great thinker to whom we owe the poem of Job, in spite of his consciousness of the utter breakdown of that which in his days passed for orthodoxy, bewildered as he is by the impossibility of solving the riddle of creation—has so ' felt the Spirit of the Highest ', that he ' Cannot confound, nor doubt him nor deny '. He possesses Ezekiel's faith, but a deeper insight than his predecessor, and, in addition, a magnificent willingness to face facts, even though he knows that he cannot reconcile the external facts upon which ' orthodoxy ' is based with his inward faith which rests on personal experience of communion with God. In like manner— even without the sure and certain hope of a resurrection to eternal life—Israelite saints, when urged to apostatize, went unflinching to martyrdom. The words which we read as addressed to Nebuchadnezzar by Shadrach, Meshach and Abednego well express the invincible faith which carried the Church of Israel unscathed through fire and water : ' If our God whom we serve be able to deliver us, from the burning fiery furnace and from thy hand, O king, he will deliver us. But if not, be it known unto thee, O king, that we will not serve thy gods, nor worship the golden image which thou hast set up.'

It will perhaps be felt that those who in this mind yielded themselves to torture and death came short of the martyr ' whose eagle eye could pierce beyond the grave ' ; it was, however, necessary that many should thus suffer before it could be clearly perceived that martyrdom is not loss but has a permanent value. Nevertheless the great lesson was learnt even in Israel ; and the prophet who expounded to his own people the meaning of martyrdom for Israel, has helped a Church drawn from all peoples towards an understanding of the sufferings of ' the Faithful Martyr, the Firstborn of the dead ', who ' was wounded for our transgressions ', and with whose ' stripes we are healed '.

It is true that no Old Testament writer—nor, for the matter of that, any one else—has been able fully to explain the presence of suffering; but in showing that the sufferings endured for the truth's sake were not in vain, the prophet has enabled us to dispense with a full interpretation of the mystery. In the Old Testament we see not only that ' the people of the saints of the Most High God '—the ' son of man ', to adopt the allegorical term—have been sent upon this earth, not to be ministered unto, but to minister, and to give their lives a ransom for many from the thraldom of superstition, wickedness, and fear; but also that, having accomplished in tribulation the work which is given them to do, they pass from the arena of conflict and suffering into vindication and reward in the presence of the God whom they have so faithfully served. Though the Old Testament contains no explicit assurance of a future life, Jesus drew the natural inference from its highest teaching when He declared, ' He is not the God of the dead, but of the living '.

Finally, the Christian Church owes an incalculable debt of gratitude to Israel, not only for the preparation of the way for Christ, but also for providing a model of adoration. The articulate worship of the Christian Church is founded on the utterances of Israel. Those utterances have not always been used with discrimination—not all the Psalms, for example, are fit for use in Christian worship—but this must not blind us to the fact that the highest devotional language of the Church is either based upon, or is taken directly from, the Old Testament. In the language of prayer and praise, in the real adoration of God, Israel has become, and is likely to continue to be, spokesman for the whole world : ' I will magnify thee, O God, my King, and I will praise thy name for ever and ever. Every day will I give thanks unto thee, and I will praise thy name for ever and ever.'

R. H. KENNETT.

JEWISH INTERPRETATION OF THE OLD TESTAMENT

There can be but few who do not desire that Jewish scholars will continue to contribute to the exposition of the Hebrew Bible. Such participation is a right and a duty. Yet this claim by no means implies the maintenance of a ' Jewish ' exegesis.

In practice, the modern Jewish student of the Hebrew Bible relies on the same works as his Christian fellow-student. The former, no less than the latter, betakes himself to Gesenius's *Dictionary* rather than to Qimḥi's *Book of Roots* for the meanings of words. The Jew, if his linguistic training qualifies him, may turn with appreciation also to Qimḥi ; and after devotion to the commentaries of Dillmann and Cheyne, Gunkel and Peake, he may still derive pleasure from the older commentaries of Rashi and Ibn Ezra. He may find spiritual sustenance in Midrash, and admiringly observe how many interpretations regarded as new are as old as Mechilta and Sifre. If he be an Arabist, the exegetical works of the Qaraites and of their Rabbinite critic Saadiah may be consulted by him not altogether without profit. Just so, the Christian student (and at least one Jewish student known to me) does not, if he be wise, altogether reject Augustine's ' Psalms ' for Briggs's, or Jerome's ' Isaiah ' for Duhm's, or depend on Allen's ' Matthew ' to the exclusion of Chrysostom's.

Though, however, Jew and Christian will be moved in such affectionate reverence for past expositors by varying loyalties, they are at one in their present homages. If Jews consult commentaries written by contemporary Christians, more than Christians refer to commentaries written by contemporary Jews, it is because the works of Christians are by far the more numerous and, on the whole, the more serviceable. Graetz did admirable work, as did S. D. Luzzatto and more recently Ehrlich and Jastrow. But as a rule liberal Jews have been timid to accept, conservative Jews reluctant to assail, modern critical conclusions. The silence was effectively broken when in 1903 Abraham Cahana published in Russia a Hebrew commentary on Genesis frankly pro-critical, and in 1905 David Hoffmann published in Germany a commentary on Leviticus as frankly anti-critical; the one upholding, the other contesting, the documentary theories as to the composition of the Pentateuch. Since then we have had works like M. Segal's ' Samuel ' and J. Hoschander's ' Esther ' which occupy an intermediate position. Again, Dr. C. G. Montefiore's *Bible for Home Reading* has won its way into general as well as into denominational regard; Jacob Barth's and Felix Perles' philological suggestions are freely cited in the Oxford Gesenius. Nor is there any essential difference of spirit on the critical side between Geiger's *Urschrift* and Driver's *Introduction*; the same being true of sections of Wiener's and Dahse's more recent anti-critical essays.

Needless is it to marshal further evidence. Exegesis of the Hebrew Bible deserves and requires a limiting denominational epithet when it is at its second not at its first best; when it is apologetic, dogmatic, controversial, and to a minor degree traditional—not when it is scientific, objective, unprejudiced, and free. ' Christian ' exegesis (in this context) can mean no more than an effort to read in the Hebrew Scriptures meanings, or draw from those meanings conclusions, antipathetic to or denied by a ' Jewish ' exegesis. Exegesis of this class was fostered by those disputes which began in the New Testament and Talmud, became prominent in Justin Martyr, and subsequently flourished in various medieval epochs. On the whole these disputes led to insincerity on both sides, for the scoring of advantages rather than ascertainment of truth was aimed at.

Monks pressed words against Rabbis, Rabbis denied contexts against Monks. The only real gain was won by Naḥmanides, who, in the famous and otherwise futile public disputation at Barcelona in 1263, established the principle that much of the so-called ' Jewish ' exegesis in the Agada was homily or opinion personal to the particular Rabbi cited, and not the authoritative decision of the mass of scholars of that particular Rabbi's generation. In other words, a good deal of the exegesis found in books written by Jews is not necessarily Jewish. This was not the case, however, with certain disputes within the community. Within the Church there has been a Roman and a Protestant exegesis, just as within the Synagogue there was a century before and a century after the Christian era a Pharisaic and Sadducean exegesis, in the Middle Ages a Rabbinite and a Qaraite exegesis, a mystical and a rational exegesis, and now an ' orthodox ' and a ' critical ' exegesis. The last-named dichotomy, however, applies to Christian no less than to Jewish circles. The divergence is parallel, not sectarian. Philological science and archaeological research have so far triumphed that, psychology apart, exegesis has largely emancipated itself from denominational if not from traditional bias. This was a triumph of the critical school.

Psychology apart. For unhappily the fruits of the scientific victory were somewhat spoilt when exegesis became psychological, and fell into the hands of scholars brilliantly gifted indeed, yet imperfectly qualified by training and disposition for the objective application of subjective methods. Perhaps, speaking historically, one might say that with the modern rejection of both the Pauline and Pharisaic philological systems of exegesis, which had much in common, there has been no reconciliation between the Pauline and Pharisaic psychological systems which were in acute opposition. To the former the Law was a way of darkness and death, to the latter it was a source of light and life. If the principle ' the letter kills ' had remained solely a standard of ethics, the heirs of Paulinism and Rabbinism could still go on their merry disputatious ways, agreeing to differ, without loss to the exact interpretation of Scripture. But the Higher Criticism transferred the antithesis between letter and spirit from the domain of ethics to that of exegesis. Recent developments have, accordingly, not only provided a fresh justification of controversial exegesis, but have in a sense made controversy unavoidable, without however reviving olden animosities. Controversy of this type arises out of temperament, it need not sink into ill-temper. To sum up the position briefly, Wellhausen was not content with a scientific philological exegesis, nor with an historical criticism that induced him to antedate the Prophets to the Pentateuch. He applied psychology. But psychology as applied to the explanation of racial genius is still an inexact instrument. Jews, whether liberals or conservatives, are here at one. They feel themselves compelled by the pressure of circumstance to invite a hearing for a ' Jewish ' Higher Criticism which should apply a psychology other than that of the accomplished Christian scholars who have otherwise done so much for the elucidation of the Hebrew Scriptures. This ' Jewish ' Criticism makes the Law equally with Prophecy a factor in religious progress. The conventional treatment of the Law as a stage of degeneration from Prophecy stimulates ' Jewish ' opposition.

Hence, after a gracious period of interdenominational agreement, we may expect a less amiable period of denominational disagreements, even though Jews do not all admit the accuracy of S. Schechter's witty if perverse characterization of Higher Criticism as Higher Anti-semitism. Exegesis, none the less, suffers when insufficient account is taken of the purpose of Law to make a holy and virtuous community. If there be one penetrating ' Jewish ' principle of interpretation of the Old Testament it is just this belief in the power of Law to moralize a whole people. There is only this to add. Anthropology, in its most recent phase, is no longer regarding ritual and idea, magic and religion, under the old aspect. Religion may after all have preceded magic, just as idea precedes ritual. Ritual may be machinery for applying principle ; Law the means of making simple prophetic ideas work in the complex life of society. An excessive antinomian proclivity in certain sections of ' Christian ' exegesis thus provokes a defensive pronomian excess in a new ' Jewish ' exegesis. Out of these excesses a mean path of moderation will be found, truth will emerge inevitably from an adjustment of the balance. The least, however, that both sides can do is to cultivate sincerity even in their advocacy of causes.

In most other respects modern Jewish exegesis is identical with Christian. The refusal to recognize, particularly in Isaiah, direct prophecies of Jesus is not nowadays specifically Jewish. Christians may favour ' typical ' suggestion ; they no longer insist on literal prediction. The Revised Version in Isa. vii. 14 still, it is true, renders *ha-'almah* by ' a virgin ', with the ineffectual marginal variant ' maiden '. The new translation, recently issued by the Jewish Publication Society of America, prefers ' the young woman ', just as the earlier Jewish Zunz Bible had ' das junge Weib '. But T. K. Cheyne (in the second edition of his ' Isaiah ', 1882, vol. i, p. 49) renders in exactly the same way (' the young woman '), and G. Buchanan Gray (*Inter. Crit. Com.*, p. 127) emphatically writes : ' Why the term *'almah* in preference, say, to *ishah* or *na'arah* was chosen, no theory yet propounded explains, but least of all the theories that require the passage to express the fact that the woman conceives and bears without ceasing to be a virgin.' To me, the use of *'almah* in Prov. xxx. 19, seems the clue ; the suggestion is that Isaiah's sign-child is the mother's first infant. Be that as it may, Christians and Jews are now agreed on what formerly was a ground of vigorous contention. Note, however, in passing that there is no ' Jewish ' interpretation of the

passage (beyond the denial of virgin birth) ; for the commentaries by ancient and medieval Jews are undecided as to
whether the child's mother is the wife of Ahaz or of Isaiah,
while Qimḥi offers both alternatives for his reader's choice.

The increasing approximation of Jewish and Christian
exegesis is further illustrated by the interpretation of the
'Servant' passages. A piquant example was afforded when
first M. Friedmann (*S'rubabel*, 1890) and then quite independently E. Sellin (*Serubabel*, 1898) explained the cryptic message
of Isa. lii–liii by aid of the cryptic personage Zerubbabel.
Thus a Jewish and a Christian scholar could arrive at the same
conclusion on a personage of the later Isaiah which, like the
child of the earlier Isaiah, had given rise to so much heated
denominational controversy. The identification, however, of
the Suffering Servant with Zerubbabel is quite improbable.
The marvel is that interdenominational consent in regard to
the Suffering Servant is not restricted to the freakish fantasy
just cited. The older Jewish exegesis, in Targum and Talmud,
interpreted Isa. liii of the Messiah, with a hint of application
(at least of Isa. vii) to Hezekiah (T. B. Sanh., 94 a). But, as
the centuries advanced, many Jewish expositors abandoned the
Messianic theory, the Gaon Saadiah seeing in Jeremiah the
original of the figure whose picture made of Isa. liii what
Neubauer and Driver describe as 'one of the principal battle-
fields between Christians and their Jewish opponents'. Why
did Jews seek another than a Messianic interpretation? They
did not do this absolutely, for the Messianic interpretation
persisted and persists. A passage from Ibn Danon deserves
citation from Neubauer and Driver's *The Fifty-Third Chapter
of Isaiah according to the Jewish Interpreters* (Oxford, 1877,
vol. ii, p. 203) :

'R. Joseph ben Kaspi was led so far as to say that those who expounded it of the Messiah, who is shortly to be revealed, gave occasion

to the heretics to interpret it of Jesus. May God, however, forgive him for not having spoken the truth! our Rabbis, the doctors of the Talmud, deliver their opinions by the power of prophecy, possessing a tradition concerning the principles of interpretation, so that their words are the truth. The principle which every expositor ought to rest upon is never to shrink from declaring the truth in order that such as are foolish may not err : for our God will not destroy anything out of his world for the sake of fools who worship his creatures.'

Ibn Danon alludes in the last clause to the famous answer of the ' Elders in Rome '—Gamaliel II, Aqiba and others—who in the year A. D. 95 were asked why God did not destroy objects of idol worship. Idolaters, the Elders replied, worship the Sun and Moon. Shall God destroy his world because of fools ? (Mishnah, *Aboda Zara*, iv. 7). Ibn Danon had his own private revelation as to the Suffering Servant. For he continues, ' I will make known what has been communicated to me from heaven, namely that the section was originally uttered with reference to Hezekiah, king of Judah and Israel, but being " a word deftly spoken " nevertheless alludes covertly to the Messiah '. So, too, according to Ibn Danon, in Num. xxii–xxv, Balaam speaks ostensibly of David but alludes covertly to the Messiah. Though, however, the Messianic interpretation persisted, it became very popular to interpret the prophecy as applying to Israel. Rashi, Ibn Ezra, Qimḥi, Isaac Abarbanel, and many others adopted this view. Naḥmanides allowed his readers to choose freely between the Messiah or Israel ; Solomon de Marini offered both alternatives—Israel *and* the Messiah being both intended. Whether the majority of Jewish expositors thought of Israel as the Suffering Servant because it seemed easier to deny the application to Jesus if they discarded *all* Messianic applications, or whether they did so because they had reached a true exegesis, it is hard to say ; probably both motives operated. Rashi explicitly says so in his commentary on the second Psalm, as I have elsewhere pointed

out. At all events, in so far as there was at all a Jewish interpretation of the Suffering Servant, it passed through three stages:
the Messianic, the Personal, the Communal. All that Jews
were agreed upon was the dogmatic negative that whoever was
meant it was not Jesus. Abraham Farissol was not the only
Jew who, while denying any Christology to Isaiah, felt that this
mere negative was unfair. The real marvel is that Christian
expositors have come to accept this negative as emphatically
as Jews ever did. Even Mowinckel who rejects the ' Israel '
ascription, denies the Christological. In the interests of a
sound, objective exegesis, the Suffering Servant is Israel to
Eduard König as much as to Abraham Ibn Ezra. The marvel
is a most honourable testimony to that love of truth, which
has not precluded theologians from receding from a strongly
entrenched position in the polemic field.

This retreat, however, by no means implies a surrender of the
' typical ' application by Christians of Isa. liii. Such comfort
and inspiration, derived not from exegesis but from a natural
desire to read the New Testament in continuity with the Old,
is an altogether legitimate expression of affection and reverence
for both Testaments. At the close of his excellent volume, the
Exiles' Book of Consolation, König writes :

' The main importance of the Exiles' Book of Consolation is this,
that the better portion of Jahweh's people, which in faith and patience
bore the sufferings of the Exile, came to be viewed as a type of Him who,
although absolutely innocent, yet took upon Himself the heaviest
sufferings, in order that He might redeem mankind from that real
exile which consists in separation from God.'

Typical application of this kind was an important element
in the older Jewish use of Scripture. As a general principle
Jews upheld that heartening linking of the generations which
sees in the experiences of one age the experiences of all ages.
Texts, relating to heroic figures of the past applied also to heroic

figures of the nearer time and of the time to come. Again, texts which had no historical reference at all, received personal, historical application; Eccles. ii. 21 ('There is a man whose labour is with wisdom') refers to the artist of the Tabernacle, Bezaleel; Prov. xxviii. 18 b to Ahithophel, David's particular foe. But such homiletic suggestions, making for edification, are too numerous to need or abide illustration. Sometimes, naturally, these applications were sincere, though not always sound, exegesis, as when Daniel's beasts are identified with wrong monarchies of the ancient world. A fine example is offered by the treatment of Ps. xcii, which is placed in the mouth of Adam. It is a paean by the first man on the first of the world's Sabbaths, when the Creator's work was done, and man entered into the garden. To sing the praise of God was man's *raison d'être* from the beginning, as it will be to the end. For the hundredth Psalm, in the Midrash, is the thanksgiving of souls in eternity. The tendency to historical application may thus aid faith as well as increase love. How old the tendency is appears from some of the headings of the Psalms, which can scarcely have been aught but a 'typical' application to incidents in David's life. The Septuagint adds further instances of its own, foreign to the Massoretic Text.

Naturally, in the Midrash such typical applications are not rigidly fixed; there are often several alternatives offered. One particular instance deserves note; namely, Ps. xxii. In the Gospel this is applied to the Passion of Jesus. In the Midrash it has a double application. In the first place it is applied to Esther, 'the hind of the dawn'. But in the second place it is applied to Israel, perhaps regarded as represented by Esther. The reader will find much that is curious in Dr. C. Taylor's treatment of Ps. xxii in his *Cairo Genizah Palimpsests* (Cambridge, 1900). The interesting point is that a communal turn is given to strongly individualized utterances. In Ps. lvii. 8 the

text runs : ' Awake up, my glory, awake, psaltery and harp.'
In the heading of the Psalm, David speaks when hiding from
Saul in the cave (1 Sam. xxii. 1). But the Midrash interprets
thus : ' The Congregation of Israel said : O world's Master !
Awake, as in the days of Esther, who was likened to the dawn,
and on us will fall the duty to sing psalms before thee with
psaltery and harp.'

The speaker is thus the ' Congregation (*Kĕneseth*) of Israel '.
We here meet another principle of interpretation, allied to
what has been superficially analysed in the preceding paragraph.
Though only of late has the theory that the ' I ' of the Psalter,
may mean Israel, become popular—in fact there is already much
reaction against the theory—it was strongly held in the older
Jewish exegesis. Personifications of Israel are frequent in the
Midrash ; Israel is the Bride, or the Dove (T. B. Bᵉrachoth,
53 b) whose ' wings are covered with silver, and her pinions
with shimmer of gold ' (Ps. lxviii. 14)—the wings are the Law by
which Israel escapes, just as the dove flies to safety. The most
common personification is the Community, the Keneseth
Israel, as an individual. An excellent summary of the exegetical
problem was contributed by Dr. C. G. Montefiore to the
Quarterly Review for July 1918. This essay illustrates the
assimilation of Jewish and Christian scholarship, and exemplifies
just that psychological nuance to which reference has been
made. Dr. Montefiore probes far more penetratingly than
a Christian would do into the relations between the ' national '
and the ' universal ' in religion. As regards the personification,
the Talmud and Midrash are full of instances. Ps. cxvi is thus
explained : The Congregation of Israel speaks : ' I am beloved
[agreeing perhaps with the LXX rendering : I am full of love]
when God hears my voice . . . I am poor [in good deeds] yet am
I thine, and it is seemly that thou save me ' (T. B. Pᵉsaḥim
118 b). The lily of Sharon (and much else in the Song of Songs)
is Israel; not only is Israel meant, but the Congregation of

Israel speaks. The forty-ninth Psalm seems intensely personal :
' I will incline mine ear to a parable, I will open my dark saying
upon the harp '—here the individual poet and moralist pours
out his soul. Yet when he proceeds to say in the next line :
' Wherefore should I fear in the days of evil,' the Midrash
remarks, ' the Congregation of Israel speaks '. Or, again, it is
Israel who, according to the Midrash, utters the poignant
yearning of Ps. lxxxiv : ' My soul longeth, yea even fainteth for
the courts of the Lord, my heart and my flesh cry out unto the
living God.' So with Ps. lxix : ' Save me, O God, for the
waters are come into my soul,' so with Ps. cxx. The hundred
and ninth Psalm, by the same exegetical method, is interpreted
nationally, not individually, and thus much of the imprecatory
sting is dulled. It is worth noting that Mendelssohn's view
that vv. 6–19 were spoken by the Psalmist's enemies against
him, not by him against them, is adopted not only by the
Jewish-American translation (observe the quotation marks on
p. 857 of that translation), but also by that eminent Christian
Divine, Prof. W. E. Barnes (see *Lex in Corde*, p. 176). Very
significant is the communal interpretation of Ps. lxxi. 2 :
' Deliver me in thy righteousness and rescue me.' The Midrash
applies this to the whole people, despite such individual touches
as v. 6 : ' By thee have I been holden up from the womb ; thou
art he that took me out of my mother's bowels.' If these be
communal, why not Ps. li. 5 as some moderns strongly insist ?
But more than this. ' The Congregation of Israel said, in the
presence of the Holy One, blessed be he, when thou deliverest
me, it is not for the righteousness and good deeds which we
have done that thou savest, but whether to-day or to-morrow
save us for thy righteousness.' Here the fact that the Psalm is
couched in singular terms prevents the arrogant claim even of
communal merit. It is an edifying application of the personification, a corrective to self-righteousness. This type of Jewish
interpretation is often sound exegesis. Dr. Montefiore

concludes the essay referred to in these terms, persuasive as judicious.

' If we allow that the *I* of the Psalter often means the individual, we shall also have to concede that occasionally it does, not, and that in many Psalms the writer speaks in a representative character, saying what is not only true of himself and of his own feelings, desires, and aspirations, but what is intended to apply also to his party, his fellow-believers or fellow-sufferers, and even to his community as a whole.'

We might even add, sometimes, to his community and not at all to himself as personally visualized.

Modern opponents of this theory—such as Gunkel and Kittel—describe it, though more or less completely adopted by Wellhausen, Smend, and Robertson Smith, as a survival of the obsolete and fantastic. There is enough, and more than enough, of the fantastic in older Jewish exegesis from which this particular theory derives, but this is not an example of it. Before, however, turning to the fantastic, we must do two things. We must see to what extent Jewish tradition still influences exegesis, and must briefly summarize the course of Jewish exegesis, following in the latter enterprise that best and safest of guides, Wilhelm Bacher.

Tradition still weighs much with Jewish expositors in their just preference of the Massoretic Text to any of the ancient versions. Some work has been done on the pre-Massoretic Text of which traces are discoverable in the Rabbinic literature ; but even when more research has been devoted to the problem of primitive readings, the Massoretic Text will undoubtedly remain irreplaceable and authoritative for most Jews. Emendations, when soundly attested, will win approval, but can never be other than hypothetical. If we turn to two recent Jewish publications we have an easy approach to the relationship between ancient and modern exegesis. When the Revised Version of the Old Testament appeared it was heartily welcomed

in Jewish circles. The abandonment of the Authorized
Version's chapter headings, was one, but not the only, ground
for this welcome ; editions of the Authorized Version without chapter headings had long been available. Nor was
the abandonment of Christological suggestions (e. g. the
substitution of the small for the capital *S* in ' son ' in Ps. ii. 7)
more than a contributory cause for satisfaction. The main
factor in the Jewish approval of the Revised Version was that,
while it retained so much of the beloved phraseology of the
Authorized Version, it revealed an almost irreproachable
objectivity, and a greatly superior scholarship, especially when
the margin was substituted for the text. Were there, however,
no grounds of objection left on dogmatic or traditional grounds ?
Did nothing remain to discriminate Jewish from Christian
exegesis, nothing to repudiate or question because of ancient
lights ?

The Jewish Religious Education Board (of London) issued
an ' Appendix to the Revised Version ', based upon two
principles : to emend the new translation (*a*) where the
Revised Version departs from the Massoretic Text, and (*b*) where
the Revised Version ' is opposed to Jewish traditional interpretation or dogmatic teaching '. Unfortunately, the *Appendix*
does not limit itself to these two principles, but includes a
number of variant translations, which in no sense are traditional
or dogmatic. Thus the traditional and dogmatic principles are
obscured. But a certain number of the suggestions of the
Appendix do fall within those categories. With regard to the
Massoretic Text, the Revised Version frequently restores it
where the Authorized Version had departed from it (e. g.
2 Chron. iii. 1 ; Job xxxvii. 7 ; Ezek. xlvi. 10 ; Amos v. 26 ;
Hag. i. 2), a striking evidence that the Massoretic Text ought
not to be rejected lightly even in difficult contexts. Curiously
enough, in 2 Sam. xvi. 12, where the Revised Version forsakes
the Massoretic Text (reading ' affliction ' or ' wrong ' for ' eye '),

the Jewish *Appendix* fails to call attention to it. Since this *Appendix* appeared, there has been issued a new *Translation* by the Jewish Publication Society of America. The *Translation*, unlike the *Appendix*, renders in the passage just cited, ' It may be that the Lord will look upon mine eye '. On the one hand, both *Translation* and *Appendix* give up the Massoretic Text of 2 Chron. xxii. 6 as untranslatable, and tacitly accept the Revised Version. On the other hand, in the opening of 1 Sam. xiii, the Revised Version emends the Massoretic Text, reading ' Saul was [*thirty*] years old when he began to reign ' ; the *Appendix* is silent ; while the *Translation* without emending discards the Massoretic Text and renders : ' Saul was —— years old,' and adds a foot-note to the dash : ' The number is wanting in the Hebrew.' Prof. Moffatt's new version in modern English seems to follow the same course. Thus there are anomalies in the treatment of the Massoretic Text by two ' Jewish ' authorities. That on the whole the Massoretic Text (and in particular by the *Appendix* the *Ķeri*) should be preferred to any emendation is natural enough. The avoidance of Belial and Jehovah is also intelligible. But while the *Appendix* substitutes ' the Adversary ' for ' Satan ', the *Translation* retains ' Satan ', another instance of Jewish vacillation. There is, in fact, no Jewish tradition against the rendering ' Satan ', especially in the prologue to Job. With regard to dogmatic and traditional motives : ' horn ' for ' trumpet ' (Num. xxix. 1, &c.), ' weeks ' for ' sabbaths ' (Lev. xxiii. 15), ' corner ' for ' border ' (Num. xv. 38), ' worship in purity ' for ' Kiss the son ' (Ps. ii. 12), these have their justification on the grounds named. But the *Translation* does not always agree with the *Appendix* in such matters. Jewish tradition requires ' thick-leaved trees ' not ' thick trees ' in Lev. xxiii. 40 ; but while the *Appendix* indicates this, the *Translation* accepts the Revised Version. In Lev. xxiii. 11 the *Appendix* naturally prefers ' the morrow after *the day of rest*' to the Revised Version's

' morrow after the *Sabbath* '. Pharisaic tradition took the reference to be to the first day of the Passover—regardless of the day of the week ; here was a bone of contention with Sadducees, and later on with Qaraites. Curiously enough, while in v. 15 the *Translation* agrees with the *Appendix*, in v. 11 it inconsistently agrees with the Revised Version. Perhaps the most remarkable instance of divergence between these two Jewish authorities is to be found in Deut. xxv. 9. It is certainly a tradition here to render ' before him ' for ' in his face ', thereby mitigating a disagreeable feature of the ceremonial refusal to consummate the levirate marriage. The *Appendix* reads ' before him ', but the *Translation* retains ' in his face '. It only remains to add that the two Jewish authorities agree in substituting ' interest ' for ' usury ', and ' fellow ' for ' friend ' in Ps. xv. 3. Why the Revised Version should have, in this place, introduced ' friend ' is hard to say. The parallelism is entirely against such a rendering. ' Like a lion ' for ' they pierced ' in Ps. xxii. 16, demanded by both Jewish authorities, is in accord with the Massoretic Text and with dogmatic opinion. With regard to the continuous translation of Isaiah lii. 13–liii. 12, it must suffice to remark that *Appendix* and *Translation* differ from each other as much as either differs from the Revised Version. And while the *Appendix* renders Gen. xlix. 10 (the ' until Shiloh come ' of the Revised Version) by ' until peace come ', the *Translation* has ' as long as men come to Shiloh '—clearly indicating the absence of a precise tradition which deserves to be described as ' Jewish '. It may be said that, on the whole, the American differs from the Revised Version far less on dogmatic than on philological grounds.

In fact Jewish interpretation of the Old Testament has passed through many phases in the course of its long history. The phases were of unequal duration and worth, and it was not always the less sound philologically that proved the less valuable spiritually. This is a solacing reflection, for so much

' interpretation ' of the Bible, by all creeds, has been grotesque misinterpretation, that it is gratifying to remember how very often faulty exegesis led to edifying practice. Mistranslation has given us some fine gems of thought and fancy. Thus, the absurdities of interpretation by Rabbinic or Patristic expositors, by Aqiba or Paul, by Philo or Calvin, by Jewish Cabbalist or Christian mystic, have conducted men less into a drab and sterile wilderness than into a fair and luxurious paradise. We could compile quite a fine *florilegium* of beauties, derived from false exegesis. But, deferring this line of thought for a moment, we may follow very briefly and sedately the phases of Jewish interpretation. For a further and fuller analysis the reader may profitably turn to W. Bacher (see *Jewish Encyclopedia*, vol. iii, pp. 162 seq.).

Oral exegesis begins with Ezra (vii. 10), who ' set his heart to *seek* the Law of the Lord '. In this verb *dārash* (seek, investigate) we have the source of *midrāsh*, ' the original name of Scriptural exegesis '. Bacher aptly terms this early exegesis the ' national science ', shows how it developed before the Canon was complete, between the Maccabean age and the opening of the Christian era, how it entered on its most fruitful period between the destruction of the Temple (A. D. 70) and the Hadrianic war against Bar Cochba (*c*. A. D. 130). Rules of exegesis, formulated by Hillel, were added to in the period last named by Ishmael, to whom as to Aqiba was due much elaboration of the exegetical machinery. Aqiba gave special significance to every word and particle of the text (influencing Aquila in this respect) ; Ishmael postulated the thesis that Scripture necessarily employs human modes of expression. The two theses are not consistent, but between them account for many of the phenomena of Jewish interpretation. Again, the early translations are a momentous contribution to our literary knowledge of Jewish exegesis, across which, however, cuts the allegorical system of Philo. Nowhere does the last-named more categorically express himself than in his *Joseph* (ch. vi) : ' all, or nearly all of the law-giving (i. e. the Penta- teuch) has an allegorical sense ' (M. i. 48). As L. Ginzberg well points out (*Jewish Encyclopedia*, i. 403), while typological exegesis is mainly symbolic and Palestinian, allegorical is mainly philosophical and Alexandrian. ' Both methods ', writes Dr. Ginzberg, ' originate in the same natural cause ; whenever the literature of a people has become an inseparable part of its intellectual possession, and the ancient and venerated letter of this literature is in the course of time no longer in consonance with more modern views, to enable the people to preserve their allegiance to the tradition it becomes necessary to make that tradition carry and contain the newer thought as well. Allegorism is thus in some sense an incipient phase of rationalism.' At all events Zeno allegorized Homer, just as Philo allegorized Moses, an enterprise in which he was followed more than a millennium later by Maimonides. Both the Palestinian typological and the Alexandrian allegorical methods are exemplified in the New Testament and the Patristic writings of the Church. But these topics lie outside the scope of the present survey.

Midrash, however, tended to pass not only beyond, but outside, the actual signification of the text. It ceased, in fact, to remain exegesis in the true sense at all. We find indeed Talmudic scholars as Kahana (a Babylonian Rabbi of the fourth century) ignorant of the difference between the primary sense of Scripture and its derived homiletical application. Similarly with the legal exegesis. At first used as a means not so much of deriving law as of justifying law by authority of the text— the real meaning of the text became lost in the ingenuities of such derivation. The centuries brought a change. Soon after the final redaction of the Talmud (*c.* A. D. 500) came the Massorites, who without throwing off allegiance to Midrashic tradition, nevertheless re-established the literal right of the text, and next the Qaraites who effected a similar end in revolt against Rabbinic tradition. The Qaraites (a sect founded by Anan in the eighth century) named themselves from *Qara*, to read, whence comes *miqra* the ' read ' text, i. e. the literary word as distinct from the oral tradition. This sect investigated the Bible anew, and while the Qaraite scholars contributed little that was original to exegesis, they served the cause profoundly by stimulating their Rabbinite opponents (notably Saadiah, 892–942) to create the scientific exegesis, based on a true philology, which flourished thereafter in Spain, and passing through Ibn Ezra (*c.* 1100–70) and others reached its high-water level in David Qimḥi (1160–1235). The philosophical and mystical exegesis supervened, but never again cast out *peshaṭ*, i. e. simple and natural exegesis. For though there was a serious gap between Isaac Abarbanel (1437–1508) and Moses Mendelssohn (1728–86) it may be claimed without overmuch exaggeration that Jewish exegesis, as brought to the culminating point in Qimḥi, remained highly influential and not merely in the Synagogue but in the Church, until the age of cuneiform and other archaeological discoveries. A tremendous change then occurred in lexicography, so far-reaching as to mark an entirely new era in interpretation.

As already remarked, it is not the purpose of this essay to discuss the influence of Jewish exegesis on the great non-Jewish translations of the Bible, the Vulgate, the Lutheran Version, or the Anglican Authorized. What is probably of more interest is the influence of that exegesis on Jews themselves. It is quite clear, from the recent article of Prof. D. Blondheim (*Revue des Études Juives*, 1924, vol. lxxviii, pp. 1 sqq.), that the LXX and Aquila continued to affect the neo-Greek versions still used by Jews whose language is Greek. But these Greek versions did not concern the two Jewish expositors who, because of their fame and popularity, represent a distinctly Jewish attitude towards the Hebrew Scriptures—namely, Saadiah and

Rashi. Saadiah's Arabic translation (with commentary) was made in the early part of the ninth century, and has rarely been equalled, never surpassed, for lucidity. He leaves no difficulties for the reader, which is to say that he often paraphrases rather than translates. But the result is that he accomplishes a clarity which is not matched by any of the modernized vernacular efforts, which succeed in increasing the intelligibility of the Anglican versions while diminishing their literary charm. Saadiah had no literary tradition to impede him, and thus was at an advantage such as no present-day English revisers can hope to enjoy. Saadiah is available in several forms, notably in the editions of Derenbourg, which give a good deal of help to non-Arabists by their French summaries or renderings. With the Mohammedan conquests, Arabic became widely used by Jews as their ordinary vernacular; Greek and Aramaic were practically driven out by the language of Islam. In his early works Saadiah deals with some problems of interpretation in arresting fashion. Why did God need to ask Cain as to the whereabouts of his brother Abel? To give Cain an opportunity to confess his sin. What about the evil thoughts implanted in man? Think rather of man's instincts to peace, truth, and love. Why was Jacob encompassed with sorrows, the death of Rachel, the loss of Joseph, and much bitterness of fate? The more, answers Saadiah to his questioner, the more thou speakest of his troubles, the more dost thou add to the praise of his endurance, justifying God's word : O Israel in whom I am glorified. Hence we are prepared for his method of translation. Translation is not commentary (though Saadiah wrote commentaries also), but it is interpretation. The reader must not be bewildered : no difficulties must be left : his enjoyment must be undisturbed by doubt. For discussion, ' let the reader turn to my other books '. Here, in the translation, ' if the insertion of a word or a letter could, in any passage, thereby make the sense clearer to those reading a translation without commentary, I have followed that course'. Thus 'God smelled the sweet savour' (of Noah's offering) becomes, as with the Targum, 'God accepted Noah's offering with favour'; 'they saw God' (Exod. xxix. 10) becomes 'they saw the light of God'; Gen. ii. 17 runs in Saadiah 'for on the day thou eatest thereof thou wilt *deserve* to die'; Gen. ii. 2 'And God ended on the seventh day his creation which he had made, and he ceased on this day to create anything like the creation which he had made', i. e. the *creatio ex nihilo* was ended, and for the future natural development ensued. Saadiah does not assume a pluperfect as some expositors have done from Calvin to Friedländer. Gen. xlix. 17 becomes in Saadiah 'Dan shall be like a serpent on the way, like an adder in a path, who bites the horse's heel so that the rider falls backwards, saying, I hope for thy help O Lord'; Exod. xxxiv. 7, *naqqēh lō yᵉnaqqěh*, 'God pardons the penitent and pardons not the impenitent, he exacts account of the sins of the fathers at the same time as those of the children'. This is the Rabbinic interpretation of 'visiting the sins of the fathers on the children'. It is not an accumulating penalty but an act of love, the penalty being deferred in the hope that the virtues of the children will wipe out the father's sins. Only if the generations fail to make amendment for the past, is the whole weight of penalty (past and present) exacted in one blow. Interesting in another way is Saadiah's rendering of Ps. xviii. 32: 'Who is God save the Lord?' He actually uses the formula of Islam, which indeed exactly translates the Hebrew, *la ilah illa allah*. Moses, God's servant, is *rasul*; the very word used of Mohammed in the formula (*la ilaha illa 'llah, wamuḥammad rasul allah*). Saadiah's, in brief, is a fine, racy rendering. But before we call his method Jewish, we must remember the precisely opposite method of Aquila, which was equally Jewish. Aquila renders word for word; Saadiah paraphrases the sense. Does not this remind us that, generally speaking, there is no *one* exclusively true principle of translation or interpretation?

Rather, several methods have their justification when we consider the various needs which the interpreters seek to serve.

We turn from the East to the West, to Rashi (1040–1105), for the only other type of Jewish interpretation which can be considered in this essay. Saadiah followed tradition in many details, in his rendering of ' eye for eye ' (to mean monetary compensation), of the levirate refusal (*ḥaliṣah*), of the date of the Pentecost. The French type did not differ from the Arabic in these and similar respects. Rashi was an interpreter ; he did not, like Saadiah, translate continuously, though he very often translated words or phrases. His French glosses, edited by Arsène Darmesteter, are of considerable value for French philology as well as for Hebrew lexicography. Rashi followed two distinct styles. In his commentary on the Talmud he is at his best ; it is no exaggerated claim that is implied when later Jewish writers spoke of him as ' *the* Commentator '. Rashi is unsurpassed in his capacity for saying enough, not less or more than suffices to explain the precise sense of the Talmudic context. When he deals with the Bible he acts otherwise. One example of his two manners may be given, not because it is particularly representative but because it deals with a Talmudic passage to which we shall soon recur. In an early page of the Tractate on Idolatry, we read how the Holy One spends three hours daily in feeding his creatures, ' from the *qarnē re'ēm* to the *bēṣē kinnim*', from the horns of the re'em to the tiniest insect. Rashi simply comments : ' *re'em*, a great beast.' This is all that is necessary for understanding the Talmudic context. Turn, however, to Deut. xxxiii. 17, where Joseph is blessed as to his offspring by comparison to an ox and to the horns of the re'em. Here Rashi is more· expansive, and, using the Midrash (*Sifre*), writes : ' An ox has powerful but unlovely horns, a re'em is less powerful but has beautiful horns ; thus Joshua is awarded the strength of the ox and the beauty of the re'em's horns.' This is not verbose, for Rashi is always terse.

Just in front of this note is a piece of pure grammar, for the *shokheni* of verse 16 is properly held identical in sense with *shokhen*. After verse 17 come specific applications of every phrase to the history of the tribe of Joseph—quite in the Midrashic manner. Often Rashi translates words into French with almost unerring accuracy; often he derives senses by a grotesquely unscientific etymology. Rashi has little of the interest in comparative religion which distinguished Maimonides, he has even less of archaeology than Ibn Ezra. But Rashi combines the methods of *peshaṭ* (simple) and *derash* (fanciful) exegesis, and he combines them into a whole of entrancing charm. This is not matched even by Naḥmanides, who, as Dr. Schechter quotes, designed his commentary on the Pentateuch to edify, ' to appease the mind of the students (labouring under persecution and troubles) when they read the portion on Sabbaths and festivals, and to attract their heart by simple explanation of sweet words '. Comfort and sweetness—these were the aims of very much of Jewish exegesis. There is a touch of mysticism in Naḥmanides, by no means so much as in the Zohar, which sees ' higher mysteries ' behind the plain texts, which plain texts are the garments not the body. While fools mistake the apparel for the man, the wise penetrate beneath the garment to the man, and beyond the man's body to his soul. But taking it all in all, Comfort and Sweetness represent the purpose of Jewish interpretation, if we add of course Conduct and Justification, conduct of man and justification of God. The justification takes a double form—it seeks to demonstrate that the precepts are not arbitrary or motiveless decrees, but explainable; and it vindicates God's providence and measures, justifying the ways of God to men.

This is all that can be said herè of the medieval interpretation, much being omitted regarding philological advances and gradual approach to a purely scientific exegesis. But what has been said may suffice to enable us to form a balanced judgement of the older Jewish exegesis which fills so many pages of all the Rabbinical books. Grotesque is a mild term to apply to it. Its verbal distortions, its subtle yet childish ingenuities, its illogical pretensions to logic, these bewilder and pain. There is no need to characterize these qualities more closely, for in his Bampton Lectures Farrar urged all that could be urged against ' methods radically untenable, producing results all but absolutely valueless ', of a system of exegesis which ' became a mere act of leading astray '. He had no higher opinion of the Patristic exegesis of the Church than of the Synagogue. The exegesis of the Church Fathers is a ' history of aberrations ', with consequential ' errors of method, of fact, of history, of grammar, and even of doctrine '. But, while he is silent as to the Pauline method, it is Pharisaic exegesis against which he turns his heaviest and most explosive artillery, the shells being packed with lighter pellets of ridicule as well as with more solid bullets of controversy.

But clearly, though the laughter and contempt are defensible this cannot be the whole truth; there must be something wrong in this unqualified condemnation. What is it that is wrong? First, it treats Pharisaic fantasy as though it were coextensive with Pharisaic exegesis; second, it overlooks the purpose which Pharisaic exegesis set before itself as the most desirable end.

Side by side with the fantastic there is much that is natural. There is, indeed, so much natural exegesis in Targum, Talmud, and Midrash, that it may well be that there once was much more of it, and that the more was suppressed from the books because it was so obvious, so lacking in excitement, and so commonly known. What is now a rivulet in a morass may have been a strong stream by flowery banks. After all, whatever be the defects of the Targum, whatever its ' prejudices ', it is, so far at all events as the Pentateuch is concerned, in the main a fairly faithful interpretation. Its very avoidance of anthropomorphisms was, as likely as not, due to the circumstance that it was in its first oral form designed for popular use in public worship. Verse by verse, in classical Hebrew and Aramaic paraphrase, the Pentateuch was recited aloud in the Synagogues; in the original text and in the vernacular translation *coram populo*. There never was indeed a time when the Jews did not possess popular translations which reproduced the natural sense. Of Aquila's Greek and the earlier LXX little is said here because they are too well known to need characterization. Of Saadiah's Arabic something has already been said ; it was matched by the French glosses, whether in the northern dialect or the southern Provençal. There was no complete French translation made for Jews till 1831, but they or their teachers adopted the plan of word-by-word rendering. This is proved by the fact that the French glosses, which illuminate the commentaries, so very often translate not the root, but the exact grammatical form of the words in the passages commented on. The evidence for this statement is absolutely convincing, and the phenomenon appears in Gershom, the 'Light of the Exile', as well as in Rashi and in the thirteenth-century Job. Qimḥi translates roots, not so these glossators.

Such facts are often overlooked or underrated by those who offer judgements favourable or unfavourable to the Rabbinic method of interpretation. Side by side with the Midrashic interpretations there was almost continuously a natural interpretation. Though the Jewish preachers preferred artificial (*derash*) to natural (*peshaṭ*) exegesis, the former did not drive out the latter. The same is true of the period when Pharisaic exegesis was at its strongest and most authoritative. We occasionally read of Rabbis who disclaim, or for whom is disclaimed, a knowledge of *peshaṭ*. There is the striking story of Abbahu and Safra (early fourth century), which implies that Safra the Babylonian was less able to explain the Scriptures than the traditions, the reason assigned being that discussions of texts between Jews and Christians were unknown in Babylonia (T. B. Abodah Zarah, 4 a). Safra simply failed in ability to explain Amos iii. 2 ; it cannot be said that Abbahu's own explanation was satisfactory. It is an interesting touch that the Palestinian (Christian ?) authorities, while they believed Abbahu's testimonial to Safra's scholarship, released the latter from taxation, a precedent which it is hopeless to expect our Inland Revenue officials to follow. Again, S. Horwitz is right in his observation regarding R. Kahana, whose case was alluded to above.

' The confession of Rab Kahana (T. B. Sabbath, 63 a) that although he knew the entire Talmud by the time he was eighteen, it was many years later before he learned the principle that a Bible verse can never lose its evident and literal meaning, is not to be taken as an indication of the general state of Bible study in his time ; on the contrary Rab Kahana wishes to indicate that he was an exception to the rule ' (*J. E.* viii. 548).

An instance or two must suffice to confirm the statement hazarded above that some simple exegesis amid the artificial is found in the older (as in the later) Midrashim. Exod. xiii. 14, ' When thy son asketh thee *maḥar* ' ; *maḥar*, notes the Mechilta (22 b), sometimes means *to-morrow*, sometimes *in after time*. Here it has the latter sense, in Exod. viii. 19 the former; in Exod. xvii. 9, it means *to-morrow*, in Joshua xxii. 24 *in after time*. This good, sound exegesis occurs in front of the pretty but fanciful analysis of the four types of son who ask concerning the Passover. Again, in Exod. xiii. 17, where various Midrashim (on *naḥam*) play on the sense ' comfort ', the Mechilta remarks : ' It means to *lead* or *drive*,' and compares Ps. lxxvii. 20, again quite soundly. There is much exegesis of this character in the Midrash, and if there is less of it than we could wish, it is because such simple notes were poetically uninteresting, and merely recorded what was quite familiar without pedantic insistence.

But the root of the matter lies in another set of considerations.

The Rabbinic hermeneutics were not so much designed to interpret as to unfold. Halachoth, practical rules of conduct, which had grown up in the course of life in the benign atmosphere of the Law, were justified by texts, not founded on those texts. They were founded not on a literal exegesis, but on a moral attitude towards the Law, the ultimate guide, but not the invariable source. Of course, much of the halachah was directly taken from the Scripture, in accordance with a natural and true exegesis. But much of the halachah grew out of the Jewish consciousness, nurtured by the Scriptures in action. So, too, with the more homiletic or edifying exegesis. The hammer, in Pharisaic metaphor, strikes into light the sparks latent in the rock. We ought assuredly to add that the hammer found in the rock a palpable source for the light otherwise impalpably obtained. A passage has already been referred to in which besides feeding all the world, God is represented as occupied in teaching young children three hours a day. This gracious idea, parallel to ' Suffer the little children to come unto me ', was really derived from the conviction of God's tenderness and love presented in the whole trend of the Hebrew Scriptures. Yet a Rabbi would seek to base it on a text (Isa. xxviii. 9) ; a sarcastic retort by the revellers is turned into a statement of divine purpose. ' Whom shall he teach knowledge ? Them that are weaned from the milk. Whom shall he make to understand doctrine ? Them that are drawn from the breasts.' Is this interpretation really grotesque, seeing the end to which it was turned ? The Pharisees themselves distinguished between the peg and the cloak ; the cloak suspended and the peg on which it was hung. Or to take another example—the seven Noaḥide precepts, which frequently meet us in Rabbinic books. These are the laws which are assumed to have been binding on all men before the revelation at Sinai, and they are still universally incumbent (in the Rabbinic view) on all who claim the name ' civilized '. Undoubtedly these laws were extracted from the spirit of the Hebrew Scriptures : to avoid idolatry and blasphemy, to establish courts of justice, not to murder, not to commit adultery, not to rob, not to eat flesh cut from a living animal (see *J. E.* vii. 648). To the ancient Hebraic conscience these laws were the fundamental basis of ordered and moral society, and if we exclude the ritual laws they remain basic. The whole conception reflects the Jewish consciousness, and yet it was seriously derived from a text by an altogether amazing exegesis. The text is Gen. ii. 16 : *And commanded,* this is directed against *idolatry,* cf. Hos. v. 11 ; *the Lord,* this is directed against *blasphemy,* cf. Lev. xxiv. 16 ; *God,* this refers to the appointment of *judges,* cf. Exod. xxii. 27 ; *the man,* this refers to *shedding blood,* cf. Gen. ix. 6 ; *saying,* this is directed against adultery, cf. Jer. iii. 1, which begins with the word ' saying ' ; *of every tree of the garden,* this is directed against *robbery* [cf. Lev. v. 24]. The law against eating flesh from a living animal is derived from Gen. ix. 4.

What are we to say of all this ? It is at least a rather effective mnemonic aid ! But as an interpretation of the letter it is futile, as an unfolding of the spirit it is fertile ; as exegesis it is negligible, as moral doctrine of permanent value. Does it really injure exegesis that, when the leader in the Synagogue prayer humbly stood below the congregation, not above it on a platform, this arrangement was justified by Ps. cxxx. 1 : ' Out of the depths I have cried unto thee, O Lord ? ' Or when Aqiba, following Nahum of Gimso, and preceding Aquila's quaint use of σύν with the accusative, proclaimed that every particle had deep significance—did he really uphold his belief in the unity of God by his impossible exegesis of the first verse of Genesis ? No doubt these tricks were useful in controversy, no doubt they tended to obscure many texts, but to argue as though for instance Pharisees derived the doctrine of the resurrection from such texts as Deut. i. 8 is to make the same mistake as to suggest a similar supposition concerning Matt. xxii. 32. The resurrection being an established dogma, it was necessary to find Scriptural support, however far-fetched and unconvincing—except to those who argued with a smile on the lips.

The Scriptures were perfect and self-consistent; an imperfect and inconsistent view, no doubt. Exegesis had by every available means to reconcile apparent divergences, and supply realized deficiencies without formally admitting them. 'Turn it and turn it, for all is therein, and thine all therein.' Sometimes an obscurantist principle this, denying science and philosophy their due place in the scheme of intellectual progress. But science and philosophy could be utilized for the purpose of reading into the Scriptures what they did not in the letter contain, but what in the spirit they justified man in discovering. Taylor in his note on the maxim just quoted (*Ābōth*, ch. v end, ed. 2, p. 96), cites the commentary *Lēb Āboth* :

'In the Bible, without doubt, are history and tale : proverb and enigma : correction and wisdom : knowledge and discretion : poetry and word-play : conviction and counsel : dirge, entreaty, prayer, praise, and every kind of supplication ; and all this in a Divine way superior to all the prolix benedictions in human books ; to say nothing of its containing in its depths the Names of the Holy One, blessed is He, and secrets of being without end.'

The author of this gorgeous eulogy was Solomon b. Isaac the Levite, born in Smyrna and a migrant to Venice. A sixteenth-century Rabbi and scholar, he was (as Dr. Elbogen informs us) not only a writer of devotional and legal works, but was ' versed in philosophy, natural science and mathematics '. All is in the Law, but this did not contract the student of the Law's outlook, or close his mind to the appeal of secular studies. Secular studies were rather part of the duty of the interpreter. How could he interpret the all, unless he strove to know the all ?

And if he must turn Scripture and turn it, for all is in it, Israel accepted the second clause also. 'Thine all is therein,' life and length of days. The Jewish women sat on Sabbath over their *ṣĕēna urĕēna*, a commentary of whimsical fancies and a medley of legends, which cheered their hearts and stirred their souls. It was (and is) life and length of days to these mothers, as to the Mater Macchabea of the fore-time. And yet life itself was dearly bought if the price be infidelity to the message and guidance which Scripture imparted. Aqiba has been ' wondered ' at for his exegesis, and he deserves the ' wonder ', using the word as unfavourably as one can. Still, it was he who said, expounding Deut. vi. 5, Shall I not be glad to yield up my life for love ? And he died in the flames kindled by the Roman executioners. He interpreted the Law by his utter self-surrender to it. In a very real sense this heroic constancy of devotion interprets the Jewish interpretation of the Hebrew Bible.

I. ABRAHAMS.

THE VALUE AND SIGNIFICANCE OF THE OLD TESTAMENT IN RELATION TO THE NEW

THE indebtedness of the New Testament to the Old is so far-reaching and so manifold that it is hard to understand how the importance of this fact can be ignored, or why it should be necessary to emphasize it afresh. In view, however, of the fact that voices have recently been raised in favour of eliminating the Old Testament altogether from popular religious teaching, it is still unfortunately necessary to protest against such a misguided policy. There is, of course, much in the New Testament which may lay claim to a certain novelty—a freshness and spontaneity of expression, and a depth of feeling and conviction, that not only sometimes create new literary forms, but also invest what is old with new vitality and power. Such a result is inevitable when a few great and dominant ideas are at work ; and that such ideas are at work in the New Testament literature needs no demonstration. The great convictions which shine through this literature are that in Jesus, His life, death, and resurrection, a new power of God had been revealed. God had indeed visited His People. This was the substance of the good news, and the source of the enthusiasm that made Christianity a power, and created a new Christian literature. And this literature, as has already been pointed out, moulded for itself new forms of literary expression. There is nothing quite like the Gospels to be found in any other literature. They are not set biographies—their very name suggests something different. They are rather manuals of instruction, intended to nourish the loyalty of believers by setting before them certain

F f

aspects of the life and teaching of Jesus the Messiah. Then, again, the Epistles possess characteristics which invest them with inimitable qualities. The Christian Church has given its verdict on these writings by regarding them as inspired—a verdict which is entirely consistent with their wonderful combination of sanity with urgency and conviction, their freedom from exaggerated language together with their deep note of passionate faith. It is not without reason that this little *corpus* of writings has achieved the position of a classic in the literature of religion.

But the Christian writers, like the wise scribe in the Gospels, knew how to bring out of their treasure things new and old. Inextricably woven with the new elements there is much that is old. These writers, for the most part Jews, had been nurtured on the Old Testament Scriptures. The Bible of Christ and His Apostles, as for all Palestinians, was the Hebrew Canon of the Old Testament. Through the old Greek translation of the Old Testament, which was appropriated by the early Christian Church, the New Testament has been profoundly influenced in various ways. The aim of this essay is to illustrate, within the limits of space available, some of the more important directions in which these effects become clear.

I

In the form in which we possess it, the New Testament is a little library of Greek writings. Some of these may—and probably do—go back to Semitic originals. Thus, for instance, the Nativity hymns of the early chapters of St. Luke's Gospel may plausibly be regarded as translations from Hebrew originals, as also may Matt. i. 20, 21.[1] It is by no means impossible that the Q element in the First Gospel—which exhibits many of the characteristics of Hebrew poetry, and

---

[1] See the present writer's *Virgin Birth of Jesus*, p. 8 f.

goes back easily into Hebrew or Aramaic composition—may also be dependent upon a Semitic original which had been worked up by a catechetical school in Palestine before it was translated into Greek, and used in this form by the compiler of the First Gospel.[1] But apart altogether from the question of possible translation from Semitic originals, what are we to say regarding the character of the Greek used in the New Testament generally, and, in particular, as to the degree in which it has been influenced by the Greek of the Old Testament (LXX)? We here enter into a region of acute controversy. According to some of the most distinguished scholars of the school that has made a special study of Hellenistic Greek in the light of modern discovery of papyri, the influence of LXX Greek, and Jewish influence generally, on the Greek of the New Testament has been much exaggerated. It is alleged from this side that the Greek of the New Testament is essentially the κοινή used in popular speech; and it is further pointed out that many locutions, supposed to be due to Jewish influence and to reflect Semitic idiom, can be paralleled in documents which have nothing to do with Jews or Jewish literature.

In his recent valuable work on the *Aramaic Origin of the Fourth Gospel* Dr. Burney has dealt with this matter, and has made a much needed protest. In particular he emphasizes afresh the probability of Jewish locutions having influenced the Egyptian κοινή itself. He says:[2]

' The fact is surely not without significance that practically the whole of the new material upon which we base our knowledge of the κοινή comes from Egypt, where there existed large colonies of Jews whose knowledge of Greek was undoubtedly influenced by the

---

[1] See the writer's *St. Matthew* (*Century Bible*, 1922), pp. 55-9, where this point is discussed.

[2] Op. cit., p. 4. See also Dr. H. B. Swete, *Apocalypse*, p. cxxiv, n. 1.

translation—Greek of the LXX, and who may not unreasonably be suspected of having influenced in some degree the character of Egyptian κοινή.'

That large parts of the Greek of the New Testament—especially the Greek of the Second and Fourth Gospels—reflect the influence of Aramaic and Hebrew idiom and modes of expression has, it seems to some of us, been proved by Dr. Burney in the full discussion he devotes to the subject in his book. He has made clear that the writers of these texts, if they wrote in Greek, thought in Aramaic.

It is not the intention of the present writer to attempt to discuss this subject at length here, but only to refer to it in some preliminary observations. But it is necessary to restate generally some facts about the relation of the Greek of the LXX to that of the New Testament. For our purpose the conclusions of Dr. H. A. A. Kennedy,[1] who is not likely to have exaggerated the indebtedness, may be accepted. Dr. Kennedy fully admits that the LXX was thoroughly familiar to the various writers of the New Testament. He also admits that ' an overwhelmingly large proportion of the vocabulary of the New Testament has already occurred in the LXX '. He accounts for this fact by assuming that both drew from a common stock of words in use generally in the κοινή. Further ' a considerable number of the words common to the LXX and New Testament are derived words, formed by the writers of the LXX. To the extent covered by these words, there is an influence of the one vocabulary on the other.' Such words as are meant are either actual Hebrew words (e. g. μάννα, πάσχα, χερουβείν) or reflect peculiar Jewish customs (e. g. ἐφημερία which in the LXX means : (1) the daily service of the priests in the Temple (e. g. Neh. xiii. 30) ; (2) the separate groups of priests who performed this service (e. g. 2 Chron. v. 10). In

---

[1] See his *Studies in New Testament Greek* (1895). This work contains some valuable statistics, and is still useful.

the New Testament it occurs in sense (2) in Luke i. 5). Finally the LXX has exercised an all-powerful influence in the creation of religious and theological terms, which are freely employed in the Greek of the New Testament. When the New Testament writers came to the task of expressing the conceptions of the new Faith in a Greek form, ' there was ', says Dr. Kennedy, ' a technical theological vocabulary actually existing '. He goes on to remark : [1]

' The early Christian writers, being almost all Jews, retained a Hebrew colouring throughout their thought. There was a basis of Hebrew ideas beneath the new superstructure. Accordingly, even in the case of purely Christian conceptions, it was thoroughly natural for the New Testament writers to frame their language on the analogy of the existing theological vocabulary which they found in the Greek version of the Old Testament.'

Such words as ἀδελφός, ἀντίληψις, δόξα, ἔθνος, ἐκκλησία, κρίσις, πάροικος, σάρξ, σωτήρ, ἀποκαλύπτω, δικαιόω, εὐλογέω, πειράζω, may be cited in this connexion.

An instructive example is the word δόξα. Dr. Kennedy notes the following meanings and usages :

I. In classical literature it = (1) expectation ; (2) sentiment ; (3) opinion ; (4) estimation, good opinion ; (5) credit.

II. In LXX δόξα almost invariably translates one of the three Hebrew words כָּבוֹד = glory, honour, &c. (150 times) ; תִּפְאֶרֶת = beauty, glory, splendour (20 times) ; and הוֹד = majesty (9 times).

III. In the New Testament the word occurs fully 150 times. It is very frequently applied to God in the sense of ' praise ' and ' honour '. A special sense which is quite unknown to Greek literature, and has arisen under LXX influence is the use of δόξα in such passages as Acts xxii. 11 (' the *glory* of that light '), 2 Cor. iii. 7, 1 Cor. xv. 41. The word reaches its most exalted meaning when it is applied to the divine glory, reminiscent of the late Jewish use of ' shekinah ' which was associated with the idea of dazzling light (cf. e. g. John i. 14).

[1] Op. cit., p. 94 f.

It must constantly be borne in mind that the Greek words which express religious and theological ideas, as we read them in the pages of the New Testament, have undergone a subtle change, in the nature of sublimation, of meaning. There has been a transvaluation of values throughout under the influence of the lofty conception of God, the ethical and strict monotheism, which was the Hebrew heritage of pious Jews. All terms which have any connexion, either mediately or immediately, with the divine, reflect this influence. Such terms as ἀγάπη, εἰρήνη, σωτηρία have undergone this kind of transformation in meaning.

We may sum up this section by saying that it is clear that the Greek version of the Old Testament which was the Bible of the early Greek-speaking Christians, and was thoroughly known by and familiar to the writers of the New Testament, has exercised a real influence on the language of these writers generally. This is shown more particularly in the technical terms which reflect Jewish usages and customs, as well as theological ideas. It is not to be denied that the language of the New Testament generally is the vigorous colloquial Greek of the time : but Jewish and Old Testament influence is marked and fundamental. Nor should it be forgotten that the Greek of the New Testament is not entirely uniform, varying as it does in different books. There are passages in the New Testament which, judged purely as specimens of Greek writing, are of surpassing power.

II

But the Greek Old Testament has played a more direct and conspicuous part in the writings of the New Testament than by its influence, either direct or indirect, on the formation of its vocabulary. In fact this version is constantly cited within the text of the New Testament itself. In this connexion it is interesting to note that the puzzling phenomenon which meets us of some citations from the Old Testament agreeing with the LXX, and some not, has been satisfactorily explained by the hypothesis that within the circles of the early Church, and subsequently, collections of proof-texts were in circulation which were used for apologetic purposes. Such a manual has been described as a kind of ' messianic *florilegium* '. Dr. Moffatt adds : [1] ' The composite Old Testament quotations in the New Testament, the early Christian literature from Barnabas and Melito to Cyprian's *Testimonia* especially, render it highly probable that *florilegia* and *catenae* of Old Testament passages were in circulation.' Probably such a *florilegium* has been used in the compilation of the First and Fourth Gospels. It appears to have been written in its original form in Aramaic, for the use of Jewish-Christians in Palestine. It was thus an Aramaic translation of certain passages of the Old Testament, but made apparently from a recension of the Hebrew text which was independent of the Masoretic. The compiler of the First Gospel used it in a Greek form. This will explain the fact that the Greek citations made from this *florilegium* are independent of the LXX. There are in the First Gospel eleven quotations of this kind, all of them introduced by a striking formula ' that it might be fulfilled ', or ' then was fulfilled ' (i. 22, ii. 6, 15, 17, 33, iv. 14, viii. 17, xii. 17, xiii. 35, xxi. 4 ff., xxvii. 9 ; cf. also xi. 10 = Mark i. 2, and such passages as John xix. 36 ff.). In this way texts were sometimes strung together, for apologetic purposes, from different contexts and books.[2] It is important to realize how early Christians used the Old Testament for apologetic purposes. The Scriptures were searched in order to find proof or illustrative texts which might be regarded as foreshadowing some event or aspect of Christ's life, work, or death. The citations were suggested by the fact. Thus there

---

[1] *Literature of the New Testament*, p. 23 f.

[2] e. g. 1 Pet. ii. 6–8 ; Rom. ix. 32–3. See Rendel Harris, *Testimonies* (Part I), p. 18.

is no reason to doubt the utterance by Jesus on the Cross of the cry, based on the opening words of Ps. xxii : *My God, my God, why hast thou forsaken me ?* But to pious Jewish Christians this was not enough. They used their ingenuity to discover in this and other psalms hints or details which might be regarded as pointing to the events of the Crucifixion. ' The taunt of the priests and the wagging of their heads, the piercing of the hands and feet, and the parting of the garments ' are all illustrated in this psalm ; and the gall and vinegar in Ps. lxix ; a citation is made also from Zech. xii. 10 (' they shall look on him whom they pierced '), and finally, the fact that the legs of the crucified were not broken is regarded as a fulfilment of the Paschal injunction in Exod. xii. 46.[1]

A remarkable example of the apologetic use of the Old Testament text is to be found in Matt. ii. 23 where the migration of the Holy Family to Nazareth is made the occasion for a curious citation which runs : *that it might be fulfilled which was spoken by the prophets, that he should be called a Nazarene.* The difficulties involved in this passage form a well-known *crux.* From the use of the plural (' by the prophets ') it seems probable that more than one passage is in the writer's mind, and the present writer has suggested [2] that possibly the Greek term here used, viz. Ναζωραῖος (which is to be carefully distinguished from the term Ναζάρηνος), has the special sense of ' Messianic One ', derived from the use of *nēṣer* in such passages as Isa. xi. 1, and possibly Isa. xlix. 6. If we can assume that the Jewish Christians developed from the technical Hebrew term *nēṣer* = ' Branch ' = Messiah an adjective *naṣôrai* = ' Messianic One ', and applied this to Jesus, this would account for the term Ναζωραῖος. They may, indeed, have derived this form from the text of Isa. xlix. 6 where the word translated ' preserved ' in its unpointed form (נצורי) can be read *naṣôrai.* So read, the passage—which

---

[1] Cf. McNeile in *Cambridge Bible Essays*, p. 241 *n.*
[2] *St. Matthew* (new ed. *Century Bible*), p. 89.

occurs in one of the ' Servant ' sections, and was undoubtedly applied to Jesus—runs as follows : *It is too light a thing that thou shouldest be my Servant to raise up the tribes of Jacob, and (shouldest be) the Nazorean (naṣôrai) to restore Israel ; I will also give thee for a light of the Gentiles,* &c.

It is suggested that the place name ' Nazarene ' (represented by the Markan form Ναζάρηνος) had acquired a somewhat contemptuous *nuance,* and was thus used by outsiders of members of the early Christian fellowship ; and that the term Ναζωραῖος was coined in order to turn the edge of the reproach : Ναζωραῖος ' the Nazorean ' (i. e. ' the Messiah ') thus became a term of honour, and was used as a counter-term to the contemptuous designation ' Nazarene '. If this explanation is accepted, it will afford one more striking instance of the free and independent way in which the passages collected in the *Testimonia* were handled.[1]

The use of the Old Testament in the Johannine Apocalypse raises some highly complex problems. The matter has been fully discussed by Dr. Charles in the first volume of his commentary. The dependence of the book either directly or indirectly upon the Old Testament is obvious upon every page. The author, or his sources, makes, as we should expect, most frequent use of the prophetical books, especially Isaiah, Jeremiah, Ezekiel, and Daniel, as well as other prophets, to a smaller extent. Next to the Prophets, the Psalms are prominent ; and the Books of the Pentateuch (esp. Exodus) are occasionally cited.[2] The character of the quotations is remarkable. Though the Greek renderings are sometimes influenced by the LXX (or possibly another Greek version), the author of the Apocalypse, according to Charles, ' translated directly

---

[1] For a full discussion of this element in the New Testament and early Christian literature, see *Testimonies* (2 vols.) by Rendel Harris ; esp. vol. i (1920).

[2] International Critical Commentary, *Revelation,* i, pp. lxv ff.

from the O.T. text '. One remarkable result of the most recent investigation seems to be that in his citations from Daniel he was influenced by the renderings of a Greek Version, which was not the LXX, but appears to have been an earlier form of the version which later was associated with the name of Theodotion.[1] In some cases the author may be dependent upon a collection of *Testimonia*. Thus in Rev. i. 7 we have a combination of Zech. xii. 10 and Dan. vii. 13 which occurs also in Matt. xxiv. 30. Both were probably drawn directly from a book of *Testimonia*. In this connexion a word may usefully be said about the Hebraic character of the Apocalypse generally. Its large use of the Old Testament Scriptures in their original form does not stand alone. It apparently also embodies sources which go back to Semitic originals, and its thought is profoundly influenced by Hebrew ideas and conceptions which go back to the Old Testament, or to literature dependent upon the Old Testament. Above all, the extraordinary character of the Greek has been rightly explained by Charles as due to Hebrew influence, which certain scholars have endeavoured to minimize.[2] Speaking of this subject Dr. Charles says :

' Its language differs from that of the LXX and other versions of the O.T., from the Greek of the Apocrypha and Pseudepigrapha, and from that of the papyri. Of course it has points in common with all these phases of later Greek, but nevertheless it possesses a very distinct character of its own. No literary document of the Greek world exhibits such a vast multitude of solecisms. . . . How are we to explain the unbridled licence of his Greek constructions? The reason clearly is that, *while he writes in Greek, he thinks in Hebrew,* and the thought has naturally affected the vehicle of expression. Moreover he has taken over some Greek sources already translated from the Hebrew

---

[1] In our present LXX texts Theodotion's version of Daniel has, as is well known, displaced that of the original LXX.

[2] e. g. the late Prof. Moulton (quoted by Charles, i, p. cxlii) who, however, it seems, changed his mind (op. cit., cxliii *n.*).

and has himself translated and adapted certain Hebrew sources. Besides, he has rendered many Hebrew expressions literally, and not idiomatically—constantly in his own original work, and occasionally in his translations.'

Dr. Charles goes on to remark that in spite of these peculiarities the literary greatness of the work stands out unmistakably. The Hebraistic character of the Greek is then illustrated in detail and completely demonstrated.

* * * *

The use of the Old Testament in one other group of New Testament writings must be referred to briefly before this section is closed—the Pauline. St. Paul is by common consent regarded as a master of Hellenistic Greek, which he could on occasion use as a literary and oratorical instrument of the highest power. He was a master of the κοινή ; and at the same time a Jew who had been in intimate contact with the Rabbinical schools of Jerusalem. How does St. Paul use the Old Testament ?

He was, of course, thoroughly familiar with the LXX, and could cite from it freely. But one of the most important results of recent investigation—if these results can be upheld—goes to show that the Apostle in his use of Old Testament material, is constantly dependent not directly upon the text of the Old Testament Books, but upon selected passages grouped in a *Testimonia* book.[1] Even the famous text quoted from Hab. ii. 4 (' *the just shall live by faith* ') depends, according to Dr. Rendel Harris, upon such a collection. It is cited in Cyprian (*Test.* i. 5) in a non-Pauline sense and application. It is clear, therefore, that the famous passage from Habakkuk, the Christian *Magna Charta* in a single line, is not confined to Pauline usage nor to Pauline interpretation. It was, in fact, one of the texts commonly employed in controversy. And some of these stock

---

[1] See Rendel Harris and Vacher Burch in *Testimonies* ii, chapters ii and iii.

texts were familiar on the Jewish side, and received Jewish explanations. When once such a collection of *Testimonia* is postulated, the explanation of a document or text may assume a new aspect. The writer is in the position of one who is handling material from outside, and utilizing it for his argument, or at any rate, for his own purposes. Thus it may be assumed that St. Paul is trying to modify the extreme harshness of the anti-Judaean document of texts in Rom. xi when he will not allow that God has abandoned His people *en bloc* ; ' he accompanies his characteristic μὴ γένοιτο with an explanation which, at least, puts the Fall and Rejection of Israel in an entirely new light. Their Fall has been the salvation of the Gentiles, their Rejection does not apply to the salvable Remnant.' ' It is clear ', adds Dr. Harris, ' that this is not the method of an extremist, anxious to make the worst case possible for a body of people from whom he has separated ; it is the position of a conciliator that is occupied by the Apostle. He still belongs to both of the disputing parties.' [1]

The existence of Books of *Testimonia* within the primitive community of Christians may be said to have been made out. It is an important fact, the full significance of which has not yet been completely worked out. The importance of the *Testimonia* is not exhausted when we say that it explains the form and collocation of certain texts. Much more than this is involved. The *Testimonia* reflect a new and remarkable exegesis of the old Hebrew Scriptures, carried out on bold and independent lines. And this method also implies certain doctrinal implications, especially of a Christological kind. What readjustments may have to be made, in the light of this new set of facts, is not yet fully clear. But Mr. Vacher Burch is able to write : ' We find that . . . a writer in the Apostolic Age is teaching Christianity from the same anti-Judaic source as Paul : and that he is grouping his teaching under the same

[1] Op. cit., p. 30.

natural divisions as the Apostle. In other words, both method and matter of this Gospel which Paul writes about are primitively Christian.' [1]

III

Before we come to consider the continuity in fundamental theological ideas between the Old Testament and the New, a word must be said about the literary influence exercised by Old Testament models on New Testament narratives and composition. The Gospels, for instance, are drawn from various sources, and in the analysis of these we are sometimes tempted to forget their essential unity, in their present form, as books. Dr. Moffatt, speaking of the First Gospel, writes : ' It is essential, at the outset, to feel the massive unity of this book, if any justice is to be done to it either from the literary or from the religious standpoint.' [2] From first to last it is dominated by an apologetic purpose. The compiler's aim is to show that Jesus, the true Messiah foreshadowed in Old Testament prophecy, while recognizing as divine the Jewish Law, ' fulfilled ' it by coming to found a Kingdom, which, transcending Jewish limitations, is of universal character and scope. It is easy to see how this idea dominates the Gospel throughout, and has determined its form and structure. At the outset the editor strikes the Messianic note that runs throughout the Gospel. Jesus was the Messianic King of Old Testament prophecy, a son of David and of Abraham (i. 1). As such he entered Jerusalem as its King (xxi. 4–5), and died as ' King of the Jews' (xxvii. 11, 29, 37, 42).[3] It is evident, in the light of this fact, how profoundly the Gospel has been influenced in its literary form by Old Testament ideas.

This is also true in detail. Thus, the opening section of the

[1] *Testimonies*, ii, p. 36.
[2] *Literature of New Testament* [2], p. 245.
[3] *St. Matthew* (*Century Bible*), p. 25.

Gospel contains a genealogy, constructed out of the Old Testament largely, and divided artificially into three divisions, each containing fourteen names, which arrangement may have been intended to suggest the name ' David ' ; for the Hebrew form of the name (דוד), consisting of three letters, by *gematria* = 14, and the sum of their numerical value (4 + 6 + 4) multiplied by their number (3) = 14 × 3. The genealogy itself, under the bare form of a category of names, thus artificially arranged in three groups, strikes the keynotes of the Gospel. Jesus—it suggests—is the Son of David, the true Messiah foreshadowed in the Old Testament. The kingdom, won by David, and lost at the exile, is regained in Jesus.

Further, it is probable that the episodes described in Matt. ii have been selected and worked up into a narrative which has been influenced, as regards its form, by the midrashic treatment of the story of Moses's birth. It is not suggested that the stories given in Matthew have no historic basis ; on the contrary, the most reasonable hypothesis is that there is a solid substratum of fact. But the form in which the episodes are presented, and perhaps some of the details, reflect the influence of traditions about Moses. In fact, the evangelist apparently intends to suggest a likeness between the divinely guided career of Moses, the instrument of Israel's redemption from Egypt, and the second Moses—the Messianic Redeemer who saves His people from their sins—the latter, of course, being of immeasurably greater significance. In Jesus a second and greater Moses has appeared (cf. Deut. xviii. 18), who is also the long awaited Messianic King.

When we turn to Luke's Nativity narrative we again find ourselves in an Old Testament atmosphere. The poems, and their setting in the two opening chapters of the Third Gospel, reflect the piety of a small circle which has been nourished upon the deepest spiritual lessons of Old Testament prophecy. ' Thus ', to quote some words used by the present writer elsewhere,[1] ' the Song of Zacharias, which may fitly be termed an Old Testament canticle, in the first strophe blesses God for the fulfilment of the promise to David, and looks for the fulfilment of the Abrahamic covenant, recalling such passages as :

There will I cause a horn to sprout for David ; I have prepared a lamp for mine Anointed, His enemies will I clothe with shame ; But upon him shall his crown be brilliant.[2]

The reference to *the holy covenant* confirmed by an oath which *He sware to our forefather Abraham* recalls the great promise made to ' the father of the faithful ' that in him *all the families of the earth should be blessed.*

In the second strophe, again, the language of Old Testament prophecy is taken up—the great passage from Deutero-Isaiah about the Herald :

Hark ! one proclaiming : make ready in the wilderness the way of Yahweh ;
Make level in the desert a highway for our God ! [3]

Or, again, the promise of light to them that sit in darkness, given in the earlier Isaiah :

The people that walked in darkness have seen a great light, They that dwell in the land of deep shadow, upon them hath the light gleamed.[4]

But the Old Testament atmosphere of these two chapters of the Third Gospel needs no further illustration. It is patent and undeniable. The poems themselves are probably translations from Hebrew originals, and were possibly composed to be sung in the circles of the Hebrew Christian Church of Palestine. The prose narrative in which they find their setting, if not actually translated from a Hebrew original, was, perhaps, constructed by St. Luke in a style and phraseology modelled on the LXX. At any rate, the narrative reflects in a wonderful

---

[1] *J. T. S.* xiii. 321 f. [2] Ps. cxxxii. 17–18.
[3] Isa. xl. 3. [4] Isa. ix. 1.

way the Old Testament atmosphere. We may even detect
a deeper influence at work than that of language. It has been
suggested that the *form* of the Lukan birth narrative has been
influenced by that of Judges xiii. 2 ff. (the announcement to
Manoah's wife of the birth of a son). There is undoubtedly
a remarkable parallelism as regards form and structure with the
Lukan narrative of the birth of the Baptist. It does not, of
course, follow that the substance of the later narrative owes
anything to the former. The fact is, the Old Testament
provided literary models of various kinds which have naturally
influenced later writings. The little genealogy at the end of
the Book of Ruth—which is obviously dominated by an
apologetic purpose—provided a model for the genealogy in
Matthew. The canticles in Luke i–ii are clearly modelled on
the Old Testament Psalms.[1]

Another Old Testament literary form which has influenced
the Gospels and the other New Testament writings is the
Apocalypse. We have already seen how profoundly the Book
of Daniel has influenced the language of the Johannine Apocalypse. The influence also extends to ideas and theological
conceptions as will be pointed out in a later section. This
literary influence can also be traced in the Gospels, at any rate
in the Synoptic Gospels, each of which has worked up into
its fabric a ' little apocalypse ' (Mark xiii and parallels). This
in the First Gospel is contained in chs. xxiv–xxv. A short
analysis will show the structure of these chapters :

xxiv. 1–2 : *The destruction of the Temple is predicted.*

xxiv. 3–36: *Discourse on the last things* (false claimants to
Messiahship shall appear ; wars and rumours of wars would
ensue, as well as troubles and convulsions ; persecution, false
prophets, and apostasy are foretold ; this is followed by the

---

[1] There are many reminiscences of Old Testament language elsewhere
in the Gospels ; e. g. in the Resurrection narratives. See W. Lockton,
The Resurrection and the Virgin Birth (1924), p. 34 f. and passim.

climax of horror—' the abomination of desolation '—appearing, flight in winter, &c. The final paragraph emphasizes the nearness of the End).

xxv. 1–46 : Three parables inculcating watchfulness, and diligence, the third depicting the final judgement. Here the whole of ch. xxv in Matthew is independent of Mark, while Matt. xxiv largely = Mark xiii.

In the purely apocalyptic sections, it is obvious that much of the imagery and representation belong to the common stock of apocalyptic writing. This applies also to the language. It is thus clear that the apocalyptic type of writing which came to a head in the Old Testament in the Book of Daniel, has exercised a real literary influence on certain parts of the New Testament literature.

IV

When we turn to the authentic utterances of Jesus Himself it is clear that while the influence of Old Testament ideas and expressions is marked—His language is steeped in them—there is nothing in the nature of a mechanical application of Old Testament language, or forced adaptation of it in an artificial way, such as meets us in some of the early Christian literature elsewhere. The ideas of Jesus are fresh and powerful, and are freely expressed in speech of plastic beauty, which fascinated and irresistibly attracted His hearers, and produced upon them the impression that once again the authoritative voice of a prophet was heard in their midst.

Christ's use of the Old Testament would require a separate essay in order to set forth the relevant *data* at all adequately.[1] Jesus's teaching and discourses are full of allusions to the stories, personages, and teachings to be found therein. It is clear that He was thoroughly familiar with its contents, and presupposes

[1] For a full and valuable discussion see Dr. A. H. McNeile's essay in *Cambridge Biblical Essays*, pp. 217–50.

a sufficient knowledge of it on the part of His hearers. But He does not employ it in the least like a typical Rabbi. The ' scribes ' of the time possessed a wonderful knowledge of the text of Scripture, and quoted it freely and ingeniously. They had developed an elaborate exegesis, and were prepared to justify every assertion they made by a proof text from the sacred text of Scripture. An instructive example of the Rabbinic method of exposition may be seen in a passage derived from the early Midrash on Exodus (*Mekhilta*), which is also of interest, incidentally, as illustrating the Rabbinic conception of faith. It occurs in a comment on Exodus xiv. 30, and runs as follows :

' *The people feared the Lord.* So long as they were in Egypt they did not fear God, but now : *the people feared the Lord, and they believed in the Lord and His servant Moses.* If they believed in Moses, much more did they believe in the Lord. From this thou mayest learn that whoever believes in the faithful Shepherd is (regarded) as if he believed in the word of Him who spake and the world was. . . . Great is faith whereby Israel believed in Him who spake and the world was ; for because Israel believed in the Lord, the Holy Spirit abode upon them, and they sang the song : for immediately after the words : *they believed in the Lord and in Moses His servant* follow the words (Exod. xv. 1) : *Then sang Moses and the children of Israel this song to the Lord.* In like manner thou findest that Abraham our father inherited this world and the world to come only by the merit of faith (אֲמָנָה) whereby he believed in the Lord, as it is said (Gen. xv. 6) *And he believed in the Lord, and He counted it to him for righteousness.* . . . R. Nehemiah says : Whoever receives unto himself one precept (of the Law) in true faith (בֶּאֱמָנָה) is worthy for the Holy Spirit to abide upon him ; for so we find in the case of our fathers that because they believed in the Lord they were deemed worthy that the Holy Spirit should abide upon them and they uttered the song. For it is said : *they believed in God and in Moses His Servant* ; and (immediately afterwards) it is said : *then sang Moses and the children of Israel,* &c. And so thou findest in the case of Abraham that he inherited this world and the world to come solely by merit of faith (בִּזְכוּת אֱמָנָה), whereby he believed in the Lord, as it is said (Gen. xv. 6) *And Abraham believed,* &c. And in the same way we find in the case of Moses, David, and Deborah that they (by reason of faith) sang a song, and the Holy Spirit abode upon them. And in like manner thou findest that solely by merit of faith was Israel redeemed from Egypt ; as it is said : *And the people believed,* &c. And so it is said (Ps. xxxi. 23) : *The Lord preserveth the faithful,* making mention of the faith of the fathers. . . . Of the righteous it is said (Isa. xxvi. 2) : *Open ye the gates that the righteous nation, which keepeth the faith, may enter in.* Into this gate all the faithful (בעלי אמונה) enter. David sings (Ps. xcii. 1) : *It is a good thing to give thanks unto the Lord, and to sing praises unto Thy name, O Most High ; to show forth Thy loving-kindness in the morning and Thy faithfulness in the nights, with an instrument of ten strings and with the psaltery, with a solemn sound upon the harp. For Thou, O Lord, hast made me glad through Thy works, and in the operation of Thy hand will I exult.* What is the cause of his joy here ? It is the reward of faith which our fathers showed in this world, wherewith they trusted by day and night. For thus is it said : *to show forth Thy loving-kindness in the morning and Thy faithfulness in the nights.* And in like manner is it said of Jehoshaphat (2 Chron. xx. 20) : *And they rose early in the morning and went forth into the wilderness of Tekoa ; and when they went forth Jehoshaphat stood up and said : Hear ye me, O Judah, and ye inhabitants of Jerusalem ! Have faith in the Lord your God, and so shall ye be established ; and have faith in His prophets, and so shall ye prosper.* And (so) it is written (Jer. v. 3) : *O Lord, do not Thine eyes look upon faith ?* And (Hab. ii. 4) : *The righteous liveth of his faith.* Also (Lam. iii. 23) : *They are new every morning, Thy faithfulness is great.* Also thou findest that the (Divine) intercourse is only accorded as the reward of faith, as it is said (Ca. iv. 8) : *Come with me from Lebanon, my bride* (" Bride " = Holy Spirit), *come with me ; of faith shalt thou be the familiar companion altogether* (lit. " *from the head* ").[1] In like

---

[1] So the words of the original (תְּשׁוּרִי מֵרֹאשׁ אֲמָנָה) are understood here. 'Bride' (כַּלָּה) is a mystical designation of the Holy Spirit or Shekinah.

manner it is said (Hos. ii. 19, 20) : *I will betroth thee unto me for ever ; yea, I will betroth thee unto me with faith* (בֶּאֱמוּנָה). Great is faith before God, for on account of faith it is that the Holy Spirit abides (upon Israel),' &c.

When Jesus cites the Law He does so with magisterial authority, either to supplement it, or to deepen its interpretation (see e. g. several examples in the ' Sermon on the Mount '). He reinterprets the Law in the light of deeper principles ; and thus overrides narrow and scribal interpretations (e. g. ' The Sabbath was made for man, not man for the Sabbath ', Mark ii. 27 ; ' This he said making all meats clean,' Mark vii. 19 ; cf. also the teaching about divorce, Mark x. 2–12). Jesus did not hesitate to reinterpret the Law against the current scribal tradition, and His method of citing and using it manifests a freedom and authority which were fresh and arresting.

But Jesus was influenced in His profoundest thoughts by the Old Testament, and more especially by the prophetic writings, and writings that were themselves influenced by the prophets. This can, perhaps, best be illustrated by the consideration of such typical terms as Messiah (' the Christ '), ' Son of Man ', ' covenant ', and ' kingdom '.

That Jesus was profoundly conscious of an intimate and unique relationship to the Father is clearly attested in the oldest tradition embedded in the Gospels. *All things have been delivered unto me of the Father : and no one knoweth the Son, save the Father ; neither doth any know the Father, save the Son, and he to whomsoever the Son willeth to reveal him* (Matt. xi. 27) is a passage that has almost a Johannine ring. ' We could hardly have stronger evidence ', says Dr. Armitage Robinson,[1] ' that our Lord himself did thus speak of himself absolutely as " the Son ".' The Sonship of Jesus is also emphasized in the story of the Temptation (Matt. iv. 1–11) and was

[1] *The Study of the Gospels*, p. 110.

a fundamental element in Jesus's consciousness. Subordinate to this seems to have been His consciousness of Messiahship. If one thing is clear in the Gospels it is that Jesus would have nothing to do with the popular conception of a national Messianic King. In this connexion His appropriation to Himself of the title *Son of Man* is significant. Founded upon the passage in Dan. vii. 13, the figure of *one like unto a Son of Man* flying with the clouds of heaven seems to have been regarded as not merely a symbol, but a person. In the thought of the original writer this was probably the case, *one like unto a Son of Man* being really a descriptive term for an angelic being—presumably Michael—who acts as Israel's representative and counterpart. The figure is thus both a symbol and a person. The heavenly Messiah—the ' Son of Man '—of the similitudes of the Book of Enoch is derived no doubt from the same tradition. Here the angelic being of Daniel, invested with Messianic attributes, becomes the pre-existent heavenly Messiah who is to judge both men and angels. It seems clear, however, that this Messianic conception was not at any time widely known or popular among the Jews. The *Son of Man* was certainly not a current name for the Messiah among the Jews generally. It was apparently cherished in certain (probably small) apocalyptic circles, to which, no doubt, some of the earliest generation of Christians belonged. It is to this circle, presumably, that Jesus owed His knowledge of the idea, and its Messianic associations, as shown by His appropriation to Himself of the title *Son of Man*. But in His hands the original conception was profoundly modified by being combined with the idea of the Suffering Servant of Isaiah liii. In the idea so modified and embodied in the term Jesus seems to have found the most adequate expression of His Messianic consciousness. It thus acquires in His mouth that combination of the ideas of humiliation and glory which is so striking a feature in His use of the expression.

That Jesus had meditated profoundly on the significance of the Suffering Servant of Isa. liii seems clear enough. In this wonderful portrait He saw His own destiny prefigured, and by a deep intuition knew that this was the mirror of His Father's will for Himself. The influence of this great passage of Scripture upon the mind of Christ can hardly be measured. That it harmonized with His deepest intuitions is unmistakable. How are we else to explain the last stages of the Master's life when He flung Himself into the work of training the Twelve in the short time that remained before the End ? The repeated predictions of the Passion and Death are too firmly embedded in the oldest tradition of the Gospels to be lightly brushed aside as unauthentic.

It is true that the whole idea of a suffering and crucified Messiah was and is to the Jews a stumbling-block. The conception was one that the Apostles themselves, as the Gospels show, were only able to grasp gradually and painfully.

The application of the great passage in Isa. liii to the Messiah is something entirely new when it emerges in the New Testament. The interpretation of the Suffering Servant that was current apparently identified him either with the pious minority in the nation (e. g. Dan. xii. 3) [1] or with the nation itself. Probably in its original connotation it really did signify the former of these interpretations. But the way had been prepared for the later Christian application by the commonly accepted Jewish exegesis of the earlier ' Servant ' poems which identified the ' Servant ' here with the Messiah. Thus the Targum renders the opening words of Isa. xlii. 1 : *Behold my Servant the Messiah*, and the use of *the Elect One* as a title of the Messiah in the Similitudes of 1 Enoch also implies the same exegesis.[2] But the Jewish expositors shrank from applying the

[1] Here the 'Servant' is identified with ' those who turn many to righteousness ', i. e. those faithful Teachers of the Law who are loyal amid tribulation and persecution.   [2] Cf. also Ps. Solomon xvii.

picture of suffering and death given in Isa. liii to the Messiah. This interpretation undoubtedly goes back to Jesus Himself and reflects some of His deepest thoughts.[1]

As regards the term ' Messiah ' itself (' the Christ ') the evidence is clear that Jesus Himself was reluctant to accept the title when there was any possibility of its being confused with the popular notion of a national and military Messianic King. On the other hand, with proper safeguards, He was not only willing to accept but to welcome it, as at Caesarea Philippi (cf. Mark viii. 27–30 and parallels). The conviction here expressed was one that had slowly formed itself in the minds of the Apostles, and is the earliest affirmation of the Christian Church's belief as to the significance of Jesus's Person. It was Jesus as ' the Christ ' of prophecy, and the Redeemer from sin, that formed the burden of the apostolic teaching ; but the category of ' Messiah ' or ' Christ ' was far from exhausting the full significance of Christ's Person. It seems clear, indeed, that in Jesus's own consciousness, the conception of ' Messiah ' was subordinate to that of Son. ' It was because He was Son that He was to become the Messiah.' [2] He was the Christ—and more.[3]

The whole Messianic idea, of course, has its roots in the Old Testament. The doctrine had developed in many directions by the New Testament period, and it is interesting to note that there was a pious circle in existence at the time of Jesus's birth which had spiritualized the idea of the coming of a Messianic King of David's line, which formed the substance of the national hope. Of this circle we catch a glimpse in the opening chapters of the Third Gospel. They were awaiting the advent of a Messiah ' who should effect the moral and spiritual redemption of His people ; who should rule as a spiritual prince in the

---

[1] Cf. Luke xxiv. 45 ff.
[2] *St. Matthew* (*Century Bible*), p. 259.
[3] Op. cit., p. 30.

hearts of a regenerate people, and so fulfil the old promises made to the House of David; and one who should extend His spiritual dominion to the ends of the earth'.[1] In this way the old Messianic passages and promises had already been re-interpreted by a small minority in Israel. The commonly accepted conception of a purely national Messianic King, was, as has already been explained, very different.

In this connexion it is interesting to notice how Jesus deals with a typical Messianic passage from the Old Testament in controversy. In the Gospels (Mark xii. 35–7 = Matt. xxii. 41–6) Jesus is represented as posing the question to the Pharisees, '*What think ye of the Christ? whose son is he?*' The expected answer is given, '*David's*'. Jesus then proceeds to quote Ps. cx (*The Lord said unto my Lord*, &c.) and draws out the inference *If David then calls him* '*Lord*', *how is he his son?* Here it is presupposed that the Messianic character of this Davidic psalm is accepted on all hands. It is clear that at this time the Messianic interpretation of the Psalm was current among the Jews. It was not in dispute. Later, however, this view was largely displaced in favour of others, and more especially of one which referred the words *my lord* to Abraham (so Rashi). But the older view occasionally reappears. Thus in the Midrash on Ps. xviii. 36, in a comment on the words *Thy right hand hath upholden me*, we read: 'R. Judan in the name of R. Chama says: "In the time to come, the Holy One—blessed be He—will make King Messiah sit at His right hand, as it is said (Ps. cx. 1): *The Lord said unto my lord, sit thou on my right hand*, &c."'

We turn to the idea of the *new covenant*. This conception comes out clearly in the Institution of the Last Supper, and obviously expressed some of the deepest thoughts of Jesus. The words, *This is my blood of the covenant, which is shed for many* (Mark xiv. 24) express an idea which is founded upon the Old Testament. The blood of a covenant, according to Old

[1] Cf. *J. T. S.* xiii. 323.

Testament ideas, was blood which had been shed sacrificially—
it was blood poured out in a sacrificial death. In employing the
term ' covenant ' in this connexion Jesus may have intended
to recall the old Mosaic covenant at Sinai : *Behold the blood
the Covenant which the Lord hath covenanted with you concerning
all these words* (Exod. xxiv. 6–8; cf. Heb. ix. 20, x. 29). The
backward reference to the Mosaic covenant is made more
explicit in the Pauline account of the Institution in 1 Cor. xi
(' *this is the new covenant in my blood* '). To use the words of
Dr. Armitage Robinson : [1] the words as uttered by Jesus
meant : ' My blood is being shed to unite you in a covenant
with God.' ' The author of the New Covenant points to the
Cross as the Sacrifice consummating and sealing.' [2] The
fundamental place occupied by the Old Testament idea of
a covenant-relation could not be made clearer. The ' new
covenant ' implies the old ; it has its roots in history and thus
strikingly illustrates the close and intimate connexion between
the Old Testament and the New.

When we turn to the idea of the *Kingdom of Heaven* or *the
Kingdom of God* which occupies a central position in Jesus's discourse, we are once more confronted with teaching which has
been developed from the Old Testament, especially through
apocalyptic. In His sermons and parables about the Kingdom
Jesus made use of Jewish terms to express His thought. But at
the same time He transformed the old material by infusing new
and profoundly ethical conceptions into it. The Jewish
equivalent of the expression ' Kingdom of God ' or ' Kingdom
of Heaven ' (' Heaven ' = ' God '), viz. *malkûth shāmāyim*, means,
as Dalman [3] has shown, the ' sovereignty ' or ' kingly rule ' of
God. It should be rendered ' sovereignty ' rather than ' kingdom '. 'The kingly rule of God was His divine sovereignty

---

[1] *Encycl. Biblica*, col. 1420.

[2] Frankland, *The Early Eucharist*, p. 32.

[3] *Words of Jesus*, pp. 91 ff.

which governed all things both in heaven and earth.' This is expressed frequently in certain psalms, as well as in definitely apocalyptic writings. Thus, e. g. Ps. ciii. 19 : *His sovereignty ruleth over all* ; and Dan. iv. 34 : *His dominion is an everlasting dominion and His sovereignty from generation to generation.*

This conception is essentially an ideal one. It embodies the grand idea that the supremacy of the divine, and all that this implies, is the consummation to which History is marching. The process by which it is to be achieved might be conceived in different ways. The Pharisees thought the most effective means for progress in this direction was to concentrate on the spread of the knowledge of the divine Law, and the extension of its practice. In this case the emphasis was laid upon the present life. Here and now men could be sanctified by deliberately putting themselves under the ' yoke ' of the Law, and by obedience to its precepts were consciously conforming themselves to the divine will, as authoritatively revealed. On the other hand, the apocalyptic writers envisaged the coming of the Kingdom as part of the eschatological drama which is to be brought about catastrophically by divine intervention. It was the apocalyptic conception of the Kingdom that was used by Jesus in His teaching, but, as has already been said, He profoundly transformed it by emphasizing its ethical and spiritual character. ' Though the sovereignty of God was to be established transcendentally, it was in its nature inward and spiritual ; and the spiritual life of men was complementary to it.' [1] It was reserved for ' the pure in heart ' (Matt. v. 8).

The Kingdom is conceived as essentially spiritual in character. It is the sovereignty of God realized in a reign of righteousness. There is nothing political or worldly about it. ' My kingdom is not of this world ' fully expresses this aspect of Christ's thought. The usurper who has seized the sovereignty of the present world-order is not Caesar but the Devil. And in the

---

[1] McNeile, *St. Matthew*, p. xxiii.

overthrow of the Evil One and all his works Jesus sees an earnest of the Kingdom's advent, already partially realized.

The Kingdom is regarded as essentially transcendental in character—it is thought of as a divine gift by Jesus. But this apocalyptic line of thought is modified by another. Though Jesus makes constant use of current eschatological metaphors— the Messianic banquet, the outer darkness, &c.—He profoundly modified the one-sided insistence upon the purely transcendental aspect by insisting upon the ethical and spiritual require- ment, which alone would make men worthy of it—self- abnegation, on the one hand, active love of God and man on the other.

Another important element in this connexion is the place of Jesus Himself in mediating the new righteousness, based upon His unique filial relation to the Father (cf. Matt. x. 32 ff., 37–9, xi. 27, xxi. 37, &c.), and in particular, the estimate He formed of the significance of His own sufferings and death. This is expressed in the ' ransom ' saying embodied in Matt. xx. 28 (= Mark x. 45) : [' *Whosoever would be first among you shall be your servant*] *even as the Son of Man came not to be ministered unto, but to minister and to give his life a ransom for many.*' This passage, if its full significance is to be realized, must be read in the light of the prophecy of the Suffering Servant (Isa. liii).

' The first part of the saying is the climax of the preceding argument that greatness in the kingdom of God is measured by service, and that this principle applies to the Son of Man who inaugurates the kingdom, as well as to its members. The second part implies that the Messianic vocation for Jesus involved not only a career of humble service, but a service which culminated in death—and in death not as a catastrophe, but as a source of eternal profit to many.' [1]

Jesus thus predicted His death as a vicarious sacrifice. He

[1] Moffatt, *Theology of the Gospels*, p. 145.

was to *suffer many things and be rejected* like the Servant; like him also He was to be *delivered up for the transgressors* (cf. Isa. liii, esp. v. 12). The Kingdom in the mind of Jesus has a double aspect, a present and a future one. It is already partially being realized, but its full and glorious consummation is to come. *Per crucem ad lucem.* It is instructive to compare this double aspect with its analogue in Rabbinic theology. There, too, God's sovereignty is conceived as being in its essence universal, and destined to receive its final and glorious manifestation at the end. But, at the same time, it is being partially but increasingly realized in the fortunes of God's Chosen People. It was first recognized on earth by Abraham. ' Before our father Abraham came into the world, God was, as it were, only the King of heaven,' runs a Rabbinic saying, ' but when Abraham came He made himself to be King over heaven and earth '.[1] Afterwards the implications of Abraham's recognition of the divine sovereignty were realized when the nation of Israel at the Red Sea and at Sinai yielded willing obedience to God as King. But the full and glorious manifestation will only come in the future. The prayer in which the aspiration is expressed that this glorious consummation shall be realized, known as *Alenu*, is one of the finest compositions in the Jewish liturgy.[2] Its most striking paragraph runs as follows :

' *We therefore hope in Thee, O Lord our God, that we may speedily behold the glory of Thy might when Thou wilt remove the abominations from the earth, and the idols will be utterly cut off, when the world will be perfected under the sovereignty (kingdom) of the Almighty, and all the children of flesh will call upon Thy name, when Thou wilt turn unto Thyself all the wicked of the earth. Let all the inhabitants of the world perceive and know, that unto Thee every knee must bow, every tongue swear. Before Thee, O Lord our God, let them bow and fall ; and unto Thy glorious name let them give honour ; let them all accept the yoke of Thy Sovereignty ;*

---

[1] *Sifre*, Deut. 113 [ed. Friedmann, 134 *b*].

[2] See Singer's *Hebrew and English Prayer Book*, pp. 76–7.

and do Thou reign over them speedily and for ever and ever. For the sovereignty is Thine, and to all eternity Thou wilt reign in glory ; as it is written in Thy Law : " THE LORD SHALL REIGN FOR EVER " (Exod. xv. 18). And it is said : " THE LORD SHALL BE SOVEREIGN OVER ALL THE EARTH ; IN THAT DAY SHALL THE LORD BE ONE, AND HIS NAME ONE " ' (Zech. xiv. 9).

The two aspects of the Kingdom are present in the teaching of Jesus. The eschatological conception preserves the vivid realization of the Kingdom as something which in its full manifestation will possess a glory and reality far transcending the sum of its stages, and essentially divine. The other aspect emphasizes its ethical character, and envisages it as something which develops historically, and is to be achieved. The two aspects (eschatological and inward) are thus converted into a unity in the teaching of Jesus.

V

A word must be said about the character of St. Paul's thought generally, and its relation to the Old Testament. That the Apostle was ' a Hebrew of the Hebrews ', and belonged to a strict Pharisaic family he states himself (Phil. iii. 5 ff.) ; and there is no reason to doubt the accuracy of this statement. Unlike the ordinary Greek-speaking Diaspora Jew he was acquainted with both Palestinian and Diaspora Judaism, having received a Rabbinic training in Jerusalem, which apparently lasted some years.[1] He was familiar with the Greek Bible (the LXX), which was recognized as authoritative Scripture in the Diaspora Synagogues, and, of course, could speak the κοινή with perfect ease and fluency, rising at times to flights of supreme eloquence. But his Hebrew and Rabbinic training

[1] Cf. Acts xxii. 3. This is part of a speech delivered at Jerusalem in Hebrew (Aramaic)—Aramaic was probably the mother tongue of the Apostle, who was in fact bilingual.

constitute a real factor in the Apostle's equipment, and his many-sidedness will not be fully understood if this fact be ignored. He sometimes, for instance, argues like a Rabbi, while at other times he speaks more in a Greek strain.

'But fundamentally he remains a Jew, whose categories of thought are rather Rabbinic and Palestinian than purely Jewish-Hellenistic. There is a remarkable contrast between St. Paul and Philo. For the great themes with which the Apostle deals and his manner of dealing with them—the problems of sin, the Fall, Election, the wrath, long-suffering and mercy of God, the prerogative of Israel, the significance of the Law, the temporal and eternal Jerusalem, the prospect of dying or surviving to the Parousia, the tribulation of the times of the End, and the Judgement—we must turn to the most Rabbinic of the Apocalypses (4 Ezra = 2 Esdras) : it will be useless to turn to Philo for any real parallels.' [1]

In all this St. Paul is dependent ultimately for his ideas and theology upon the Old Testament. What could be more Jewish and in line with Hebrew thought than his doctrine of the resurrection? It is, indeed, generally admitted that his eschatology, at any rate, in the earlier Epistles, is thoroughly Jewish. Dr. St. John Thackeray truly remarks : [2]

'There is perhaps no aspect of the Pauline theology in which the influence of the Apostle's Rabbinic training is so clearly marked as the use which is made of the Old Testament. It appears at first sight paradoxical that whereas the Law is constantly spoken of as done away in Christ and as powerless to produce man's salvation, yet the Apostle as constantly bases his arguments for the truth of Christianity on the Law in the wider sense of the term. The Epistle which may be regarded as summing up the main ideas of St. Paul begins and ends with a reference to the ' holy ' and ' prophetical ' writings which fore-

---

[1] See the present writer's article ' Judaism and Hellenism ' in *Church Quarterly Review*, Oct. 1923, p. 130.

[2] *The Relation of St. Paul to Contemporary Jewish Thought*, p. 180 f. See ch. xv of this work for a discussion of St. Paul's use of the Old Testament.

told the coming of Christ (cf. Rom. i. 2, xvi. 26). The proof for his arguments is sought again and again in the Old Testament. He never for a moment thought of disparaging the Scriptures to which the Jew appealed, on the contrary he recognized that the chief privilege of his nation was the possession of the oracles of God ; but he maintained that these oracles had been misinterpreted. . . . He met the Jew on his own ground and bade him search the Scriptures in the light of the coming of Christ.'

We have already seen that St. Paul was familiar with the LXX, and regularly cites it. He also, as we have seen, was familiar with the *Testimonia* collection of proof-passages derived from the Old Testament. How far, indeed, it is possible to distinguish between the Apostle's free and independent use of the Old Testament, and his citations which depend upon the *Testimonia* has not yet been clearly determined. Some advocates of the claims of the *Testimonia* seem to the present writer to overestimate the influence of this element at the expense of the Apostle's originality. The Pauline writings are so distinctive and peculiar in their style, so entirely unlike any other writings in the New Testament or elsewhere, that it is difficult to believe that their use of Old Testament texts is largely second-hand. Here, as elsewhere, the Apostle's strikingly original personality must have asserted itself.

In general St. Paul uses the Old Testament often to illustrate and enforce an argument quite in the manner of the Rabbinical teachers ; he sometimes abandons the original and literal sense, quotes without reference to the context, and employs methods of exegesis which would not be used to-day. Perhaps the most striking examples are those passages—few in number—where he interprets the Law allegorically, the literal sense being altogether abandoned in favour of a figurative interpretation which points to something specifically Christian.

The allegorical method seems to have grown up first at Alexandria, where it was applied to the interpretation of the

Homeric poems, and afterwards to the exposition of certain
parts of the Jewish Law. Its object was to overcome certain
awkward or unacceptable elements of an ancient text by giving
them a higher symbolic or spiritual meaning. This method,
as is well known, is carried to great lengths by Philo. Its
dangers are obvious, involving as its logical and extreme
application might well do, the entire dissipation of the original
meaning of a text. It has to be remembered that the allegorical
method had spread from Alexandria into Palestine during
the first century of our era. But it was current there only
in a restricted form, and was employed only under stringent
safeguards. Perhaps the most important example of the use
of this method is its employment in the interpretation of
Canticles which, as a Book of Scripture, was admitted into the
Canon only on the ground of an allegorical interpretation, in
which the community of Israel was regarded as Yahweh's Bride.
A development of this interpretation is to be seen in St. Paul's
language about the Church, regarded as the Bride of Christ.[1]

St. Paul employs the allegorical method in the case of a few
passages ; the principal are, 1 Cor. ix. 9 ff., 1 Cor. x. 1-10, and
the most elaborate of all, Gal. iv. 21-31. Here the sparing use
of this method by the Apostle is a striking fact. It stands in
marked contrast with that of Philo, who allegorizes everywhere and all the time. Moreover, the details of St. Paul's
allegorical exegesis do not harmonize with Philo's.[2] We conclude, therefore, that the Apostle derived his knowledge of the
method not directly from Alexandria, but from his general
Rabbinic training.

To sum up, St. Paul's thought was fundamentally Jewish—
not Hellenic or Hellenized in any deep sense—and his great
ideas go back to the Old Testament. He does, it is true, use
Stoic terms and, to some extent, the terminology of the

---

[1] Cf. Eph. v (esp. v. 32).
[2] See Bishop Lightfoot on the Galatians passage.

mystery-religions ; but in all such cases the language is charged with new meaning and new content. The determinative element is Jewish.

That this really is the case is proved by the fact that in the subapostolic age, and subsequently, when Greek thought really did exercise a decisive influence upon Christianity, the Pauline theology failed to be understood, and exercised no real influence. It was only partially rediscovered by St. Augustine, and later by the Reformers.

VI

In conclusion, we may sum up by saying that the connexion between the Old Testament and the New is of a vital and organic character. They stand in a single line of development. New Testament literature is indebted to the Old Testament not only on the score of language and literary form, but in the more vital sphere of theological ideas. In this respect the New Testament marks a somewhat revolutionary development. It is a remarkable fact that the emphasis is laid by the New Testament writers rather upon the prophetic and purely religious elements than upon the Law and legalism. Many years ago Dr. Sanday [1] quoted with approval the following statement :

' It was the Soferim and Perushim, the Scribes and Pharisees, when they made the end into the beginning, when they put the Torah first ' who ' created the illusion which was to last for centuries that the religion of Israel began with a Law. No one who starts from this assumption will ever come to understand the Old Testament. He who would really trace the development of the higher religion from the older popular religion of Israel must start from the Elder prophets.'

It is certainly significant that Jesus Himself, not, of course, on critical, but on purely moral and religious grounds, puts the Prophets above the Law, in the sense that He interprets the

[1] Sanday, *The Oracles of God* (1891), p. 155.

Law in the spirit of a Prophet. As the present writer has written elsewhere :

' It must not be forgotten that our Lord's attitude towards the old religion of Israel was that of the prophet rather than the priest. The fulfilment of the Law of which He spoke was essentially prophetic in character. He breathed into it fresh life, deepened and extended its moral significance and claim. And above all, He took up a position towards it of sovereign freedom. It is in the prophetic Scriptures that He finds the most adequate expression of His own Messianic consciousness, especially in Isaiah liii. The people instinctively recognised in the new teacher the voice of a prophet. And in fact the whole character of the Christian movement depicted in the New Testament is prophetic. The Day of Pentecost marked the outpouring of the prophetic spirit and gifts. " The testimony of Jesus is the spirit of prophecy." ' [1]

The New Testament is thus the true sequel of the Old. It is not the only possible sequel, as the existence of Rabbinic Judaism shows ; but it largely embodies the spirit and genius of an older type of Judaism which was seeking to emancipate itself from purely nationalistic limitations in order to become the World Religion.

But the New Testament literature is something more than mere literature. It does not consist of a series of artistically constructed creations, produced by literary artists living in detachment from the world. It was forged amid the conflicts and the everyday movements of the busy life of mankind, in which great issues were being fought out, and in which the tragic side was not lacking. Amid the dust and turmoil of the conflict the little Christian community fought its way to a position of commanding importance as a creative force in a changing environment. The records of this tremendous struggle are enshrined in what we call the New Testament. We have seen how large a part the apologetic element plays in

[1] *Expositor*, July 1919, p. 10 f.

this literature. This is one of the results of the conflict in which the Christian community was engaged. How decisive a part the Old Testament played in this conflict we have already seen. This can be fully realized only when it is remembered that behind the literature lies an organized community with a continuous life. One of the greatest achievements of modern critical method is the rediscovery of the Old Testament. In the light of modern criticism the religion of Israel stands out before us in a clear line of development, which can be fully traced. Not the least noteworthy result that has been reached is to be seen in the fact that the religion of the New Testament expresses and emphasizes at their true value the most vital elements of the religion of Israel as made clear by modern criticism. In a very real and true sense we can still say *Novum Testamentum in vetere latet : vetus Testamentum in novo patet.*

G. H. Box.

THE HORIZONS
OF OLD TESTAMENT STUDY[1]

WITH sufficient accuracy for our present purpose Old Testament study may be said to comprise the study of language,
literature, history, and religion. It is hardly more than a
truism to remark that the study of any language, literature,
history, and religion by itself, if not impossible, must yet be
inadequate and unsatisfactory. 'What does he know of England
that only England knows?' and what is the knowledge of a
single language, or the history of a single people or period, so
long as it remains unillumined by the knowledge of other
languages and periods? A Society that exists for the study
of the Old Testament cannot and will not wish to lose sight
of these.

Old Testament study comprises the study of language. I
advisedly use the term indefinitely. The languages of the Old
Testament are two—Hebrew and Aramaic—but the languages
that fall within or on the horizons of Old Testament study are
not so easy to count. On the more distant horizon lie all those
languages into which the Old Testament has been translated ;
some years ago the British and Foreign Bible Society alone
claimed to have translated the Bible into 400 languages, and
doubtless by now this number has been exceeded. Only

[1] A paper read as a Presidential Address before the Society for Old
Testament study on January 3, 1922. The manuscript was found amongst
Dr. Gray's papers some months after his death, and is probably incomplete.
The manuscript ends, however, in the middle of a page, and it seems possible
that the concluding paragraphs of the Address were actually delivered
extempore. Their general trend is indicated by the passage in brackets
at the end of the paper.

a few of these claim in general the attention of Old Testament students, though I can well believe that some very interesting light might be cast on Old Testament ideas by a comparison of the ease or difficulty which various translators into the most diverse languages have found in rendering various words and phrases. It is probable that words and phrases which can only with almost infinite difficulty, and even so with most unsatisfactory results, be rendered in one language, turn almost of themselves without any difficulty into another, and vice versa. What is the affinity of thought or the reverse lying behind these difficulties ? Can the wider connexions of thought in these remoter languages throw light, not merely on particular Hebrew words, but on the warp and woof of Hebrew thought ? But all this lies too far beyond my own knowledge to dwell further on it.

The languages that come closer to our central study, the languages which must be known, I do not say all of them by each Old Testament student, but certainly all of them by some of the co-workers in our field, if the study of the Old Testament is to be adequately carried through, are of three classes : (1) the languages cognate with Hebrew, in other words the Semitic languages : (2) the languages which though not Semitic are those into which important ancient versions were made ; and (3) such other languages, not already included in the first two classes, as are used in ancient documents having a direct relation to Old Testament study, these being principally Sumerian, ancient Egyptian, and ancient Persian, to which we may hope not so long hence to add Hittite.

The languages of the first two classes, at least most of them, were already studied by the great scholars of the seventeenth century and some of their works we continue to use to-day, such as Walton's Polyglott, a fact which is at once a tribute to their learning and their appreciation of the breadth and meaning of Old Testament study, and a reminder of how much remains to be done in this direction to-day. We may as well

still use Walton for the very good reason that for large parts of
the Old Testament there are as yet no really critical texts, for
example of the Targums, so important for certain sides of Old
Testament study, or of the Syriac version, or even of texts
which, without being critical in the fullest sense, at least antiquate the texts of Walton. In speaking of such texts I think
especially of the Septuagint for a critical text of which we have
still merely *Vorarbeiten*, but in Swete's Septuagint at least
a faithful reproduction of the text of a particular MS. with
the variants of other important MSS. ; and so far as it has gone
in the longer Cambridge Septuagint an ampler collection of
variants which for those parts goes far to antiquate another
great work of a former generation, viz. Holmes and Parsons.
Among other great desiderata in this matter of versions are
accessible editions of the Syro-Hexaplar and of at least the more
important Coptic versions. In the case of all the versions,
moreover, an immense amount of all kinds of investigation
into the language of them, their relation to the Hebrew text,
their place in the history of exegesis remains to be done ; at
present we constantly move on uncertain or treacherous ground,
and our study of particular points or sides of our study is
hampered and prolonged by the fact that in innumerable
places where the uncertainty and danger is sufficiently well
known we are not warned off by danger posts : it is strange
for example that we must grope about and waste valuable time
when using any text of the Septuagint of Job, if we want to
know whether a particular passage was in it or not : no warning
asterisks prevent the unwary from falling into the error of
taking as the work of the early translator what is really that of
the later.

If we now turn for a moment to the cognate languages, we
recall at once that we have here an immense advantage over
early generations of scholars in the discovery of Assyrian ; and
to this I think we must add, as though not of equal yet of great

importance the discovery of early Aramaic inscriptions and documents. In another respect much has been done, viz. in the comparative study of the languages. Castell, in his for certain purposes still useful *Lexicon Heptaglotton*, brought together the words of the several languages, but the investigation of the laws of language had yet to come. And yet here again how much remains to be done! The comparative study of the Semitic languages still lags behind that of the Indo-European. And in the several languages, though much has been done, much remains to do. It is strange but true that we have no full and complete dictionary of Arabic, and that those which exist offer pitfalls enough for the Old Testament student who hastily consults them and have curiously misled even what should have been the more deliberate investigation of commentators on the Bible. It is less strange, but inconvenient, that there exists no lexicon or concordance of the South Arabian inscriptions which have yet much to contribute to certain sides of Old Testament study. Assyriology marches on unrestingly, and the existing Assyrian lexicons become increasingly inadequate : various Hebrew words receive, or seem to receive, illumination in more or less scattered and remote articles—that very intractable material, the titles of the Psalms, is a recent example—but all this remains uncollected, and relatively inaccessible and often actually unapplied in the treatment of the Old Testament. All this leads up to a very urgent need in Old Testament study and offers a very practical need to which a Society such as ours should not be indifferent. We stand in very serious need of a new edition of the Hebrew lexicon. If it is important to keep our eyes on the horizons of Old Testament study, it is also and even more important to focus the light ; and the right place to gather the contributions from various languages to Hebrew lexicography is the Hebrew lexicon. Yet what are a few of the startling facts when we consider this question ? It is thirty years since the first part of the Hebrew lexicon, which we all use and to whose editors we are all so deeply indebted, was issued. This means that for example, the Tel-el-Amarna glosses could be but incompletely utilized, the Hebrew of Ecclesiasticus, the Code of Hammurabi, the Hebrew names in the Nippur documents not at all ; while the work was actually closed before the papyri of Elephantine were available to make their important contributions to the Aramaic words and the Hebrew names. Important too has been the advance made in balancing the preponderance—though not in my judgement so great an over-preponderance as some would allege—of Arabic in the comparative study of the Semitic languages by giving a greater recognition to the bearing on the subject of Assyrian. Here then is a great need ; and here as elsewhere finance is a great barrier. I am not suggesting that our Society should add to its other ambitions the editing of a new dictionary ; but it may certainly serve to define and articulate the need. Should, for example, a new Brown-Driver-Briggs follow rather more the model of Gesenius-Buhl with less exhaustive Biblical references and so with less bulk and therefore less expensive and capable of being revised at more frequent intervals ?

To pass from this rapid glance at the linguistic horizons to a still briefer glance at literature. In this respect our modern world of scholarship has been more revolutionized than in language. From being the oldest literature the Old Testament has become comparatively young ; and in the older literatures we find important parallels alike to the form and to the substance of Hebrew literature. Here again an older scholar prepared the way for the reception of the new light that the past century has brought. If we recall such names as Walton and Castell in connexion with language, we may well in connexion with literature, with the discrimination of some at least of its forms, and an exacter determination of their limits, recall that of Robert Lowth. But to Lowth all these forms of literature found their earliest expression in the Old Testament. To us this is no longer the case : parallelism was no unique literary mode of the Hebrews ; it was already old in Babylon before the Hebrews came to be : and so in a measure at least was the use of rhythm. But the study of parallelism—though in view of the almost mechanical repetition of Lowth's examples that is so frequently to be met with, the contrary might be thought to be the case—and of Hebrew rhythm is not a closed chapter : much remains to be done, and perhaps more light yet is to be sought in especially the cognate literatures. The great feature of the study of Old Testament literature during the past century has certainly been the source-analysis of the various books ; and this has been carried, it might seem, as far as it can go, and often to such a degree of minuteness that the results can command but little conviction. Yet comparatively recently fresh points of view have been gained which reopen some older questions or put them in a fresh light : and here perhaps we are rather at the beginning than at the end of inquiry. I think for example of the extremely interesting question of the different elements of tradition, of the simple sagas and the associated sagas, which lie behind not only our existing books but behind the earliest written sources which it is reasonable to postulate. This is a fascinating if treacherous region ; but it may yet be possible to discover with reasonable care paths to a better understanding of the Old Testament literature.

But the object of comparison is to discover not only similarities and anticipations, but differences ; to understand the peculiar genius and spirit of a people as well as the material on which it has worked. This is of supreme importance in the case of Israel with its religion : but on the side of literature interesting questions arise. To what extent was the form, or the substance of the Book of Job anticipated outside Israel ? Is Meyer right in his judgement that alone of the ancient

nations Israel and Greece created, as distinct from mere
chronicles and records, an historical *literature* ?

I will not, even briefly, make further reference to history :
but a word or two on religion. Here again we may recall one
older name, that of John Spencer ; whether or not we may go
as far as Robertson Smith in regarding him as the founder of
the science of Comparative Religion, his *De Legibus Hebraeorum
Ritualibus et earum Rationibus* is a noble parallel in its width of
outlook and its comprehensive collection of material to other
older works. But here again both discovery and improvement
of method have carried us farther forward, and set fresh
problems. Great attention has been directed to the study of
origins ; and the study has thrown much light on many
features of Hebrew religion, which were previously almost
invariably misinterpreted. And this particular line of study
yet calls for much further investigation : it will be affected by
increasing and more discriminating knowledge of the religion
of other Semites—Babylonians, Syrians, Arabs northern and
southern : it will also be affected by the more extended
investigations of Anthropology. Here unquestionably the
horizons of Old Testament study are very wide and distant.
But there is another aspect of the study of Old Testament
religion. If it is important to trace a rite to its origin, it is
equally important to determine if we can the religious associations and interpretation of a rite, often very different from the
original, at various periods ; for so we trace the movement and
become familiar with the spirit of the religion. Nowhere better
perhaps can we hope to see the peculiarity of a religion than
by comparing the way in which it and other religions deflect
the same or similar rites from their original meaning and
re-interpret them, or in which they severally and differently
develop the same or similar ideas. And for this purpose,
particularly in the study of the greater ideas, Old Testament
study must not only look back to origins, but forwards and

outwards to the greater historical religions, considering for example in what different ways its idea of the uniqueness of God is reached or approximated to, in what ways it continues limited by its origins, in Persia, in Islam, in later Judaism, in the Christian religion.

I am already turning from what I may call the horizons behind to the horizons before, or to speak otherwise from Old Testament study as part of the wider study of ancient Semitic and Oriental antiquity to Old Testament study as part of, or as intimately connected with, New Testament study. I do not wish to raise again a question which I have raised at other times, as to the expediency of enlarging the scope of our Society and of any publications it may ultimately undertake either so as to become a Society of Semitic studies on the one hand or of Biblical study on the other ; but I would suggest that it is of the first importance for the fruitfulness of our more especial study and for the good of New Testament study, to which we cannot be indifferent, to keep our eyes constantly towards this horizon. I do not know that I share what I believe is the feeling of some members of our Society that we need such a Society as a means of mutual defence against theologians and others who would drive Old Testament study from the field ; but I have no doubt that if defence is required one of the soundest lines of defence is to keep well to the front the fact, too apt to be lost sight of or not duly appreciated, that the study of the Old Testament and the study of the New Testament are most intimately connected. No doubt this has been to some extent obscured by another tendency towards isolation on the part of both Old Testament and New Testament students : a chasm seemed to lie between them because the intervening history and literature were neglected. But this tendency has been greatly checked of late years, though not all the effects of the earlier attitude are yet removed. For example, Has the significance of the Book of Jubilees for the history of the Pentateuch and the development of Jewish legal theory and practice received even yet anything like the attention it deserves ? But even though the chasm in time, smaller as we now know than till recently was thought, between the latest writings of the Old Testament and the earliest of the New Testament were less filled than it is with literature which alike in form and in substance does more than merely bridge the chasm, the intimate connexion of Old Testament and New Testament, carrying with it the need for close association of the study of the two, would really exist. All the great ideas of the Old Testament await their fuller unfolding in the New Testament, and the student of the one can as little afford to lose sight of the end as the student of the other of the beginnings of their interest. This no doubt finds a good deal of recognition. But the connexion goes farther back to the very languages which express the ideas of the Old Testament. The New Testament is in large part scarcely less than the Old a Semitic literature ; Hebrew or Aramaic lies behind a large part of it either as the original language of its sources or as the mould in which the writer thought, even though he used Greek words to express his thought. New Testament like Old Testament study is study of language, literature, history, religion : and the languages which are, whether this be sufficiently recognized or not, of primary importance for the study of the New Testament are the same as those for the Old Testament—Hebrew, Aramaic, and Greek. The ultimate Aramaic element in the Synoptics is now generally admitted ; but the admission carries with it the necessity, not indeed of re-establishing the Aramaic of all the sayings in the Gospels, a task which will never be more than very tentatively carried through, though it may not be aggravated by quite such difficulties as Dalman's suspicion as to the possibility of knowledge of the Aramaic of the first century suggests, but the necessity of thinking all the terms in which the great ideas are expressed in connexion with their Aramaic associations. In some respects one of the most notable among recent books even for the Old Testament student has been Dr. Charles' *Commentary on the Apocalypse* : and I say this not as at all necessarily accepting all or most of his conclusions ; but as a study in the Greek of one who thinks in Semitic forms—and so much I think he has made out—it is a very important complement to the Hebrew thinkers and teachers writing in Hebrew whose writings fill the Old Testament. It is, I believe, no secret that we are in the immediate future to have a reconstruction of the Aramaic original of the Fourth Gospel. As to whether as well as such a reconstructed original there was ever an Aramaic original, I need not here express an opinion. But the attempt, whether it fails or succeeds, is likely to do service in bringing out the extent to which and the manner in which the Fourth Gospel forms part of the Semitic literature of the New Testament. Aramaic sources of Acts have been sought, but once again, whether successfully found or not, I will not now try to determine. There remains the Pauline literature. St. Paul was a Hebrew of the Hebrews, yet in some respects and at times at least the Pauline epistles perhaps leave upon us the impression of being the least Semitic of any parts of the New Testament. But this is probably not the last impression left after a careful examination of the relation of the Epistles to Semitic writings. The parallels to Rabbinic thought in St. Paul have often been discussed : much less so, I believe, the parallels to Rabbinic style. Yet this is a matter worth investigation. It is provoked by Dr. Moffatt's translation. Large parts of the Pauline Epistles are thrown into lines, as are the really parallelistic quotations from the Old Testament. [Some evidence of the extent to which Rabbinic methods of exegesis influenced St. Paul's approach to and treatment of certain passages at least in the Old Testament may seem to be indicated by his symbolic identification of Hagar with Mt. Sinai in Galatians iv, and possibly also by allusions and expositions elsewhere, particularly in the same Epistle. It may be true that the lapse of time and a wider and closer acquaintance with the non-Jewish world modified to some extent his outlook in his later years, but it is nowhere possible to form an adequate judgement on his work or to reach a satisfactory appreciation of his thought without fully realizing his Hebrew ancestry and training. For an interpretation of St. Paul, no less than any other writer in the New Testament, familiarity with the language and thought of the Old Testament is indispensable.]

G. BUCHANAN GRAY.

BIBLIOGRAPHY

FOR ESSAY I

ALBRIGHT, W. F.   Egypt and the Early History of the Negeb, *Journal of the Palestinian Oriental Society*, 1924, pp. 131 ff.

ALT, A.   Israel und Aegypten, 1909.

BÖHL, F. M. T.   Kananäer und Hebräer, 1911.

BURNEY, C. F.   The Book of Judges, 1918.

—— Israel's Settlement in Canaan, 1917.

Cambridge Ancient History, vol. i, 1923 ; vol. ii, 1924; vol. iii, 1925.

COOK, S. A.   Inscriptions from Ophel, *Palestine Exploration Fund Quarterly*, 1924, pp. 183 ff.

COWLEY, A. E.   Aramaic Papyri of the Fifth Century B. C., 1923.

—— The Hittites, 1920.

—— Origin of the Semitic Alphabet, *Journal of Egyptian Archaeology* (*JEA*), 1916, pp. 17 ff.

DUSSAUD, R.   Les Inscriptions phéniciennes du tombeau d'Ahiram. *Syria*, v, pp. 135–57.

FISHER, C. S.   Bethshean, *Philadelphia Museum Journal*, 1923, pp. 227 ff.

FORRER, E.   Chronologie der neuassyrischen Zeit, *Mitteilungen der Vorderasiatischen Gesellschaft*, 1915.

GADD, C. J.   The Fall of Nineveh, 1923.

GARDINER, A. H.   Origin of the Semitic Alphabet, *JEA*, 1916, pp. 1 ff.

—— The Geography of the Exodus, *Recueil Champollion*, 1922, pp. 203 ff., and *JEA*, 1924, pp. 87 ff.

GRESSMANN, H.   Altorientalische Texte und Bilder zum Alten Testament, 1909.

—— Die Anfänge Israels, 2. Aufl., 1922.

HALL, H. R.   Ancient History of the Near East, 6th ed., with addenda. 1924.

—— Egypt and the External World in the Time of Akhenaten, *JEA*, 1921, pp. 39 ff.

—— The Hittites and Egypt, in *Anatolian Studies presented to W. M. Ramsay*, 1923.

—— The Peoples of the Sea, *Recueil Champollion*, pp. 297 ff.

HEYES, H.   Bibel und Aegypten, 1904.

HOGARTH, D. G.   The Hittite Monuments of Southern Asia Minor, in *Anatolian Studies*, pp. 225 ff.

JIRKU, A.   Altorientalischer Kommentar zum Alten Testament, 1923.

—— Die Wanderungen der Hebräer, 1924.

MEYER, E.   Geschichte des Altertums, i, 4. Aufl., 1921.

—— Die Israeliten und ihre Nachbarstämme, 1906.

MACALISTER, R. A. S.   The Philistines, their History and Civilization, 1913.

NAVILLE, E.   The Geography of the Exodus, *JEA*, 1924, pp. 18 ff.

OLMSTEAD, A. T.   History of Assyria, 1923.

PEET, T. E.   Egypt and the Old Testament, 1922.

STÄHELIN.   Die Philister, 1918.

THOMSEN.   Die neueren Forschungen in Palästina und Syrien, 1925.

WEILL, R.   L'Installation des Israélites en Palestine et la Légende des Patriarches, 1921.

FOR ESSAY II

The literature is so large and often so miscellaneous that a mere list can hardly be attempted.   ROBERTSON SMITH's great pioneering work (see p. 42) should be read with LAGRANGE's fine Études sur les Religions Sémitiques (2nd ed., 1905).   For the religion of Egypt and of Babylonia-Assyria, see respectively BREASTED (p. 68) and JASTROW (p. 64).   Much valuable material will be found in G. A. BARTON's A Sketch of Semitic Origins (1902), J. G. FRAZER's Adonis, Attis, and Osiris (3rd ed., 1914) and in the relevant articles (e. g. Arabs, Canaanites, Phoenicians) in HASTINGS' *Encyclopaedia of Religion and Ethics* (*ERE*).   Readers of German should consult GRESSMANN's Altorientalische Texte und Bilder zum Alten Testament (1909), BAUDISSIN's Adonis und Esmun (1911), with LAGRANGE's valuable review, Rev. Bibl., 1912, pp. 117–27, and JIRKU's Altorientalischer Kommentar zum Alten Testament (1923).   The writings of Winckler, Gunkel, and Gressmann established a new stage in the interpretation of Old Testament symbolism and thought ; for criticism see the Introduction by C. H. W. JOHNS to The Old Testament in the Light of the Ancient East (1911) by A. JEREMIAS ; also K. FULLERTON, *Journal of Biblical Literature*, xli, 1922, pp. 71 ff. ; N. SCHMIDT, *ibid.*, pp. 102 ff. ; A. S. PEAKE, The Roots of Hebrew Prophecy and Jewish Apocalyptic, 1923 ; W. L. WARDLE, Israel and Babylon, 1925.   The tendencies to reinterpretation of the Old Testament along the lines suggested by the external evidence have, as mentioned above, sometimes taken extreme forms, whether ' conservative ' or ' radical ' ; the author of the essay has given his own views in the *Cambridge Ancient History* (*CAH*) on Pre-Israelite Palestine in the Amarna Period (ii. 336–51), and on Israel before the Prophets (iii, Chap. XIX).   Fuller bibliographies are given in that work.   For the question of Semitic monotheism cf. *CAH*, i. 198 ff. ; see also the instructive paper on Monotheism among Primitive Peoples by PAUL RADIN (1924).

FOR ESSAY III

I.

BARTH, J.   Die Nominalbildung in der semitischen Sprache, 1889.

BAUER, H.   Die Tempora im Semitischen, 1912.

BROCKELMANN, C.   Grundriss der vergleichenden Grammatik der semitischen Sprachen, 1908.

KÖNIG, E.   Hebräisch und Semitisch, 1901.

LAGARDE, P. de.   Uebersicht über die im Aramäischen, Arabischen und Hebräischen übliche Bildung der Nomina, 1889.

O'LEARY, D.   Comparative Grammar of the Semitic Languages, 1923.

TORCZYNER, H.   Die Entstehung des semitischen Sprachtypus, 1906.

WRIGHT, W.   Lectures on the Comparative Grammar of the Semitic Languages, 1890.

ZIMMERN, H.   Vergleichende Grammatik der semitischen Sprachen, 1898.

II.

BÖHL, F.   Die Sprache der Amarnabriefe, 1909.

—— Kananäer und Hebräer, 1911.

DELITZSCH, F.   The Hebrew Language viewed in the Light of Assyrian Research, 1883.

—— Prolegomena eines neuen Hebräisch-Aramäischen Wörterbuchs, 1886.

—— Philologische Forderungen an die hebräische Lexicographie, 1917.

EBELING, F.   Das Verbum der El-Amarna-Briefe, 1910.

III.

BAUER, H., and LEANDER, P.   Historische Grammatik der Hebräischen Sprache, 1922.

DAVIDSON, A. B.   Introductory Hebrew Grammar, 22nd ed., revised by J. E. McFADYEN.

—— Hebrew Syntax, 1894.

DRIVER, S. R.   A Treatise on the Use of the Tenses in Hebrew, 1892.

JOÜON, P. P.   Grammaire de l'Hébreu Biblique, 1923.

KAUTZSCH, E.   Gesenius' Hebrew Grammar, 2nd Eng. ed., 1910.

KÖNIG, E.   Historisch-kritisches Lehrgebäude der Hebräischen Sprache, 1881, 1895, 1897.

—— Stilistik, Rhetorik, Poetik in Bezug auf die biblische Litteratur komparativisch dargestellt, 1900.

BROWN, F., DRIVER, S. R., BRIGGS, C. A.   A Hebrew and English Lexicon of the Old Testament, 1906.

BUHL, F.   W. Gesenius' Hebräisches und Aramäisches Handwörterbuch über das Alte Testament, 1921.

KÖNIG, E.   Hebräisches und Aramäisches Wörterbuch zum Alten Testament, 1910.

BAUER, H.   Zur Frage der Sprachmischung im Hebräischen, 1924.

LANDESDORFER, S.   Sumerisches Sprachgut im Alten Testament, 1916.

JIRKU, A.   Die Wanderungen der Hebräer, 1924.

IV.

KAUTZSCH, E.   Grammatik des Biblisch-Aramäischen, 1884.

MARTI, K.   Kurzgefasste Grammatik der Biblisch-Aramäischen Sprache, 1896.

STRACK, H. L.   Grammatik des Biblisch-Aramäischen mit . . . Texten und einem Wörterbuch, 1921.

STEVENSON, W. B.   Grammar of Palestinian Jewish Aramaic, 1924.

DALMAN, G.   Grammatik des Jüdisch-Palästinischen Aramäisch, 1905.

483

FOR ESSAY IV

—— Jerusalem under the High Priests, 1904.
Böhl, F.   Kananäer und Hebräer, 1911.
Burney, C. F.   The Book of Judges, 1918 (Sections 5 and 6 of Introduction).
—— Israel's Settlement in Canaan, 1918.
Cook, S. A.   Articles in the Cambridge Ancient History.
Gadd, C. J.   The Fall of Nineveh, 1923.
Gressmann, H.   Altorientalische Texte und Bilder zum Alten Testamente, 1909.
Hrozny, F.   Code Hittite, 1922.
Kittel, R.   Geschichte des Volkes Israel, 1925.
Knudtzon, J. A.   Die El-Amarna-Tafeln, 1907–15.
Lehmann-Haupt, C. H.   Israel, 1911.
Macalister, R. A. S.   The Philistines, 1913.
Meyer, E.   Die Israeliten und ihre Nachbarstämme, 1906.
—— Geschichte des Altertums.
Naville, E.   The Store-City of Pithom, 1885.
Peet, T. E.   Egypt and the Old Testament, 1922.
Petrie, W. M. F.   Israel and Egypt, 1911.
Sellin, E.   Geschichte des israelitisch-jüdischen Volkes, i, 1924.
Smith, H. P.   Old Testament History, 1903.
Vincent, H.   Canaan d'après l'Exploration récente, 1907.
Wellhausen, J.   Israelitische und jüdische Geschichte, 1894, 7th ed. 1914.
Wilke, F.   Das Skythenproblem, 1913.
Winckler, H.   Geschichte Israels, 1895–1900.
—— Vorläufige Nachrichten über die Ausgrabungen in Boghazköi, 1907.

FOR ESSAYS V AND VI

A list of the older books is not necessary, but the Introductions to the Old Testament by Driver (9th ed., 1913), Cornill (Eng. trans., 1907), Steuernagel (1912) with the more elementary works of Bennett, Gray, (1913), and McFadyen (1905) should be mentioned. One of the best guides to the beginner is still W. Robertson Smith's Old Testament in the Jewish Church (2nd ed., 1892). For the Hexateuch, Kuenen's The Hexateuch (Eng. trans.) 1886, Wellhausen's Die Composition des Hexateuchs (2nd ed., 1889), and his Prolegomena to the History of Israel (Eng. trans. from 3rd ed.), 1885, are fundamental. The best English work is Carpenter and Harford, The Composition of the Hexateuch (1902); but excellent guidance for the general reader is given by Addis, The Documents of the Hexateuch (1892–8); Chapman, An Introduction to the Pentateuch (1911); Simpson, Pentateuchal Criticism (1914). Books defending a substantially conservative position are Orr, The Problem of the Old Testament (1905); Finn, The Unity of the Pentateuch (n.d.). It must be remembered that commentaries contain much valuable critical material. The leading English series is The International Critical Commentary, but important contributions are to be found in the Westminster Commentaries, The Cambridge Bible, and the Century Bible. The leading German commentaries are NOWACK's Hand-Kommentar zum Alten Testament, MARTI's Kurzer Hand-Commentar zum Alten Testament, SELLIN's Kommentar zum Alten Testament. Nor should the dictionaries of the Bible or the *Encyclopaedia Britannica* be neglected. The list which follows contains a selection representing the more recent developments as sketched in Chapter VI.

CORNILL, C. H. Zur Einleitung in das Alte Testament, 1912.

COWLEY, A. E. Aramaic Papyri of the Fifth Century B. C., 1923.

DAHSE, J. Textkritische Materialien zur Hexateuchfrage, 1912.

EICHRODT, W. Die Quellen der Genesis von neuem untersucht, 1916.

EERDMANS, B. D. Alttestamentliche Studien, 1908–12.

EISSFELDT, O. Hexateuch-Synopse, 1922.

—— Die Quellen des Richterbuches, 1925.

EYXAPIΣTHPION. Studien zur Religion und Literatur des Alten und Neuen Testaments Hermann Gunkel zum 60. Geburtstage dargebracht, 1923.

GRESSMANN, H. Der Ursprung der israelitisch-jüdischen Eschatologie, 1905.

—— Mose und seine Zeit, 1913.

GUNKEL, H. Schöpfung und Chaos in Urzeit und Endzeit, 1895.

—— Ausgewählte Psalmen, 1904.

—— Die israelitsche Literatur, in Die Kultur der Gegenwart, 1906.

—— Die Propheten, 1917.

HARFORD, J. BATTERSBY. Since Wellhausen (*Expositor*, July–December 1925).

HÖLSCHER, G. Die Profeten, 1914.

—— Hesekiel, der Dichter und das Buch, 1924.

—— Geschichte der israelitischen und jüdischen Religion, 1922.

KENNETT, R. H. Deuteronomy and the Decalogue, 1920.

LÖHR, M. Untersuchungen zum Hexateuchproblem, 1924–25.

MEYER, E. Der Papyrusfund von Elephantine, 1912.

MOORE, G. F. The Rise of Normative Judaism, I. *Harvard Theol. Rev.*, 1924.

MOWINCKEL, S. Psalmenstudien, 1921–4.

OESTREICHER, T. Das deuteronomische Grundgesetz, 1923.

PETERS, J. P. The Psalms as Liturgies, 1922.

ROBINSON, T. H. Prophecy and the Prophets in Ancient Israel, 1923.

SELLIN, E. Einleitung in das Alte Testament, 3rd ed., 1920; Eng. trans. by W. MONTGOMERY, Introduction to the Old Testament, 1923.

—— Zur Einleitung in das Alte Testament, 1912.

—— Mose und seine Bedeutung für die israelitisch-jüdische Religionsgeschichte, 1922.

—— Geschichte des israelitisch-jüdischen Volkes, i, 1924.

SKINNER, J. The Divine Names in Genesis, 1914.

—— Prophecy and Religion, 1922.

Smend, J. Die Erzählung des Hexateuchs auf ihre Quellen untersucht, 1912.
Staerk, W. Das Problem des Deuteronomiums.
Torrey, C. C. Ezra Studies, 1910.
Welch, A. C. The Code of Deuteronomy, 1924.
Wiener, H. M. Essays in Pentateuchal Criticism, 1910.
—— The Origin of the Pentateuch.
Wilson, R. D. Studies in the Book of Daniel, 1917.
Zeitschrift für die alttestamentliche Wissenschaft, ed. H. Gressmann.

FOR ESSAYS VII, VIII, AND IX

Bertholet, A. Biblische Theologie des Alten Testaments, ii, 1911 (see Stade).
—— Kulturgeschichte Israels, 1919.
Budde, K. Religion of Israel to the Exile, 1899.
—— Die altisraelitische Religion, 1912 (3rd German ed. of above).
Causse, A. Les Prophètes d'Israël et les Religions de l'Orient, 1913.
Cheyne, T. K. Jewish Religious Life after the Exile, 1898.
Cornill, C. H. The Prophets of Israel, 1895.
Duhm, B. Israels Propheten, 1916.
Gordon, A. R. The Prophets of the Old Testament, 1916.
Gressmann, H. Der Ursprung der israelitisch-jüdischen Eschatologie, 1905.
—— Mose und seine Zeit, 1913.
Gunkel, H. Schöpfung und Chaos in Urzeit und Endzeit, 1895.
—— Die Propheten, 1917.
Hamilton, H. F. The People of God, vol. i, 1912.
Hölscher, G. Die Profeten, 1914.
—— Geschichte der israelitischen und jüdischen Religion, 1922.
Kautzsch, E. Article 'Religion of Israel' in *Hastings' Dictionary of the Bible*, Extra Volume, 1904.
Kennett, R. H. Article 'Israel' in *Hastings' Encyclopaedia of Religion and Ethics*, vol. vii, 1914.
—— History of the Jewish Church from Nebuchadnezzar to Alexander the Great, in *Cambridge Biblical Essays*, 1909.
Kittel, R. The Religion of the People of Israel, 1925.
König, E. Geschichte der Alttestamentlichen Religion, 2nd ed., 1915.
—— Geschichte des Reiches Gottes bis auf Jesus Christus, 1908.
Marti, K. Geschichte der israelitischen Religion, 1907.
—— The Religion of the Old Testament, 1907.
Meyer, E. Ursprung und Anfänge des Christentums, vol. ii, 1921.
Montefiore, C. G. The Old Testament and After, 1923.
Oesterley, W. O. E. Immortality and the Unseen World, 1921.
Pace, E. Ideas of God in Israel, 1924.
Peake, A. S. The Problem of Suffering in the Old Testament, 1904.
—— The Roots of Hebrew Prophecy and Jewish Apocalyptic, 1923.

ROBINSON, H. W. The Religious Ideas of the Old Testament, 1913.
ROBINSON, T. H. Prophecy and the Prophets in Ancient Israel, 1923.
SELLIN, E. Die alttestamentliche Religion im Rahmen der andern alt-
orientalischen, 1908.
—— Der alttestamentliche Prophetismus, 1912.
SKINNER, J. Prophecy and Religion, 1922.
SMEND, R. Lehrbuch der alttestamentlichen Religionsgeschichte, 2nd ed.,
1899.
SMITH, G. A. Jeremiah, 1924.
SMITH, H. P. The Religion of Israel, 1914.
SMITH, W. R. The Prophets of Israel, new edition, edited by T. K. CHEYNE,
1895.
STADE, B. Biblische Theologie des Alten Testaments, i, 1905 (see BER-
THOLET).
VOLZ, P. Der Geist Gottes, 1910.
WELCH, A. C. The Religion of Israel under the Kingdom, 1912.

FOR ESSAY X

BAUDISSIN, W. W. Studien zur semitischen Religionsgeschichte, 1876.
CURTISS, S. I. Primitive Semitic Religion To-day, 1902.
GOLDZIHER. Muhammedanische Studien, 1888–90.
KITTEL, R. Zur hebräischen Archäologie, 1908.
LAGRANGE, M. J. Études sur les Religions Sémitiques, 2nd ed., 1905.
LOISY, A. Essai historique sur le Sacrifice, 1920.
SMITH, W. R. The Religion of the Semites, 1894.
GRESSMANN, HÖLSCHER, STADE. See on Essays VII–IX.

FOR ESSAY XI

BRIGGS, C. A. The Use of נֶפֶשׁ in the Old Testament, *Journal of Biblical
Literature* (*JBL*), xvi, Part I, 1897.
—— The Use of רוּחַ in the Old Testament, *JBL*, xix, Part II, 1900.
BURTON, E. D. Spirit, Soul, and Flesh, 1918.
KÖBERLE, J. Natur und Geist nach der Auffassung des Alten Testaments,
1901.
LODS, A. La Croyance à la Vie Future, 1906.
ROBINSON, H. W. Hebrew Psychology in relation to Pauline Anthro-
pology (*Mansfield College Essays*), 1909.
—— The Christian Doctrine of Man (Chap. I), 1913.
—— Religious Ideas of the Old Testament (Chap. IV), 1913.
—— The Psychology and Metaphysic of ' Thus saith Yahweh ', *ZATW*
Bd. xli, 1923.
—— The Old Testament Approach to the Life after Death, *The Congrega-
tional Quarterly*, April 1925.
SCHOEMAKER, W. R. The Use of רוּחַ and of πνεῦμα, *JBL*, xxiii, Part I,
1904.

TORGE, P. Seelenglaube und Unsterblichkeitshoffnung im Alten Testament, 1909.
OESTERLEY, STADE, and VOLZ as for Essays VII–IX.

FOR ESSAY XII

BRUCE, A. B. The Chief End of Revelation, 1881.
CARPENTER, J. E. The Bible in the Nineteenth Century, 1905.
FULLERTON, K. Prophecy and Authority, A Study in the History of the Doctrine and Interpretation of Scripture, 1919.
KAUTZSCH, E. Die bleibende Bedeutung des Alten Testaments, 1901.
MARTINEAU, J. The Seat of Authority in Religion, 2nd ed., 1890.
ORR, J. Revelation and Inspiration, 1910.
PEAKE, A. S. The Bible, Its Origin, Its Significance, and Its Abiding Worth, 1913.
ROTHE, R. Zur Dogmatik, 2nd ed., 1869.
SABATIER, A. The Religions of Authority and the Religion of the Spirit, 1904.
SMITH, G. A. Modern Criticism and the Preaching of the Old Testament, 1901.
SMITH, H. P. Essays in Biblical Interpretation, 1921.
SMITH, W. R. The Old Testament in the Jewish Church, 2nd ed., 1892.

FOR ESSAY XIII

The best work on Jewish Exegesis was done by the late Professor WILHELM BACHER, of Buda-Pesth. (i) For early Rabbinic Exegesis, Die Agada der Tannaiten (2 vols. 1884–90, 2nd ed. of vol. i, 1903) ; Die Agada der Palästinensischen Amoräer (3 vols., 1892–9) ; Die Agada der Babylonischen Amoräer (1878). (ii) For medieval Jewish Exegesis, a number of monographs, including volumes on Ibn Janah (1889), pre-Maimonist Exegesis (1892), the Exegesis of Maimonides (1896), on Ibn Ezra (1894), and many other essays. (iii) For General Jewish Exegesis, an elaborate series of chapters, occupying pp. 121–339 in the *Anthologie* edited by J. Winter and Aug. Wünsche (1894). There are many extracts (in German) from the annotators discussed. Professor Bacher also contributed (in English) an admirable article to the *Jewish Encyclopedia*, s.v. ' Bible Exegesis ' (vol. iii, pp. 162 ff. ; there is a valuable bibliography on p. 174). Of the more recent Jewish Exegesis from Moses Mendelssohn onwards there is a useful account by M. KAYSERLING in the Winter-Wünsche *Anthologie*, vol. iii, pp. 741 ff. See further The Story of Biblical Translations (1917) by MAX L. MARGOLIS. The volume A Short Survey of the Literature of Rabbinical and Mediaeval Judaism (1920) by W. O. E. OESTERLEY and G. H. Box includes a very useful account of the Targumim, Midrashim, and Medieval Grammar and Exegesis. The reader will find valuable information in the articles in the *Encyclopaedia Britannica* and the *Jewish Encyclopedia* on the various commentators named in the course of the essay.

FOR ESSAY XIV

BLASS, F. Grammar of New Testament Greek, 2nd ed., 1905.

BURNEY, C. F. The Aramaic Origin of the Fourth Gospel, 1922.

DALMAN, G. The Words of Jesus considered in the light of Post-Biblical Jewish Writings and the Aramaic Language, 1902.

DEISSMANN, A. Bible Studies, 1901.

—— Licht vom Osten, 4th ed., 1923. English translation from the 3rd ed. Light from the Ancient East, 1910.

KENNEDY, H. A. A. Sources of New Testament Greek, 1895.

HARRIS, J. R., and BURCH, V. Testimonies, Part I, 1916 ; Part II, 1920.

MOULTON, J. H. A Grammar of New Testament Greek, vol. i, 3rd ed., 1908.

THACKERAY, H. St. J., A Grammar of the Old Testament in Greek, vol. i, 1909.

TOY, C. H. Quotations in the New Testament, 1884.

WENDLAND, P. Die Hellenistisch-Römische Kultur in ihren Beziehungen zu Judentum und Christentum, 2nd ed., 1912.

—— Die urchristlichen Literaturformen, 2nd ed. 1912.

INDEX

Index

507

Tenses 78, 81, 92–9, 105 f., 116, 120, 381
Tent 257, 332, 340
Teraphim 247 f., 342
Terebinth 324, 327
Testimonia 439–44, 463
Tetragrammaton 192, 304
Textual criticism 154, 185 f.
Thackeray, St. John, 462 f.
Thebes (city in Egypt) 37 f.
Theriomorphism 56, 58
Thekri 25, 27 f.
Theocracy 172 f.
Theodotion 442
Theology 267, 284
Theophany 261 f., 367
Thucydides 184
Thutmosis III 2, 9, 12, 20
Tid'al 18, 21
Tiglath Pileser III 36
Tiglath Pileser IV 36 f., 140, 266
Tigris 102, 258
Time 120
Tiras 29
Tirhakah 38
Tithe 267, 312, 330
Tobiah 292
Tobit 306
—, Book of, 306, 312
Togarmah 29
Toi 33
Torah 230, 233–5, 297
Totemism 56–8, 223, 323
Trade routes 33 f., 43, 131, 133
Tradition 18, 59, 121 f., 125–7, 135, 223–6, 230 f., 409, 414, 419–21, 423, 426, 446, 452 f., 474
Trajan 97
Trance 373 f.
Translation 415–24, 426, 469 f.
Tree 46, 222, 239 f., 274, 286, 323–6
Tree of Life 49
Tribe 121 f., 125–35, 223, 237, 251, 259, 397
Trichotomy 362
Trito-Isaiah 296 f., 299, 301 f., 309, 311, 315, 317
Trumpet 44

Tubal 28
Tursha 25, 27
Tutenkhamon 69
Two brothers, the, 54
Tylor 353
Tyre 34, 137 f., 261, 291, 295, 309

Umman-Manda 29
Unamon 28
Uncleanness 46, 81, 245 f., 274 f., 310, 312
Universalism 68, 188, 308, 399 f., 445
Ur 15, 18, 121 f., 224
Uriah the Hittite 24
Uriah, friend of Isaiah, 209
Urijah 368
Urim and Tummim 90 f., 332
Uvakhshatra 38 ; see Kyaxares

Valeton 211
Varuna 23, 52, 61, 71
Versions, the, 185, 470 f.
Vicarious suffering 287 f.
Vineyard 251, 259
Virgin birth 407 f.
Vision 120, 206 f., 273–5, 282, 302, 308, 359, 367, 372–5
Vocabulary 380
Volz 196 f., 207 f., 221
Vow 330, 343 f.
Vulgate 420

Walls of Jerusalem 291 f., 318
Walton's Polyglott 470 f., 473
War 125, 235, 243 f., 246 f., 276, 393, 448
Wardle, W. L., 59
Washasha 25
Weasel 57
Welch, A. C., 169, 183, 191, 199, 202–4, 349
Wellhausen 151, 154, 189 f., 211, 215, 218, 269, 276, 406, 414
Wells 222, 239
Weltanschauung 59
Widow's son, the, 357
Wiener 191